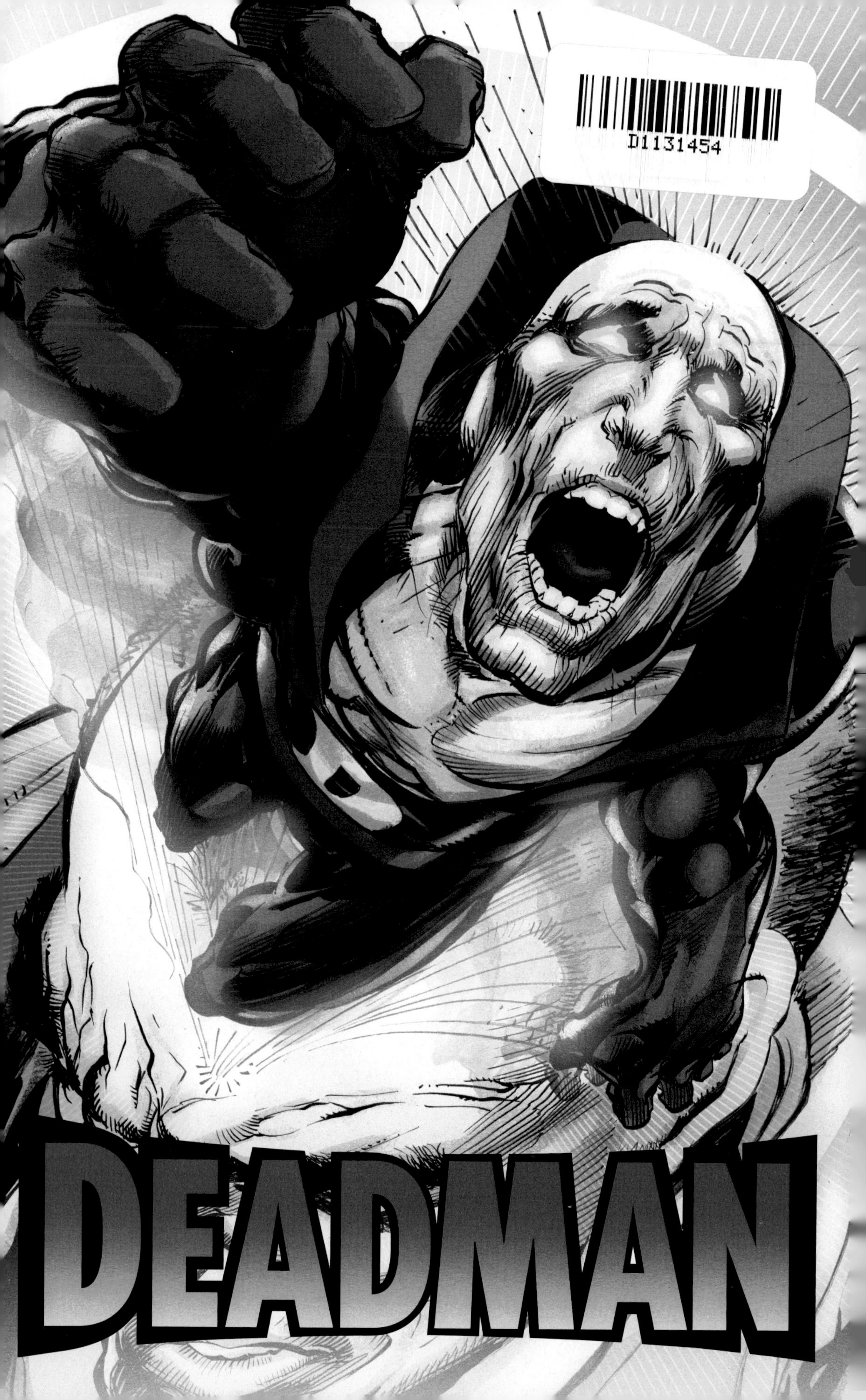
DEADMAN

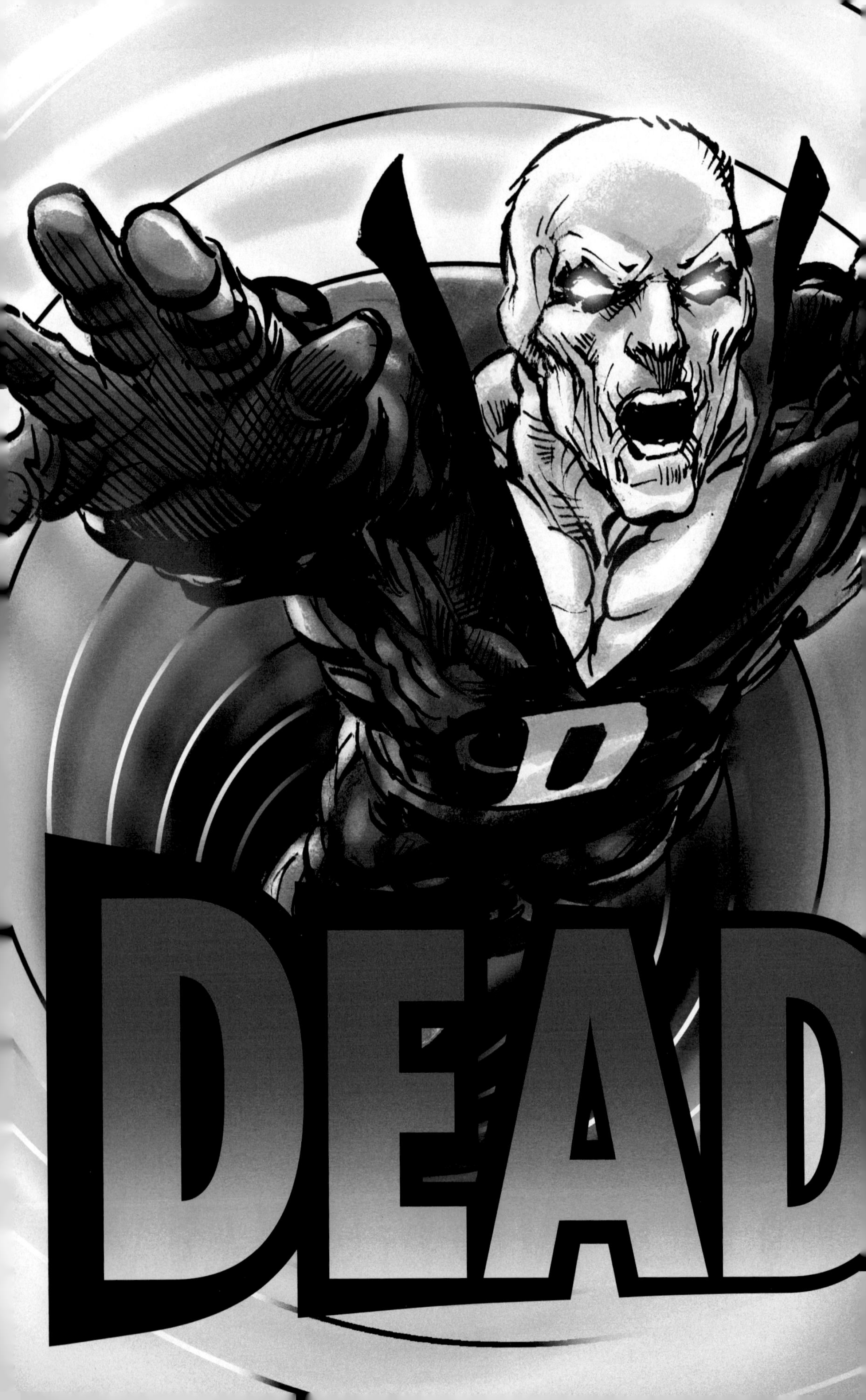
DEAD

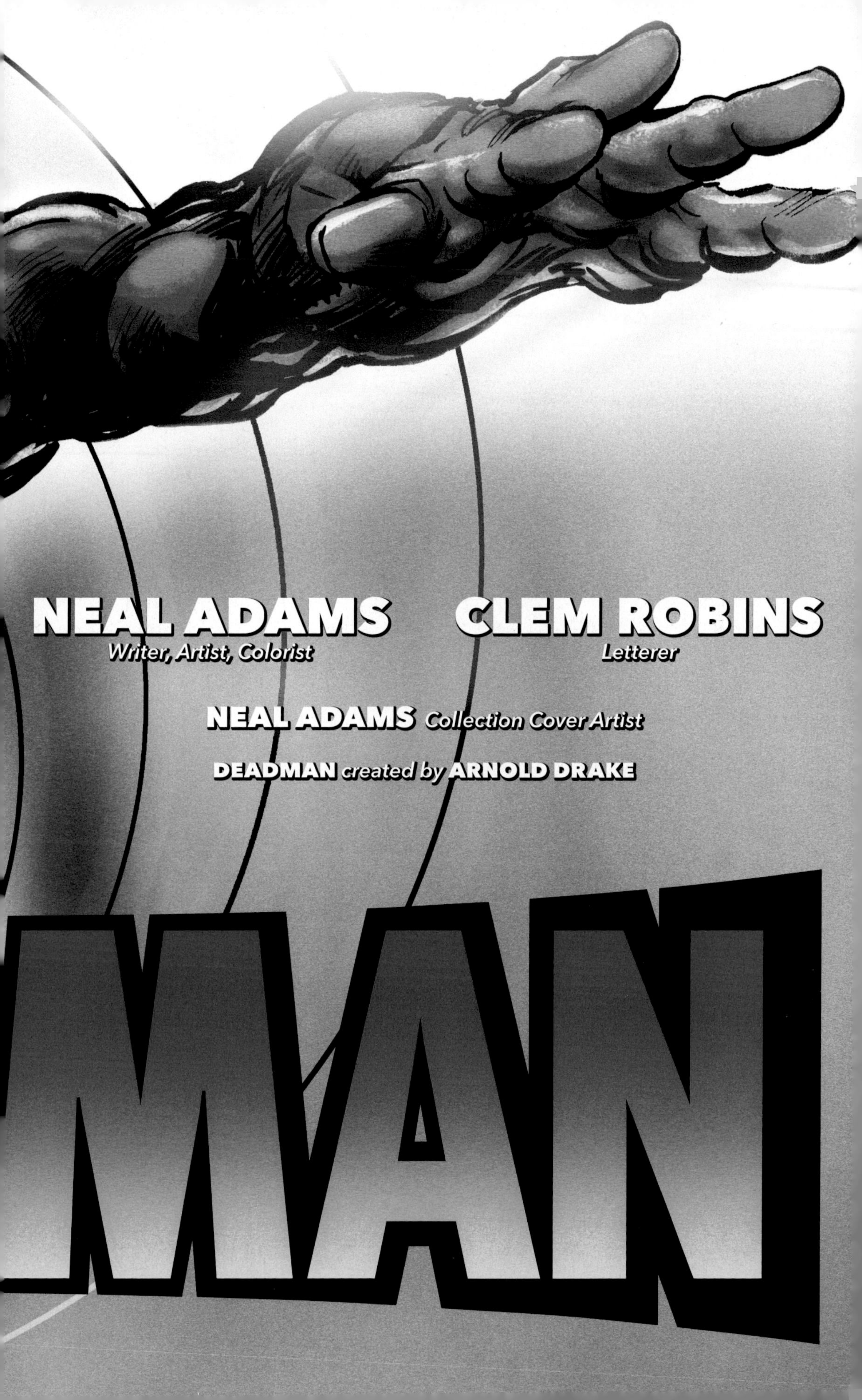
MAN

NEAL ADAMS
Writer, Artist, Colorist

CLEM ROBINS
Letterer

NEAL ADAMS *Collection Cover Artist*

DEADMAN *created by* **ARNOLD DRAKE**

DEADMAN

Published by DC Comics. Compilation and all new material Copyright © 2018 DC Comics.
All Rights Reserved. Originally published in single magazine form in DEADMAN 1-6.
Copyright © 2017, 2018 DC Comics. All Rights Reserved. All characters, their distinctive
likenesses and related elements featured in this publication are trademarks of DC Comics.
The stories, characters and incidents featured in this publication are entirely fictional.
DC Comics does not read or accept unsolicited submissions of ideas, stories or artwork.

DC Comics, 2900 West Alameda Ave., Burbank, CA 91505

Printed by LSC Communications
Kendallville, IN, USA. 7/6/18. First Printing.
ISBN: 978-1-4012-8141-0

Library of Congress Cataloging-in-Publication Data is available.

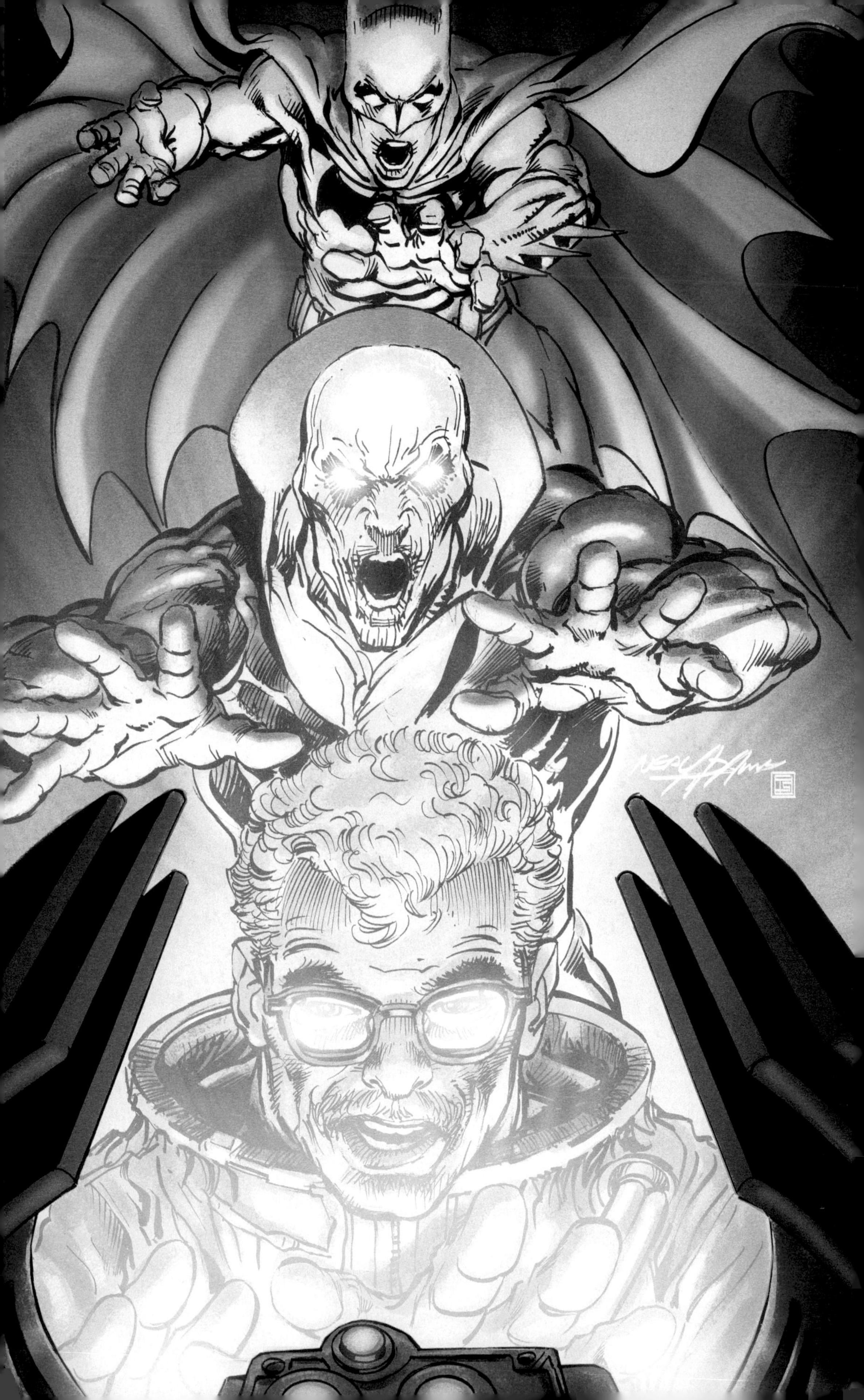

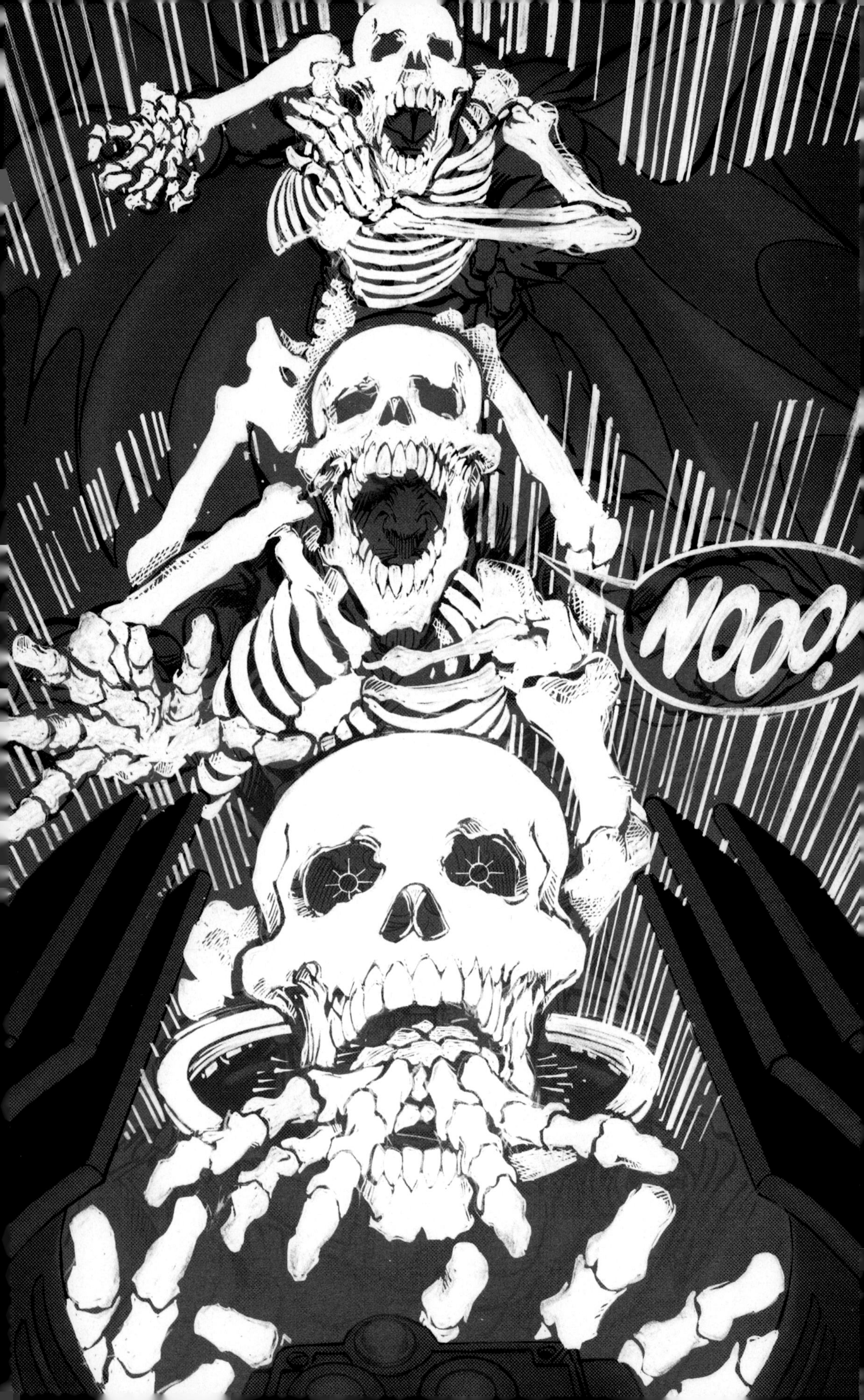
NOOO!

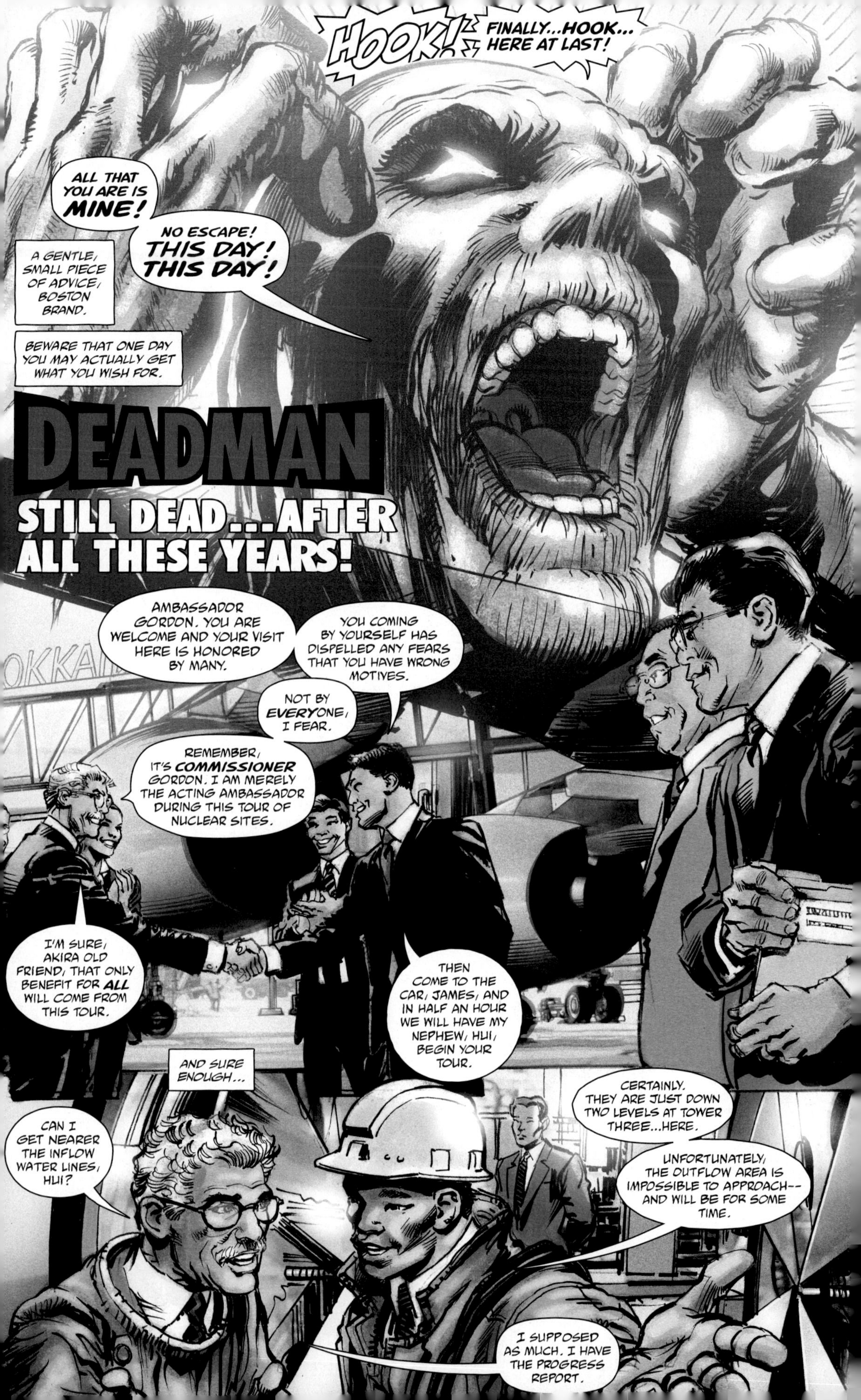

HOOK!
FINALLY...HOOK... HERE AT LAST!
ALL THAT YOU ARE IS MINE!
NO ESCAPE! THIS DAY! THIS DAY!
A GENTLE, SMALL PIECE OF ADVICE, BOSTON BRAND.
BEWARE THAT ONE DAY YOU MAY ACTUALLY GET WHAT YOU WISH FOR.
DEADMAN
STILL DEAD...AFTER ALL THESE YEARS!
AMBASSADOR GORDON. YOU ARE WELCOME AND YOUR VISIT HERE IS HONORED BY MANY.
YOU COMING BY YOURSELF HAS DISPELLED ANY FEARS THAT YOU HAVE WRONG MOTIVES.
NOT BY EVERYONE, I FEAR.
REMEMBER, IT'S COMMISSIONER GORDON. I AM MERELY THE ACTING AMBASSADOR DURING THIS TOUR OF NUCLEAR SITES.
I'M SURE, AKIRA OLD FRIEND, THAT ONLY BENEFIT FOR ALL WILL COME FROM THIS TOUR.
THEN COME TO THE CAR, JAMES, AND IN HALF AN HOUR WE WILL HAVE MY NEPHEW, HUI, BEGIN YOUR TOUR.
AND SURE ENOUGH...
CAN I GET NEARER THE INFLOW WATER LINES, HUI?
CERTAINLY. THEY ARE JUST DOWN TWO LEVELS AT TOWER THREE...HERE.
UNFORTUNATELY, THE OUTFLOW AREA IS IMPOSSIBLE TO APPROACH--AND WILL BE FOR SOME TIME.
I SUPPOSED AS MUCH. I HAVE THE PROGRESS REPORT.

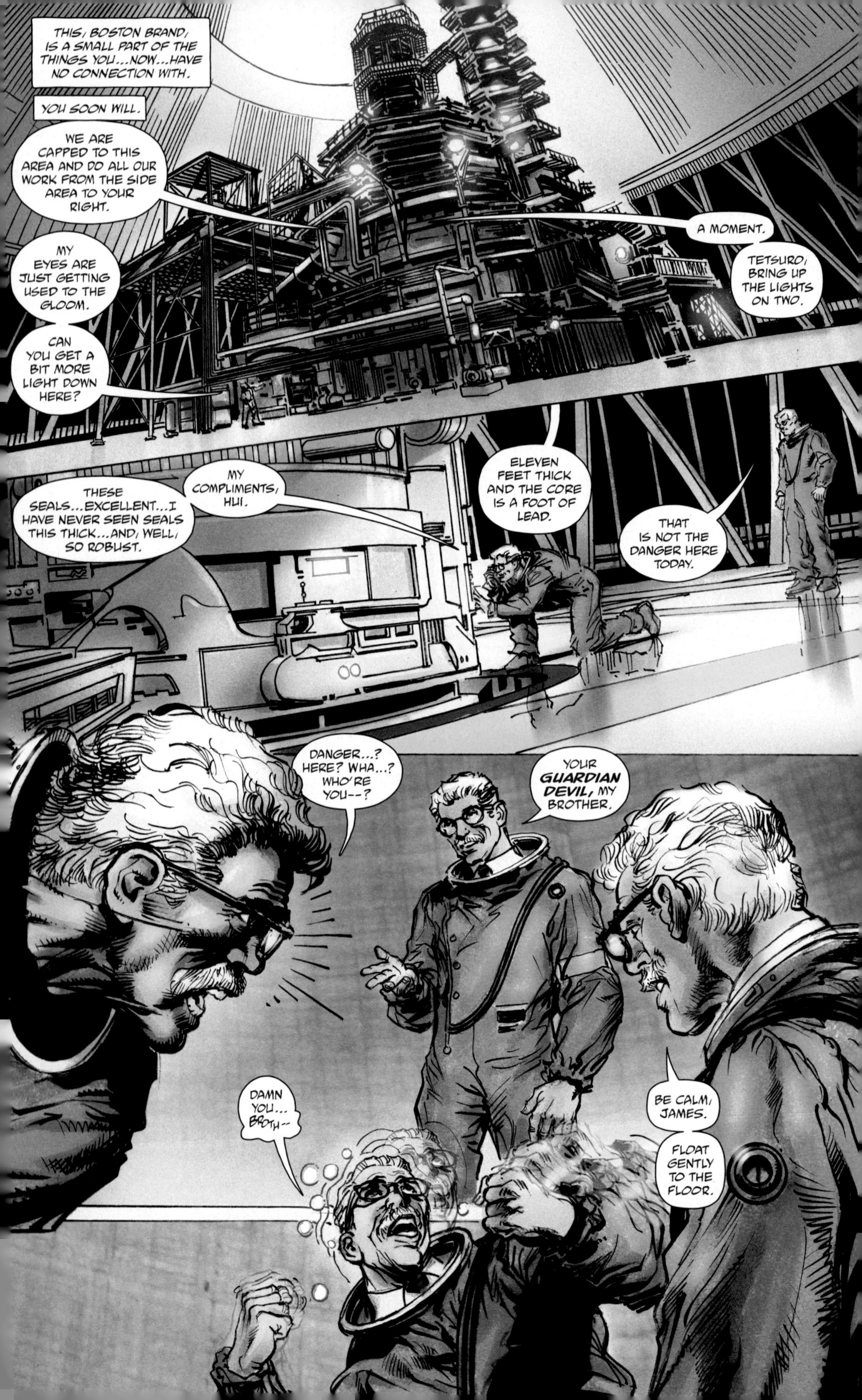
THIS, BOSTON BRAND, IS A SMALL PART OF THE THINGS YOU...NOW...HAVE NO CONNECTION WITH.
YOU SOON WILL.
WE ARE CAPPED TO THIS AREA AND DO ALL OUR WORK FROM THE SIDE AREA TO YOUR RIGHT.
A MOMENT.
TETSURO, BRING UP THE LIGHTS ON TWO.
MY EYES ARE JUST GETTING USED TO THE GLOOM.
CAN YOU GET A BIT MORE LIGHT DOWN HERE?
THESE SEALS...EXCELLENT...I HAVE NEVER SEEN SEALS THIS THICK...AND, WELL, SO ROBUST.
MY COMPLIMENTS, HUI.
ELEVEN FEET THICK AND THE CORE IS A FOOT OF LEAD.
THAT IS NOT THE DANGER HERE TODAY.
DANGER...? HERE? WHA...? WHO'RE YOU--?
YOUR GUARDIAN DEVIL, MY BROTHER.
DAMN YOU... BROTH--
BE CALM, JAMES.
FLOAT GENTLY TO THE FLOOR.

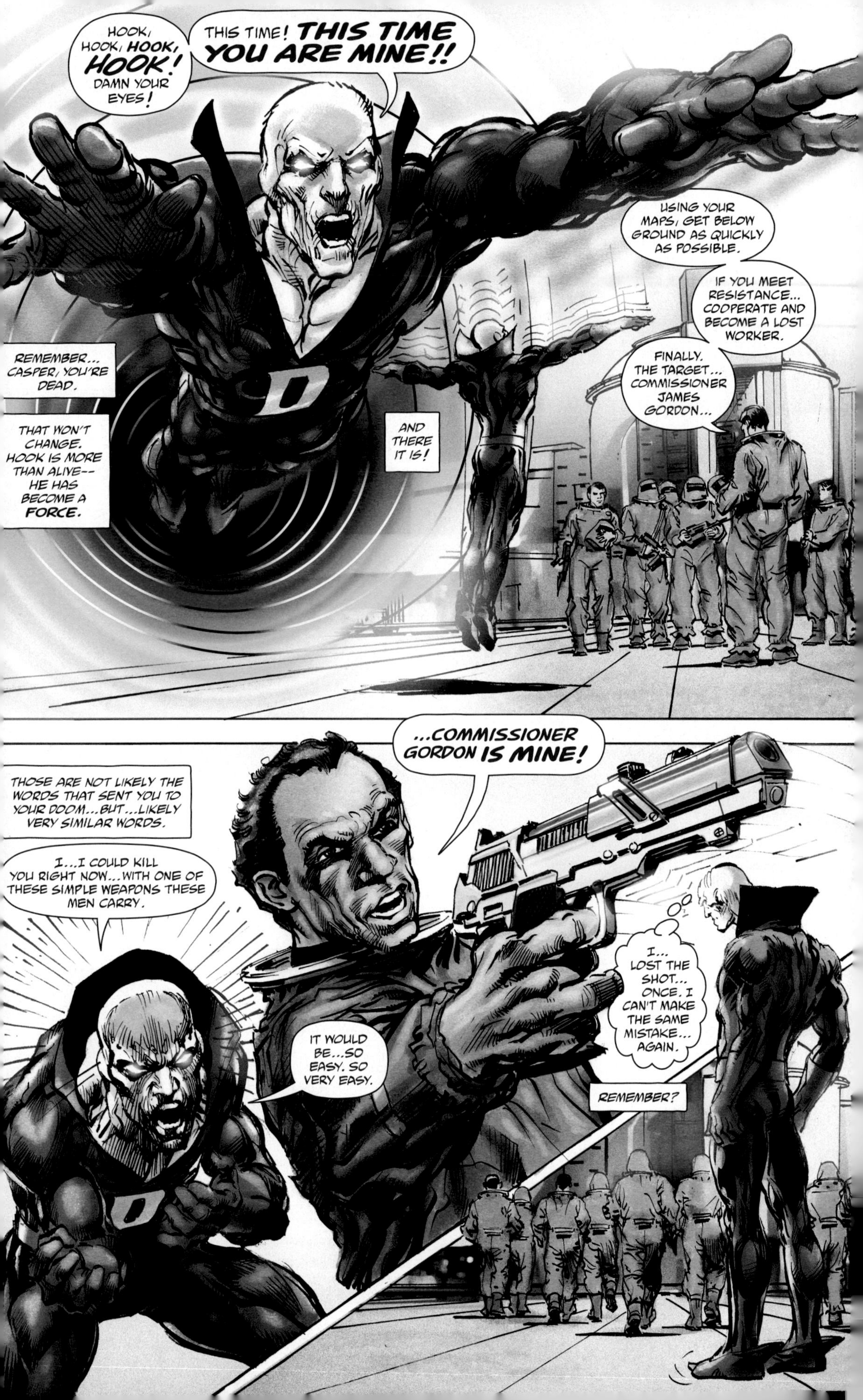

HOOK, HOOK, HOOK, HOOK! DAMN YOUR EYES!
THIS TIME! THIS TIME YOU ARE MINE!!
REMEMBER... CASPER, YOU'RE DEAD.
THAT WON'T CHANGE. HOOK IS MORE THAN ALIVE-- HE HAS BECOME A FORCE.
AND THERE IT IS!
USING YOUR MAPS, GET BELOW GROUND AS QUICKLY AS POSSIBLE.
IF YOU MEET RESISTANCE... COOPERATE AND BECOME A LOST WORKER.
FINALLY. THE TARGET... COMMISSIONER JAMES GORDON...
...COMMISSIONER GORDON IS MINE!
THOSE ARE NOT LIKELY THE WORDS THAT SENT YOU TO YOUR DOOM...BUT...LIKELY VERY SIMILAR WORDS.
I...I COULD KILL YOU RIGHT NOW...WITH ONE OF THESE SIMPLE WEAPONS THESE MEN CARRY.
IT WOULD BE...SO EASY. SO VERY EASY.
I... LOST THE SHOT... ONCE. I CAN'T MAKE THE SAME MISTAKE... AGAIN.
REMEMBER?

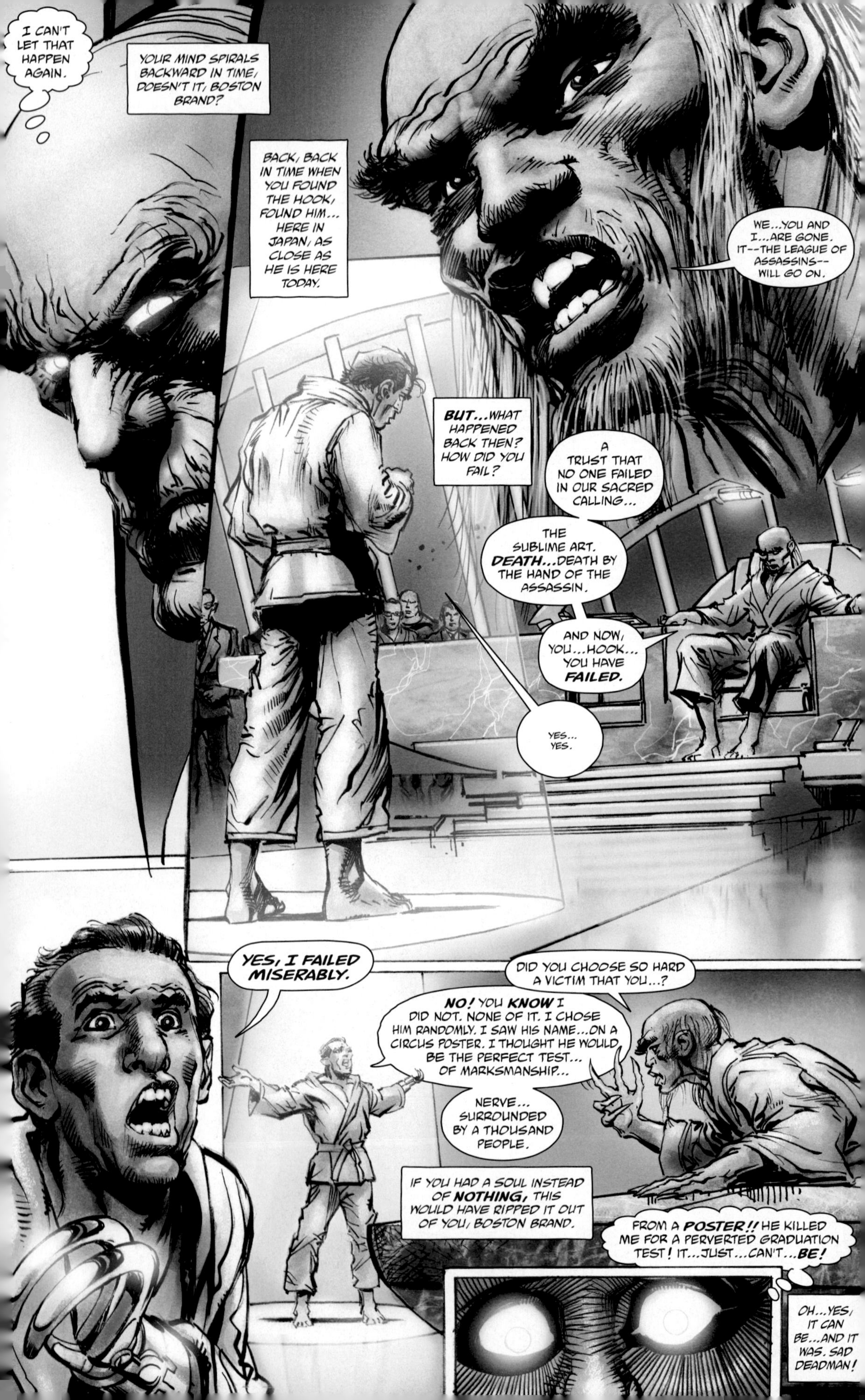

I CAN'T LET THAT HAPPEN AGAIN.
YOUR MIND SPIRALS BACKWARD IN TIME, DOESN'T IT, BOSTON BRAND?
BACK, BACK IN TIME WHEN YOU FOUND THE HOOK, FOUND HIM... HERE IN JAPAN, AS CLOSE AS HE IS HERE TODAY.
WE...YOU AND I...ARE GONE. IT--THE LEAGUE OF ASSASSINS--WILL GO ON.
BUT...WHAT HAPPENED BACK THEN? HOW DID YOU FAIL?
A TRUST THAT NO ONE FAILED IN OUR SACRED CALLING...
THE SUBLIME ART. DEATH...DEATH BY THE HAND OF THE ASSASSIN.
AND NOW, YOU...HOOK... YOU HAVE FAILED.
YES... YES.
YES, I FAILED MISERABLY.
DID YOU CHOOSE SO HARD A VICTIM THAT YOU...?
NO! YOU KNOW I DID NOT. NONE OF IT. I CHOSE HIM RANDOMLY. I SAW HIS NAME...ON A CIRCUS POSTER. I THOUGHT HE WOULD BE THE PERFECT TEST... OF MARKSMANSHIP...
NERVE... SURROUNDED BY A THOUSAND PEOPLE.
IF YOU HAD A SOUL INSTEAD OF NOTHING, THIS WOULD HAVE RIPPED IT OUT OF YOU, BOSTON BRAND.
FROM A POSTER!! HE KILLED ME FOR A PERVERTED GRADUATION TEST! IT...JUST...CAN'T...BE!
OH...YES, IT CAN BE...AND IT WAS. SAD DEADMAN!

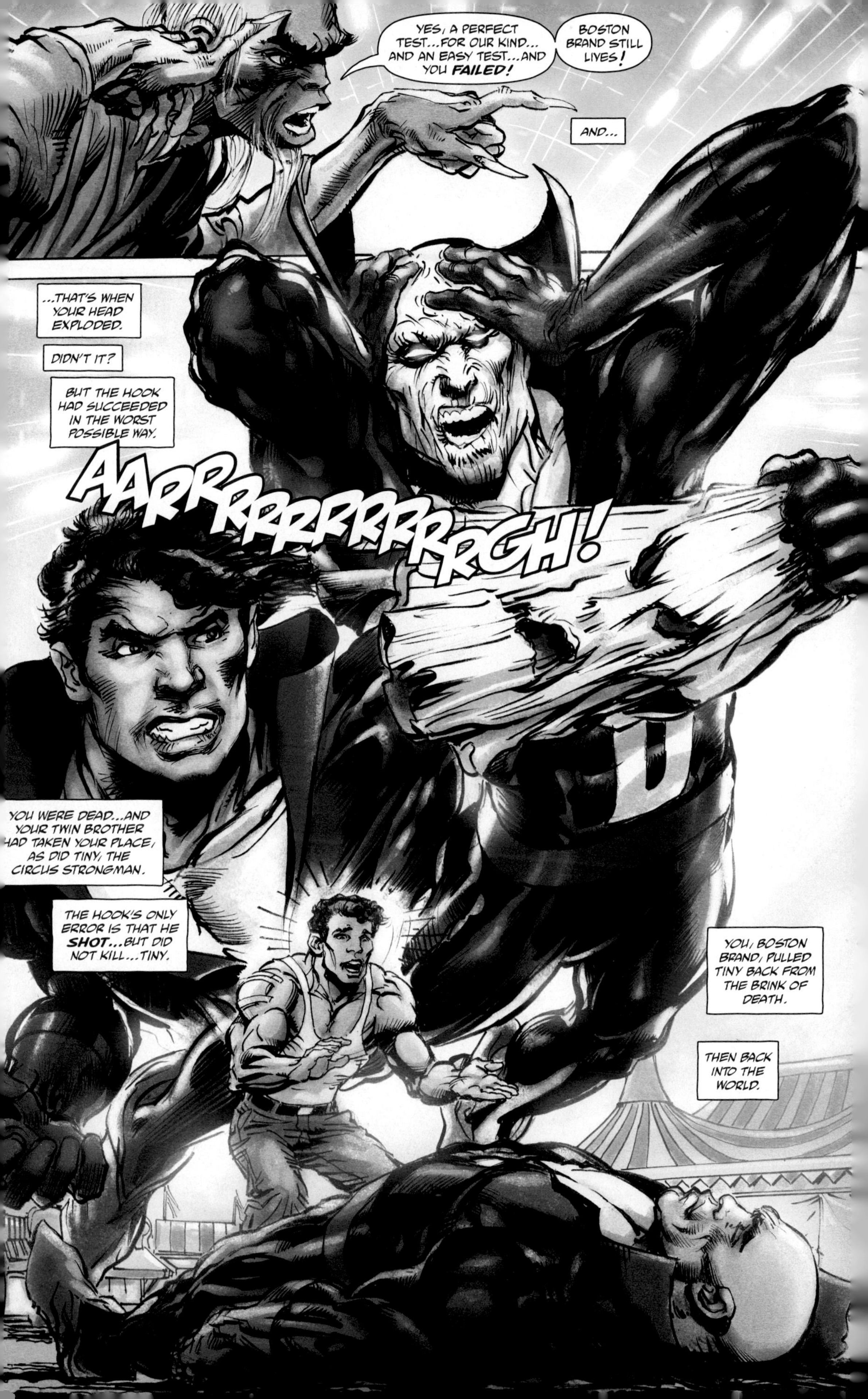
YES, A PERFECT TEST...FOR OUR KIND... AND AN EASY TEST...AND YOU **FAILED!**
BOSTON BRAND STILL LIVES!
AND...
...THAT'S WHEN YOUR HEAD EXPLODED.
DIDN'T IT?
BUT THE HOOK HAD SUCCEEDED IN THE WORST POSSIBLE WAY.
AARRRRRRRRRRGH!
YOU WERE DEAD...AND YOUR TWIN BROTHER HAD TAKEN YOUR PLACE, AS DID TINY, THE CIRCUS STRONGMAN.
THE HOOK'S ONLY ERROR IS THAT HE **SHOT...** BUT DID NOT KILL...TINY.
YOU, BOSTON BRAND, PULLED TINY BACK FROM THE BRINK OF DEATH.
THEN BACK INTO THE WORLD.

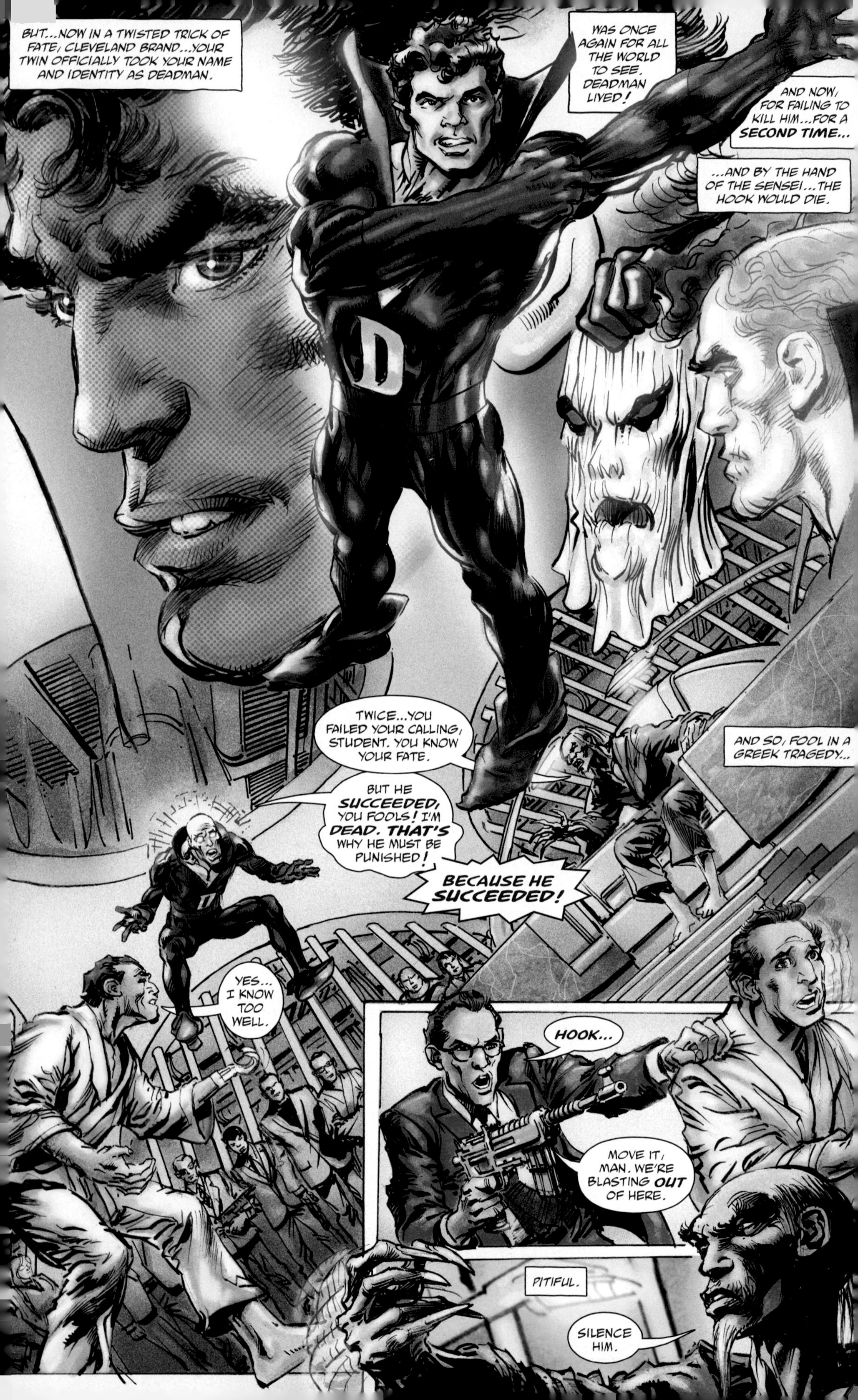
BUT...NOW IN A TWISTED TRICK OF FATE, CLEVELAND BRAND...YOUR TWIN OFFICIALLY TOOK YOUR NAME AND IDENTITY AS DEADMAN.
WAS ONCE AGAIN FOR ALL THE WORLD TO SEE. DEADMAN LIVED!
AND NOW, FOR FAILING TO KILL HIM...FOR A SECOND TIME...
...AND BY THE HAND OF THE SENSEI...THE HOOK WOULD DIE.
TWICE...YOU FAILED YOUR CALLING, STUDENT. YOU KNOW YOUR FATE.
BUT HE SUCCEEDED, YOU FOOLS! I'M DEAD. THAT'S WHY HE MUST BE PUNISHED!
BECAUSE HE SUCCEEDED!
AND SO, FOOL IN A GREEK TRAGEDY...
YES... I KNOW TOO WELL.
HOOK...
MOVE IT, MAN. WE'RE BLASTING OUT OF HERE.
PITIFUL.
SILENCE HIM.

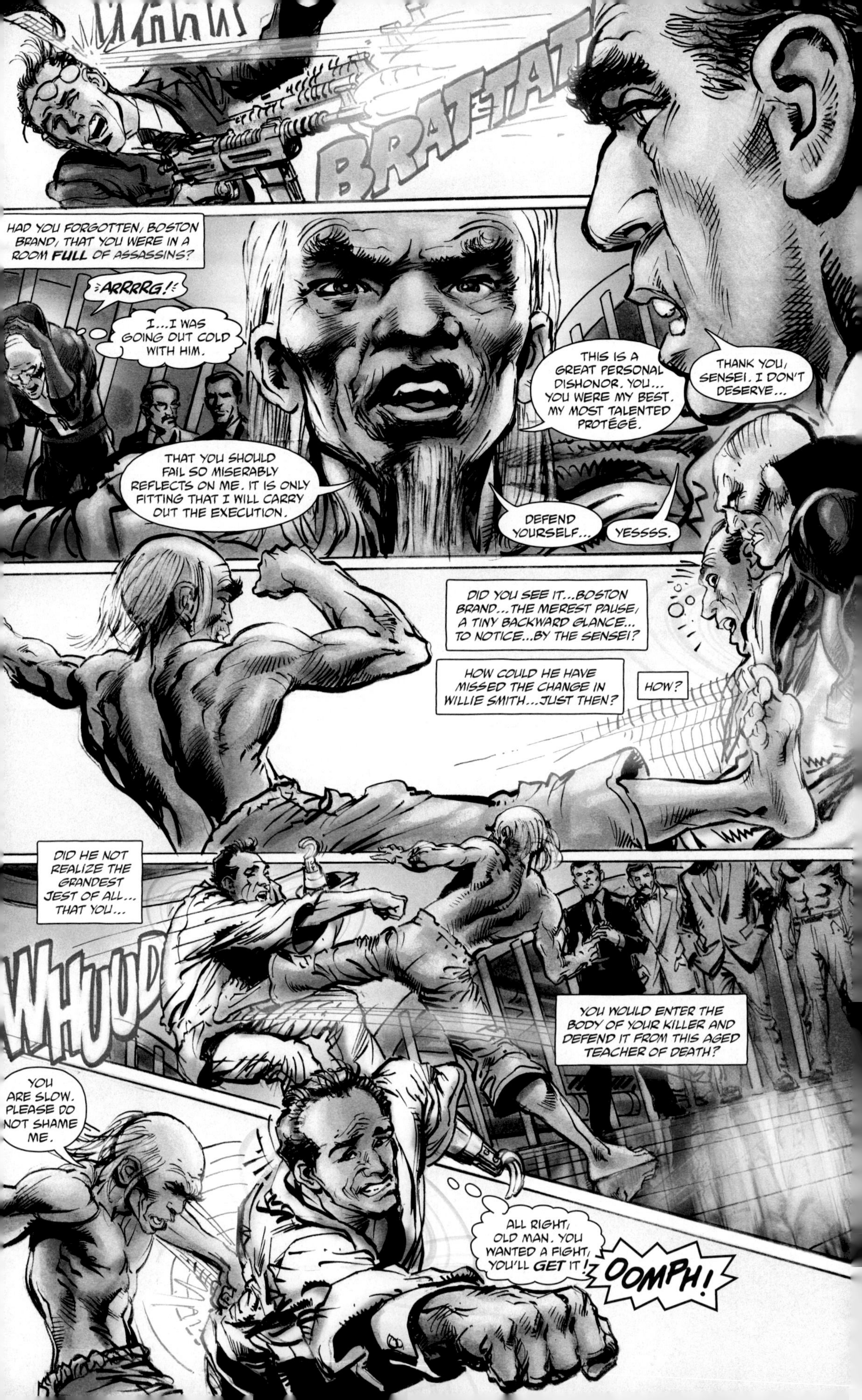

BRATTAT
HAD YOU FORGOTTEN, BOSTON BRAND, THAT YOU WERE IN A ROOM FULL OF ASSASSINS?
ARRRRG!
I...I WAS GOING OUT COLD WITH HIM.
THIS IS A GREAT PERSONAL DISHONOR. YOU... YOU WERE MY BEST. MY MOST TALENTED PROTÉGÉ.
THANK YOU, SENSEI. I DON'T DESERVE...
THAT YOU SHOULD FAIL SO MISERABLY REFLECTS ON ME. IT IS ONLY FITTING THAT I WILL CARRY OUT THE EXECUTION.
DEFEND YOURSELF...
YESSSS.
DID YOU SEE IT...BOSTON BRAND...THE MEREST PAUSE, A TINY BACKWARD GLANCE... TO NOTICE...BY THE SENSEI?
HOW COULD HE HAVE MISSED THE CHANGE IN WILLIE SMITH...JUST THEN?
HOW?
DID HE NOT REALIZE THE GRANDEST JEST OF ALL... THAT YOU...
WHUD
YOU WOULD ENTER THE BODY OF YOUR KILLER AND DEFEND IT FROM THIS AGED TEACHER OF DEATH?
YOU ARE SLOW. PLEASE DO NOT SHAME ME.
ALL RIGHT, OLD MAN. YOU WANTED A FIGHT, YOU'LL GET IT!
OOMPH!

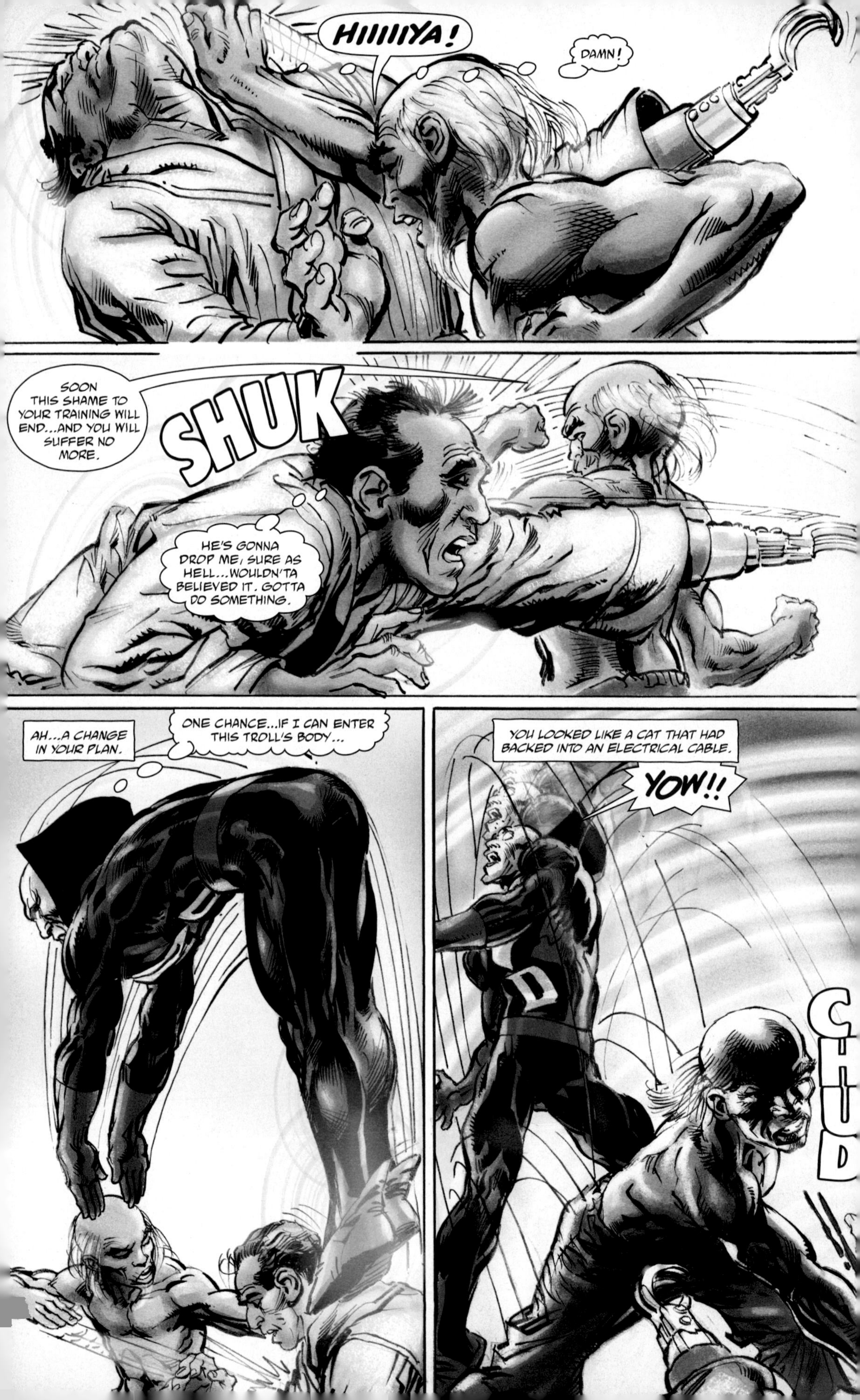

HIIIIIYA!
DAMN!
SOON THIS SHAME TO YOUR TRAINING WILL END...AND YOU WILL SUFFER NO MORE.
SHUK
HE'S GONNA DROP ME, SURE AS HELL...WOULDN'TA BELIEVED IT. GOTTA DO SOMETHING.
AH...A CHANGE IN YOUR PLAN.
ONE CHANCE...IF I CAN ENTER THIS TROLL'S BODY...
YOU LOOKED LIKE A CAT THAT HAD BACKED INTO AN ELECTRICAL CABLE.
YOW!!
CHUD

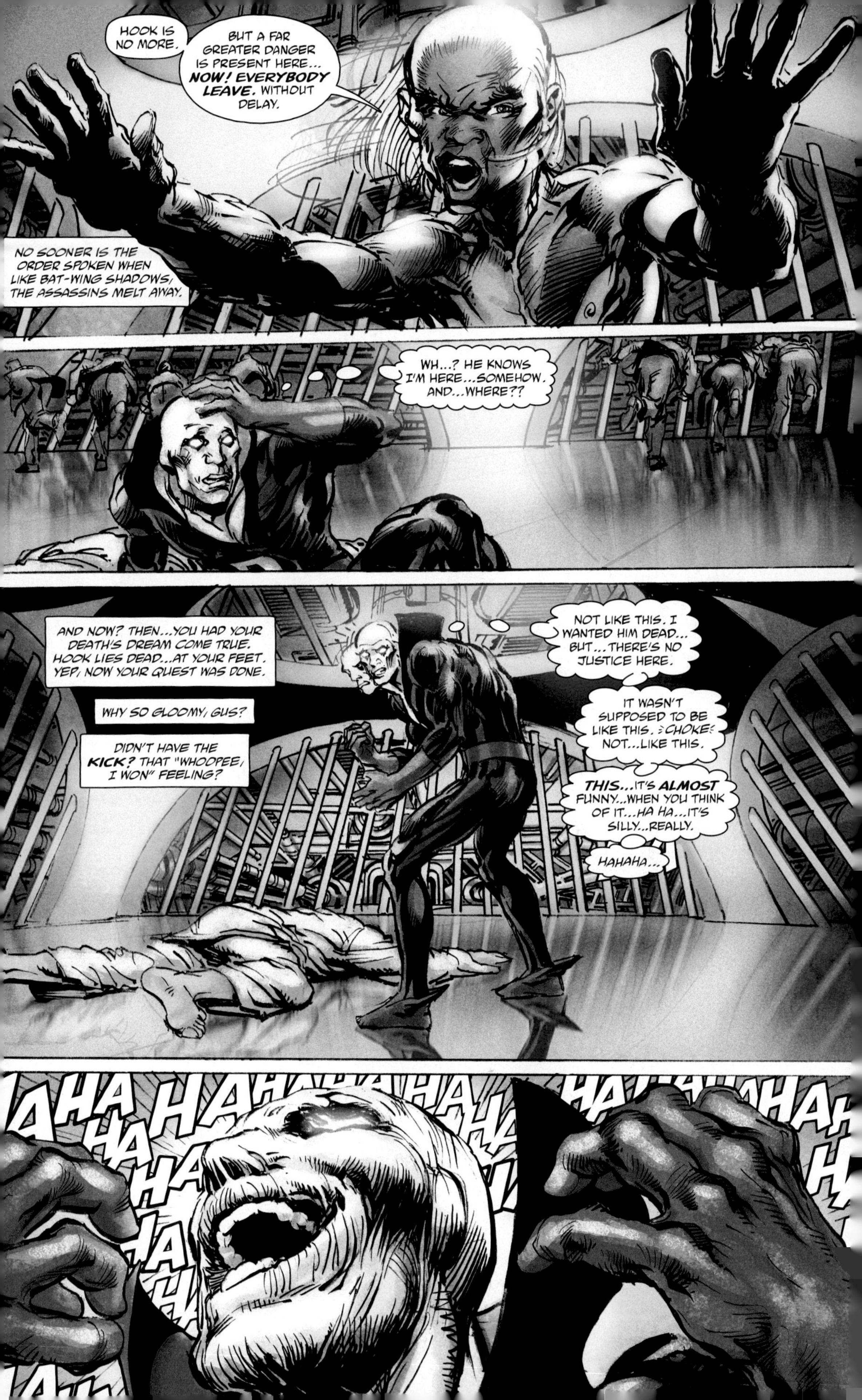
HOOK IS NO MORE.
BUT A FAR GREATER DANGER IS PRESENT HERE... **NOW! EVERYBODY LEAVE.** WITHOUT DELAY.
NO SOONER IS THE ORDER SPOKEN WHEN LIKE BAT-WING SHADOWS, THE ASSASSINS MELT AWAY.
WH...? HE KNOWS I'M HERE...SOMEHOW. AND...WHERE??
AND NOW? THEN...YOU HAD YOUR DEATH'S DREAM COME TRUE. HOOK LIES DEAD...AT YOUR FEET. YEP, NOW YOUR QUEST WAS DONE.
WHY SO GLOOMY, GUS?
DIDN'T HAVE THE **KICK?** THAT "WHOOPEE, I WON" FEELING?
NOT LIKE THIS. I WANTED HIM DEAD... BUT...THERE'S NO JUSTICE HERE.
IT WASN'T SUPPOSED TO BE LIKE THIS. ≈CHOKE≈ NOT...LIKE THIS.
THIS... IT'S **ALMOST** FUNNY...WHEN YOU THINK OF IT...HA HA...IT'S SILLY...REALLY.
HAHAHA...
HA HA HAHAHAHA HA HA HA HA HA HA HA HAHAHAHAHA HA

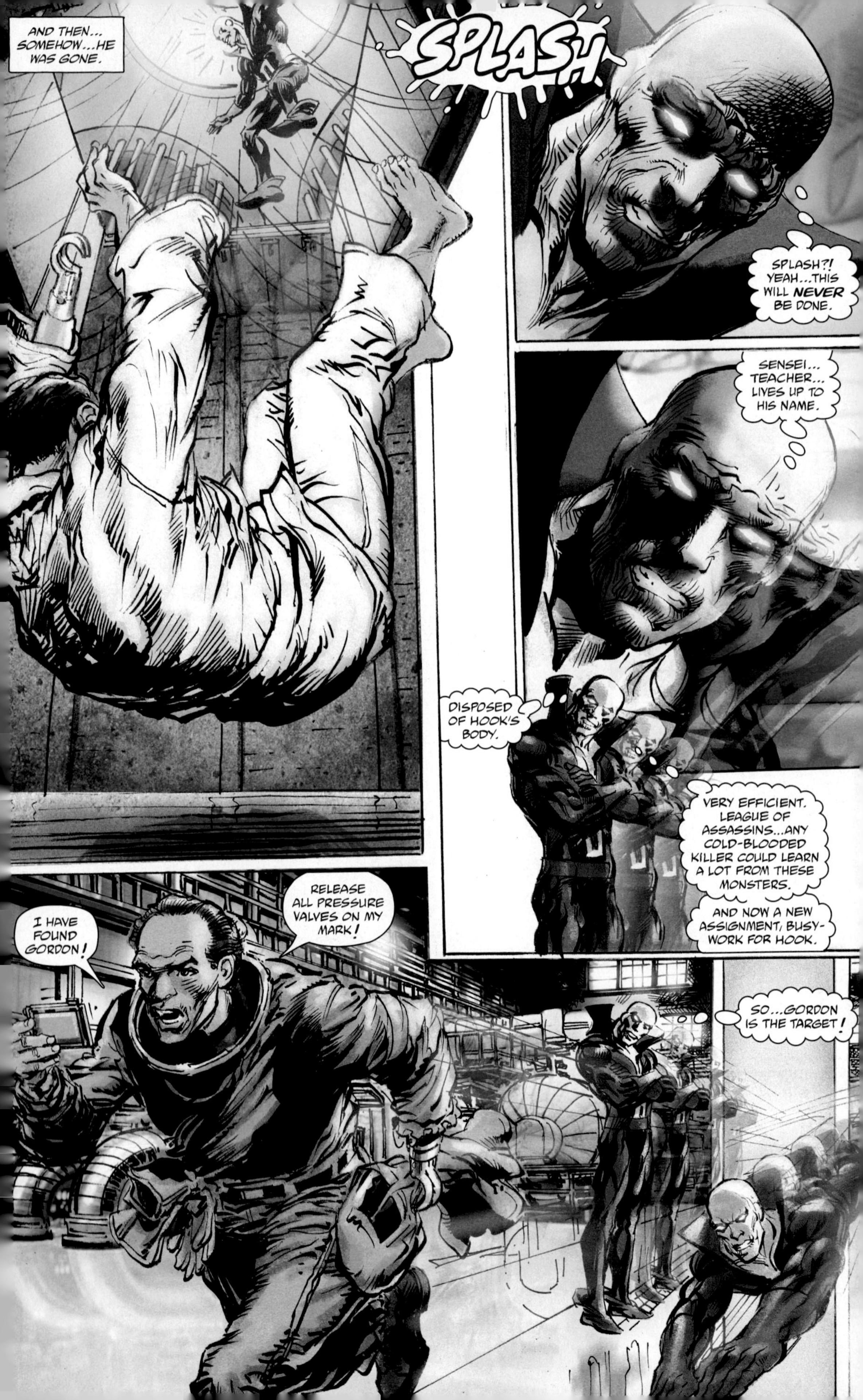
AND THEN... SOMEHOW...HE WAS GONE.
SPLASH
SPLASH?! YEAH...THIS WILL NEVER BE DONE.
SENSEI... TEACHER... LIVES UP TO HIS NAME.
DISPOSED OF HOOK'S BODY.
VERY EFFICIENT. LEAGUE OF ASSASSINS...ANY COLD-BLOODED KILLER COULD LEARN A LOT FROM THESE MONSTERS.
AND NOW A NEW ASSIGNMENT, BUSY-WORK FOR HOOK.
I HAVE FOUND GORDON!
RELEASE ALL PRESSURE VALVES ON MY MARK!
SO...GORDON IS THE TARGET!

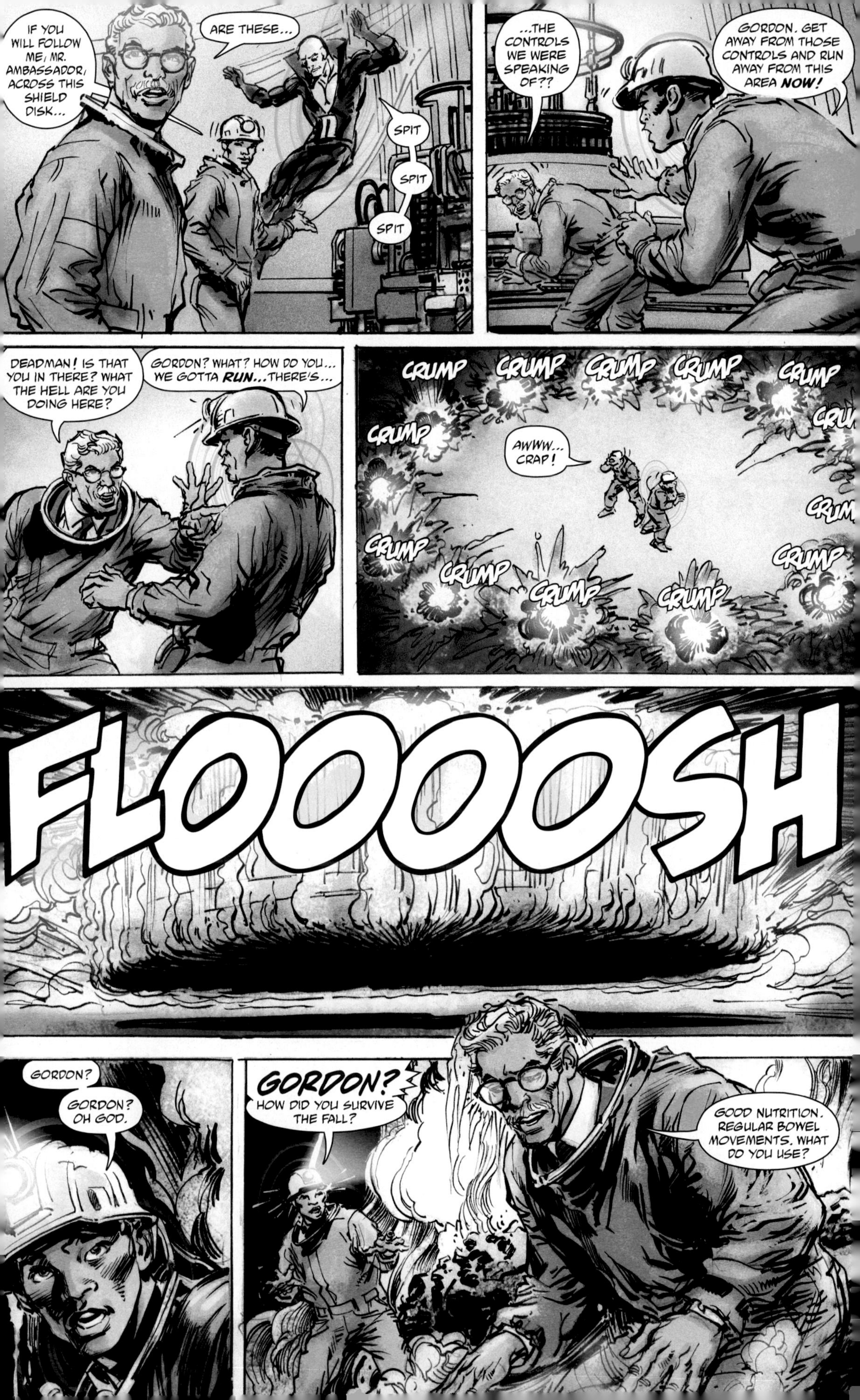
IF YOU WILL FOLLOW ME, MR. AMBASSADOR, ACROSS THIS SHIELD DISK...
ARE THESE...
SPIT
SPIT
SPIT
...THE CONTROLS WE WERE SPEAKING OF??
GORDON. GET AWAY FROM THOSE CONTROLS AND RUN AWAY FROM THIS AREA NOW!
DEADMAN! IS THAT YOU IN THERE? WHAT THE HELL ARE YOU DOING HERE?
GORDON? WHAT? HOW DO YOU... WE GOTTA RUN... THERE'S...
CRUMP CRUMP CRUMP CRUMP CRUMP
CRUMP
AWWW... CRAP!
CRUMP CRUMP CRUMP CRUMP CRUMP
FLOOOOSH
GORDON?
GORDON? OH GOD.
GORDON?
HOW DID YOU SURVIVE THE FALL?
GOOD NUTRITION. REGULAR BOWEL MOVEMENTS. WHAT DO YOU USE?

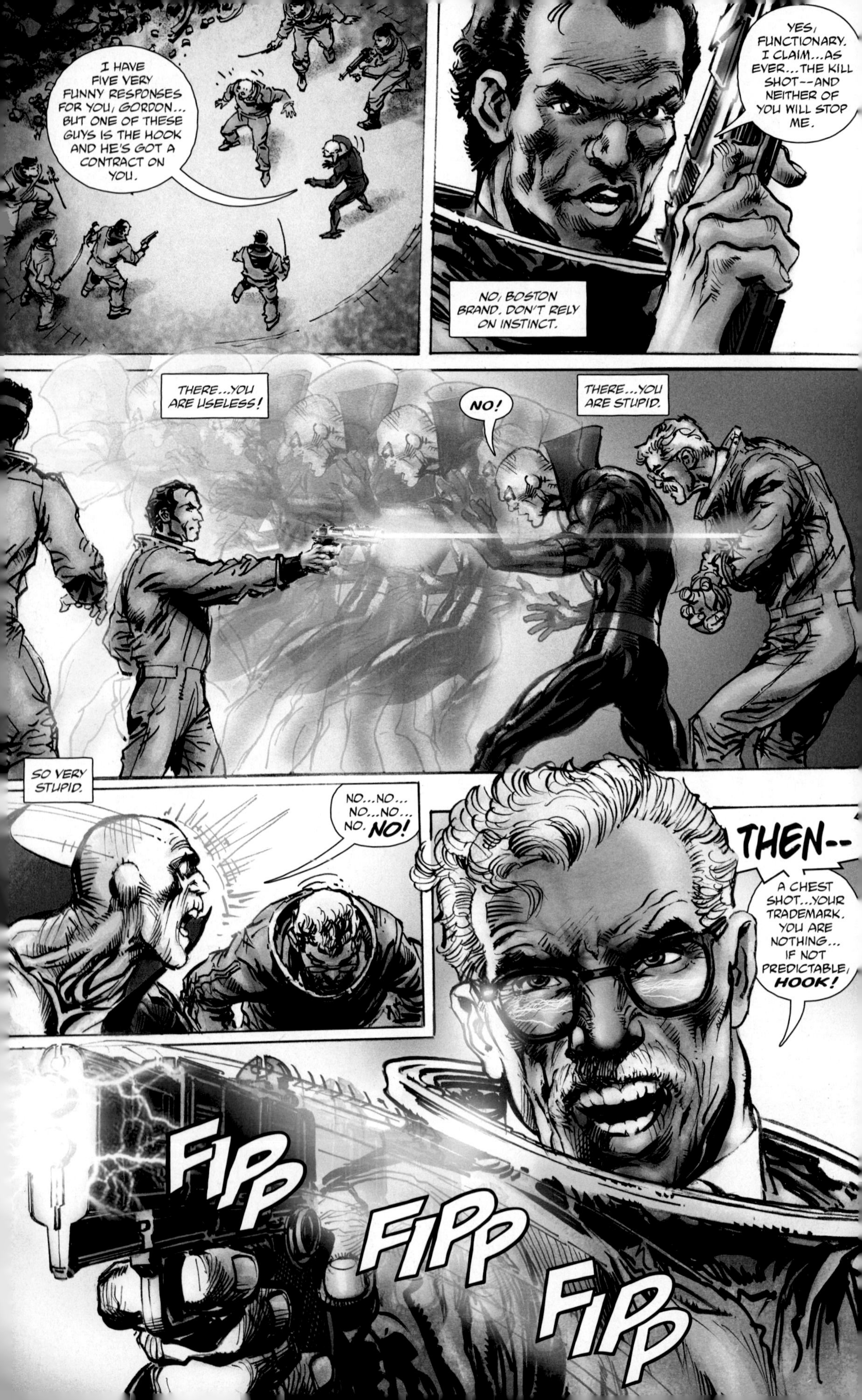
I HAVE FIVE VERY FUNNY RESPONSES FOR YOU, GORDON... BUT ONE OF THESE GUYS IS THE HOOK AND HE'S GOT A CONTRACT ON YOU.
YES, FUNCTIONARY. I CLAIM...AS EVER...THE KILL SHOT--AND NEITHER OF YOU WILL STOP ME.
NO, BOSTON BRAND. DON'T RELY ON INSTINCT.
THERE...YOU ARE USELESS!
NO!
THERE...YOU ARE STUPID.
SO VERY STUPID.
NO...NO... NO...NO... NO. NO!
THEN--
A CHEST SHOT...YOUR TRADEMARK. YOU ARE NOTHING... IF NOT PREDICTABLE, HOOK!
FIPP
FIPP
FIPP

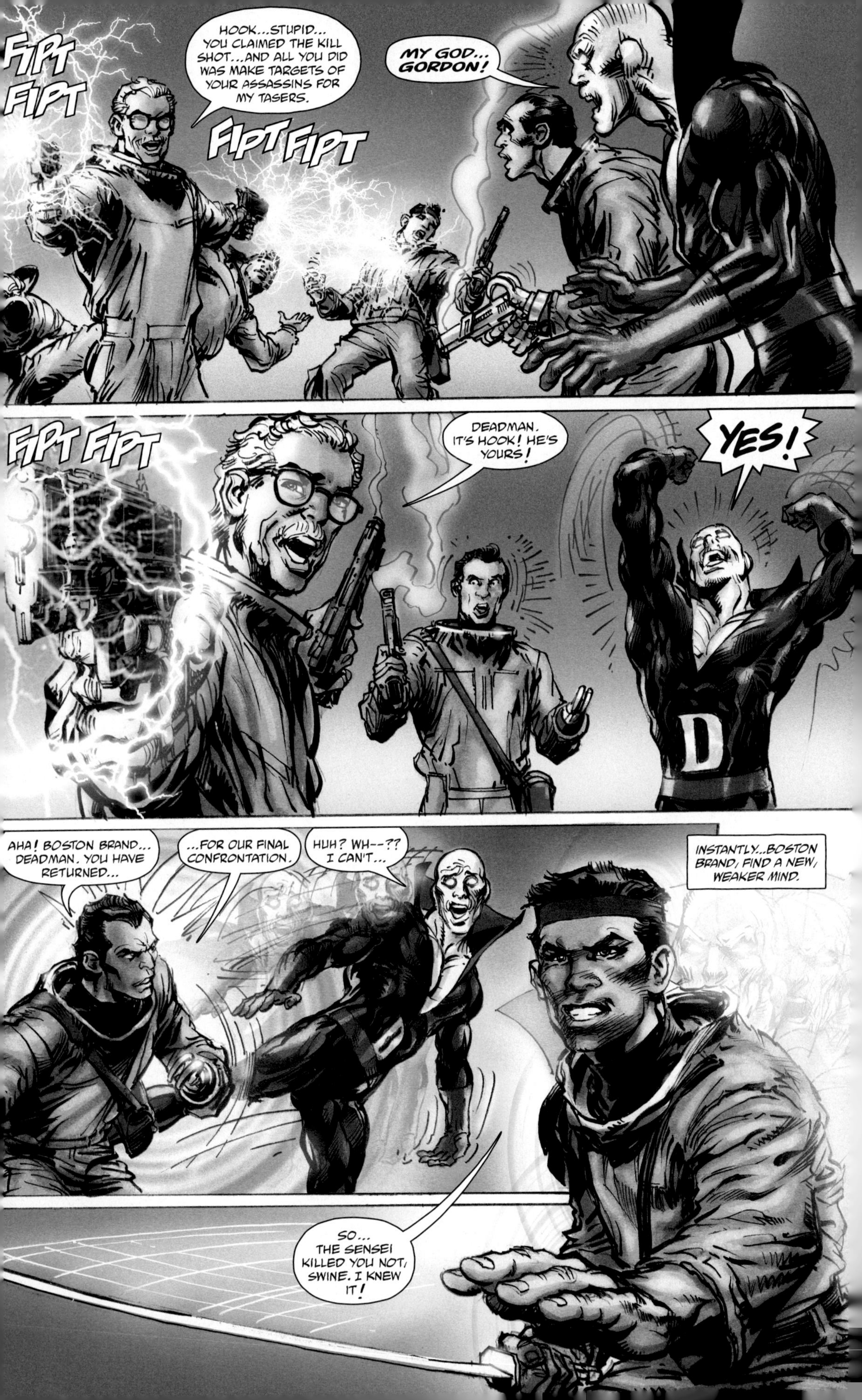
FIPT FIPT
HOOK...STUPID... YOU CLAIMED THE KILL SHOT...AND ALL YOU DID WAS MAKE TARGETS OF YOUR ASSASSINS FOR MY TASERS.
FIPT FIPT
MY GOD... GORDON!
FIPT FIPT
DEADMAN. IT'S HOOK! HE'S YOURS!
YES!
AHA! BOSTON BRAND... DEADMAN. YOU HAVE RETURNED...
...FOR OUR FINAL CONFRONTATION.
HUH? WH--?? I CAN'T...
INSTANTLY...BOSTON BRAND, FIND A NEW, WEAKER MIND.
SO... THE SENSEI KILLED YOU NOT, SWINE. I KNEW IT!

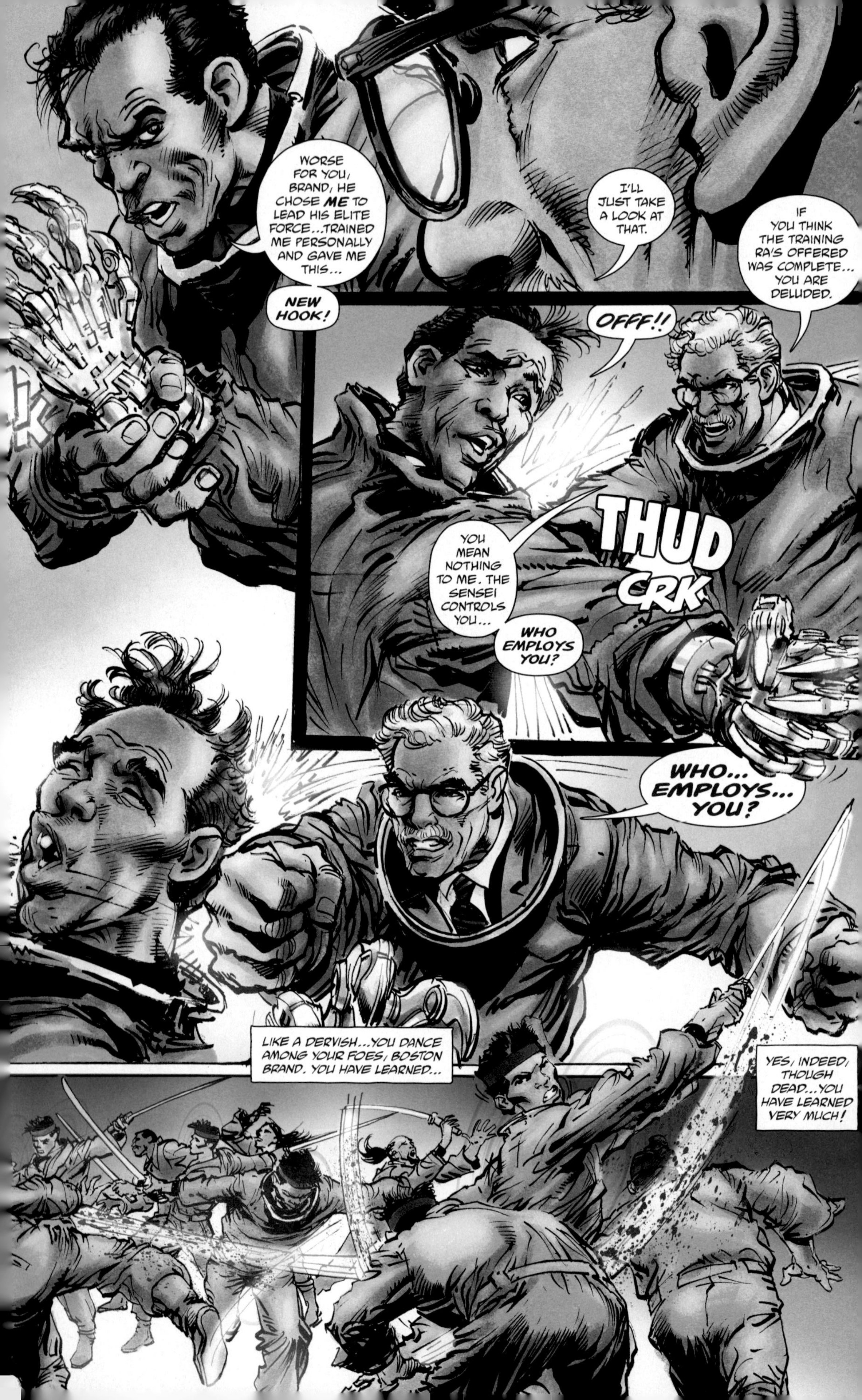
WORSE FOR YOU, BRAND, HE CHOSE ME TO LEAD HIS ELITE FORCE...TRAINED ME PERSONALLY AND GAVE ME THIS...
NEW HOOK!
I'LL JUST TAKE A LOOK AT THAT.
IF YOU THINK THE TRAINING RA'S OFFERED WAS COMPLETE... YOU ARE DELUDED.
OFFF!!
THUD
CRK
YOU MEAN NOTHING TO ME. THE SENSEI CONTROLS YOU...
WHO EMPLOYS YOU?
WHO... EMPLOYS... YOU?
LIKE A DERVISH...YOU DANCE AMONG YOUR FOES, BOSTON BRAND. YOU HAVE LEARNED...
YES, INDEED, THOUGH DEAD...YOU HAVE LEARNED VERY MUCH!

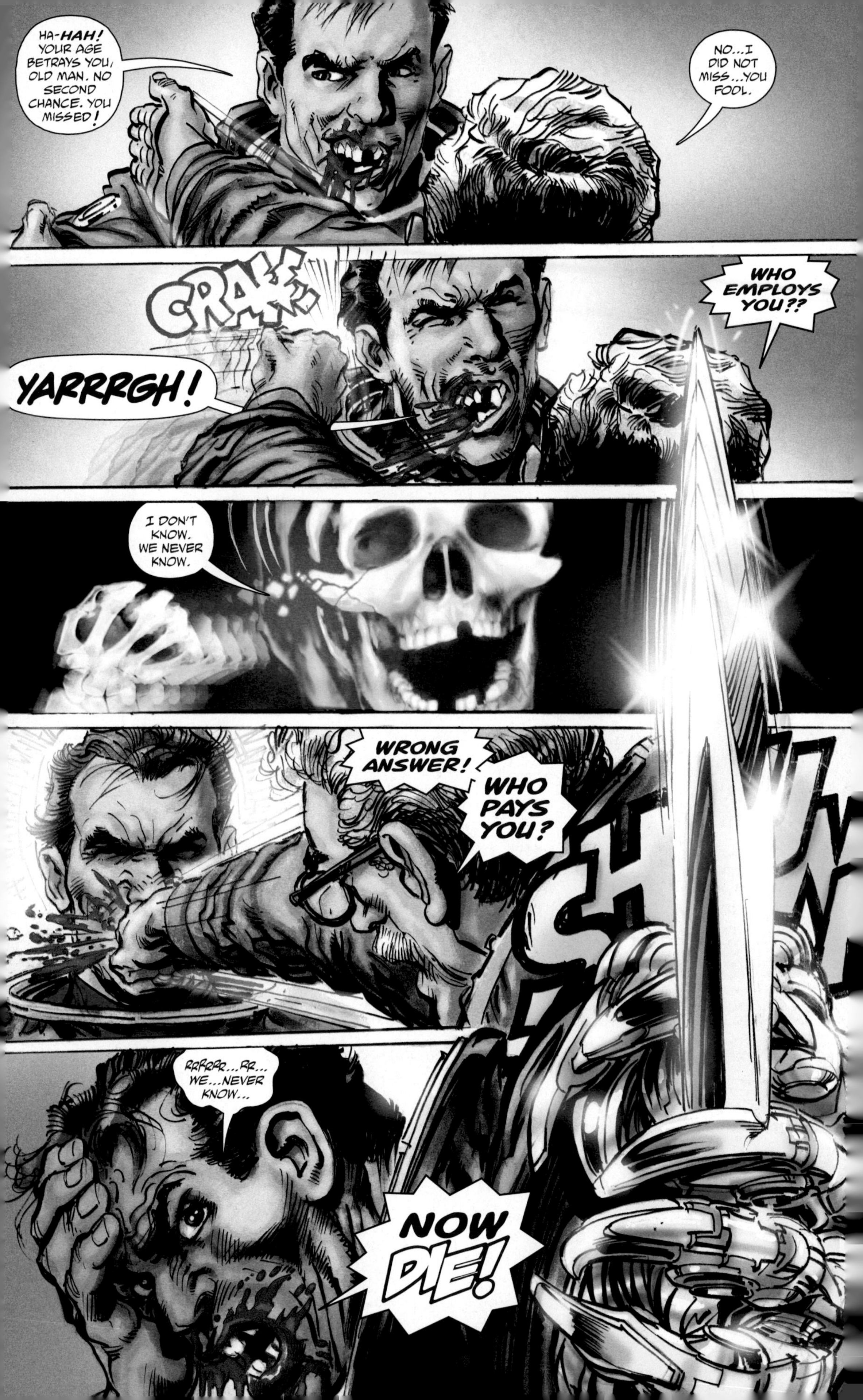
HA-HAH! YOUR AGE BETRAYS YOU, OLD MAN. NO SECOND CHANCE. YOU MISSED!
NO...I DID NOT MISS...YOU FOOL.
CRAK!
WHO EMPLOYS YOU??
YARRRGH!
I DON'T KNOW. WE NEVER KNOW.
WRONG ANSWER!
WHO PAYS YOU?
RRRRRR...RR... WE...NEVER KNOW...
NOW DIE!

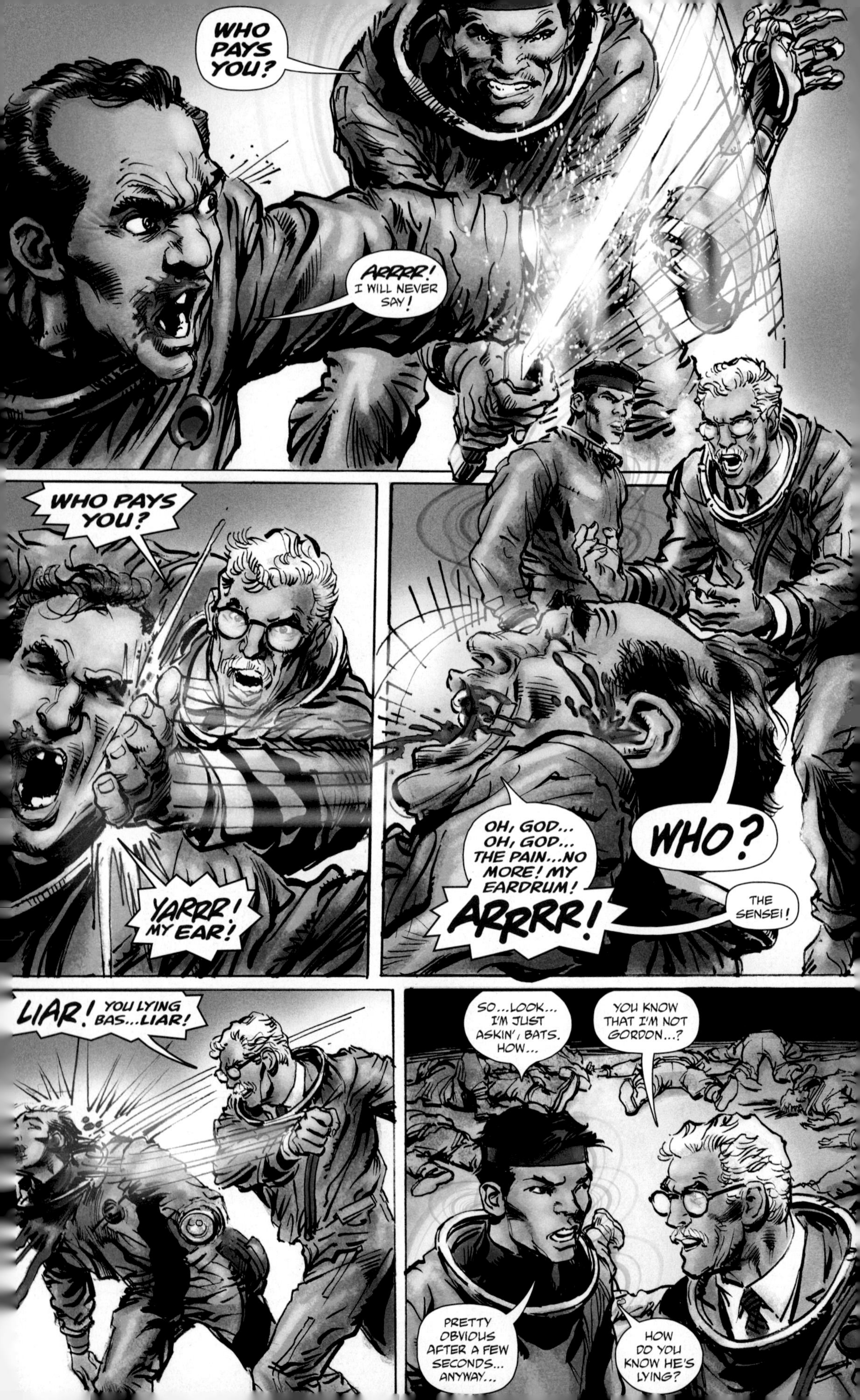
WHO PAYS YOU?
ARRRR! I WILL NEVER SAY!
WHO PAYS YOU?
YARRR! MY EAR!
OH, GOD... OH, GOD... THE PAIN...NO MORE! MY EARDRUM!
ARRRR!
WHO?
THE SENSEI!
LIAR! YOU LYING BAS...LIAR!
SO...LOOK... I'M JUST ASKIN', BATS. HOW...
YOU KNOW THAT I'M NOT GORDON...?
PRETTY OBVIOUS AFTER A FEW SECONDS... ANYWAY...
HOW DO YOU KNOW HE'S LYING?

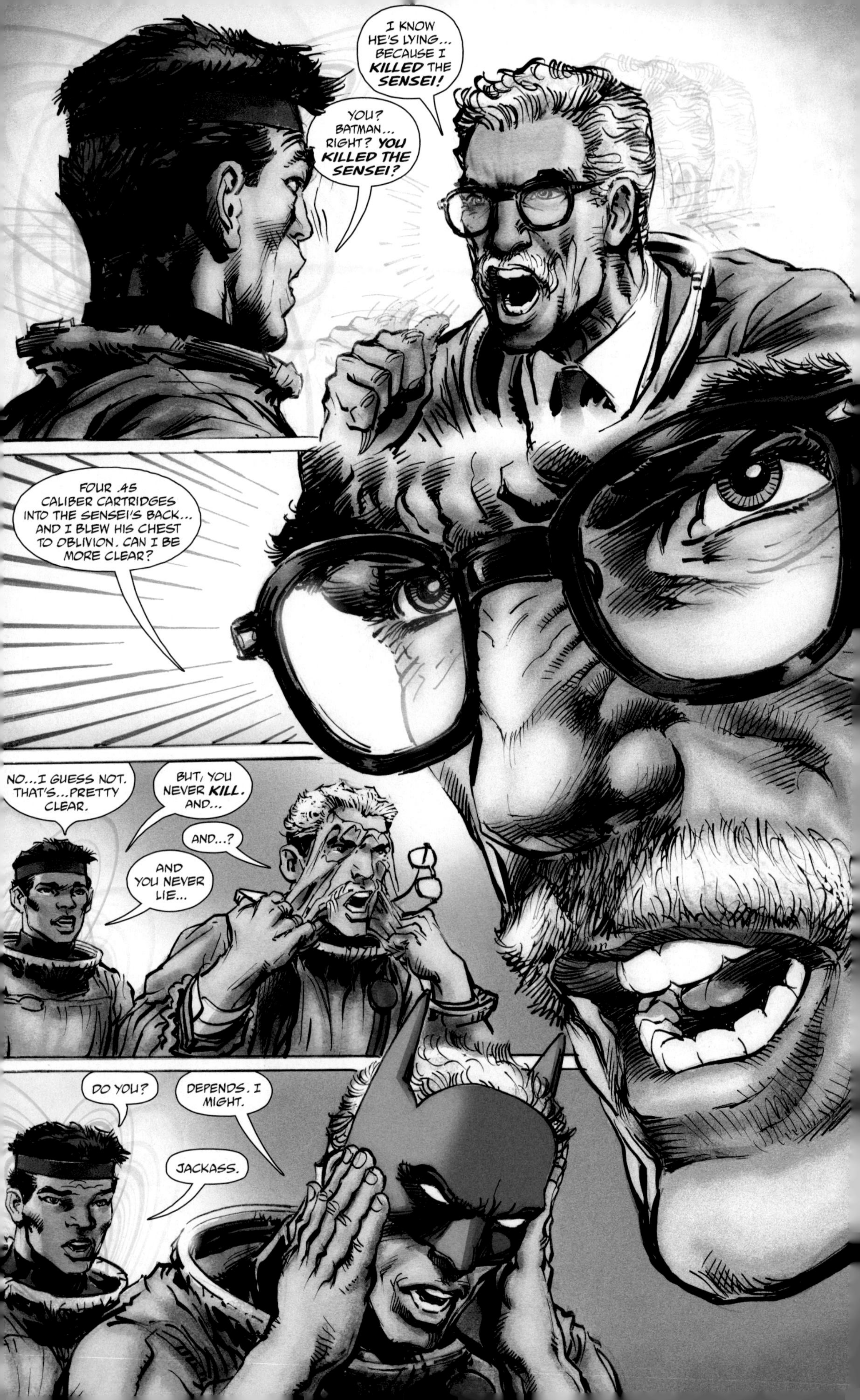
I KNOW HE'S LYING... BECAUSE I KILLED THE SENSEI!
YOU? BATMAN... RIGHT? YOU KILLED THE SENSEI?
FOUR .45 CALIBER CARTRIDGES INTO THE SENSEI'S BACK... AND I BLEW HIS CHEST TO OBLIVION. CAN I BE MORE CLEAR?
NO...I GUESS NOT. THAT'S...PRETTY CLEAR.
BUT, YOU NEVER KILL. AND...
AND...?
AND YOU NEVER LIE...
DO YOU?
DEPENDS. I MIGHT.
JACKASS.

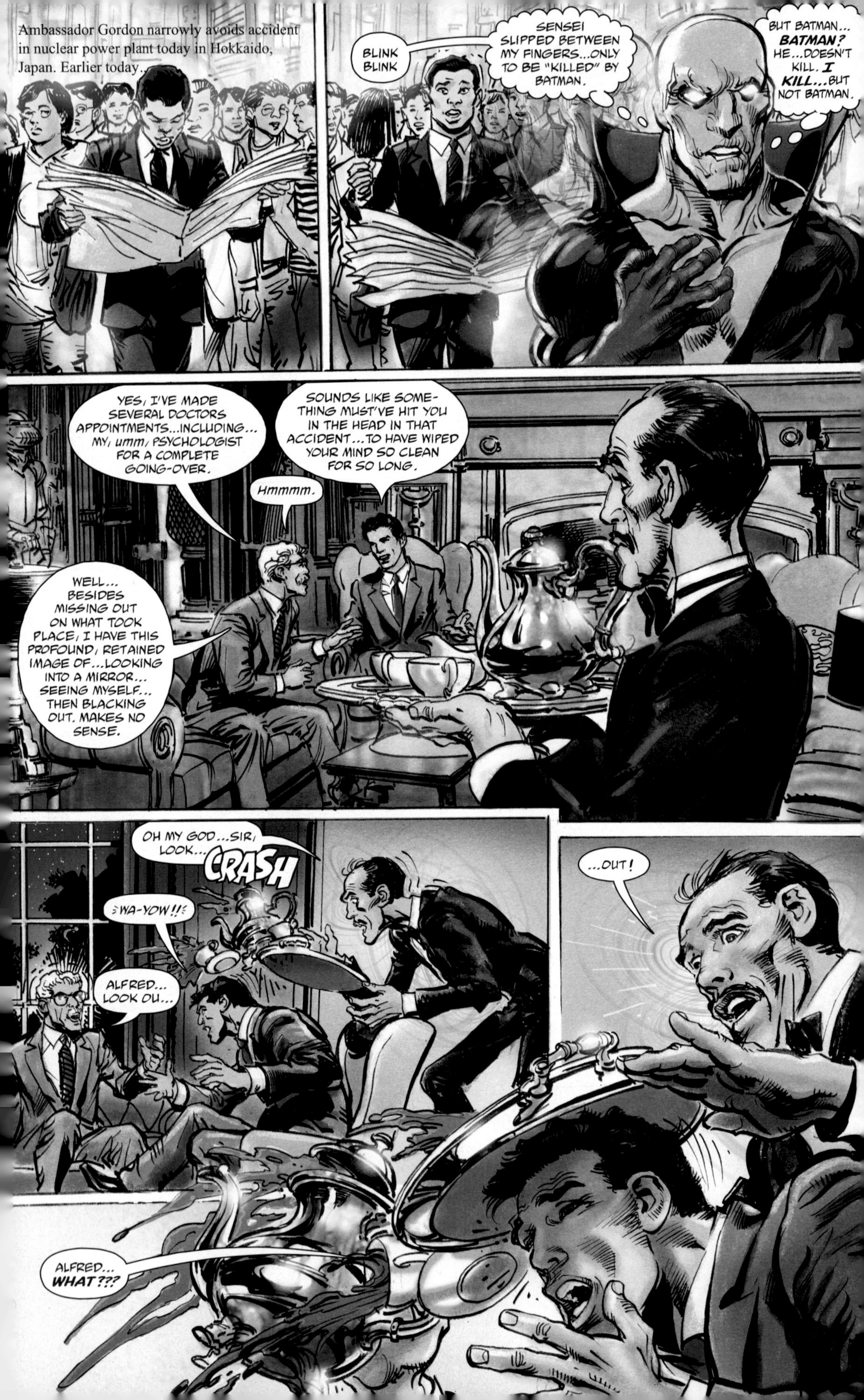
Ambassador Gordon narrowly avoids accident in nuclear power plant today in Hokkaido, Japan. Earlier today...
BLINK BLINK
SENSEI SLIPPED BETWEEN MY FINGERS...ONLY TO BE "KILLED" BY BATMAN.
BUT BATMAN... BATMAN? HE...DOESN'T KILL. I KILL...BUT NOT BATMAN.
YES, I'VE MADE SEVERAL DOCTORS APPOINTMENTS...INCLUDING... MY, umm, PSYCHOLOGIST FOR A COMPLETE GOING-OVER.
Hmmmm.
SOUNDS LIKE SOME-THING MUST'VE HIT YOU IN THE HEAD IN THAT ACCIDENT...TO HAVE WIPED YOUR MIND SO CLEAN FOR SO LONG.
WELL... BESIDES MISSING OUT ON WHAT TOOK PLACE, I HAVE THIS PROFOUND, RETAINED IMAGE OF...LOOKING INTO A MIRROR... SEEING MYSELF... THEN BLACKING OUT. MAKES NO SENSE.
OH MY GOD...SIR, LOOK...
CRASH
WA-YOW!!
ALFRED... LOOK OU...
...OUT!
ALFRED... WHAT???

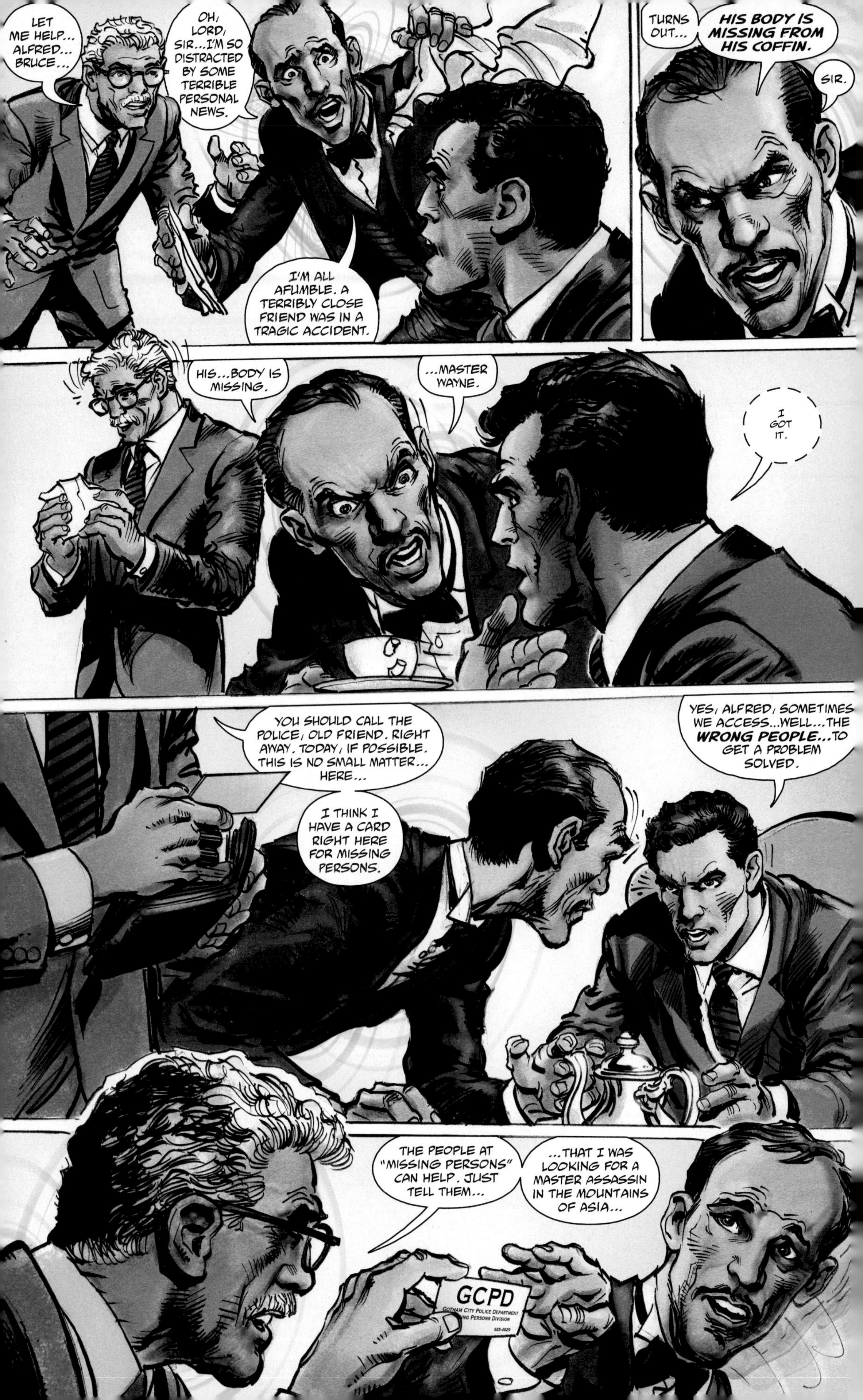
LET ME HELP... ALFRED... BRUCE...
OH, LORD, SIR...I'M SO DISTRACTED BY SOME TERRIBLE PERSONAL NEWS.
I'M ALL AFUMBLE. A TERRIBLY CLOSE FRIEND WAS IN A TRAGIC ACCIDENT.
TURNS OUT...
HIS BODY IS MISSING FROM HIS COFFIN.
SIR.
HIS...BODY IS MISSING.
...MASTER WAYNE.
I GOT IT.
YOU SHOULD CALL THE POLICE, OLD FRIEND. RIGHT AWAY. TODAY, IF POSSIBLE. THIS IS NO SMALL MATTER... HERE...
I THINK I HAVE A CARD RIGHT HERE FOR MISSING PERSONS.
YES, ALFRED, SOMETIMES WE ACCESS...WELL...THE WRONG PEOPLE...TO GET A PROBLEM SOLVED.
THE PEOPLE AT "MISSING PERSONS" CAN HELP. JUST TELL THEM...
...THAT I WAS LOOKING FOR A MASTER ASSASSIN IN THE MOUNTAINS OF ASIA...
GCPD
GOTHAM CITY POLICE DEPARTMENT
555-4529

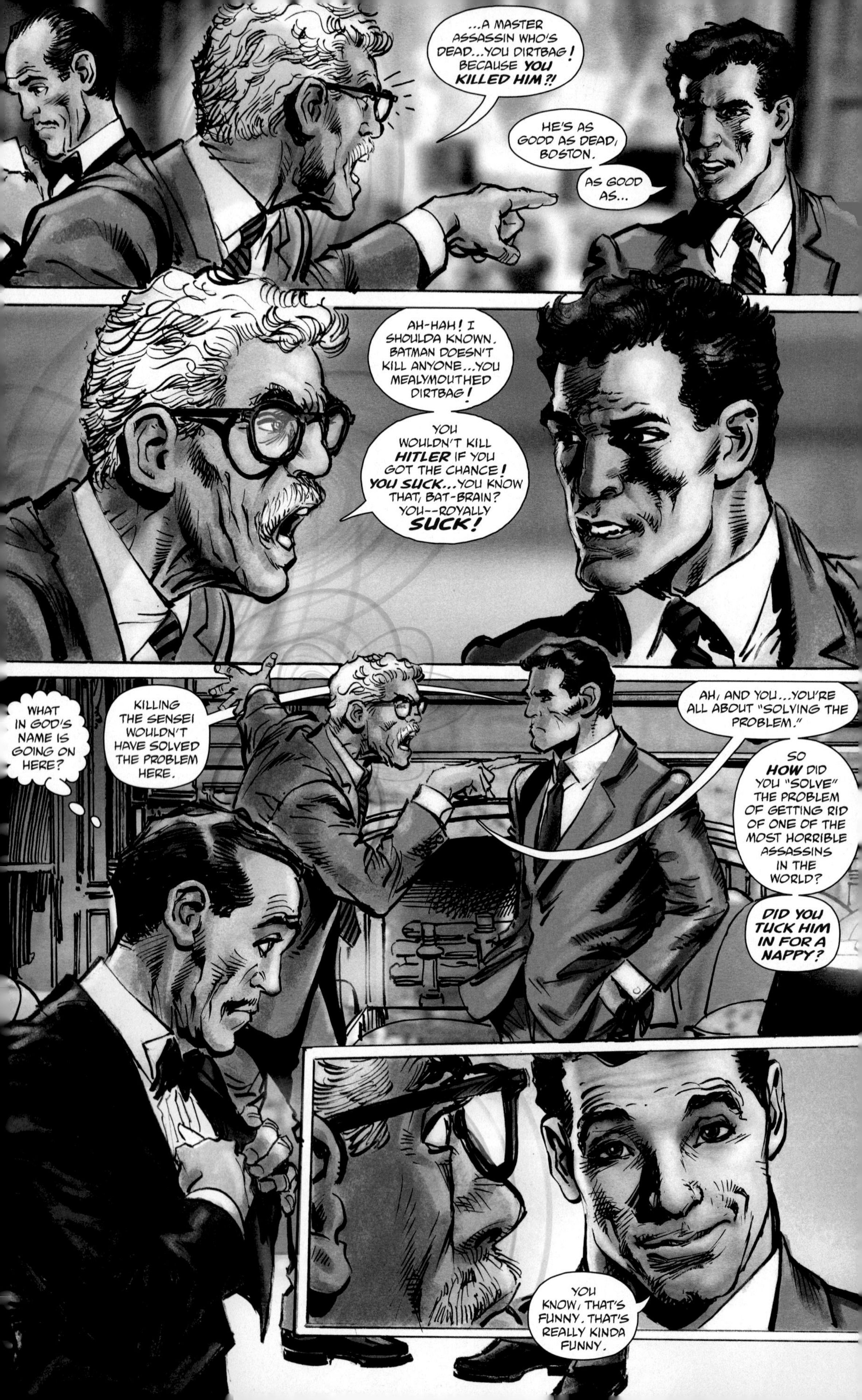
...A MASTER ASSASSIN WHO'S DEAD...YOU DIRTBAG! BECAUSE YOU KILLED HIM?!
HE'S AS GOOD AS DEAD, BOSTON.
AS GOOD AS...
AH-HAH! I SHOULDA KNOWN. BATMAN DOESN'T KILL ANYONE...YOU MEALYMOUTHED DIRTBAG!
YOU WOULDN'T KILL HITLER IF YOU GOT THE CHANCE! YOU SUCK...YOU KNOW THAT, BAT-BRAIN? YOU--ROYALLY SUCK!
WHAT IN GOD'S NAME IS GOING ON HERE?
KILLING THE SENSEI WOULDN'T HAVE SOLVED THE PROBLEM HERE.
AH, AND YOU...YOU'RE ALL ABOUT "SOLVING THE PROBLEM."
SO HOW DID YOU "SOLVE" THE PROBLEM OF GETTING RID OF ONE OF THE MOST HORRIBLE ASSASSINS IN THE WORLD?
DID YOU TUCK HIM IN FOR A NAPPY?
YOU KNOW, THAT'S FUNNY. THAT'S REALLY KINDA FUNNY.

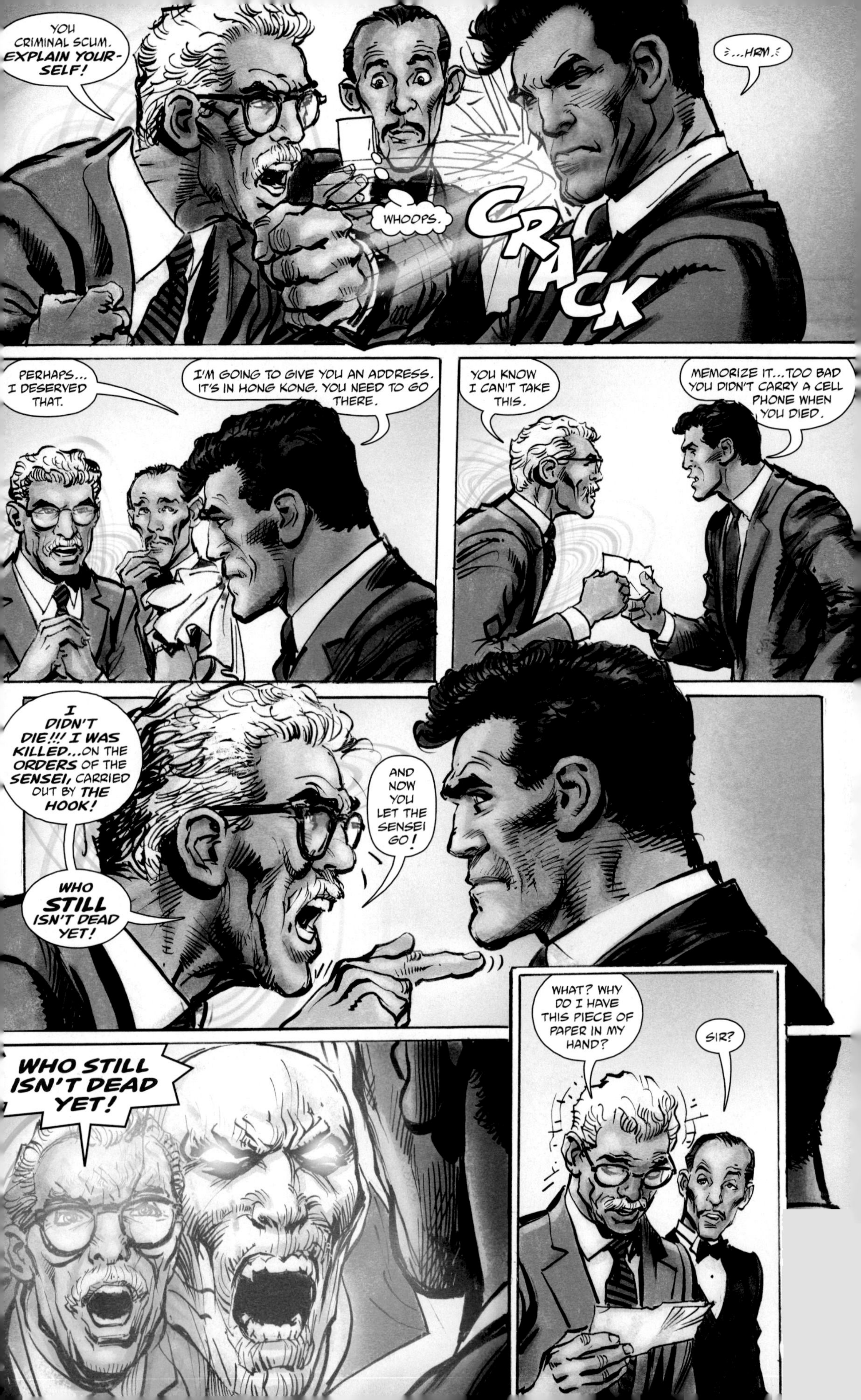

YOU CRIMINAL SCUM. EXPLAIN YOURSELF!
WHOOPS.
CRACK
...HRM...
PERHAPS... I DESERVED THAT.
I'M GOING TO GIVE YOU AN ADDRESS. IT'S IN HONG KONG. YOU NEED TO GO THERE.
YOU KNOW I CAN'T TAKE THIS.
MEMORIZE IT...TOO BAD YOU DIDN'T CARRY A CELL PHONE WHEN YOU DIED.
I DIDN'T DIE!!! I WAS KILLED...ON THE ORDERS OF THE SENSEI, CARRIED OUT BY THE HOOK!
AND NOW YOU LET THE SENSEI GO!
WHO STILL ISN'T DEAD YET!
WHO STILL ISN'T DEAD YET!
WHAT? WHY DO I HAVE THIS PIECE OF PAPER IN MY HAND?
SIR?

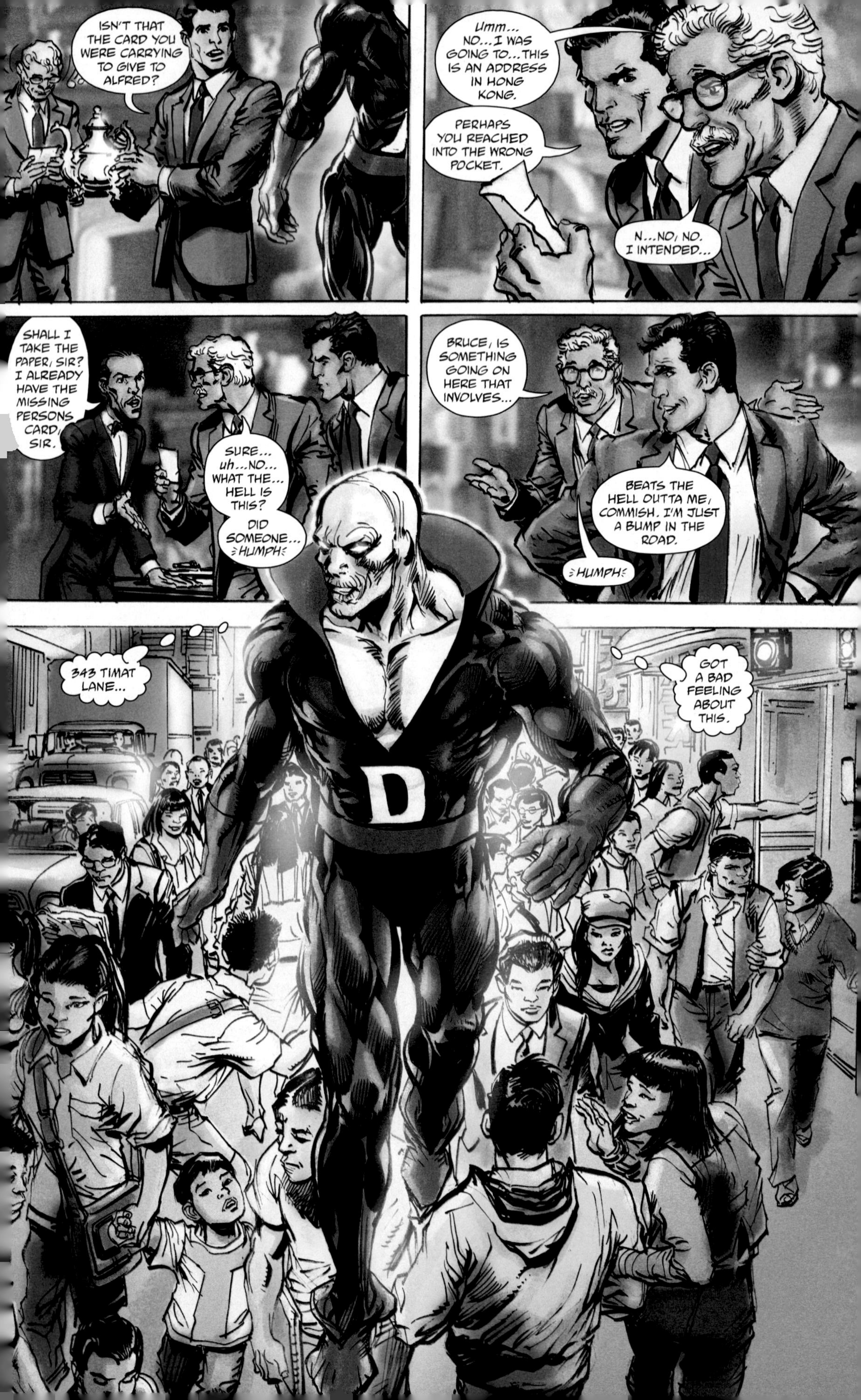
ISN'T THAT THE CARD YOU WERE CARRYING TO GIVE TO ALFRED?
Umm... NO...I WAS GOING TO...THIS IS AN ADDRESS IN HONG KONG.
PERHAPS YOU REACHED INTO THE WRONG POCKET.
N...NO, NO. I INTENDED...
SHALL I TAKE THE PAPER, SIR? I ALREADY HAVE THE MISSING PERSONS CARD, SIR.
SURE... uh...NO... WHAT THE... HELL IS THIS?
DID SOMEONE... HUMPH
BRUCE, IS SOMETHING GOING ON HERE THAT INVOLVES...
BEATS THE HELL OUTTA ME, COMMISH. I'M JUST A BUMP IN THE ROAD.
HUMPH
343 TIMAT LANE...
GOT A BAD FEELING ABOUT THIS.

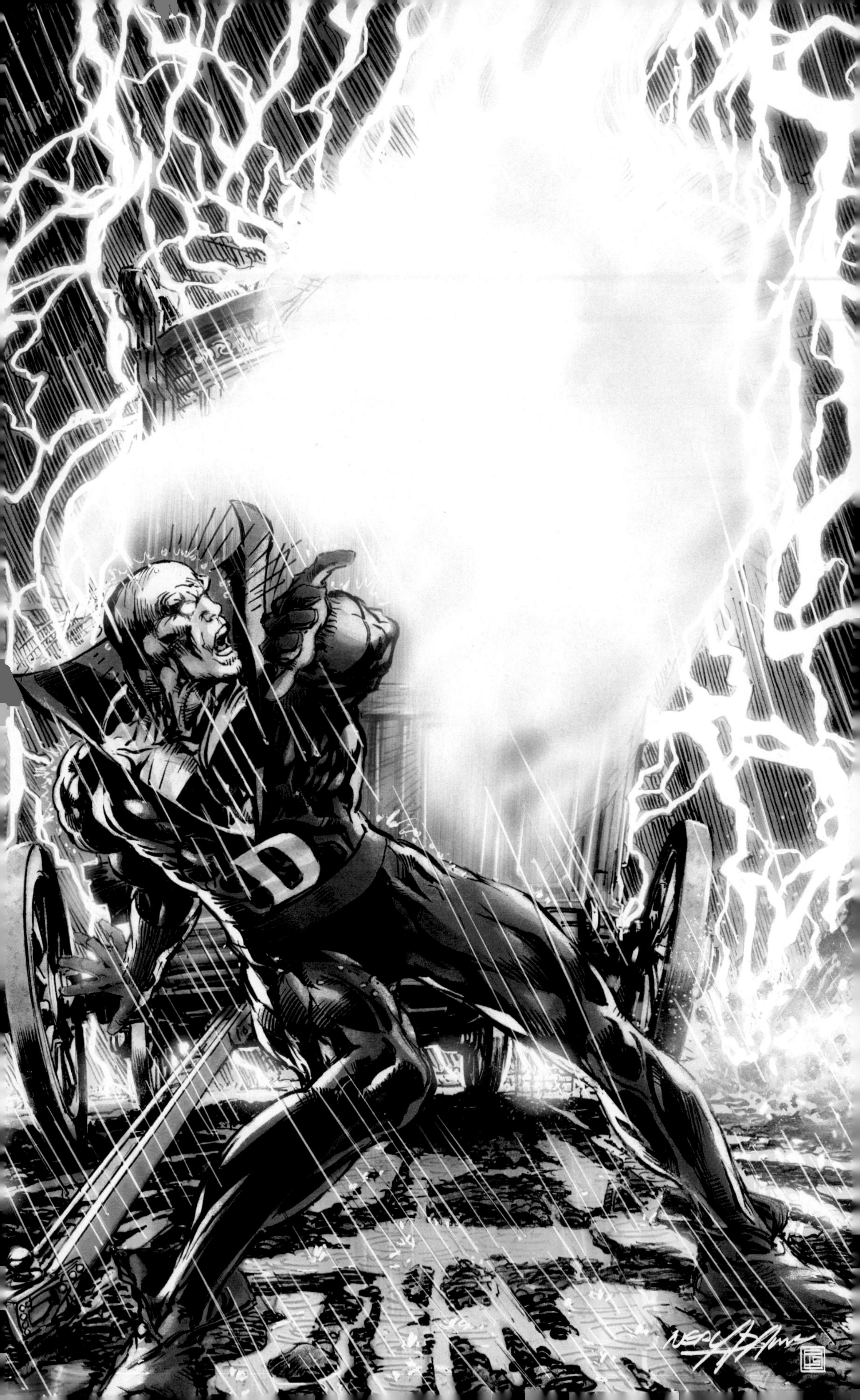

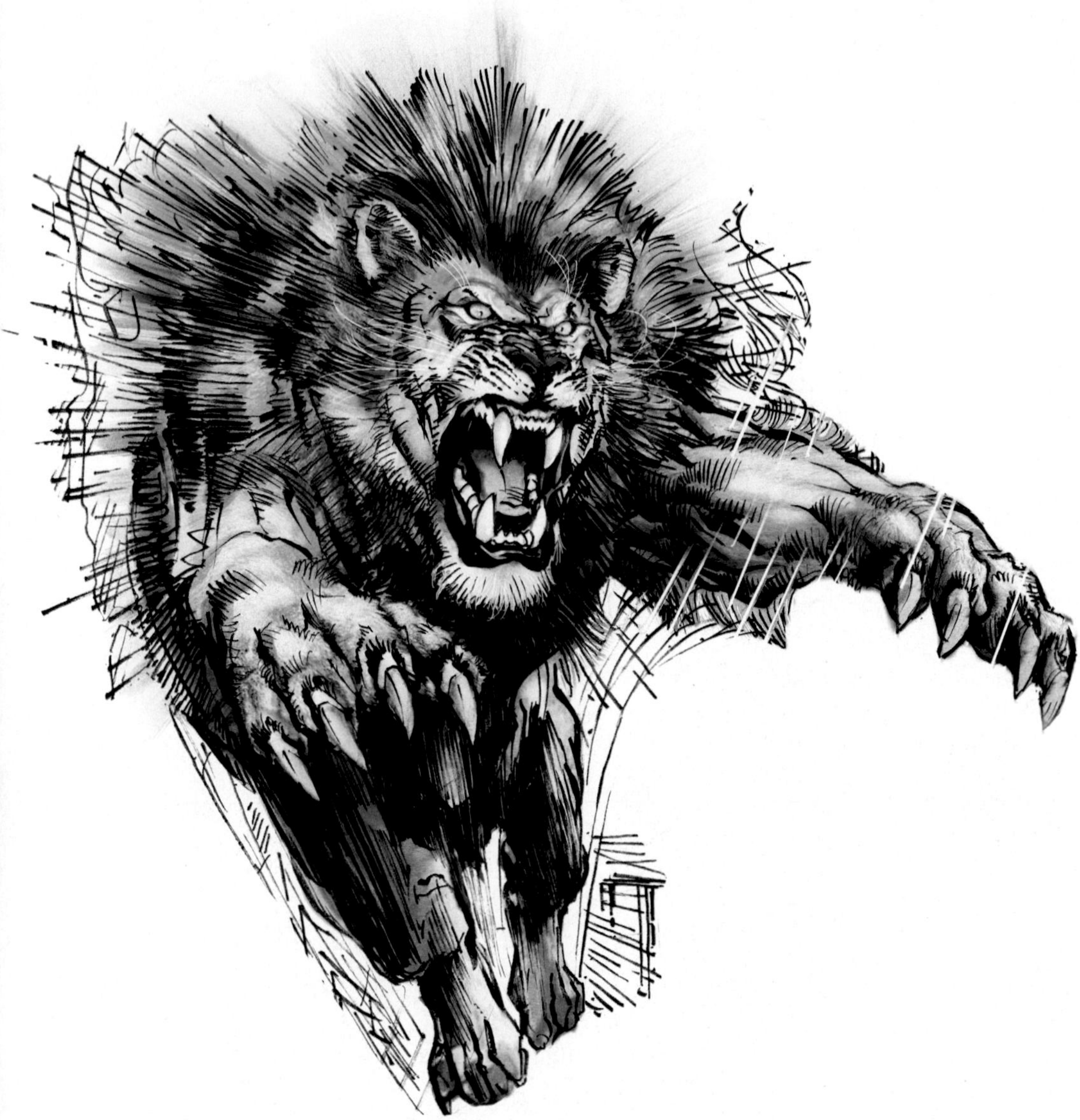

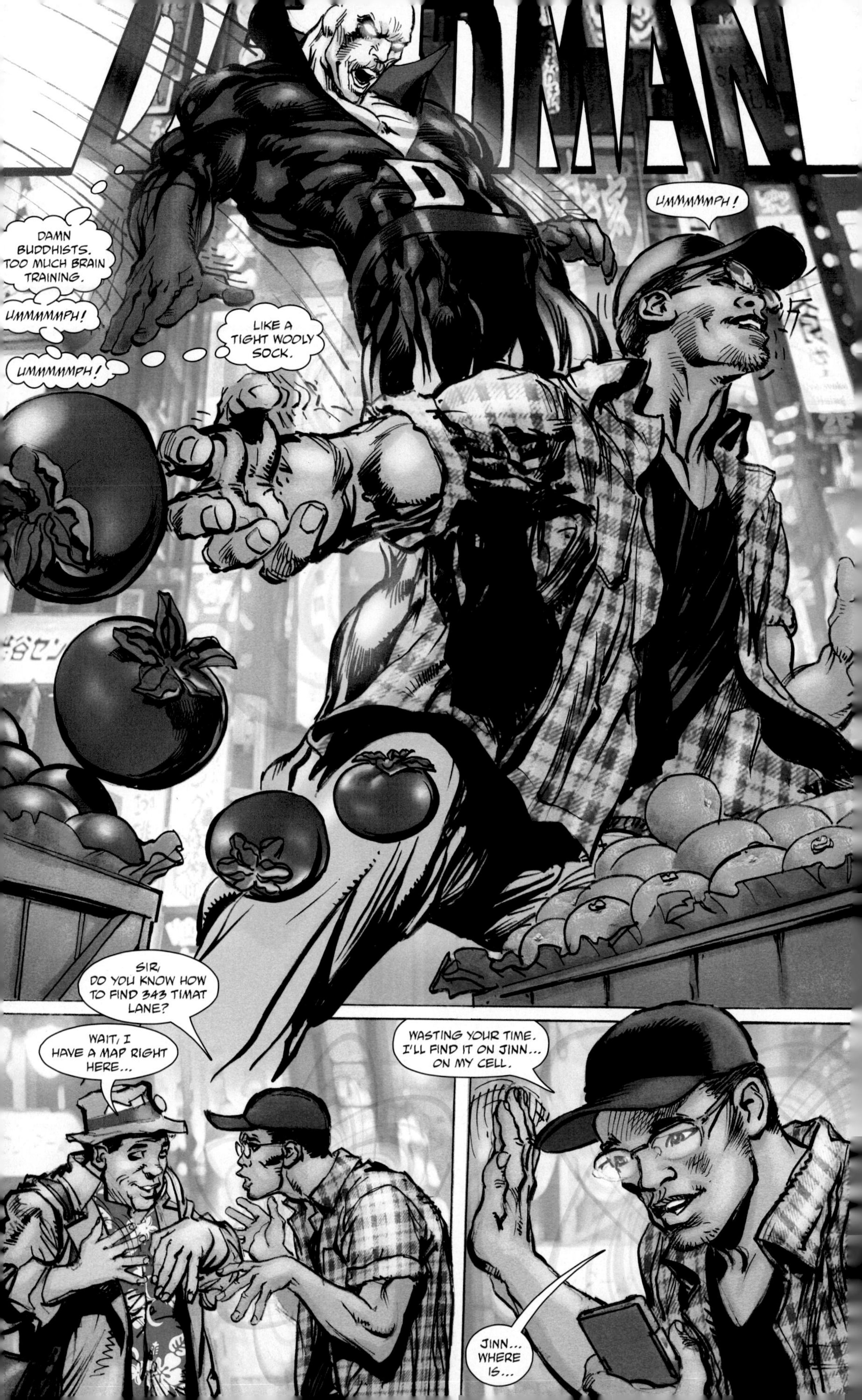
DEADMAN
UMMMMMPH!
DAMN BUDDHISTS. TOO MUCH BRAIN TRAINING.
UMMMMMPH!
LIKE A TIGHT WOOLY SOCK.
UMMMMMPH!
SIR, DO YOU KNOW HOW TO FIND 343 TIMAT LANE?
WAIT, I HAVE A MAP RIGHT HERE...
WASTING YOUR TIME. I'LL FIND IT ON JINN... ON MY CELL.
JINN... WHERE IS...

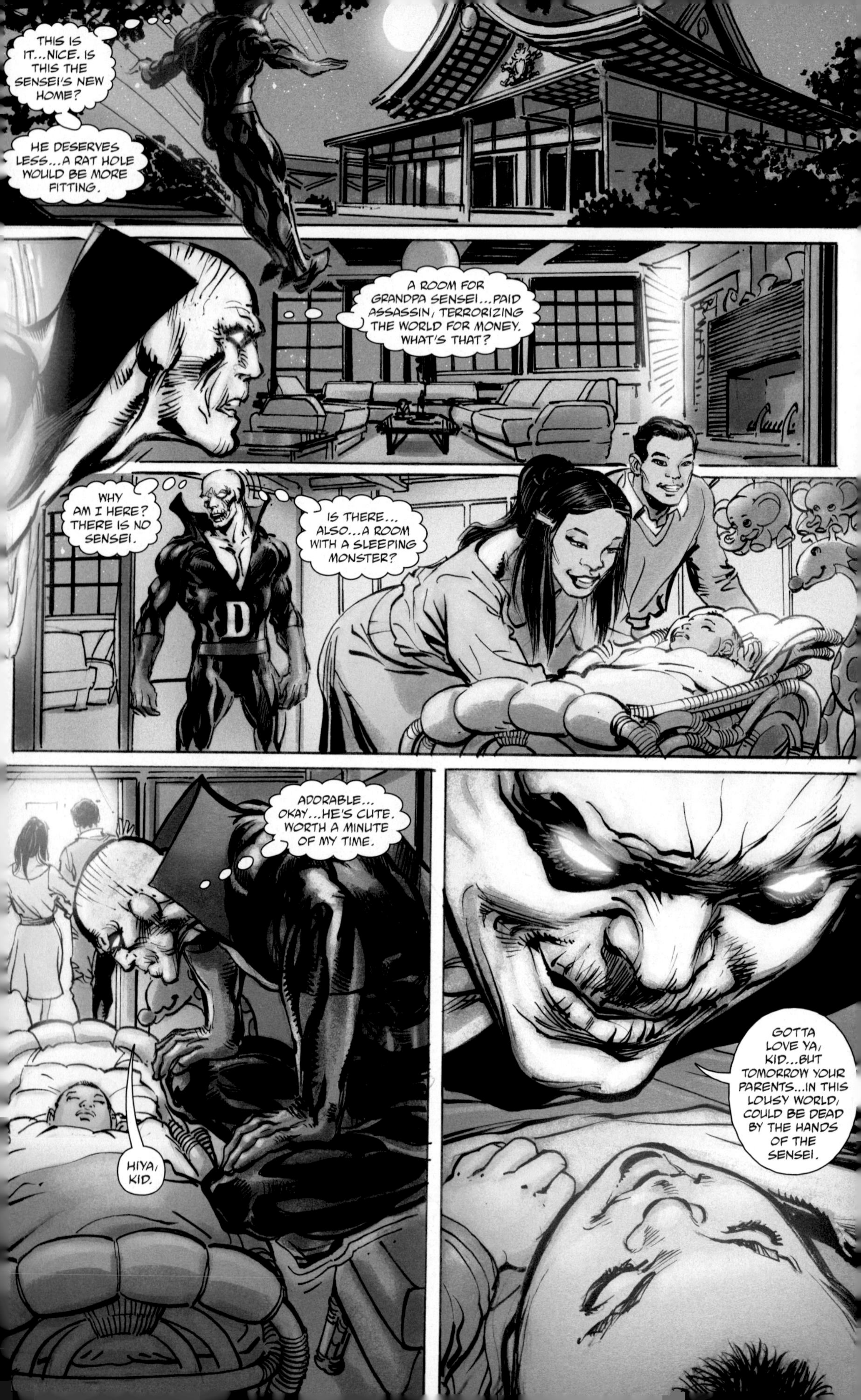

THIS IS IT...NICE. IS THIS THE SENSEI'S NEW HOME?
HE DESERVES LESS...A RAT HOLE WOULD BE MORE FITTING.
A ROOM FOR GRANDPA SENSEI...PAID ASSASSIN, TERRORIZING THE WORLD FOR MONEY. WHAT'S THAT?
WHY AM I HERE? THERE IS NO SENSEI.
IS THERE... ALSO...A ROOM WITH A SLEEPING MONSTER?
D
ADORABLE... OKAY...HE'S CUTE. WORTH A MINUTE OF MY TIME.
HIYA, KID.
GOTTA LOVE YA, KID...BUT TOMORROW YOUR PARENTS...IN THIS LOUSY WORLD, COULD BE DEAD BY THE HANDS OF THE SENSEI.

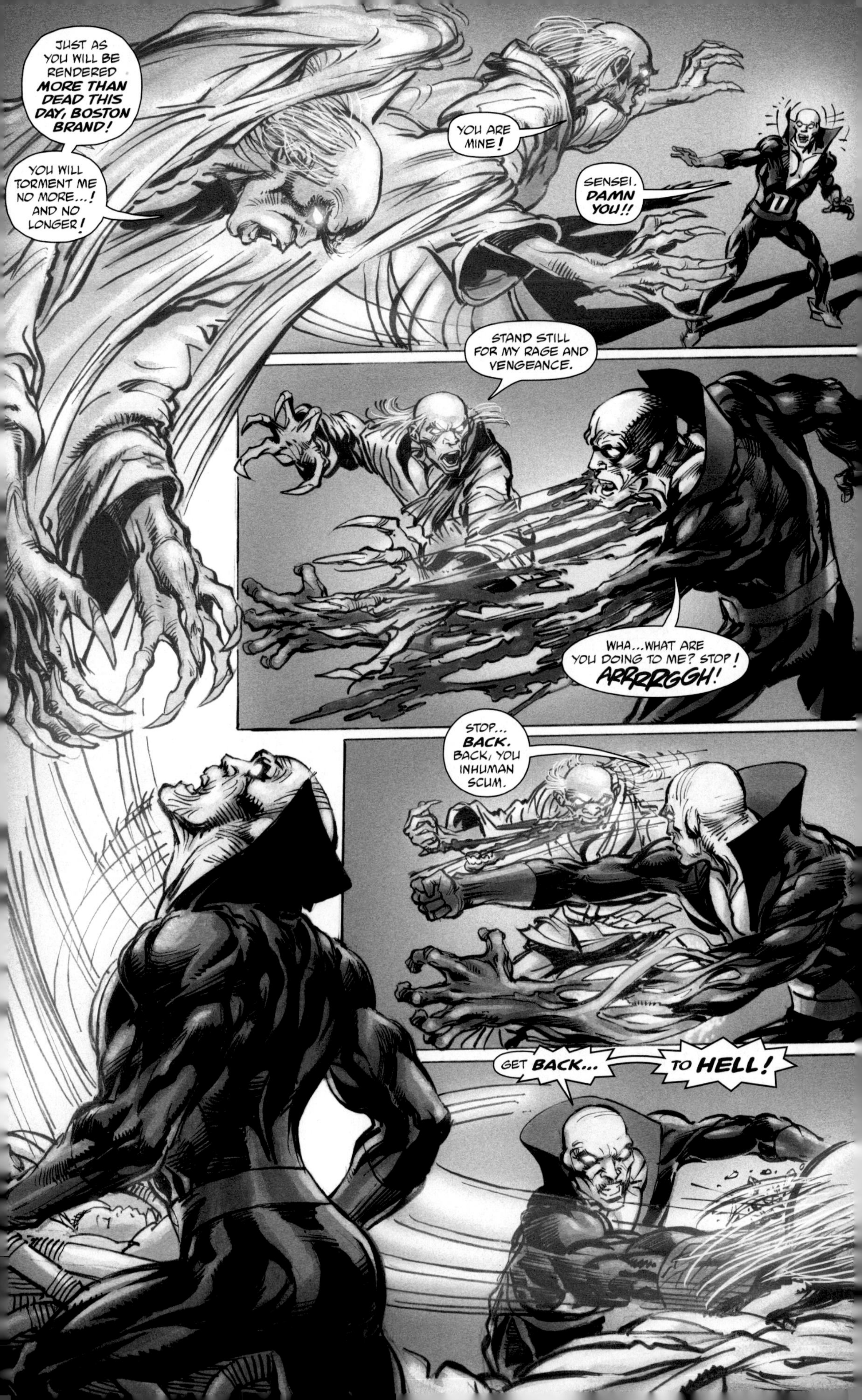

JUST AS YOU WILL BE RENDERED **MORE THAN DEAD THIS DAY, BOSTON BRAND!**
YOU WILL TORMENT ME NO MORE...! AND NO LONGER!
YOU ARE MINE!
SENSEI. **DAMN YOU!!**
STAND STILL FOR MY RAGE AND VENGEANCE.
WHA...WHAT ARE YOU DOING TO ME? STOP! **ARRRRGGH!**
STOP... **BACK.** BACK, YOU INHUMAN SCUM.
GET **BACK...**
TO **HELL!**

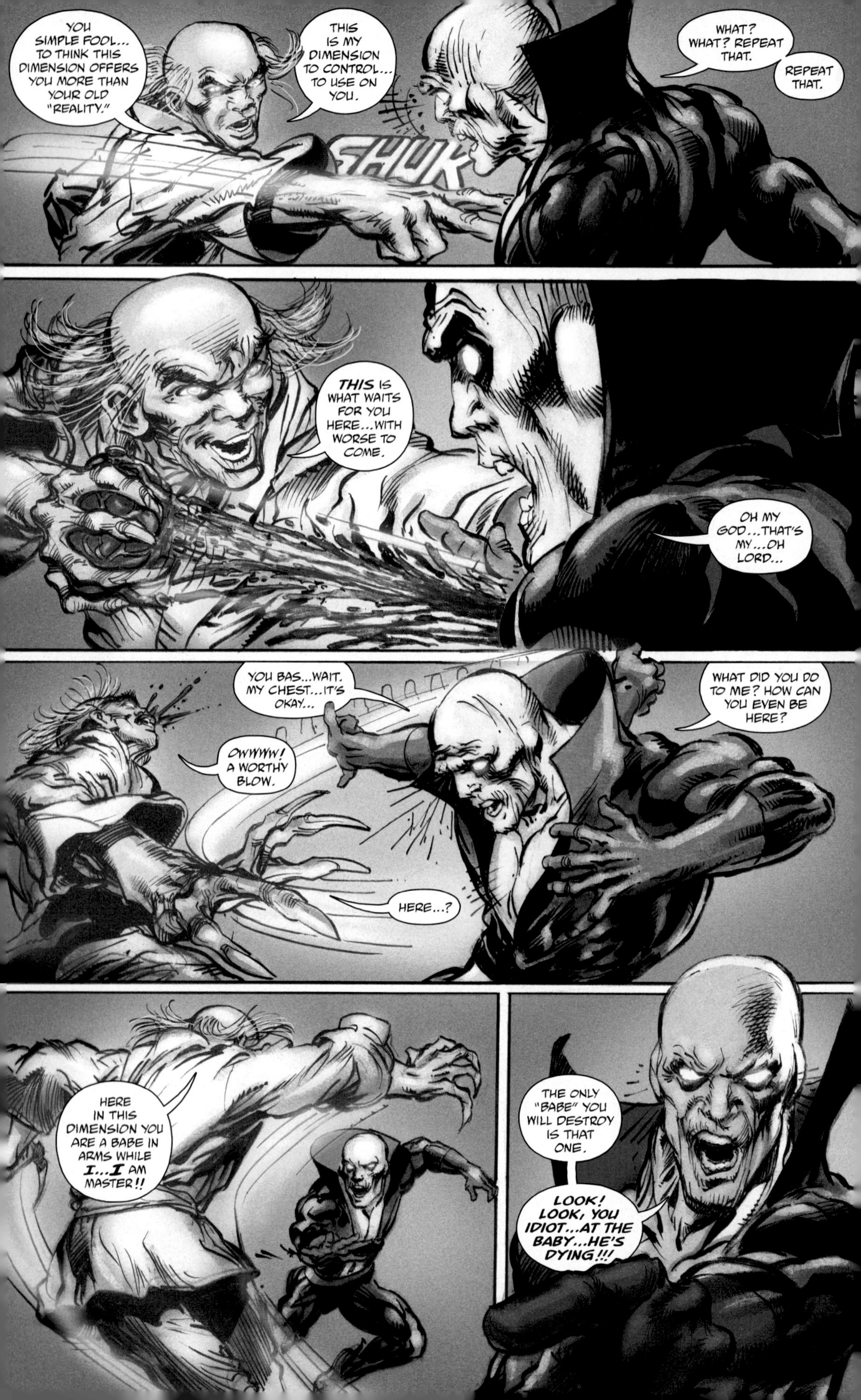
YOU SIMPLE FOOL... TO THINK THIS DIMENSION OFFERS YOU MORE THAN YOUR OLD "REALITY."
THIS IS MY DIMENSION TO CONTROL... TO USE ON YOU.
SHUK
WHAT? WHAT? REPEAT THAT.
REPEAT THAT.
THIS IS WHAT WAITS FOR YOU HERE...WITH WORSE TO COME.
OH MY GOD...THAT'S MY...OH LORD...
YOU BAS...WAIT. MY CHEST...IT'S OKAY...
WHAT DID YOU DO TO ME? HOW CAN YOU EVEN BE HERE?
OWWWW! A WORTHY BLOW.
HERE...?
HERE IN THIS DIMENSION YOU ARE A BABE IN ARMS WHILE I...I AM MASTER!!
THE ONLY "BABE" YOU WILL DESTROY IS THAT ONE.
LOOK! LOOK, YOU IDIOT...AT THE BABY...HE'S DYING!!!

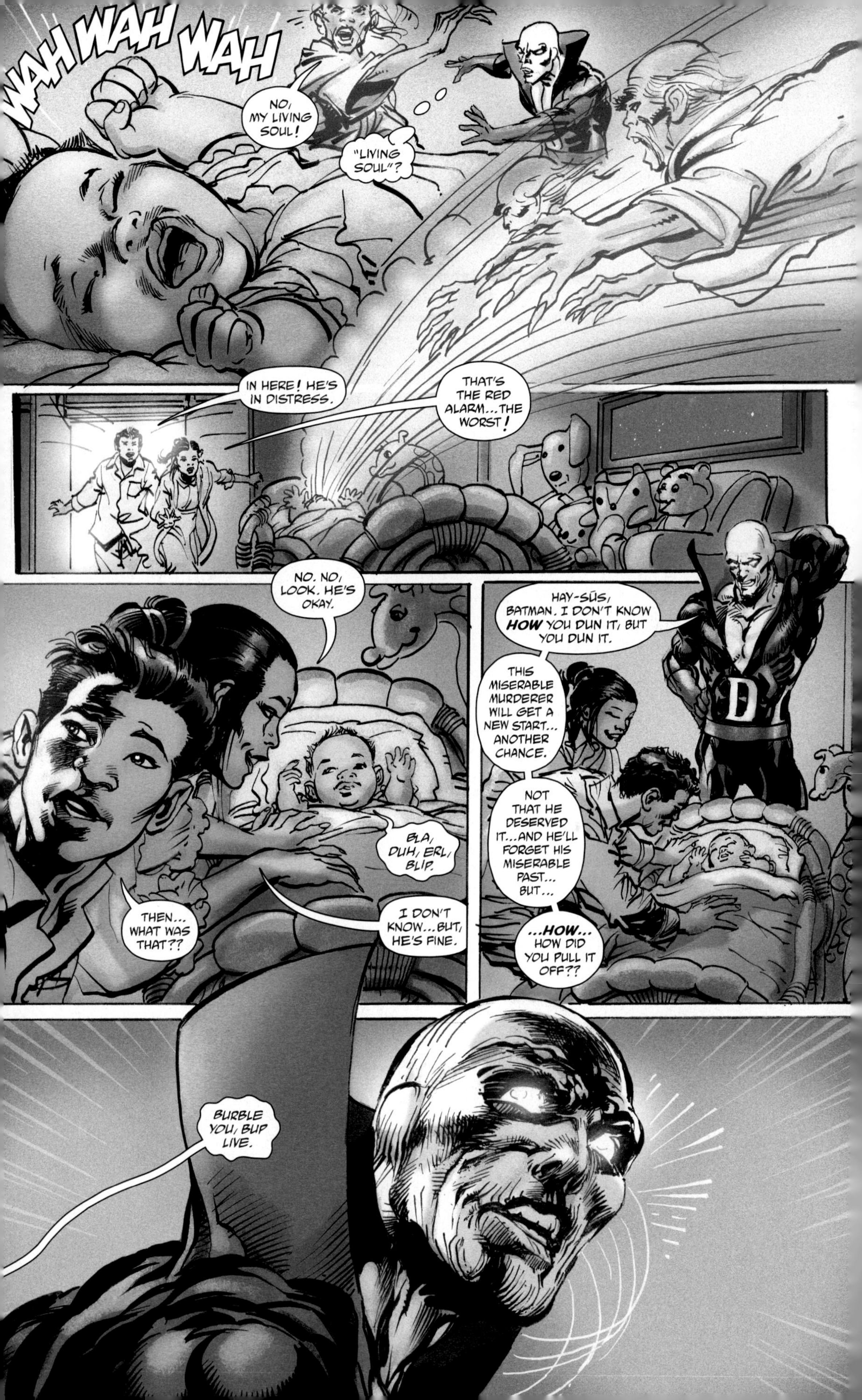
WAH WAH WAH WAH
NO, MY LIVING SOUL!
"LIVING SOUL"?
IN HERE! HE'S IN DISTRESS.
THAT'S THE RED ALARM...THE WORST!
NO. NO, LOOK. HE'S OKAY.
BLA, DUH, ERL, BLIP.
THEN... WHAT WAS THAT??
I DON'T KNOW...BUT, HE'S FINE.
HAY-SŪS, BATMAN. I DON'T KNOW **HOW** YOU DUN IT, BUT YOU DUN IT.
THIS MISERABLE MURDERER WILL GET A NEW START... ANOTHER CHANCE.
NOT THAT HE DESERVED IT...AND HE'LL FORGET HIS MISERABLE PAST... BUT...
...HOW... HOW DID YOU PULL IT OFF??
BURBLE YOU, BLIP LIVE.

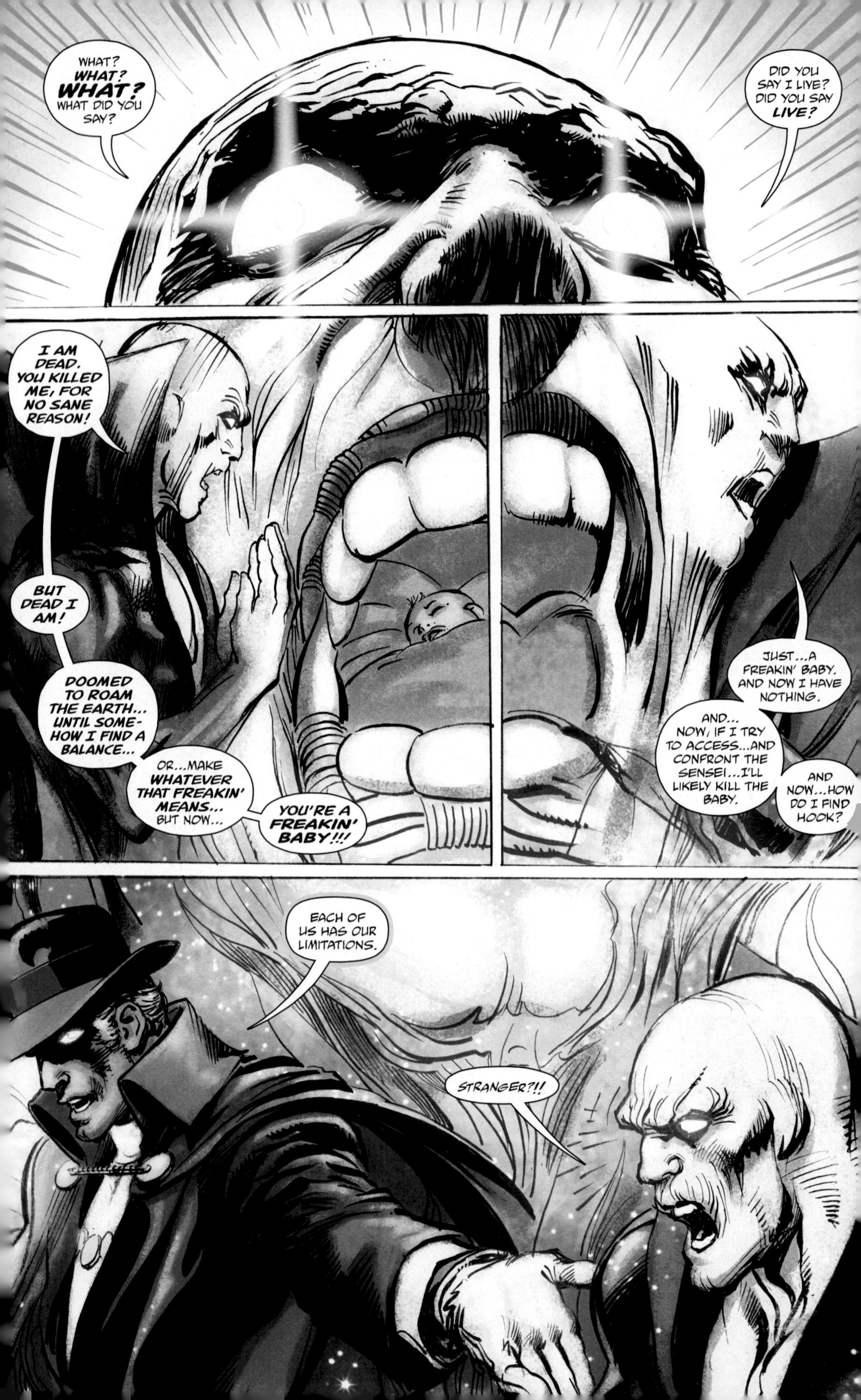
WHAT? WHAT? WHAT? WHAT DID YOU SAY?
DID YOU SAY I LIVE? DID YOU SAY LIVE?
I AM DEAD. YOU KILLED ME, FOR NO SANE REASON!
BUT DEAD I AM!
DOOMED TO ROAM THE EARTH... UNTIL SOME-HOW I FIND A BALANCE...
OR...MAKE WHATEVER THAT FREAKIN' MEANS... BUT NOW...
YOU'RE A FREAKIN' BABY!!!
JUST...A FREAKIN' BABY. AND NOW I HAVE NOTHING.
AND... NOW, IF I TRY TO ACCESS...AND CONFRONT THE SENSEI...I'LL LIKELY KILL THE BABY.
AND NOW...HOW DO I FIND HOOK?
EACH OF US HAS OUR LIMITATIONS.
STRANGER?!!

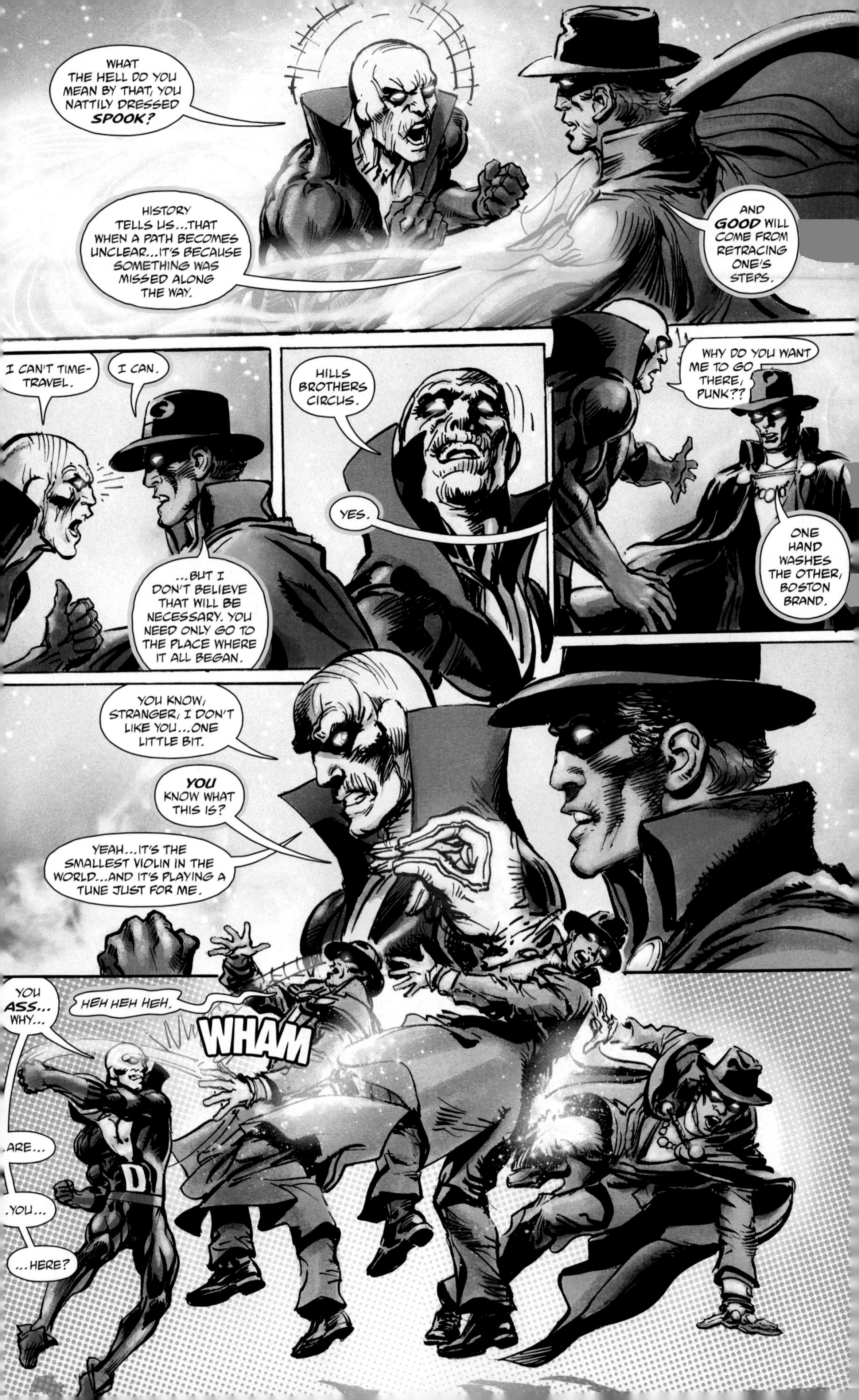
WHAT THE HELL DO YOU MEAN BY THAT, YOU NATTILY DRESSED SPOOK?
HISTORY TELLS US...THAT WHEN A PATH BECOMES UNCLEAR...IT'S BECAUSE SOMETHING WAS MISSED ALONG THE WAY.
AND GOOD WILL COME FROM RETRACING ONE'S STEPS.
I CAN'T TIME-TRAVEL.
I CAN.
...BUT I DON'T BELIEVE THAT WILL BE NECESSARY. YOU NEED ONLY GO TO THE PLACE WHERE IT ALL BEGAN.
HILLS BROTHERS CIRCUS.
YES.
WHY DO YOU WANT ME TO GO THERE, PUNK??
ONE HAND WASHES THE OTHER, BOSTON BRAND.
YOU KNOW, STRANGER, I DON'T LIKE YOU...ONE LITTLE BIT.
YOU KNOW WHAT THIS IS?
YEAH...IT'S THE SMALLEST VIOLIN IN THE WORLD...AND IT'S PLAYING A TUNE JUST FOR ME.
YOU ASS... WHY...
HEH HEH HEH.
WHAM
...ARE...
...YOU...
...HERE?

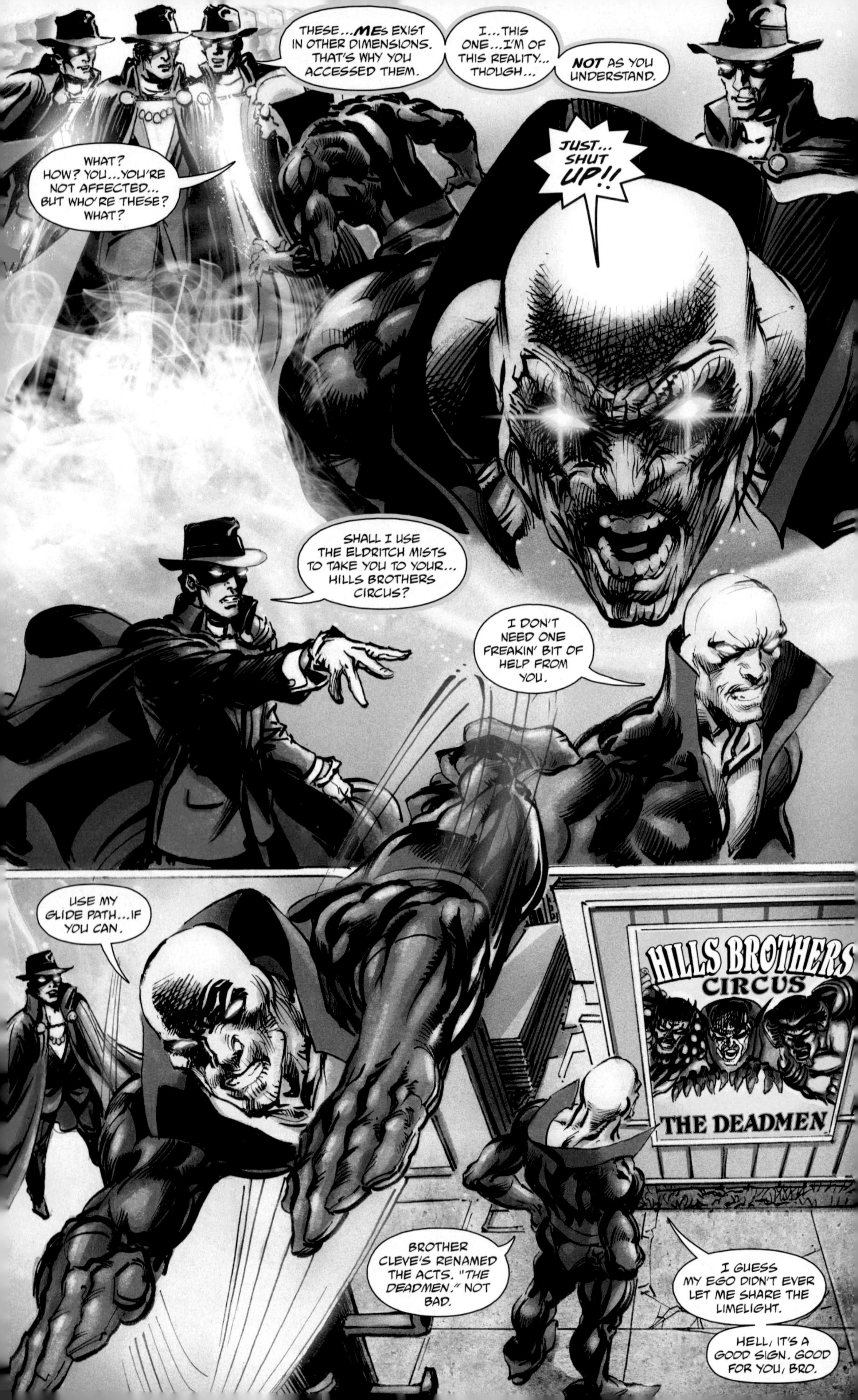
THESE...MEs EXIST IN OTHER DIMENSIONS. THAT'S WHY YOU ACCESSED THEM.
I...THIS ONE...I'M OF THIS REALITY... THOUGH...
NOT AS YOU UNDERSTAND.
WHAT? HOW? YOU...YOU'RE NOT AFFECTED... BUT WHO'RE THESE? WHAT?
JUST... SHUT UP!!
SHALL I USE THE ELDRITCH MISTS TO TAKE YOU TO YOUR... HILLS BROTHERS CIRCUS?
I DON'T NEED ONE FREAKIN' BIT OF HELP FROM YOU.
USE MY GLIDE PATH...IF YOU CAN.
HILLS BROTHERS CIRCUS
THE DEADMEN
BROTHER CLEVE'S RENAMED THE ACTS. "THE DEADMEN." NOT BAD.
I GUESS MY EGO DIDN'T EVER LET ME SHARE THE LIMELIGHT.
HELL, IT'S A GOOD SIGN. GOOD FOR YOU, BRO.

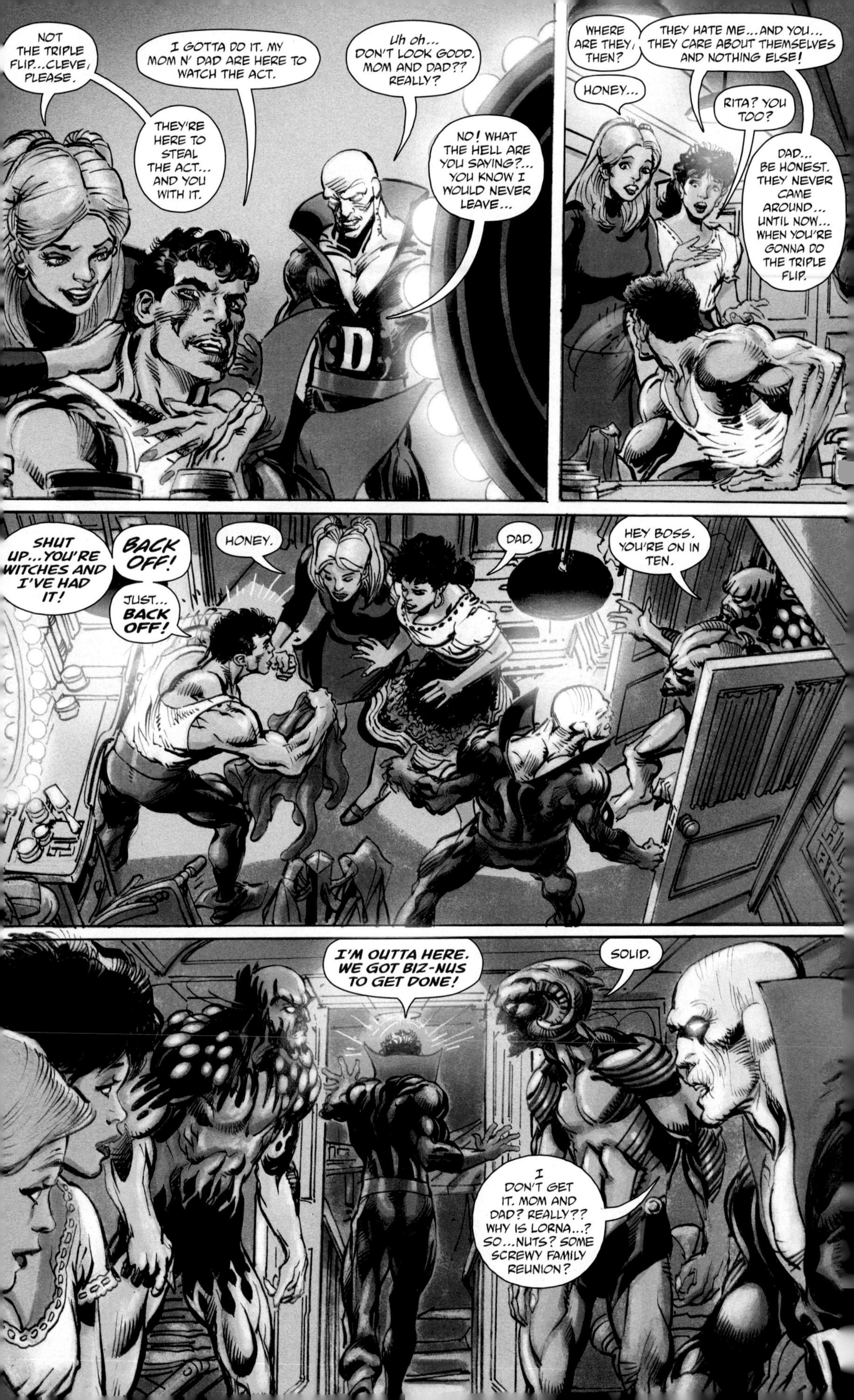
NOT THE TRIPLE FLIP...CLEVE, PLEASE.
I GOTTA DO IT. MY MOM N' DAD ARE HERE TO WATCH THE ACT.
THEY'RE HERE TO STEAL THE ACT... AND YOU WITH IT.
Uh oh... DON'T LOOK GOOD. MOM AND DAD?? REALLY?
NO! WHAT THE HELL ARE YOU SAYING?... YOU KNOW I WOULD NEVER LEAVE...
WHERE ARE THEY, THEN?
THEY HATE ME...AND YOU... THEY CARE ABOUT THEMSELVES AND NOTHING ELSE!
HONEY...
RITA? YOU TOO?
DAD... BE HONEST. THEY NEVER CAME AROUND... UNTIL NOW... WHEN YOU'RE GONNA DO THE TRIPLE FLIP.
SHUT UP...YOU'RE WITCHES AND I'VE HAD IT!
BACK OFF!
JUST... BACK OFF!
HONEY.
DAD.
HEY BOSS. YOU'RE ON IN TEN.
I'M OUTTA HERE. WE GOT BIZ-NUS TO GET DONE!
SOLID.
I DON'T GET IT. MOM AND DAD? REALLY?? WHY IS LORNA...? SO...NUTS? SOME SCREWY FAMILY REUNION?

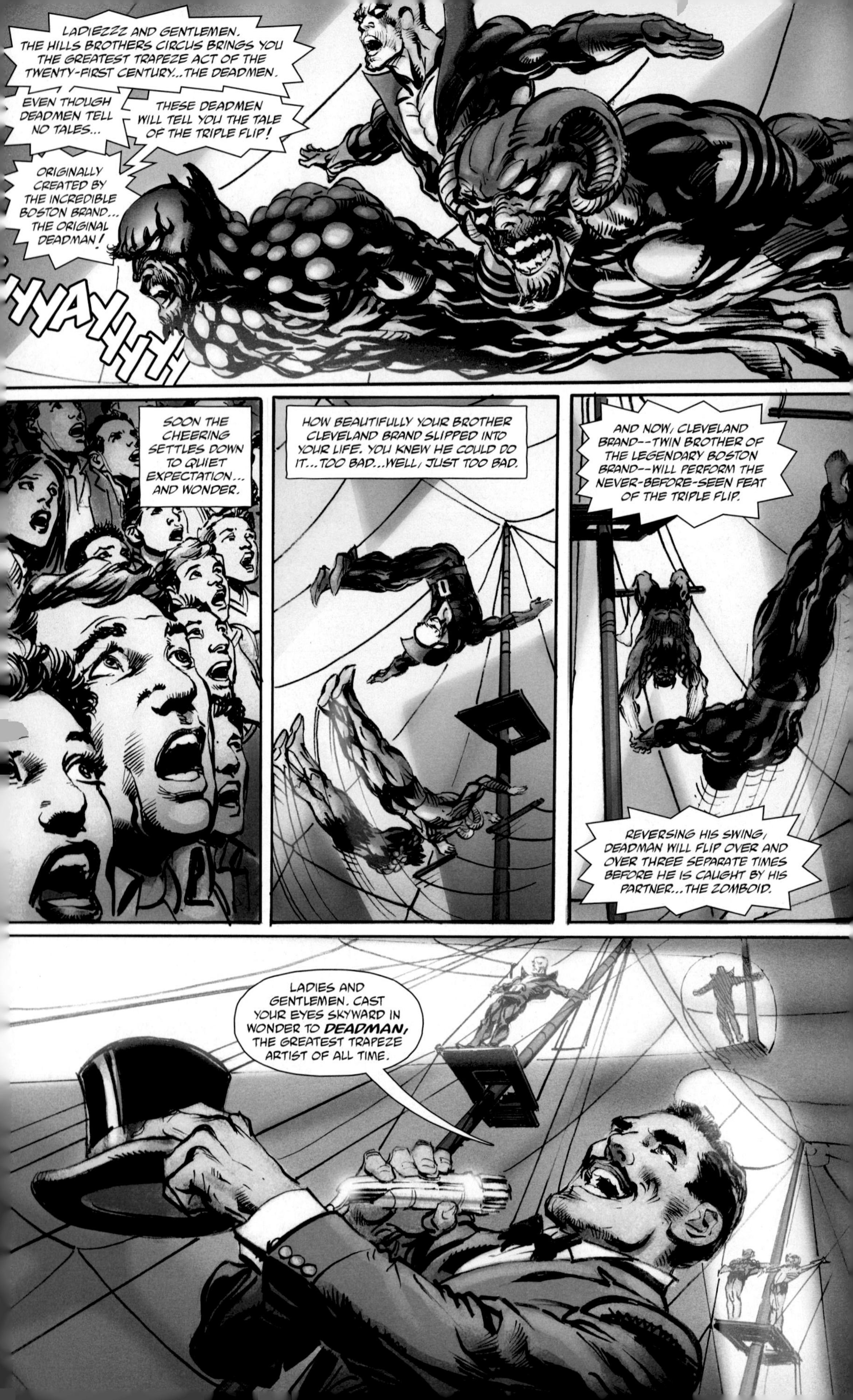
LADIEZZZ AND GENTLEMEN. THE HILLS BROTHERS CIRCUS BRINGS YOU THE GREATEST TRAPEZE ACT OF THE TWENTY-FIRST CENTURY...THE DEADMEN.
EVEN THOUGH DEADMEN TELL NO TALES...
THESE DEADMEN WILL TELL YOU THE TALE OF THE TRIPLE FLIP!
ORIGINALLY CREATED BY THE INCREDIBLE BOSTON BRAND... THE ORIGINAL DEADMAN!
YYAYYYYY
SOON THE CHEERING SETTLES DOWN TO QUIET EXPECTATION... AND WONDER.
HOW BEAUTIFULLY YOUR BROTHER CLEVELAND BRAND SLIPPED INTO YOUR LIFE. YOU KNEW HE COULD DO IT...TOO BAD...WELL, JUST TOO BAD.
AND NOW, CLEVELAND BRAND--TWIN BROTHER OF THE LEGENDARY BOSTON BRAND--WILL PERFORM THE NEVER-BEFORE-SEEN FEAT OF THE TRIPLE FLIP.
REVERSING HIS SWING, DEADMAN WILL FLIP OVER AND OVER THREE SEPARATE TIMES BEFORE HE IS CAUGHT BY HIS PARTNER...THE ZOMBOID.
LADIES AND GENTLEMEN. CAST YOUR EYES SKYWARD IN WONDER TO DEADMAN, THE GREATEST TRAPEZE ARTIST OF ALL TIME.

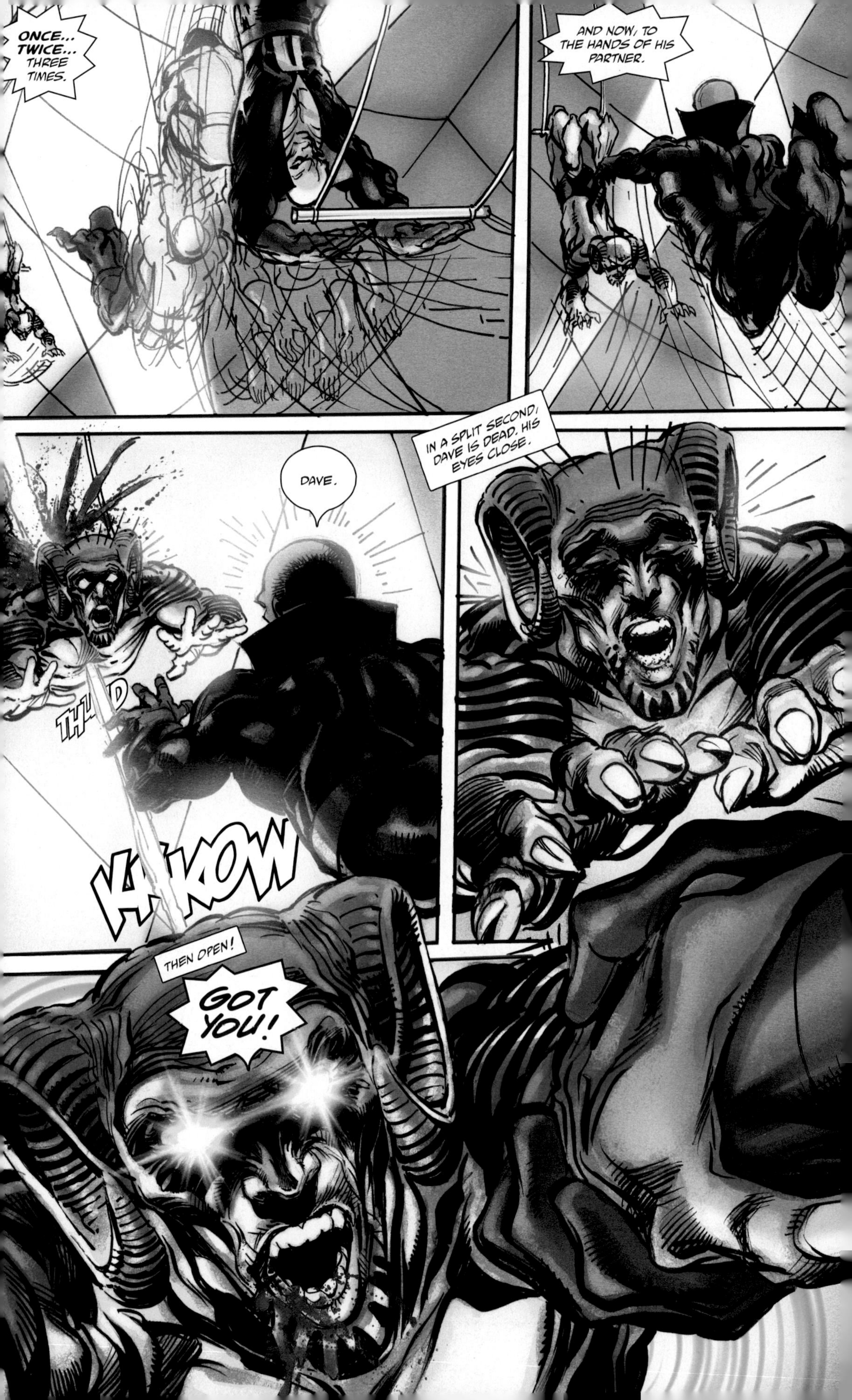
ONCE... TWICE... THREE TIMES.
AND NOW, TO THE HANDS OF HIS PARTNER.
DAVE.
THUD
KA-KOW
IN A SPLIT SECOND, DAVE IS DEAD. HIS EYES CLOSE.
THEN OPEN!
GOT YOU!

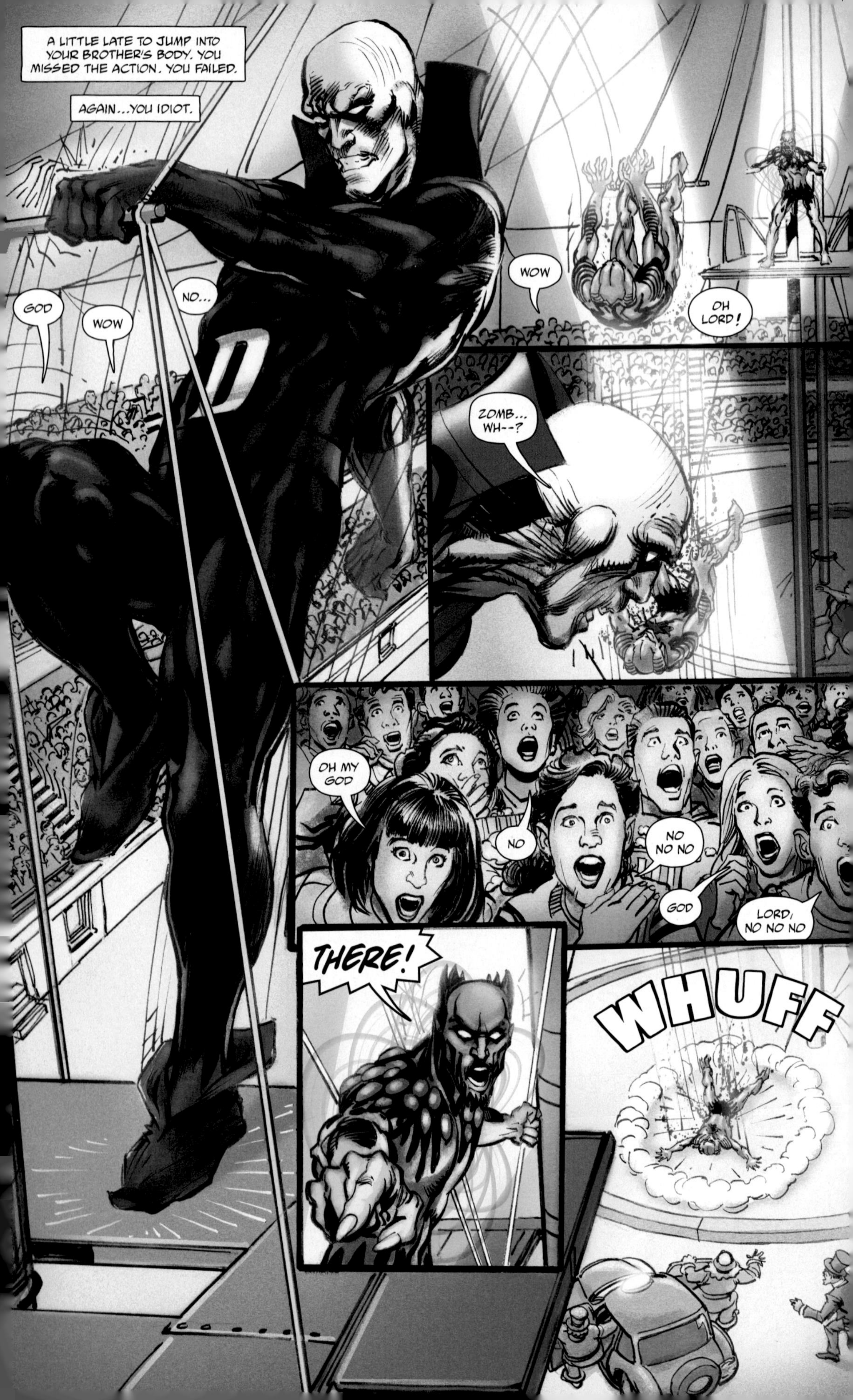

A LITTLE LATE TO JUMP INTO YOUR BROTHER'S BODY. YOU MISSED THE ACTION. YOU FAILED.
AGAIN...YOU IDIOT.
GOD
WOW
NO...
WOW
OH LORD!
ZOMB... WH--?
OH MY GOD
NO
NO NO NO
GOD
LORD, NO NO NO
THERE!
WHUFF

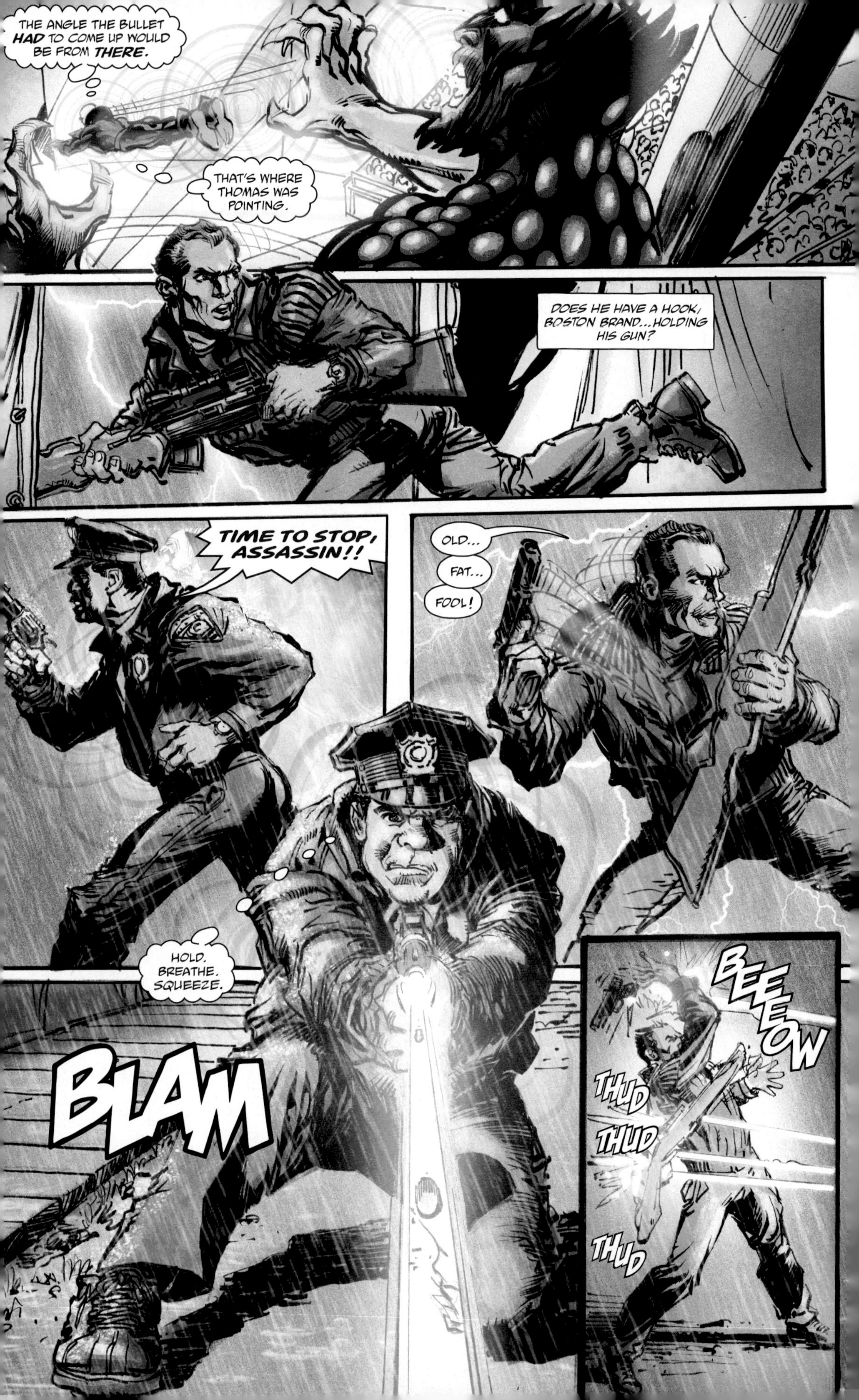
THE ANGLE THE BULLET HAD TO COME UP WOULD BE FROM THERE.
THAT'S WHERE THOMAS WAS POINTING.
DOES HE HAVE A HOOK, BOSTON BRAND...HOLDING HIS GUN?
TIME TO STOP, ASSASSIN!!
OLD...
FAT...
FOOL!
HOLD. BREATHE. SQUEEZE.
BLAM
BEEEOW
THUD
THUD
THUD

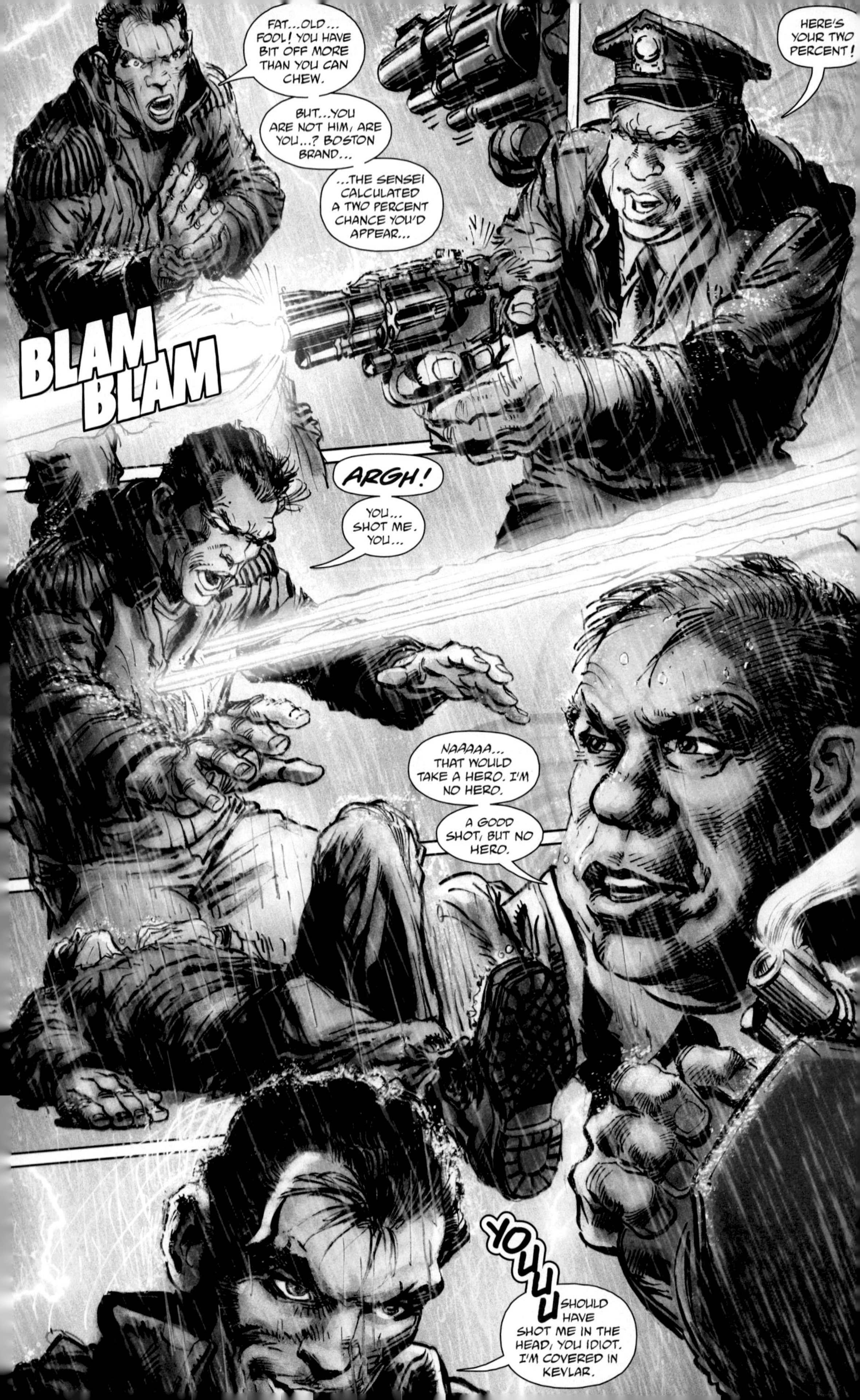
FAT...OLD... FOOL! YOU HAVE BIT OFF MORE THAN YOU CAN CHEW.
BUT...YOU ARE NOT HIM, ARE YOU...? BOSTON BRAND...
...THE SENSEI CALCULATED A TWO PERCENT CHANCE YOU'D APPEAR...
HERE'S YOUR TWO PERCENT!
BLAM BLAM
ARGH!
YOU... SHOT ME. YOU...
NAAAAA... THAT WOULD TAKE A HERO. I'M NO HERO.
A GOOD SHOT, BUT NO HERO.
YOUUU SHOULD HAVE SHOT ME IN THE HEAD, YOU IDIOT. I'M COVERED IN KEVLAR.

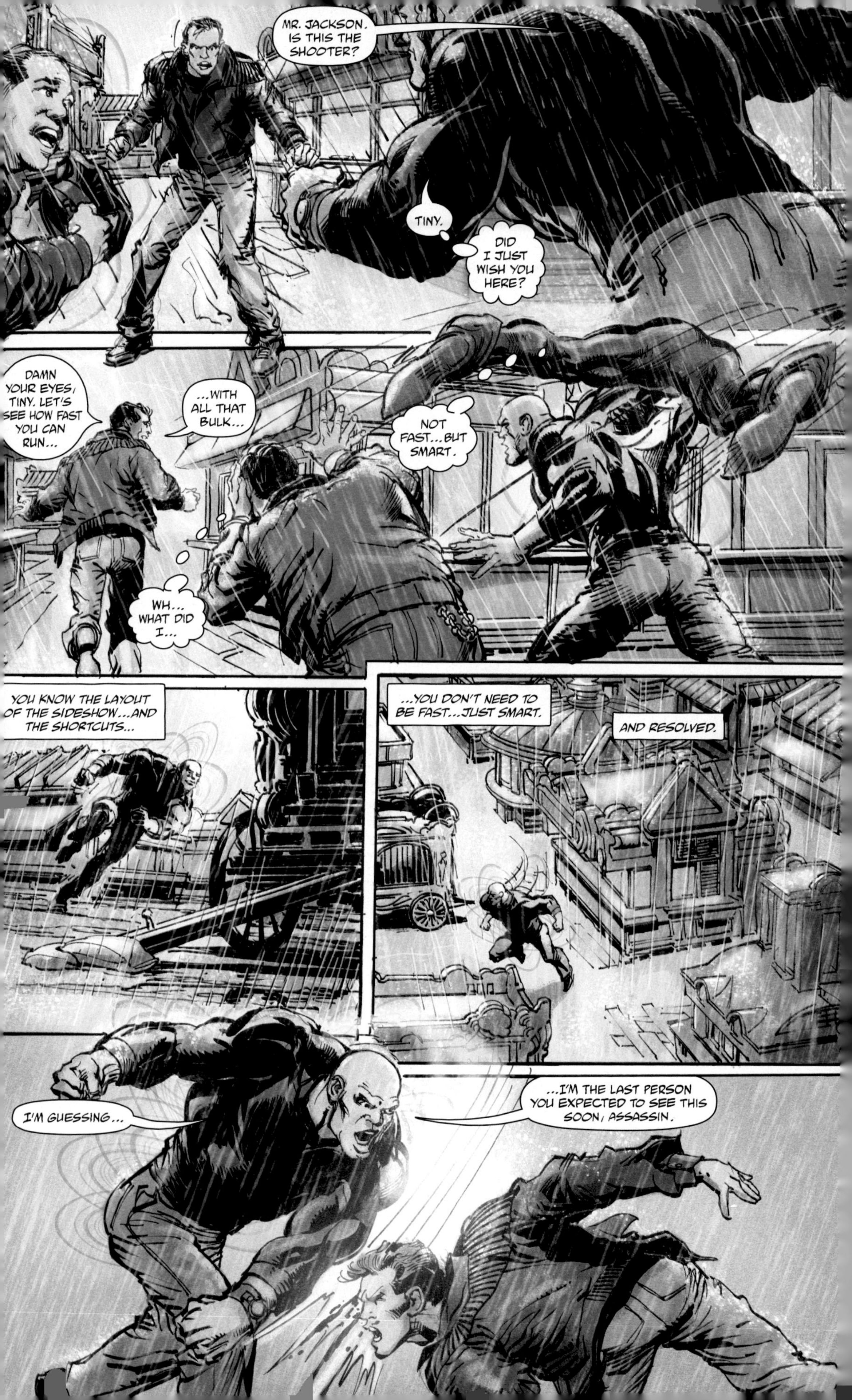
MR. JACKSON. IS THIS THE SHOOTER?
TINY.
DID I JUST WISH YOU HERE?
DAMN YOUR EYES, TINY. LET'S SEE HOW FAST YOU CAN RUN...
...WITH ALL THAT BULK...
NOT FAST...BUT SMART.
WH... WHAT DID I...
YOU KNOW THE LAYOUT OF THE SIDESHOW...AND THE SHORTCUTS...
...YOU DON'T NEED TO BE FAST...JUST SMART.
AND RESOLVED.
I'M GUESSING...
...I'M THE LAST PERSON YOU EXPECTED TO SEE THIS SOON, ASSASSIN.

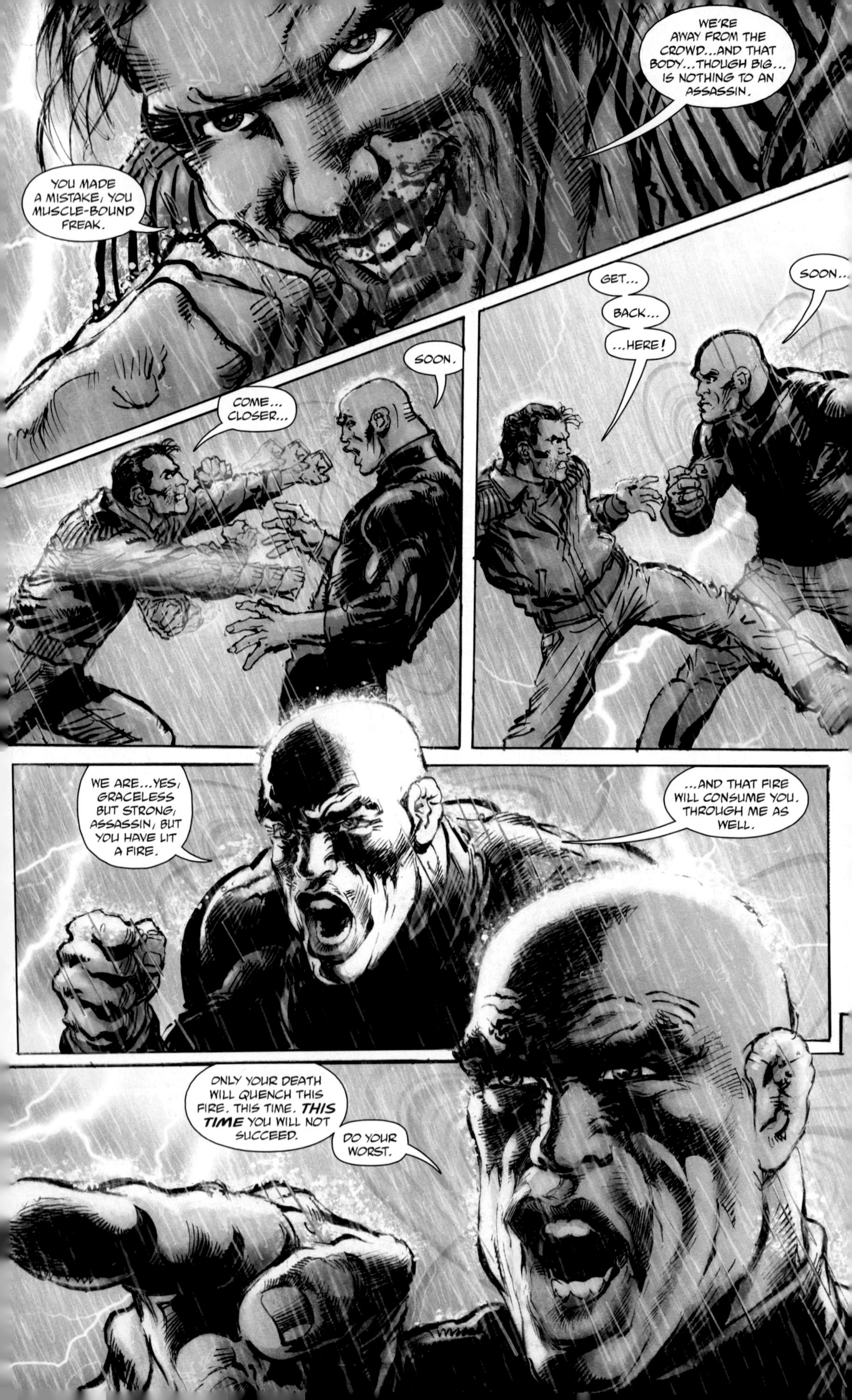
WE'RE AWAY FROM THE CROWD...AND THAT BODY...THOUGH BIG...IS NOTHING TO AN ASSASSIN.
YOU MADE A MISTAKE, YOU MUSCLE-BOUND FREAK.
COME... CLOSER...
SOON.
GET...
BACK...
...HERE!
SOON...
WE ARE...YES, GRACELESS BUT STRONG, ASSASSIN, BUT YOU HAVE LIT A FIRE.
...AND THAT FIRE WILL CONSUME YOU. THROUGH ME AS WELL.
ONLY YOUR DEATH WILL QUENCH THIS FIRE. THIS TIME. THIS TIME YOU WILL NOT SUCCEED.
DO YOUR WORST.

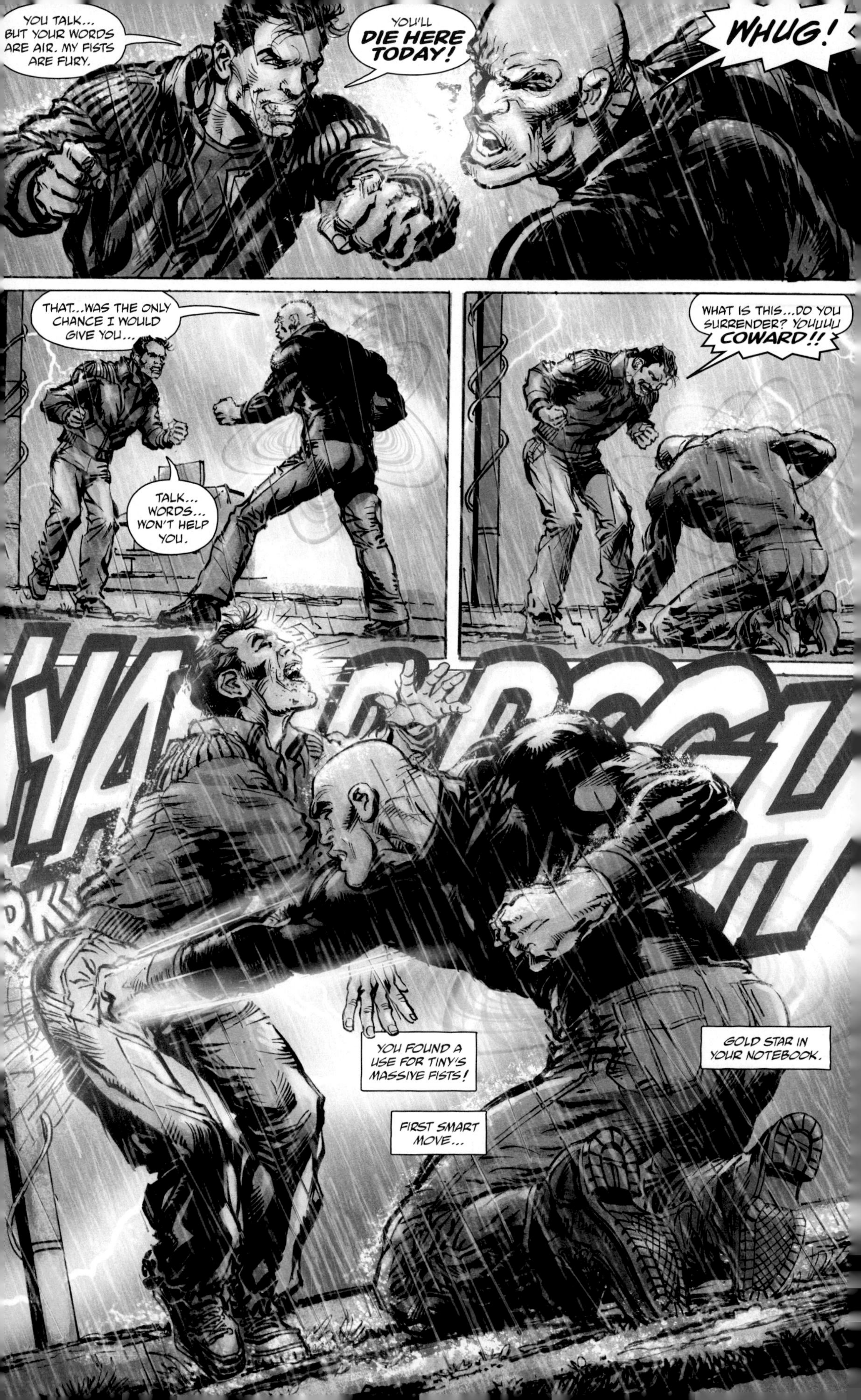

YOU TALK... BUT YOUR WORDS ARE AIR. MY FISTS ARE FURY.
YOU'LL DIE HERE TODAY!
WHUG!
THAT...WAS THE ONLY CHANCE I WOULD GIVE YOU...
TALK... WORDS... WON'T HELP YOU.
WHAT IS THIS...DO YOU SURRENDER? YOUUUU COWARD!!
YOU FOUND A USE FOR TINY'S MASSIVE FISTS!
FIRST SMART MOVE...
GOLD STAR IN YOUR NOTEBOOK.

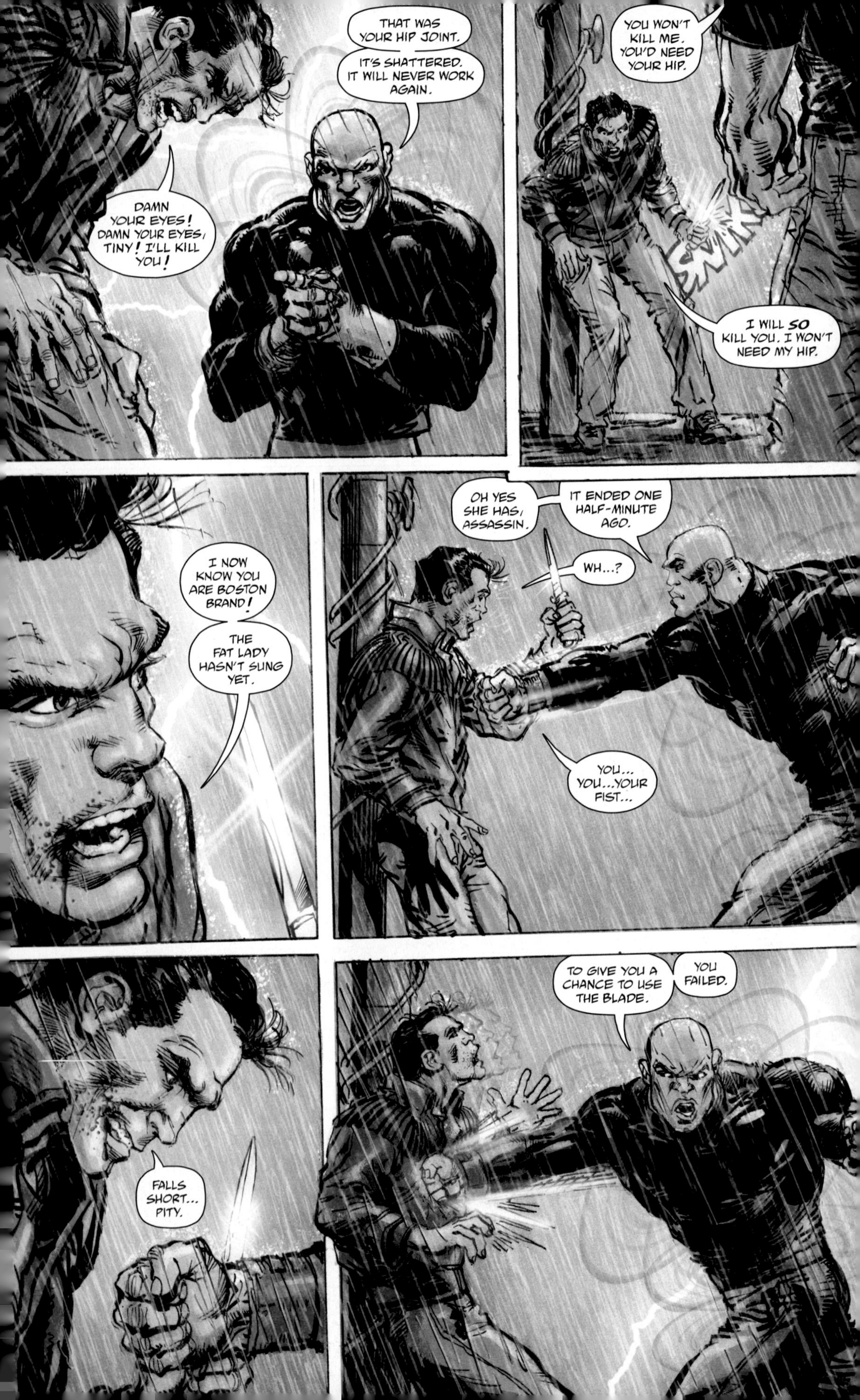
THAT WAS YOUR HIP JOINT.
IT'S SHATTERED. IT WILL NEVER WORK AGAIN.
DAMN YOUR EYES! DAMN YOUR EYES, TINY! I'LL KILL YOU!
YOU WON'T KILL ME. YOU'D NEED YOUR HIP.
I WILL SO KILL YOU. I WON'T NEED MY HIP.
I NOW KNOW YOU ARE BOSTON BRAND!
THE FAT LADY HASN'T SUNG YET.
OH YES SHE HAS, ASSASSIN.
IT ENDED ONE HALF-MINUTE AGO.
WH...?
YOU... YOU...YOUR FIST...
FALLS SHORT... PITY.
TO GIVE YOU A CHANCE TO USE THE BLADE.
YOU FAILED.

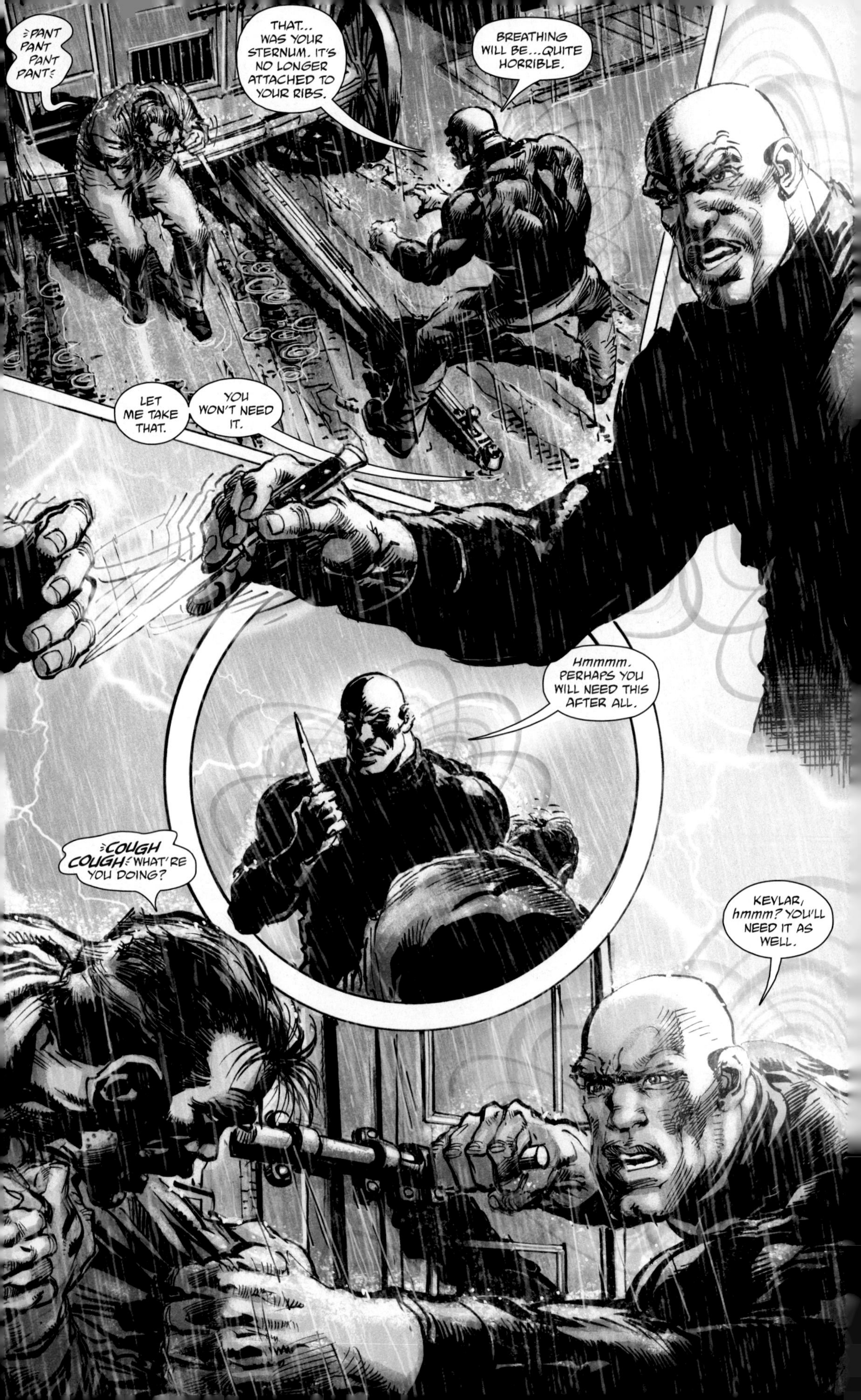
PANT PANT PANT PANT
THAT... WAS YOUR STERNUM. IT'S NO LONGER ATTACHED TO YOUR RIBS.
BREATHING WILL BE...QUITE HORRIBLE.
LET ME TAKE THAT.
YOU WON'T NEED IT.
Hmmmm. PERHAPS YOU WILL NEED THIS AFTER ALL.
COUGH COUGH WHAT'RE YOU DOING?
KEVLAR, hmmm? YOU'LL NEED IT AS WELL.

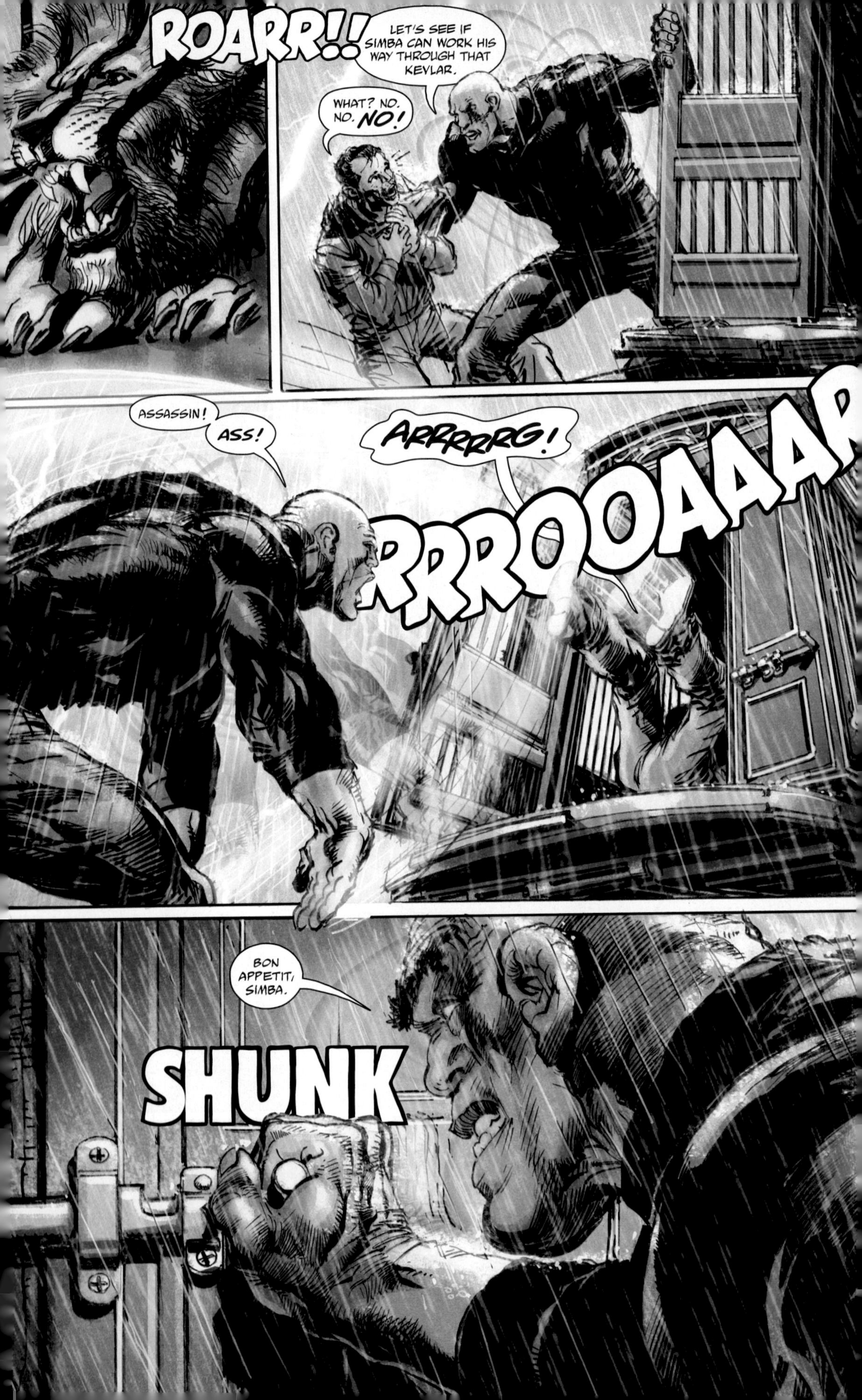
ROARR!!
LET'S SEE IF SIMBA CAN WORK HIS WAY THROUGH THAT KEVLAR.
WHAT? NO. NO. NO!
ASSASSIN!
ASS!
ARRRRRG!
RRROOAAAR
BON APPETIT, SIMBA.
SHUNK

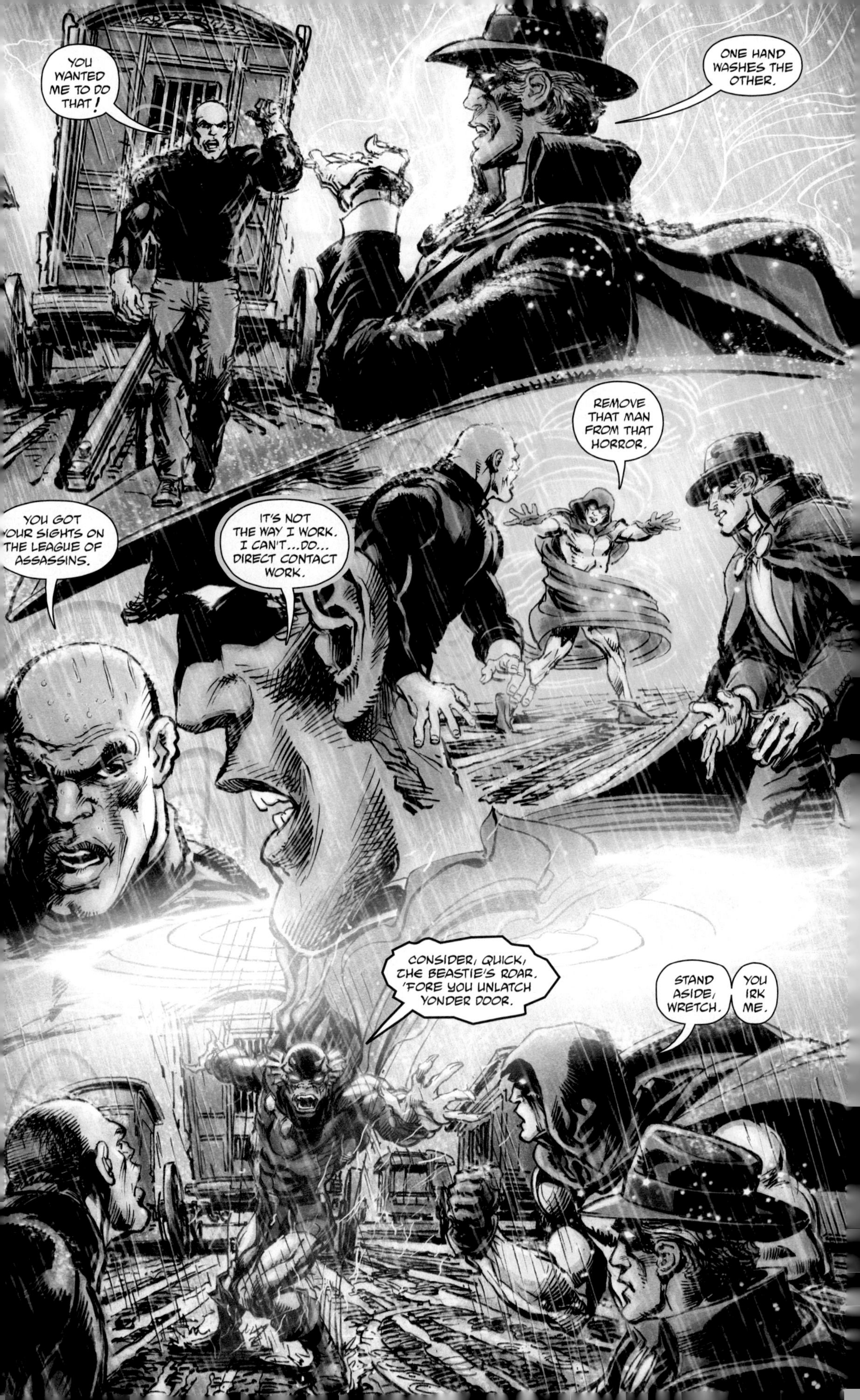
YOU WANTED ME TO DO THAT!
ONE HAND WASHES THE OTHER.
REMOVE THAT MAN FROM THAT HORROR.
YOU GOT YOUR SIGHTS ON THE LEAGUE OF ASSASSINS.
IT'S NOT THE WAY I WORK. I CAN'T...DO... DIRECT CONTACT WORK.
CONSIDER, QUICK, THE BEASTIE'S ROAR, 'FORE YOU UNLATCH YONDER DOOR.
STAND ASIDE, WRETCH.
YOU IRK ME.

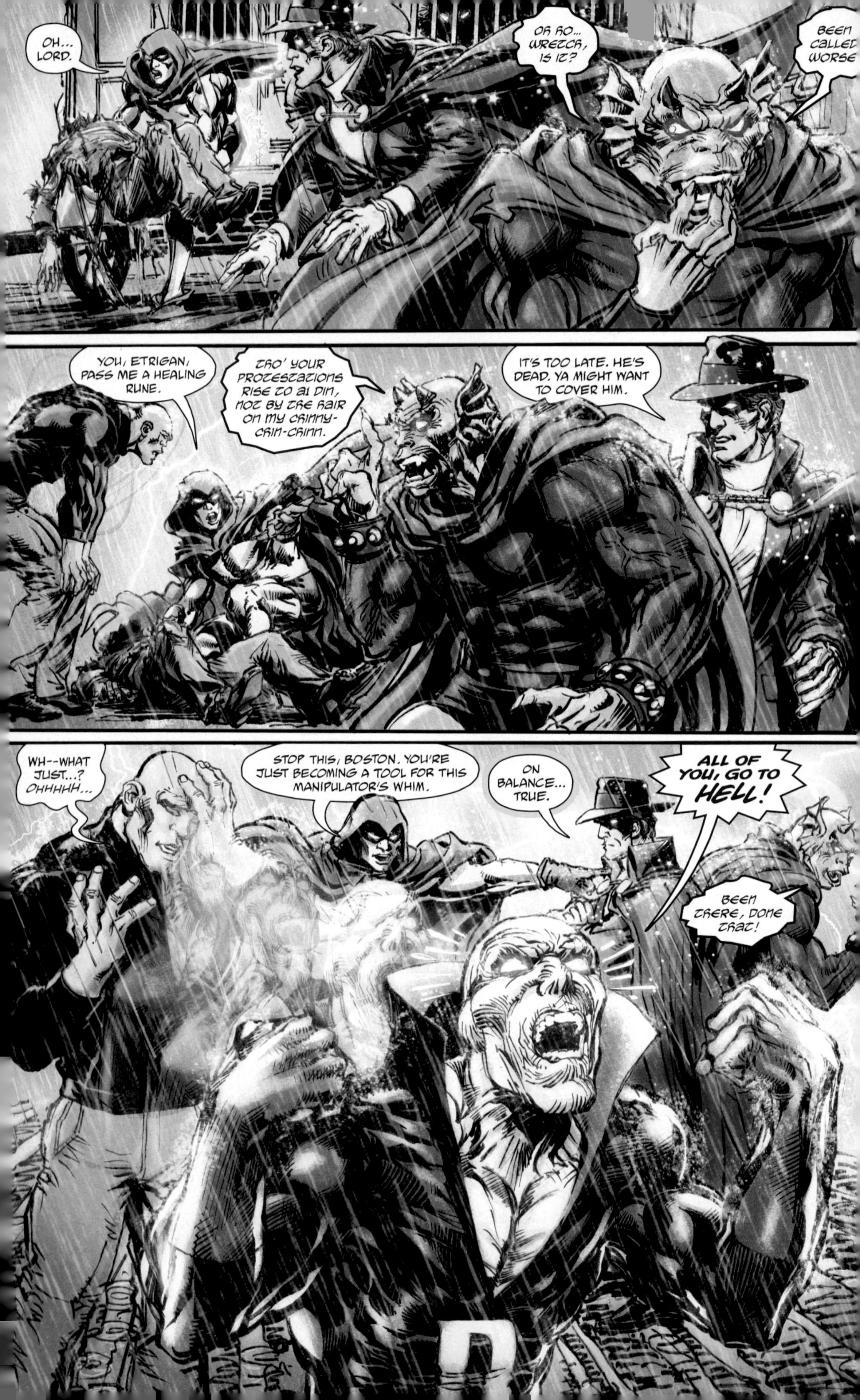
OH... LORD.
OH HO... WRETCH, IS IT?
BEEN CALLED WORSE
YOU, ETRIGAN, PASS ME A HEALING RUNE.
THO' YOUR PROTESTATIONS RISE TO AI DIN, NOT BY THE HAIR ON MY CHINNY-CHIN-CHIN.
IT'S TOO LATE. HE'S DEAD. YA MIGHT WANT TO COVER HIM.
WH--WHAT JUST...? OHHHHH...
STOP THIS, BOSTON. YOU'RE JUST BECOMING A TOOL FOR THIS MANIPULATOR'S WHIM.
ON BALANCE... TRUE.
ALL OF YOU, GO TO HELL!
BEEN THERE, DONE THAT!

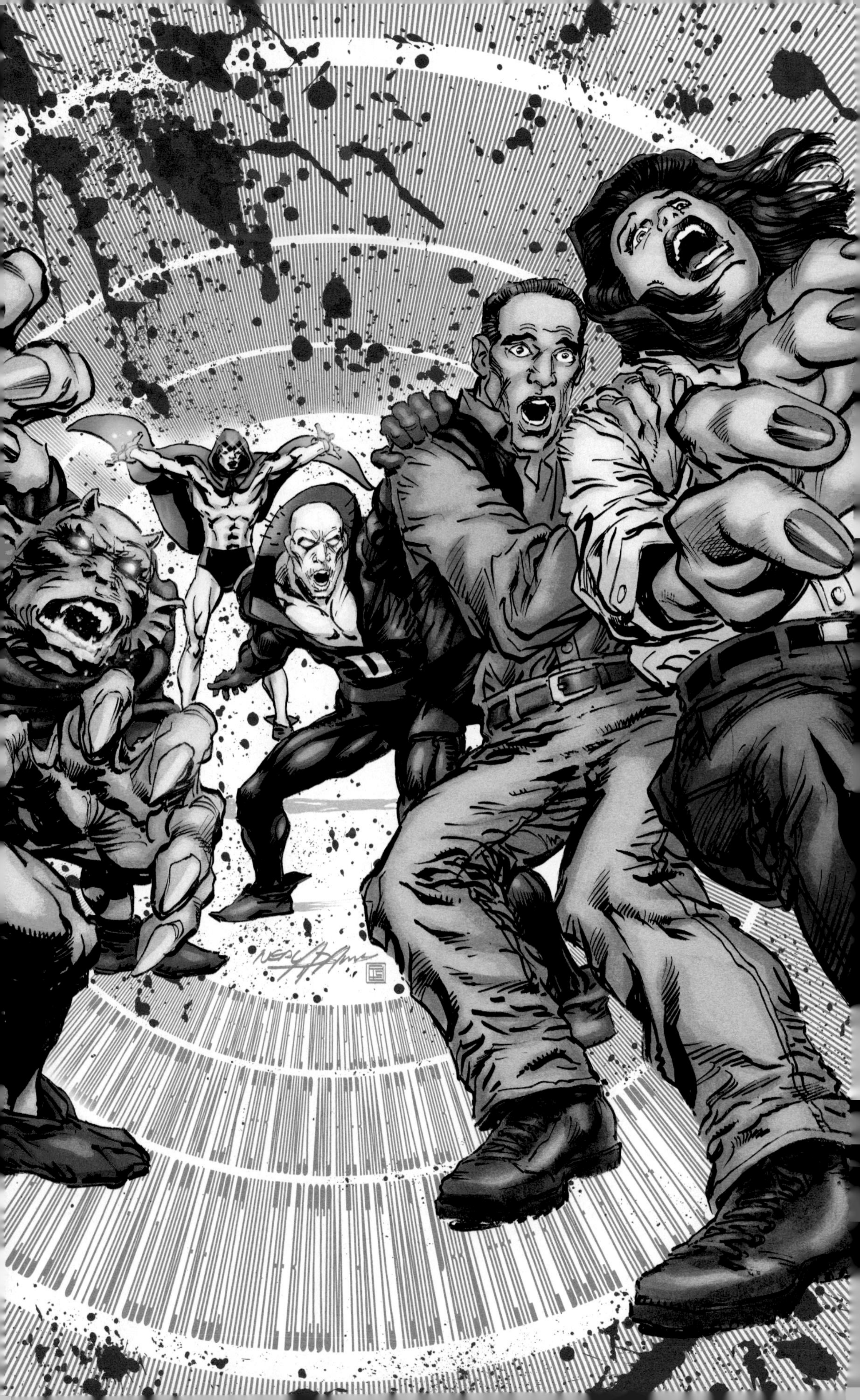

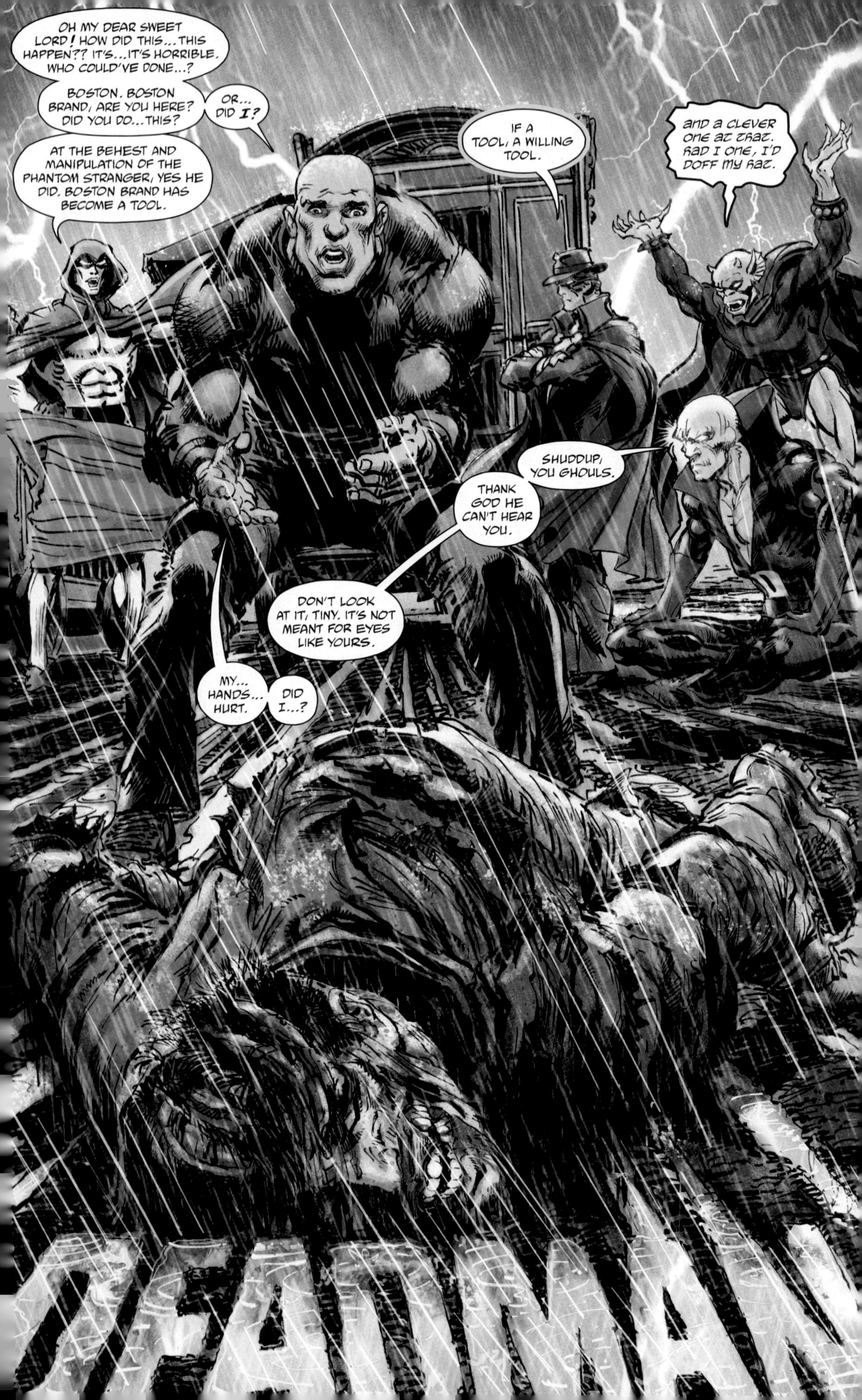
OH MY DEAR SWEET LORD! HOW DID THIS... THIS HAPPEN?? IT'S... IT'S HORRIBLE. WHO COULD'VE DONE...?
BOSTON. BOSTON BRAND, ARE YOU HERE? DID YOU DO... THIS?
OR... DID I?
AT THE BEHEST AND MANIPULATION OF THE PHANTOM STRANGER, YES HE DID. BOSTON BRAND HAS BECOME A TOOL.
IF A TOOL, A WILLING TOOL.
AND A CLEVER ONE AT THAT. HAD I ONE, I'D DOFF MY HAT.
SHUDDUP, YOU GHOULS.
THANK GOD HE CAN'T HEAR YOU.
DON'T LOOK AT IT, TINY. IT'S NOT MEANT FOR EYES LIKE YOURS.
MY... HANDS... HURT.
DID I...?

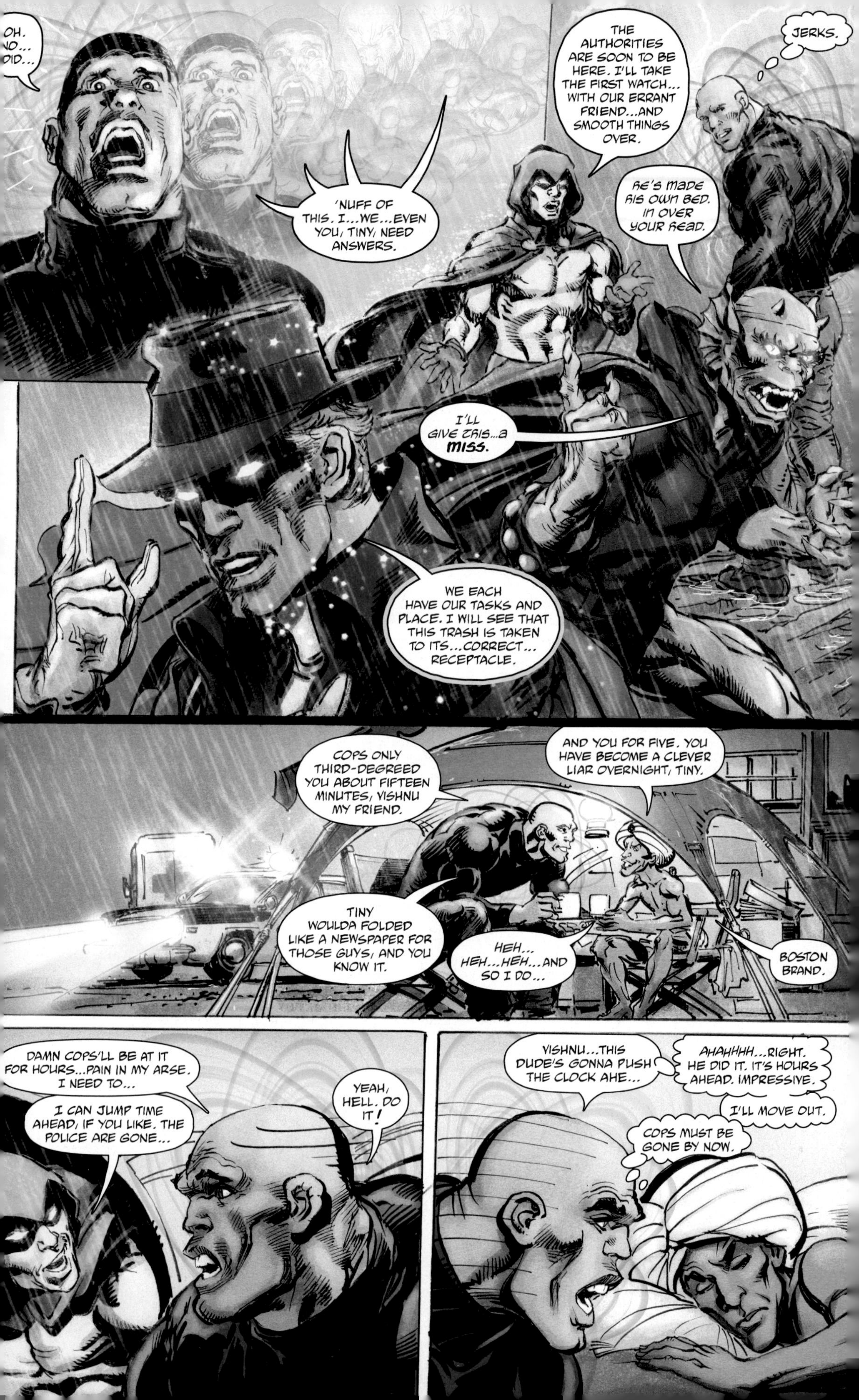
OH. NO... DID...
'NUFF OF THIS. I...WE...EVEN YOU, TINY, NEED ANSWERS.
THE AUTHORITIES ARE SOON TO BE HERE. I'LL TAKE THE FIRST WATCH... WITH OUR ERRANT FRIEND...AND SMOOTH THINGS OVER.
JERKS.
HE'S MADE HIS OWN BED. IN OVER YOUR HEAD.
I'LL GIVE THIS...a MISS.
WE EACH HAVE OUR TASKS AND PLACE. I WILL SEE THAT THIS TRASH IS TAKEN TO ITS...CORRECT... RECEPTACLE.
COPS ONLY THIRD-DEGREED YOU ABOUT FIFTEEN MINUTES, VISHNU MY FRIEND.
AND YOU FOR FIVE. YOU HAVE BECOME A CLEVER LIAR OVERNIGHT, TINY.
TINY WOULDA FOLDED LIKE A NEWSPAPER FOR THOSE GUYS, AND YOU KNOW IT.
HEH... HEH...HEH...AND SO I DO...
BOSTON BRAND.
DAMN COPS'LL BE AT IT FOR HOURS...PAIN IN MY ARSE. I NEED TO...
I CAN JUMP TIME AHEAD, IF YOU LIKE. THE POLICE ARE GONE...
YEAH, HELL. DO IT!
VISHNU...THIS DUDE'S GONNA PUSH THE CLOCK AHE...
AHAHHHH...RIGHT. HE DID IT. IT'S HOURS AHEAD. IMPRESSIVE.
I'LL MOVE OUT.
COPS MUST BE GONE BY NOW.

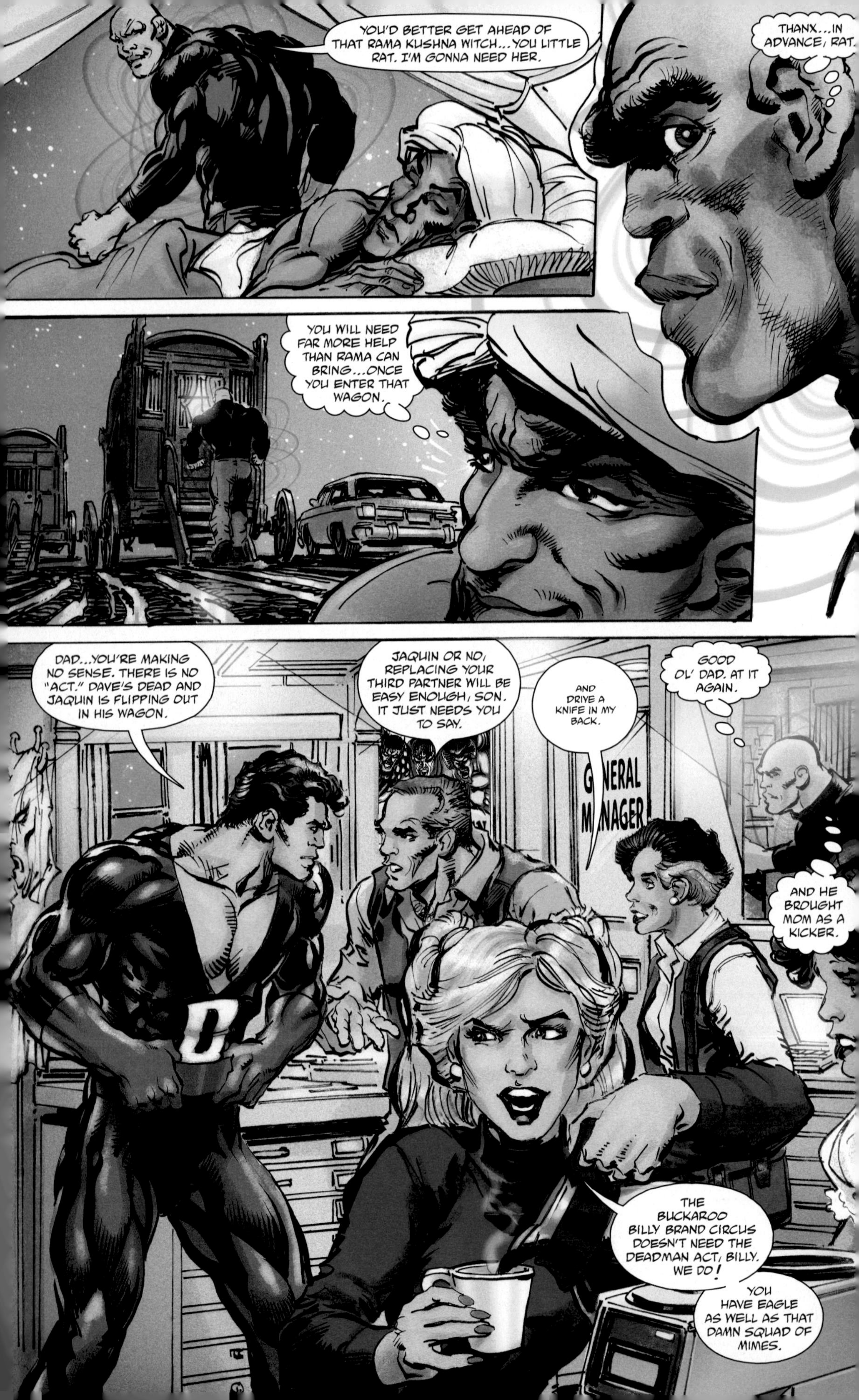
YOU'D BETTER GET AHEAD OF THAT RAMA KUSHNA WITCH...YOU LITTLE RAT. I'M GONNA NEED HER.
THANX...IN ADVANCE, RAT.
YOU WILL NEED FAR MORE HELP THAN RAMA CAN BRING...ONCE YOU ENTER THAT WAGON.
DAD...YOU'RE MAKING NO SENSE. THERE IS NO "ACT." DAVE'S DEAD AND JAQUIN IS FLIPPING OUT IN HIS WAGON.
JAQUIN OR NO, REPLACING YOUR THIRD PARTNER WILL BE EASY ENOUGH, SON. IT JUST NEEDS YOU TO SAY.
AND DRIVE A KNIFE IN MY BACK.
GOOD OL' DAD. AT IT AGAIN.
AND HE BROUGHT MOM AS A KICKER.
GENERAL MANAGER
THE BUCKAROO BILLY BRAND CIRCUS DOESN'T NEED THE DEADMAN ACT, BILLY. WE DO!
YOU HAVE EAGLE AS WELL AS THAT DAMN SQUAD OF MIMES.

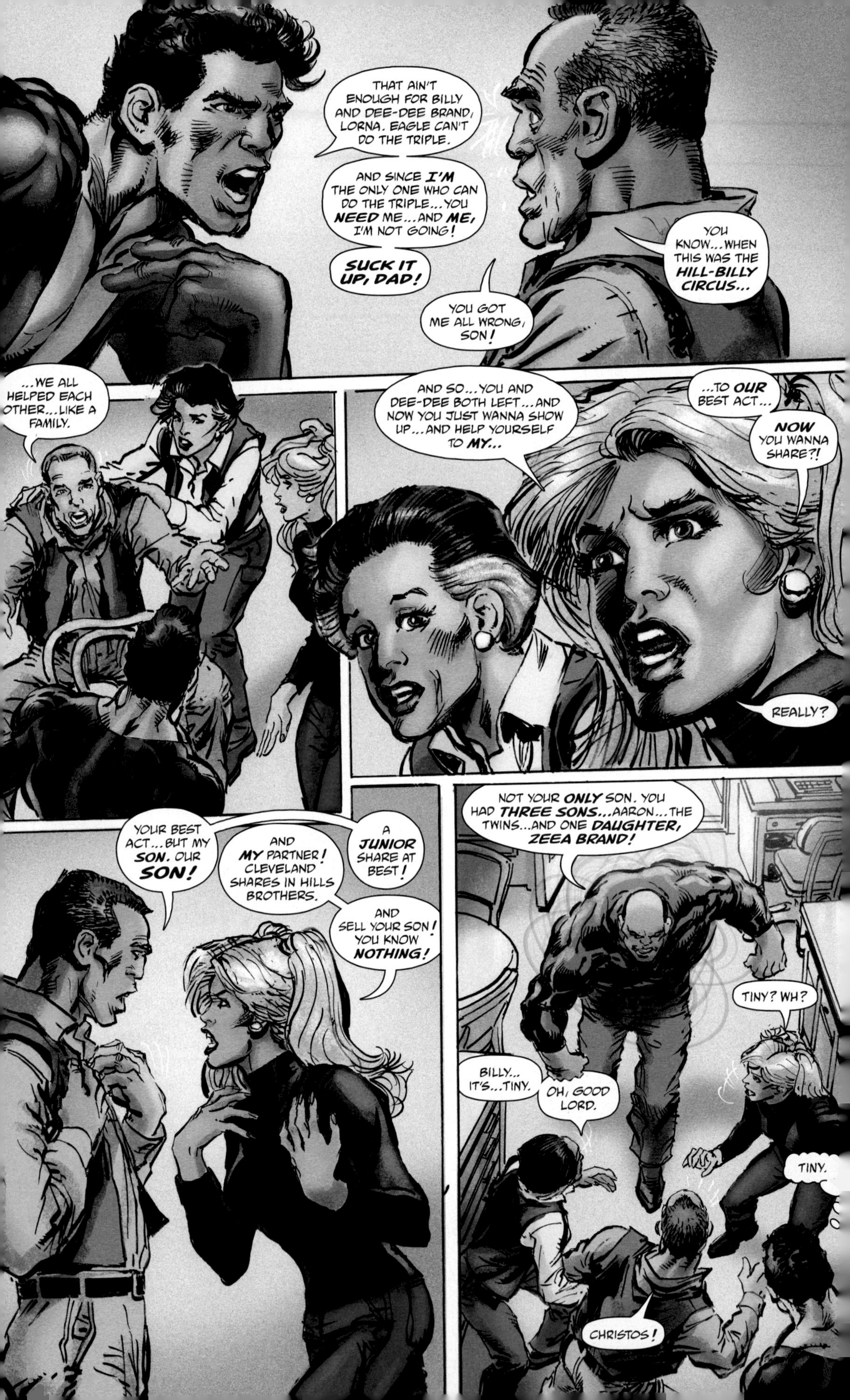
THAT AIN'T ENOUGH FOR BILLY AND DEE-DEE BRAND, LORNA. EAGLE CAN'T DO THE TRIPLE.
AND SINCE I'M THE ONLY ONE WHO CAN DO THE TRIPLE... YOU NEED ME... AND ME, I'M NOT GOING!
SUCK IT UP, DAD!
YOU GOT ME ALL WRONG, SON!
YOU KNOW... WHEN THIS WAS THE HILL-BILLY CIRCUS...
...WE ALL HELPED EACH OTHER... LIKE A FAMILY.
AND SO... YOU AND DEE-DEE BOTH LEFT... AND NOW YOU JUST WANNA SHOW UP... AND HELP YOURSELF TO MY...
...TO OUR BEST ACT...
NOW YOU WANNA SHARE?!
REALLY?
YOUR BEST ACT... BUT MY SON. OUR SON!
AND MY PARTNER! CLEVELAND SHARES IN HILLS BROTHERS.
A JUNIOR SHARE AT BEST!
AND SELL YOUR SON! YOU KNOW NOTHING!
NOT YOUR ONLY SON. YOU HAD THREE SONS... AARON... THE TWINS... AND ONE DAUGHTER, ZEEA BRAND!
TINY? WH?
BILLY... IT'S... TINY.
OH, GOOD LORD.
TINY.
CHRISTOS!

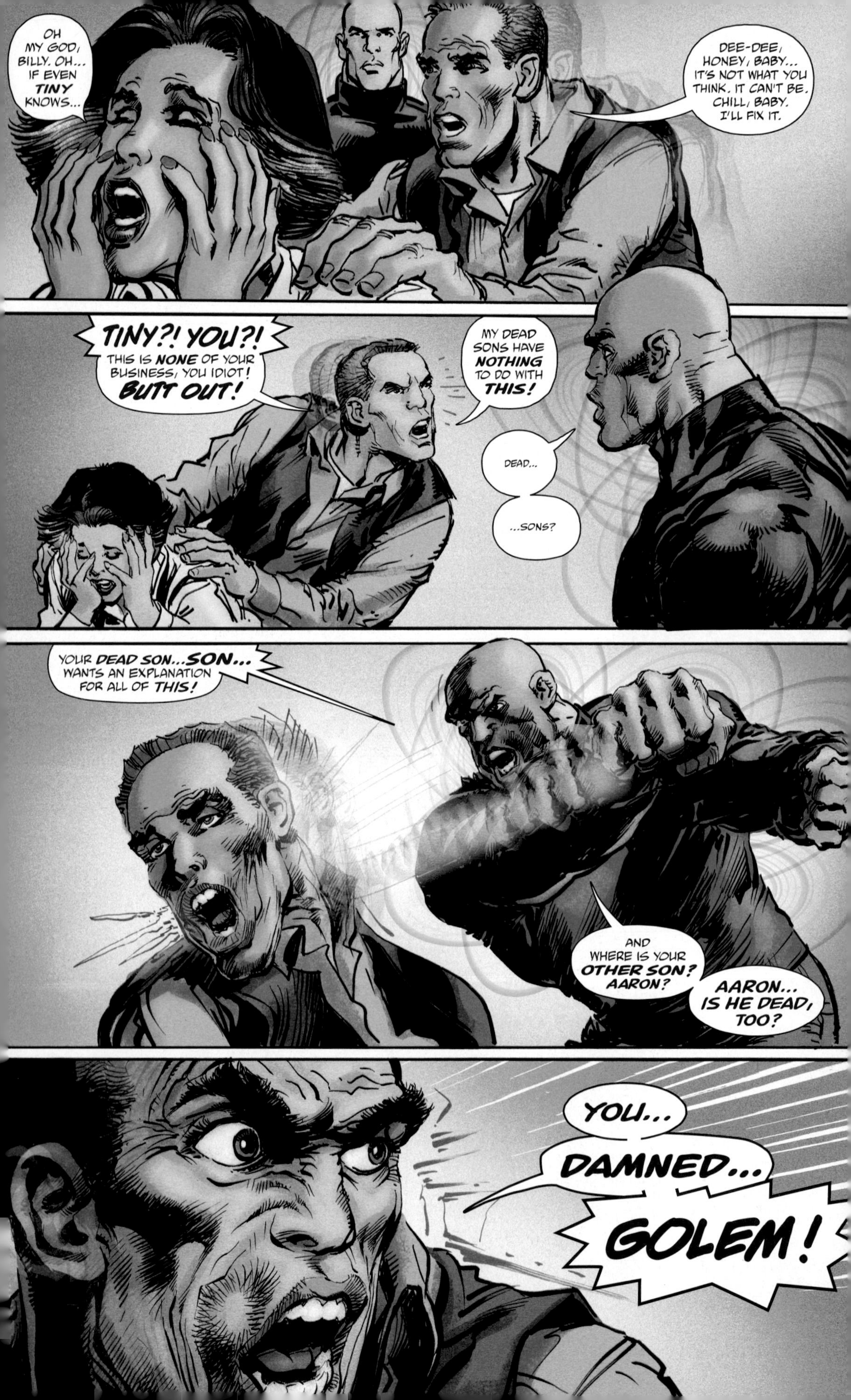
OH MY GOD, BILLY. OH... IF EVEN TINY KNOWS...
DEE-DEE, HONEY, BABY... IT'S NOT WHAT YOU THINK. IT CAN'T BE. CHILL, BABY. I'LL FIX IT.
TINY?! YOU?! THIS IS NONE OF YOUR BUSINESS, YOU IDIOT! BUTT OUT!
MY DEAD SONS HAVE NOTHING TO DO WITH THIS!
DEAD...
...SONS?
YOUR DEAD SON...SON... WANTS AN EXPLANATION FOR ALL OF THIS!
AND WHERE IS YOUR OTHER SON? AARON?
AARON... IS HE DEAD, TOO?
YOU...
DAMNED...
GOLEM!

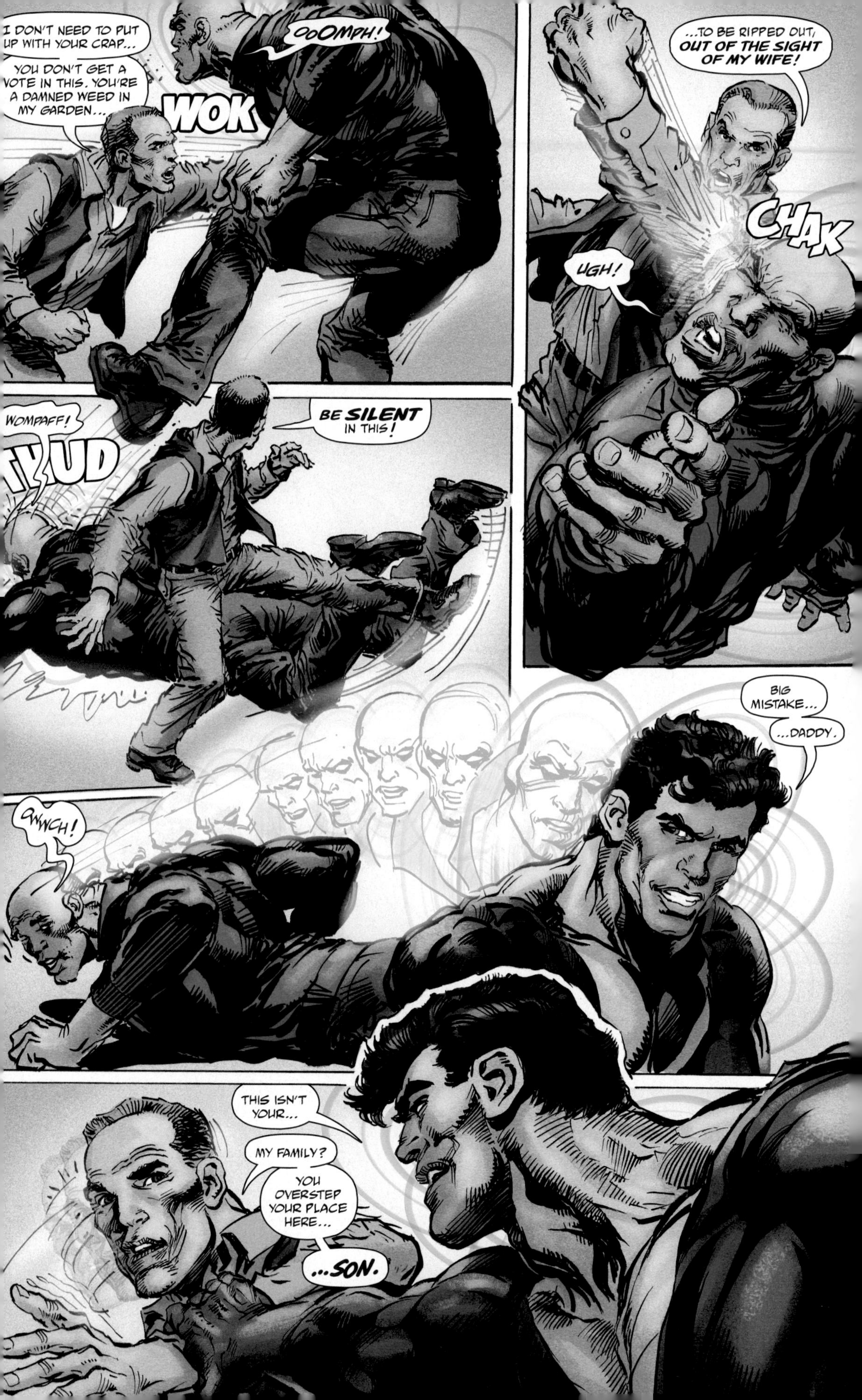
I DON'T NEED TO PUT UP WITH YOUR CRAP...
YOU DON'T GET A VOTE IN THIS. YOU'RE A DAMNED WEED IN MY GARDEN...
OOOMPH!
WOK
...TO BE RIPPED OUT, OUT OF THE SIGHT OF MY WIFE!
CHAK
UGH!
WOMPAFF!
THUD
BE SILENT IN THIS!
BIG MISTAKE...
...DADDY.
AWWCH!
THIS ISN'T YOUR...
MY FAMILY?
YOU OVERSTEP YOUR PLACE HERE...
...SON.

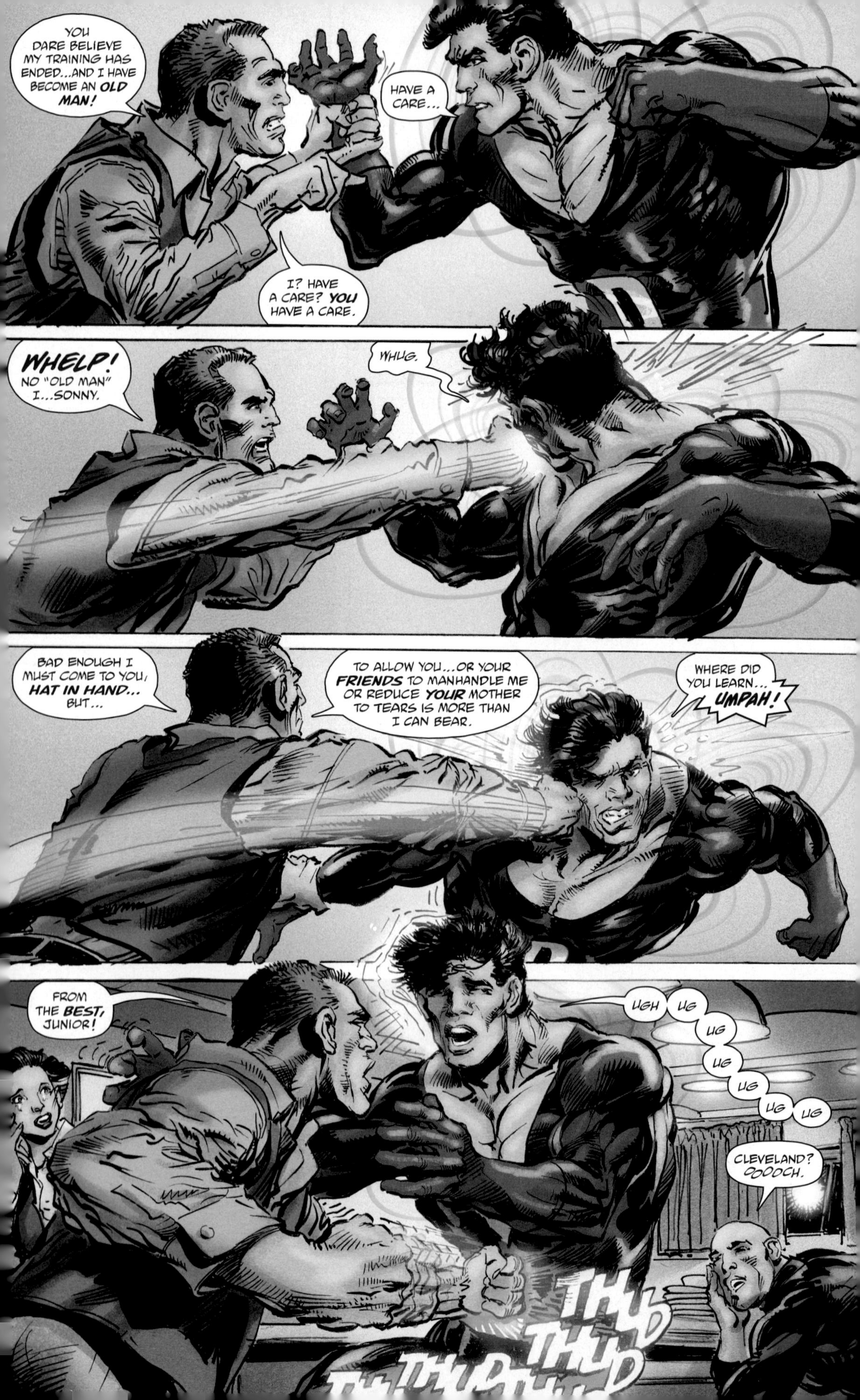

YOU DARE BELIEVE MY TRAINING HAS ENDED...AND I HAVE BECOME AN OLD MAN!
HAVE A CARE...
I? HAVE A CARE? YOU HAVE A CARE.
WHELP! NO "OLD MAN" I...SONNY.
WHUG.
BAD ENOUGH I MUST COME TO YOU, HAT IN HAND... BUT...
TO ALLOW YOU...OR YOUR FRIENDS TO MANHANDLE ME OR REDUCE YOUR MOTHER TO TEARS IS MORE THAN I CAN BEAR.
WHERE DID YOU LEARN... UMPAH!
FROM THE BEST, JUNIOR!
UGH UG UG UG UG UG UG
CLEVELAND? OOOOCH.
THUD THUD THUD THUD

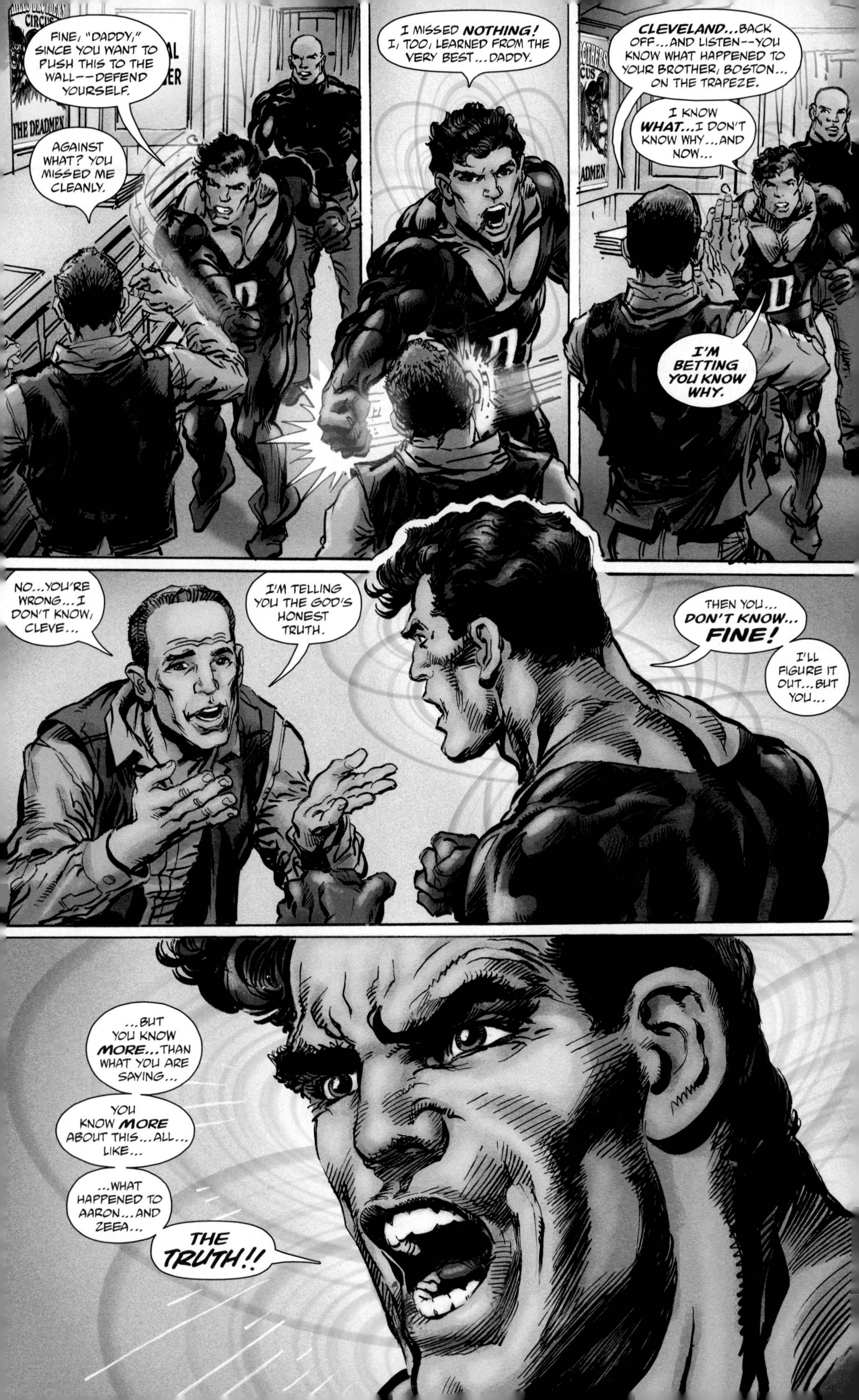
CIRCUS
THE DEADMEN
FINE, "DADDY," SINCE YOU WANT TO PUSH THIS TO THE WALL--DEFEND YOURSELF.
AGAINST WHAT? YOU MISSED ME CLEANLY.
I MISSED **NOTHING!** I, TOO, LEARNED FROM THE VERY BEST... DADDY.
CLEVELAND...BACK OFF...AND LISTEN--YOU KNOW WHAT HAPPENED TO YOUR BROTHER, BOSTON... ON THE TRAPEZE.
I KNOW **WHAT...**I DON'T KNOW WHY...AND NOW...
I'M BETTING YOU KNOW WHY.
NO...YOU'RE WRONG...I DON'T KNOW, CLEVE...
I'M TELLING YOU THE GOD'S HONEST TRUTH.
THEN YOU... **DON'T KNOW... FINE!**
I'LL FIGURE IT OUT...BUT YOU...
...BUT YOU KNOW **MORE...**THAN WHAT YOU ARE SAYING...
YOU KNOW **MORE** ABOUT THIS...ALL... LIKE...
...WHAT HAPPENED TO AARON...AND ZEEA...
THE TRUTH!!

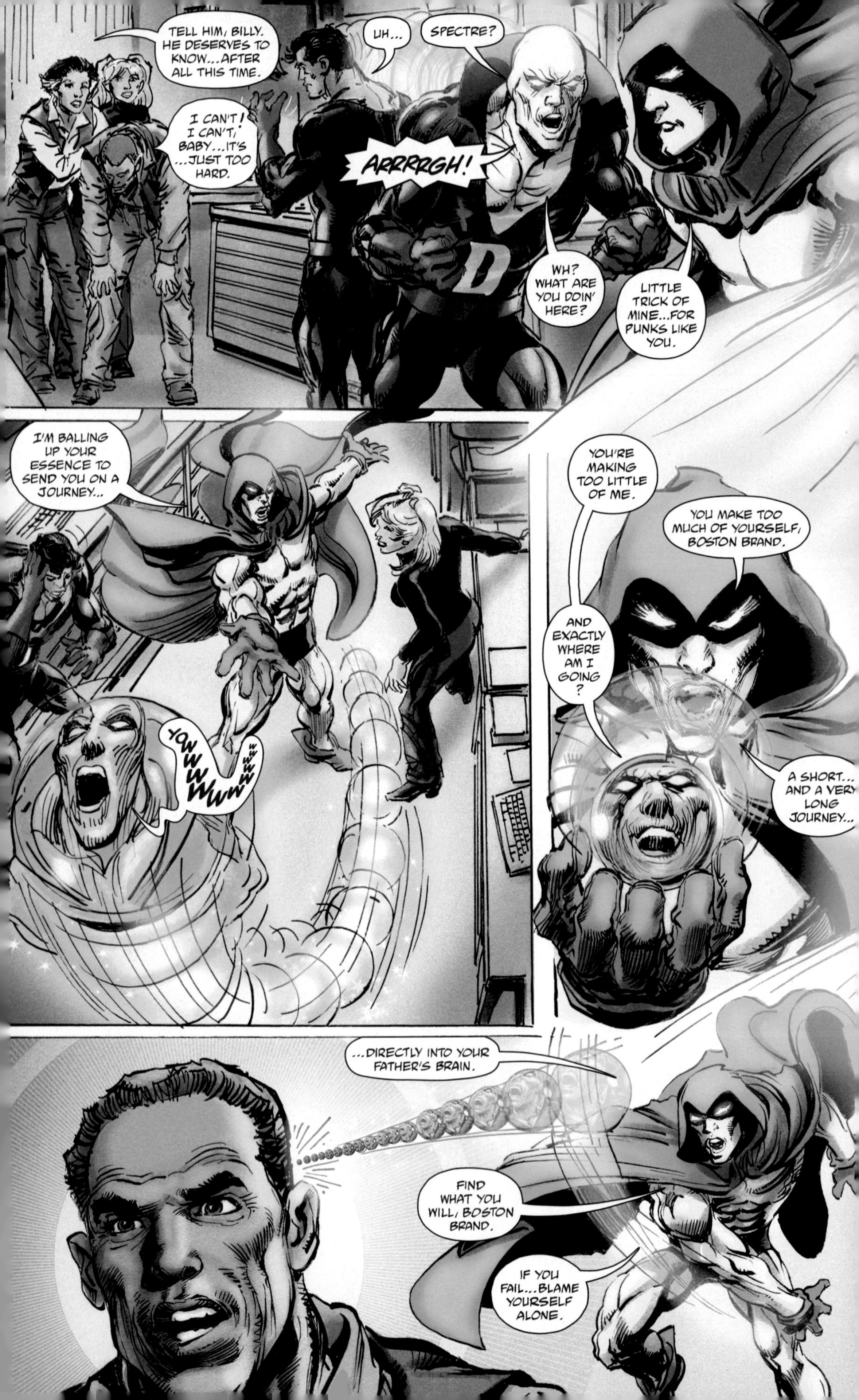
TELL HIM, BILLY. HE DESERVES TO KNOW...AFTER ALL THIS TIME.
I CAN'T! I CAN'T, BABY...IT'S ...JUST TOO HARD.
UH...
SPECTRE?
ARRRRGH!
WH? WHAT ARE YOU DOIN' HERE?
LITTLE TRICK OF MINE...FOR PUNKS LIKE YOU.
I'M BALLING UP YOUR ESSENCE TO SEND YOU ON A JOURNEY...
YOWWWWWWWWWW
YOU'RE MAKING TOO LITTLE OF ME.
YOU MAKE TOO MUCH OF YOURSELF, BOSTON BRAND.
AND EXACTLY WHERE AM I GOING?
A SHORT... AND A VERY LONG JOURNEY...
...DIRECTLY INTO YOUR FATHER'S BRAIN.
FIND WHAT YOU WILL, BOSTON BRAND.
IF YOU FAIL...BLAME YOURSELF ALONE.

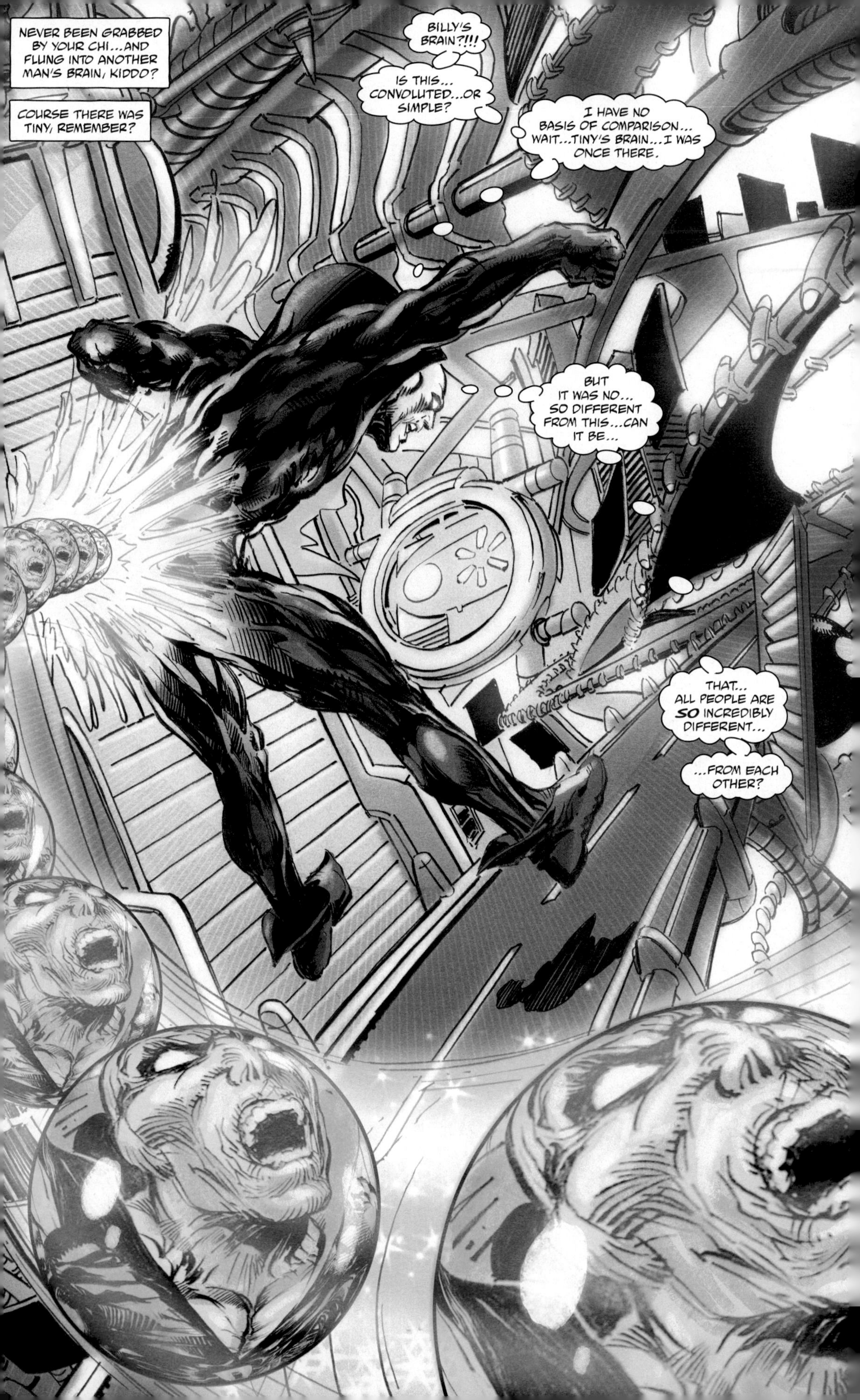

NEVER BEEN GRABBED BY YOUR CHI...AND FLUNG INTO ANOTHER MAN'S BRAIN, KIDDO?
COURSE THERE WAS TINY, REMEMBER?
BILLY'S BRAIN?!!!
IS THIS... CONVOLUTED...OR SIMPLE?
I HAVE NO BASIS OF COMPARISON... WAIT...TINY'S BRAIN...I WAS ONCE THERE.
BUT IT WAS NO... SO DIFFERENT FROM THIS...CAN IT BE...
THAT... ALL PEOPLE ARE **SO** INCREDIBLY DIFFERENT...
...FROM EACH OTHER?

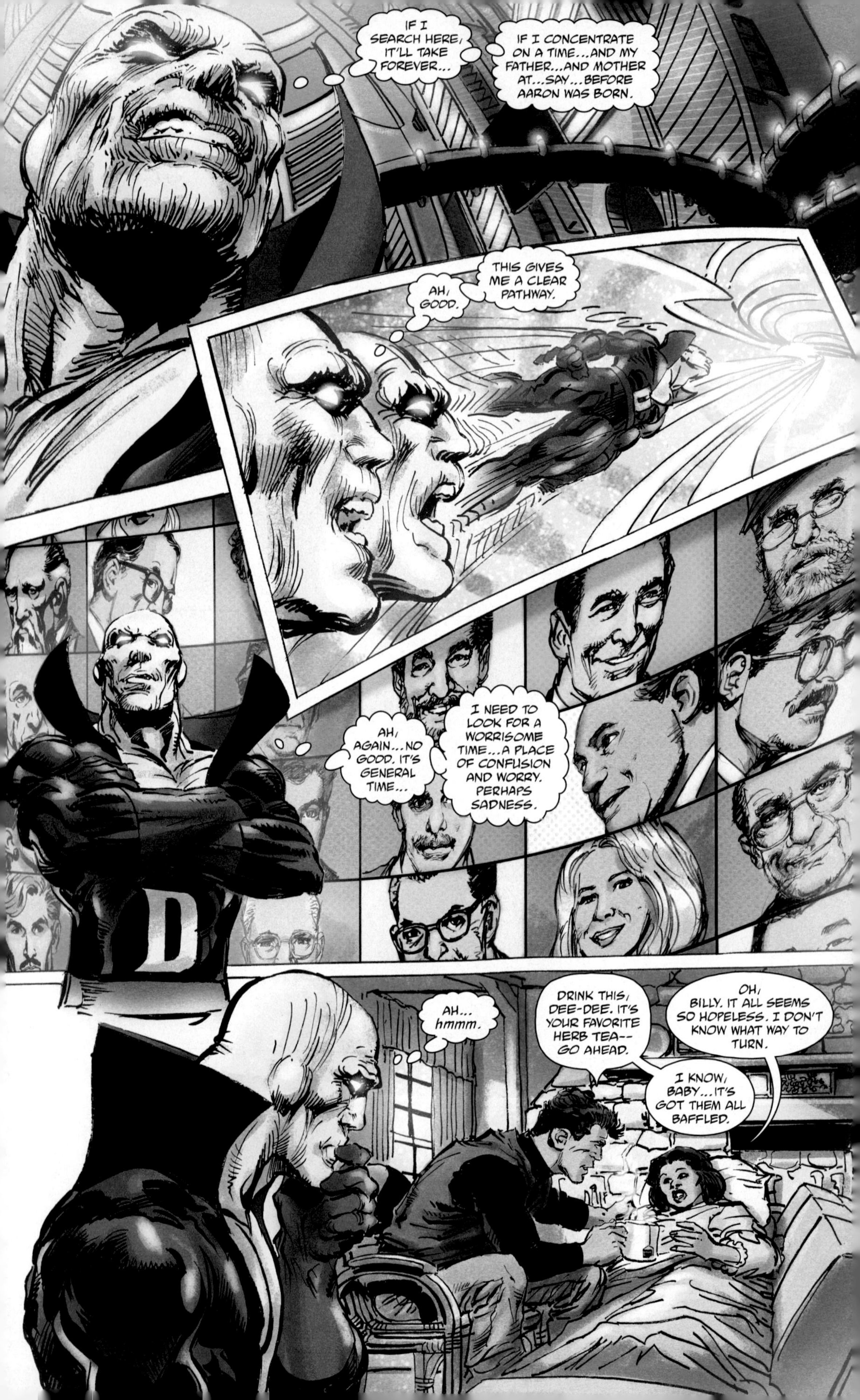
IF I SEARCH HERE, IT'LL TAKE FOREVER...
IF I CONCENTRATE ON A TIME...AND MY FATHER...AND MOTHER AT...SAY...BEFORE AARON WAS BORN.
AH, GOOD.
THIS GIVES ME A CLEAR PATHWAY.
AH, AGAIN...NO GOOD. IT'S GENERAL TIME...
I NEED TO LOOK FOR A WORRISOME TIME...A PLACE OF CONFUSION AND WORRY. PERHAPS SADNESS.
AH... hmmm.
DRINK THIS, DEE-DEE. IT'S YOUR FAVORITE HERB TEA--GO AHEAD.
OH, BILLY. IT ALL SEEMS SO HOPELESS. I DON'T KNOW WHAT WAY TO TURN.
I KNOW, BABY...IT'S GOT THEM ALL BAFFLED.

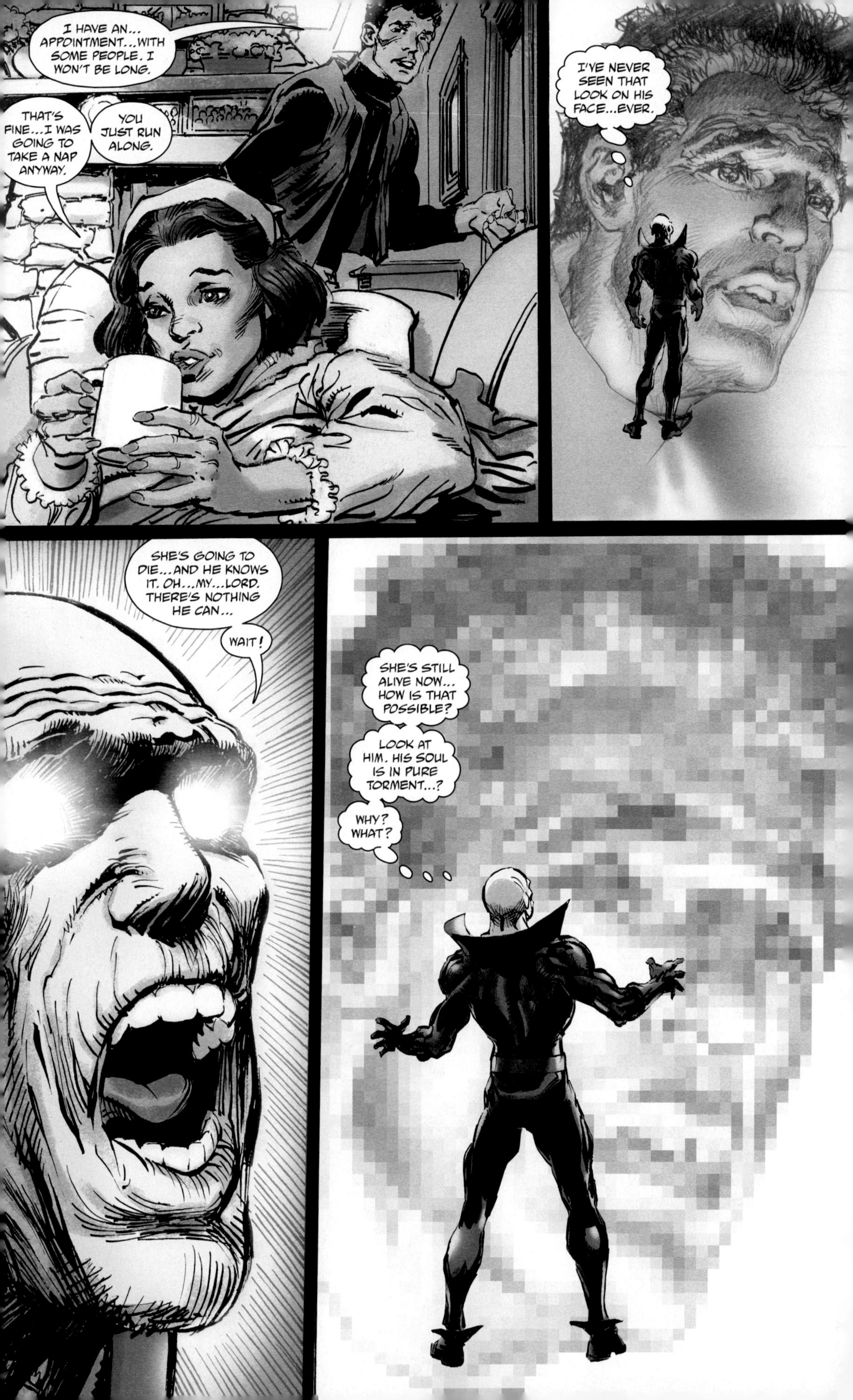
I HAVE AN... APPOINTMENT... WITH SOME PEOPLE. I WON'T BE LONG.
THAT'S FINE... I WAS GOING TO TAKE A NAP ANYWAY.
YOU JUST RUN ALONG.
I'VE NEVER SEEN THAT LOOK ON HIS FACE... EVER.
SHE'S GOING TO DIE... AND HE KNOWS IT. OH... MY... LORD. THERE'S NOTHING HE CAN...
WAIT!
SHE'S STILL ALIVE NOW... HOW IS THAT POSSIBLE?
LOOK AT HIM. HIS SOUL IS IN PURE TORMENT...?
WHY? WHAT?

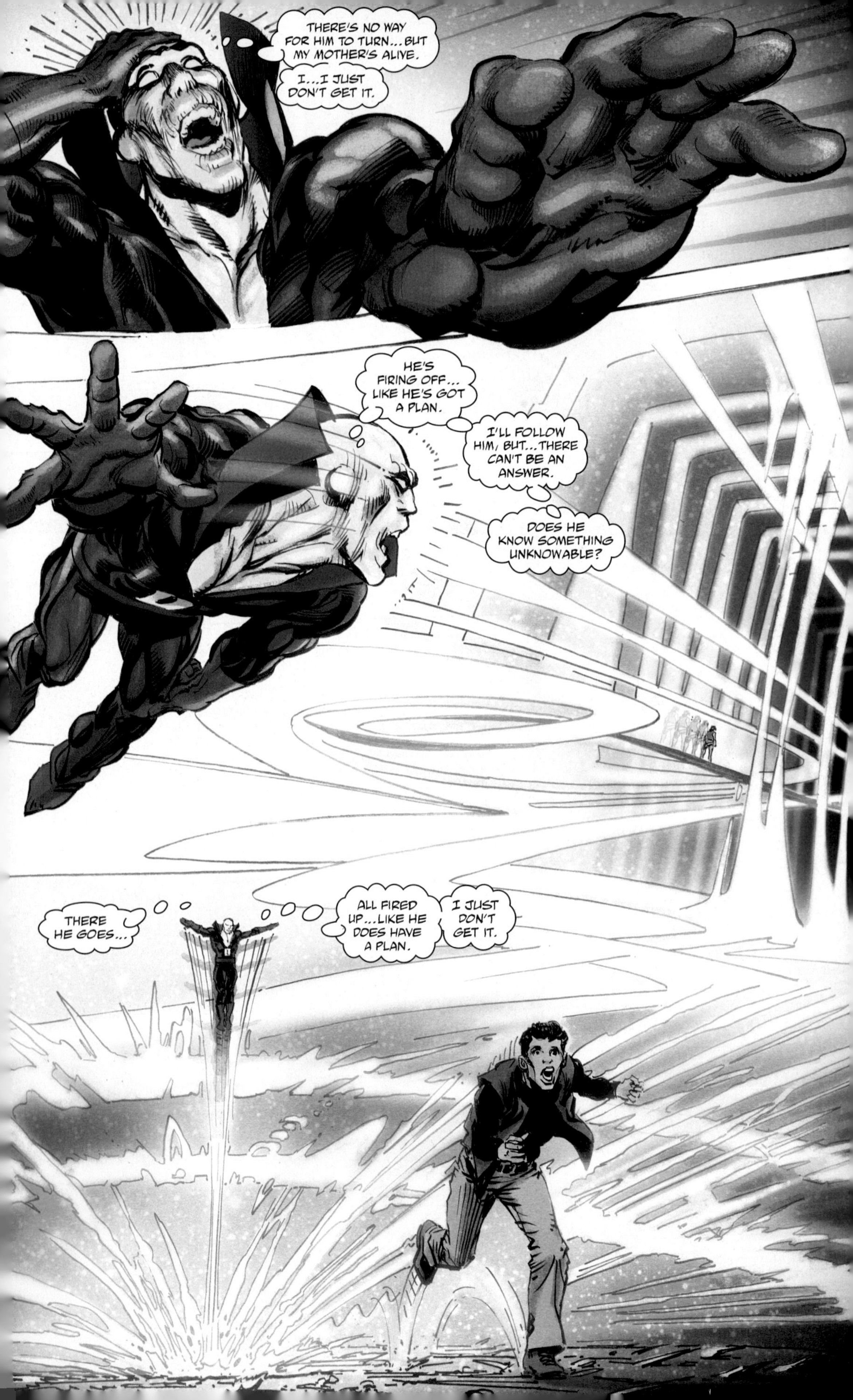
THERE'S NO WAY FOR HIM TO TURN... BUT MY MOTHER'S ALIVE.
I...I JUST DON'T GET IT.
HE'S FIRING OFF... LIKE HE'S GOT A PLAN.
I'LL FOLLOW HIM, BUT...THERE CAN'T BE AN ANSWER.
DOES HE KNOW SOMETHING UNKNOWABLE?
THERE HE GOES...
ALL FIRED UP...LIKE HE DOES HAVE A PLAN.
I JUST DON'T GET IT.

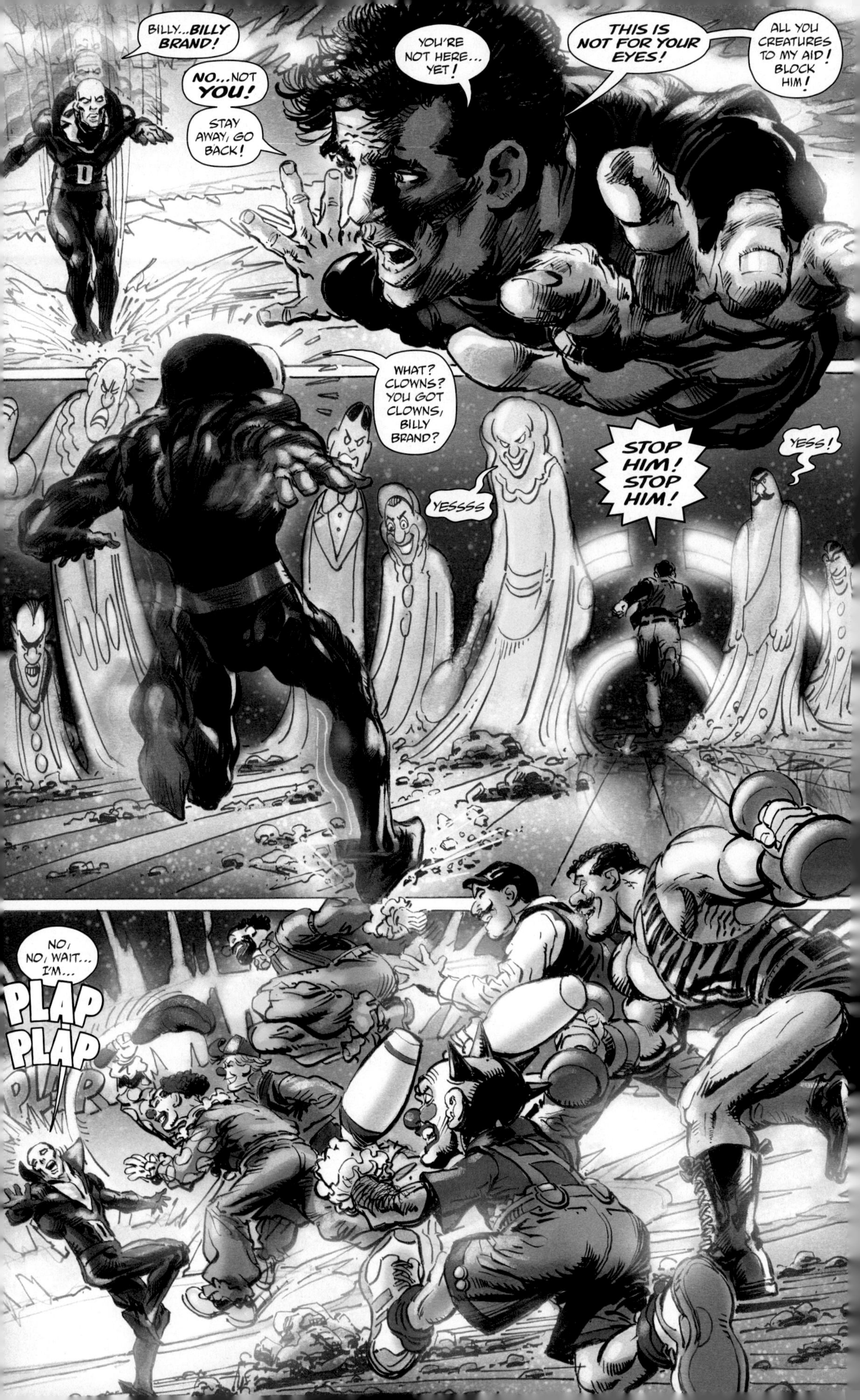
BILLY...BILLY BRAND!
NO...NOT YOU!
STAY AWAY, GO BACK!
YOU'RE NOT HERE... YET!
THIS IS NOT FOR YOUR EYES!
ALL YOU CREATURES TO MY AID! BLOCK HIM!
WHAT? CLOWNS? YOU GOT CLOWNS, BILLY BRAND?
YESSSS
STOP HIM! STOP HIM!
YESS!
NO, NO, WAIT... I'M...
PLAP
PLAP
PLAP

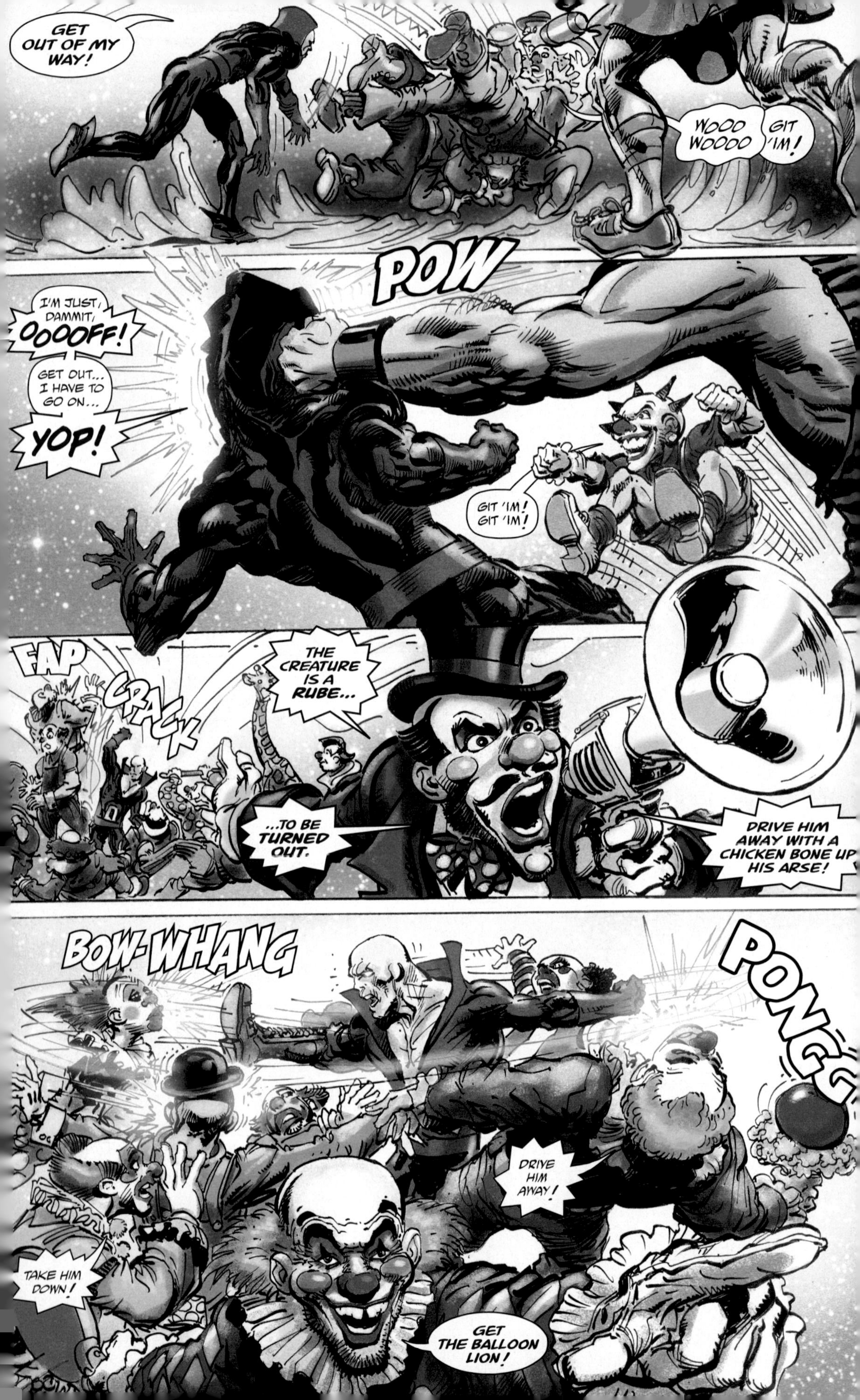
GET OUT OF MY WAY!
WOOO WOOOO
GIT 'IM!
POW
I'M JUST, DAMMIT, OOOOFF!
GET OUT... I HAVE TO GO ON...
YOP!
GIT 'IM! GIT 'IM!
FAP
CRACK
THE CREATURE IS A RUBE...
...TO BE TURNED OUT.
DRIVE HIM AWAY WITH A CHICKEN BONE UP HIS ARSE!
BOW-WHANG
PONGG
DRIVE HIM AWAY!
TAKE HIM DOWN!
GET THE BALLOON LION!

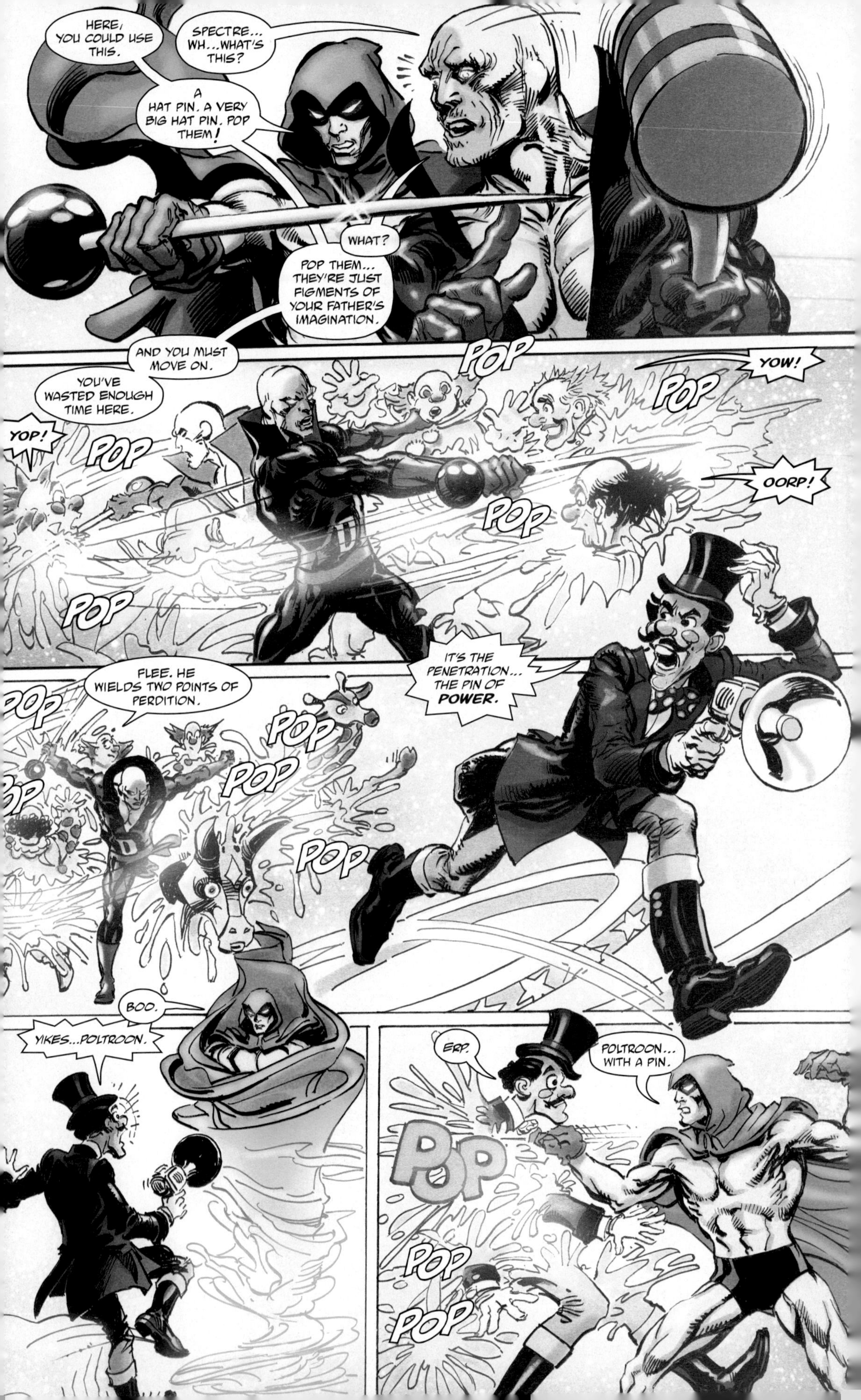
HERE, YOU COULD USE THIS.
SPECTRE... WH...WHAT'S THIS?
A HAT PIN. A VERY BIG HAT PIN. POP THEM!
WHAT?
POP THEM... THEY'RE JUST FIGMENTS OF YOUR FATHER'S IMAGINATION.
AND YOU MUST MOVE ON.
YOU'VE WASTED ENOUGH TIME HERE.
POP
YOW!
POP
YOP!
POP
OORP!
POP
POP
FLEE. HE WIELDS TWO POINTS OF PERDITION.
IT'S THE PENETRATION... THE PIN OF POWER.
POP
POP
POP
BOO.
YIKES...POLTROON.
ERP.
POLTROON... WITH A PIN.
POP
POP
POP

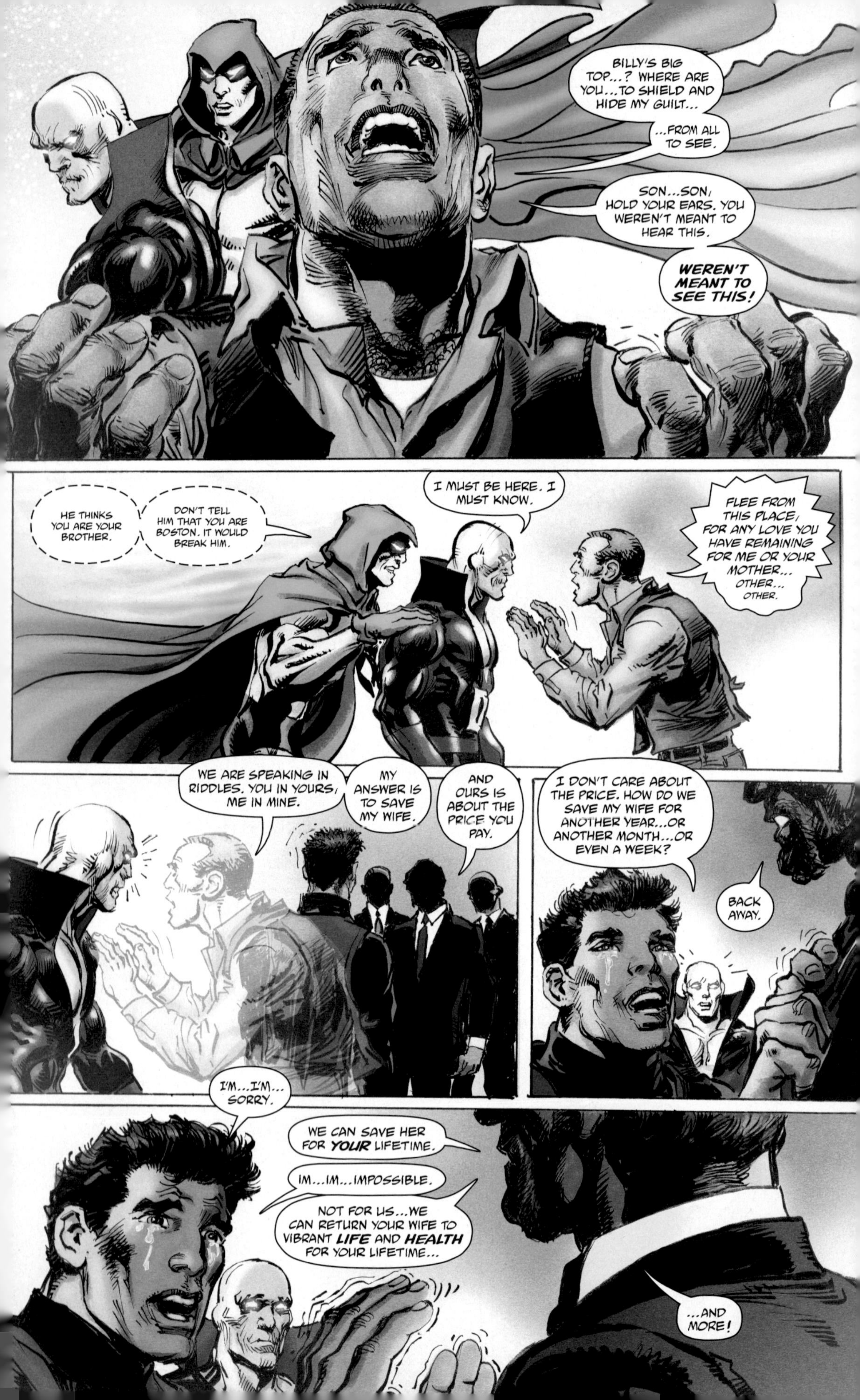

BILLY'S BIG TOP...? WHERE ARE YOU...TO SHIELD AND HIDE MY GUILT...
...FROM ALL TO SEE.
SON...SON, HOLD YOUR EARS. YOU WEREN'T MEANT TO HEAR THIS.
WEREN'T MEANT TO SEE THIS!
HE THINKS YOU ARE YOUR BROTHER.
DON'T TELL HIM THAT YOU ARE BOSTON. IT WOULD BREAK HIM.
I MUST BE HERE. I MUST KNOW.
FLEE FROM THIS PLACE, FOR ANY LOVE YOU HAVE REMAINING FOR ME OR YOUR MOTHER... OTHER... OTHER.
WE ARE SPEAKING IN RIDDLES. YOU IN YOURS, ME IN MINE.
MY ANSWER IS TO SAVE MY WIFE.
AND OURS IS ABOUT THE PRICE YOU PAY.
I DON'T CARE ABOUT THE PRICE. HOW DO WE SAVE MY WIFE FOR ANOTHER YEAR...OR ANOTHER MONTH...OR EVEN A WEEK?
BACK AWAY.
I'M...I'M... SORRY.
WE CAN SAVE HER FOR YOUR LIFETIME.
IM...IM...IMPOSSIBLE.
NOT FOR US...WE CAN RETURN YOUR WIFE TO VIBRANT LIFE AND HEALTH FOR YOUR LIFETIME...
...AND MORE!

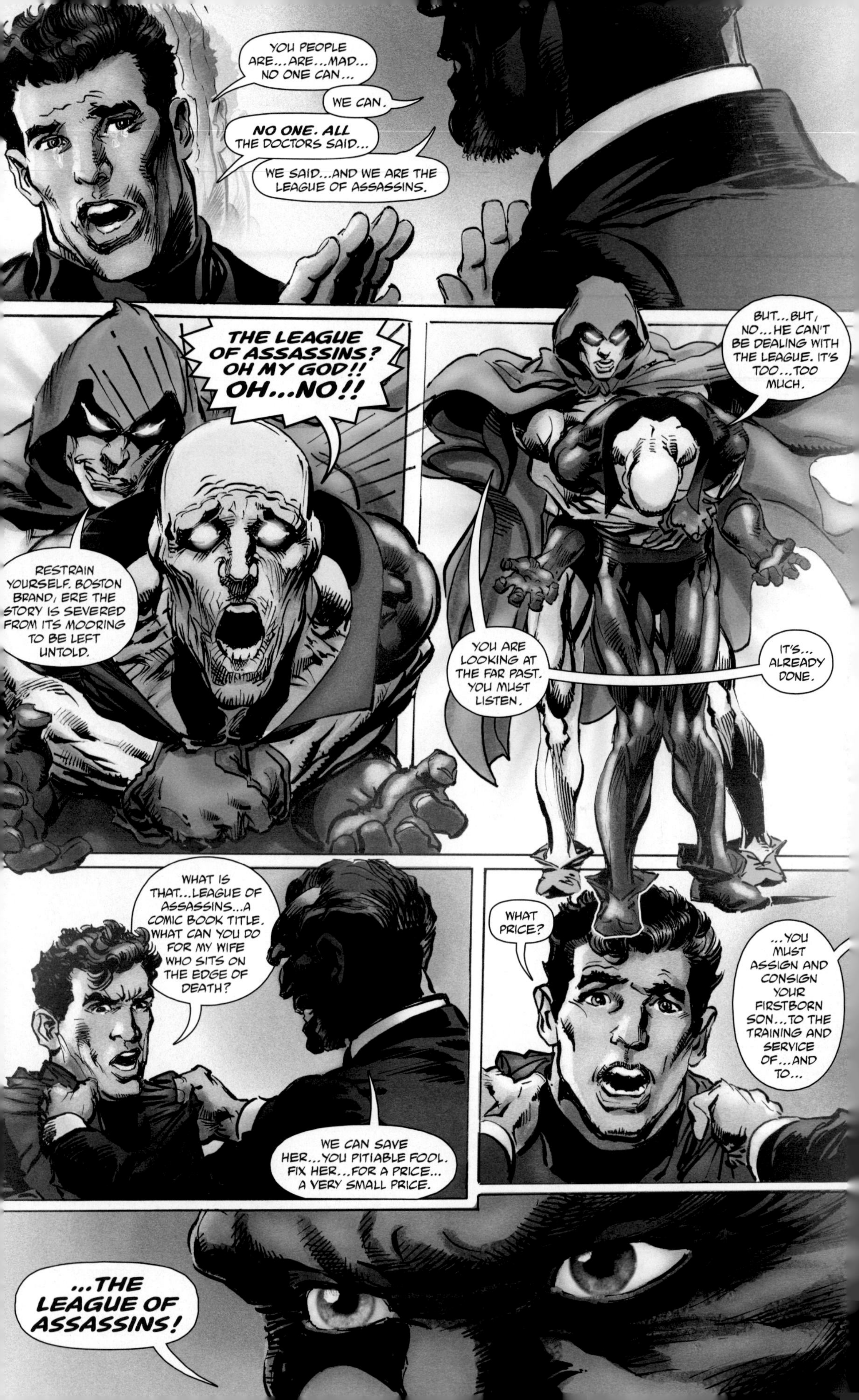
YOU PEOPLE ARE...ARE...MAD... NO ONE CAN...
WE CAN.
NO ONE. ALL THE DOCTORS SAID...
WE SAID...AND WE ARE THE LEAGUE OF ASSASSINS.
THE LEAGUE OF ASSASSINS? OH MY GOD!! OH...NO!!
RESTRAIN YOURSELF, BOSTON BRAND, ERE THE STORY IS SEVERED FROM ITS MOORING TO BE LEFT UNTOLD.
BUT...BUT, NO...HE CAN'T BE DEALING WITH THE LEAGUE. IT'S TOO...TOO MUCH.
YOU ARE LOOKING AT THE FAR PAST. YOU MUST LISTEN.
IT'S... ALREADY DONE.
WHAT IS THAT...LEAGUE OF ASSASSINS...A COMIC BOOK TITLE. WHAT CAN YOU DO FOR MY WIFE WHO SITS ON THE EDGE OF DEATH?
WE CAN SAVE HER...YOU PITIABLE FOOL. FIX HER...FOR A PRICE... A VERY SMALL PRICE.
WHAT PRICE?
...YOU MUST ASSIGN AND CONSIGN YOUR FIRSTBORN SON...TO THE TRAINING AND SERVICE OF...AND TO...
...THE LEAGUE OF ASSASSINS!

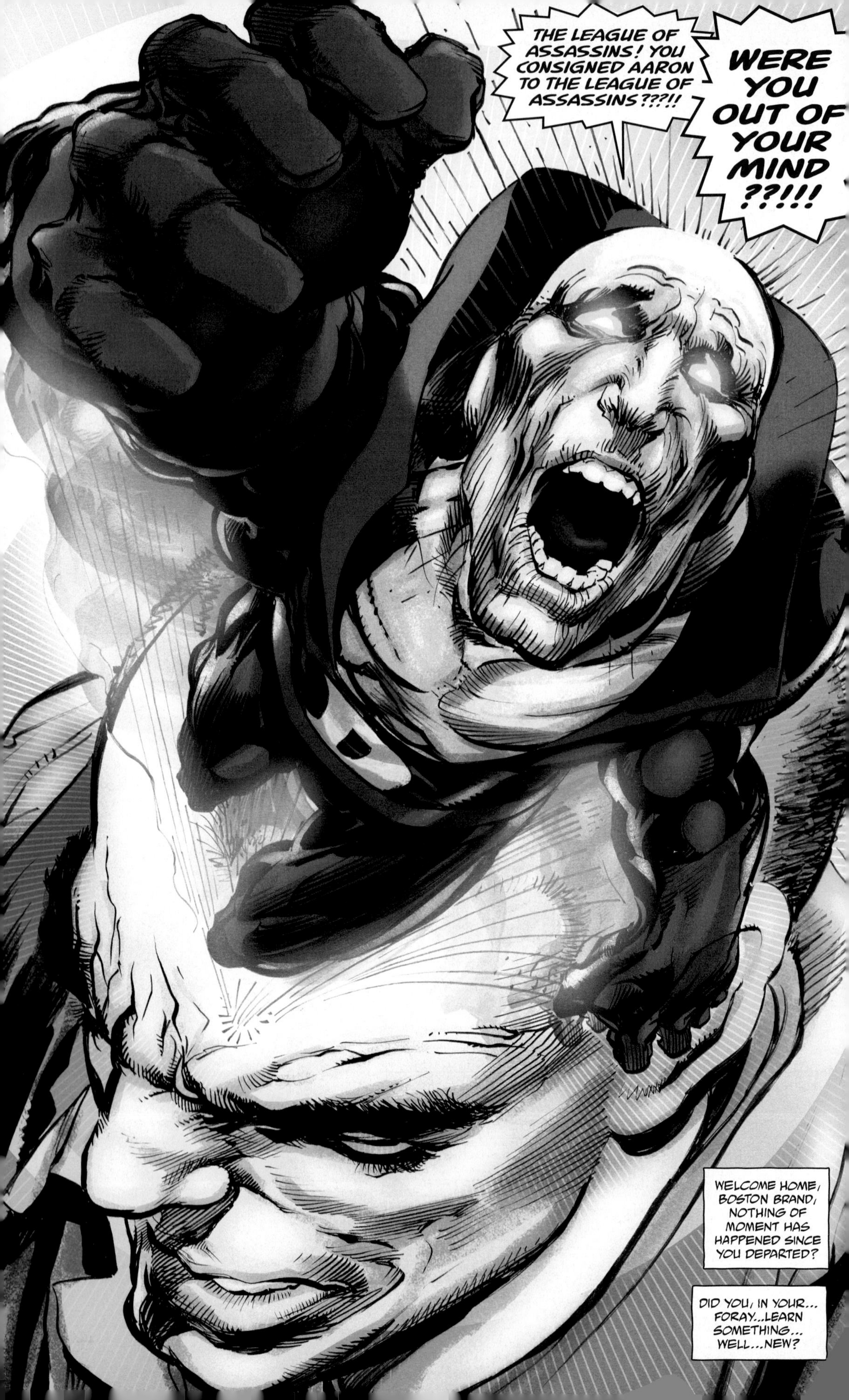
THE LEAGUE OF ASSASSINS! YOU CONSIGNED AARON TO THE LEAGUE OF ASSASSINS???!!
WERE YOU OUT OF YOUR MIND ??!!!
WELCOME HOME, BOSTON BRAND. NOTHING OF MOMENT HAS HAPPENED SINCE YOU DEPARTED?
DID YOU, IN YOUR... FORAY...LEARN SOMETHING... WELL...NEW?

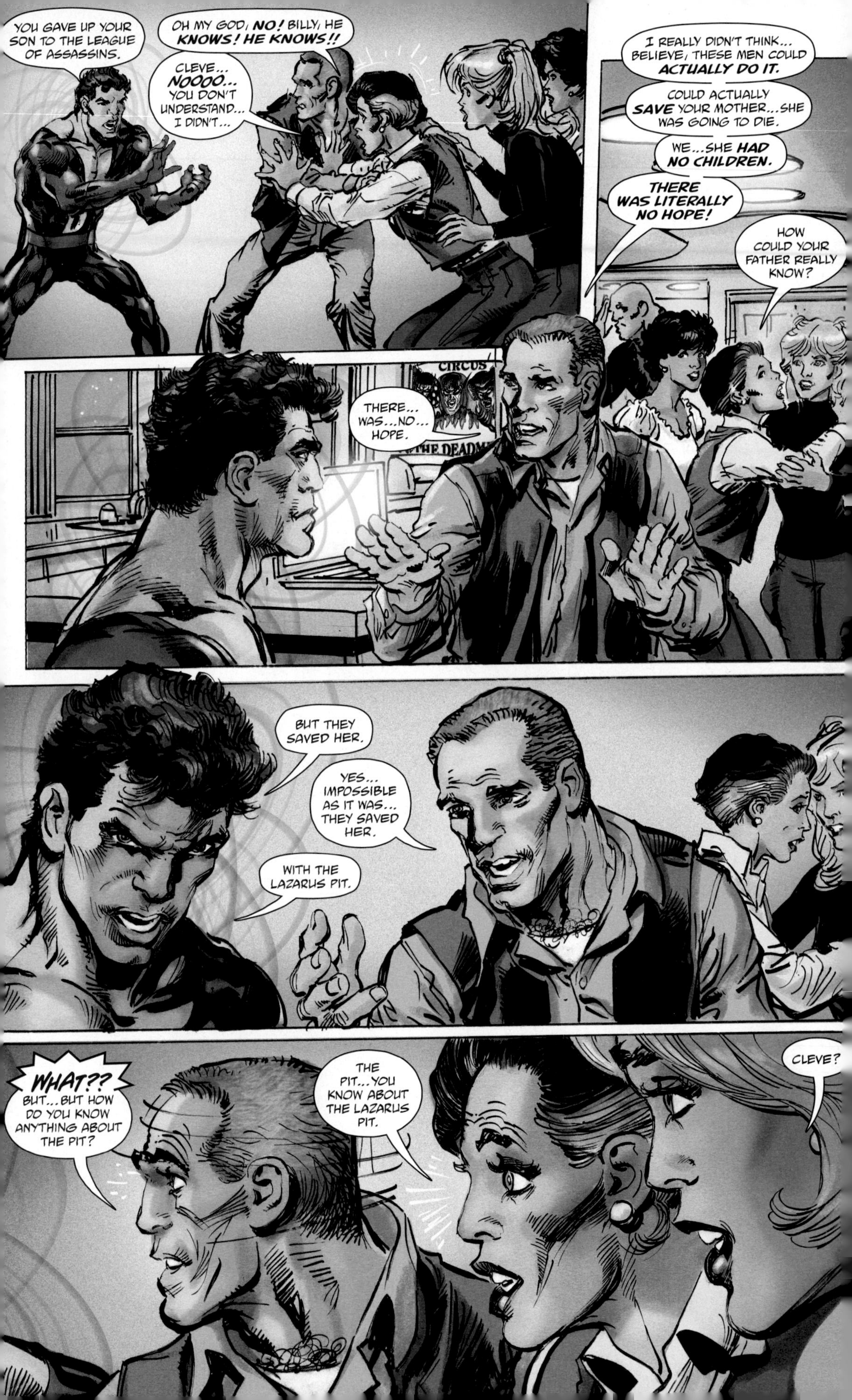
YOU GAVE UP YOUR SON TO THE LEAGUE OF ASSASSINS.
OH MY GOD, NO! BILLY, HE KNOWS! HE KNOWS!!
CLEVE... NOOOO... YOU DON'T UNDERSTAND... I DIDN'T...
I REALLY DIDN'T THINK... BELIEVE, THESE MEN COULD ACTUALLY DO IT.
COULD ACTUALLY SAVE YOUR MOTHER...SHE WAS GOING TO DIE.
WE...SHE HAD NO CHILDREN.
THERE WAS LITERALLY NO HOPE!
HOW COULD YOUR FATHER REALLY KNOW?
CIRCUS
THE DEADM
THERE... WAS...NO... HOPE.
BUT THEY SAVED HER.
YES... IMPOSSIBLE AS IT WAS... THEY SAVED HER.
WITH THE LAZARUS PIT.
WHAT?? BUT...BUT HOW DO YOU KNOW ANYTHING ABOUT THE PIT?
THE PIT...YOU KNOW ABOUT THE LAZARUS PIT.
CLEVE?

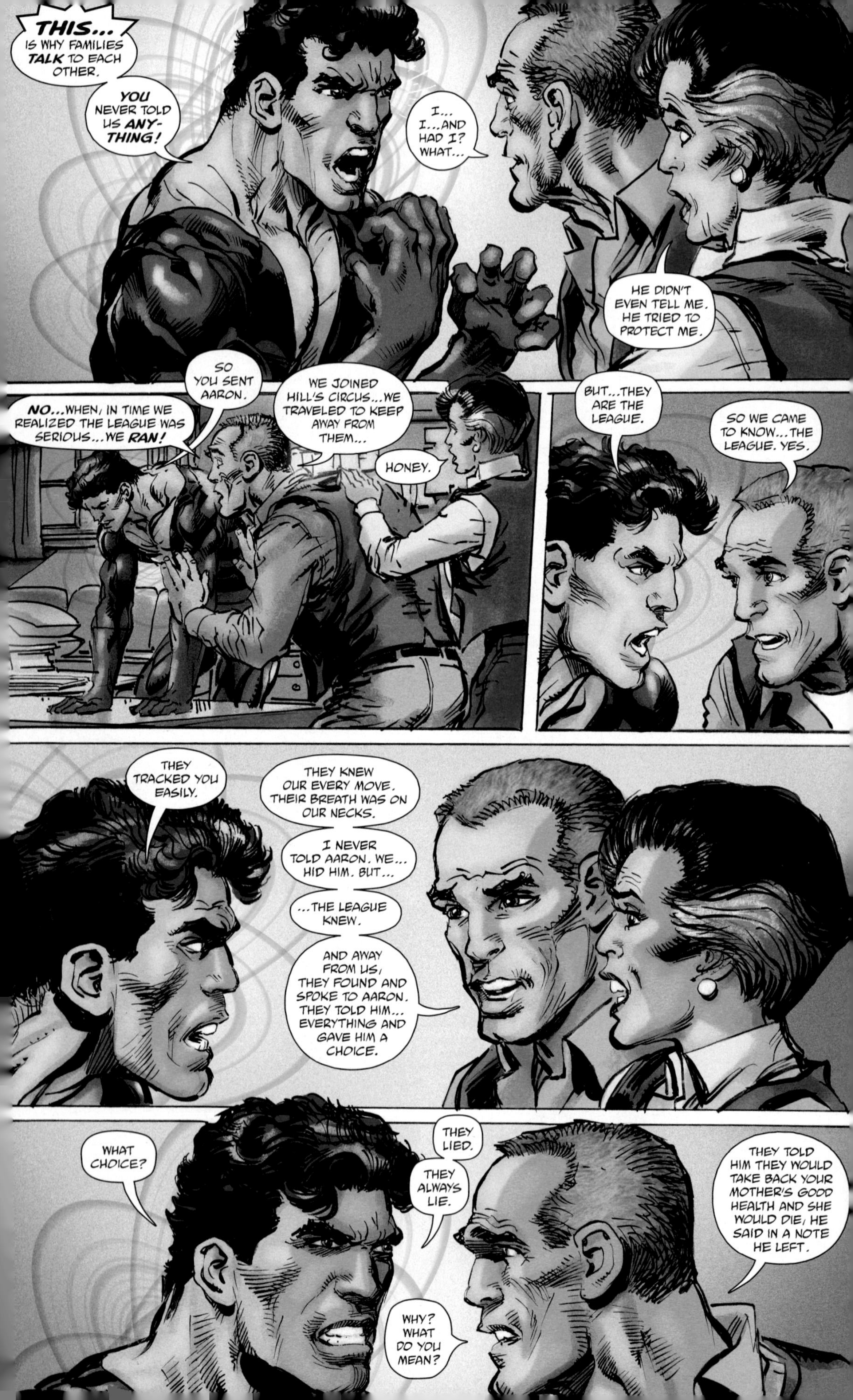
THIS... IS WHY FAMILIES TALK TO EACH OTHER.
YOU NEVER TOLD US ANY-THING!
I... I...AND HAD I? WHAT...
HE DIDN'T EVEN TELL ME. HE TRIED TO PROTECT ME.
NO...WHEN, IN TIME WE REALIZED THE LEAGUE WAS SERIOUS...WE RAN!
SO YOU SENT AARON.
WE JOINED HILL'S CIRCUS...WE TRAVELED TO KEEP AWAY FROM THEM...
HONEY.
BUT...THEY ARE THE LEAGUE.
SO WE CAME TO KNOW...THE LEAGUE. YES.
THEY TRACKED YOU EASILY.
THEY KNEW OUR EVERY MOVE. THEIR BREATH WAS ON OUR NECKS.
I NEVER TOLD AARON. WE... HID HIM. BUT...
...THE LEAGUE KNEW.
AND AWAY FROM US, THEY FOUND AND SPOKE TO AARON. THEY TOLD HIM... EVERYTHING AND GAVE HIM A CHOICE.
WHAT CHOICE?
THEY LIED.
THEY ALWAYS LIE.
THEY TOLD HIM THEY WOULD TAKE BACK YOUR MOTHER'S GOOD HEALTH AND SHE WOULD DIE, HE SAID IN A NOTE HE LEFT.
WHY? WHAT DO YOU MEAN?

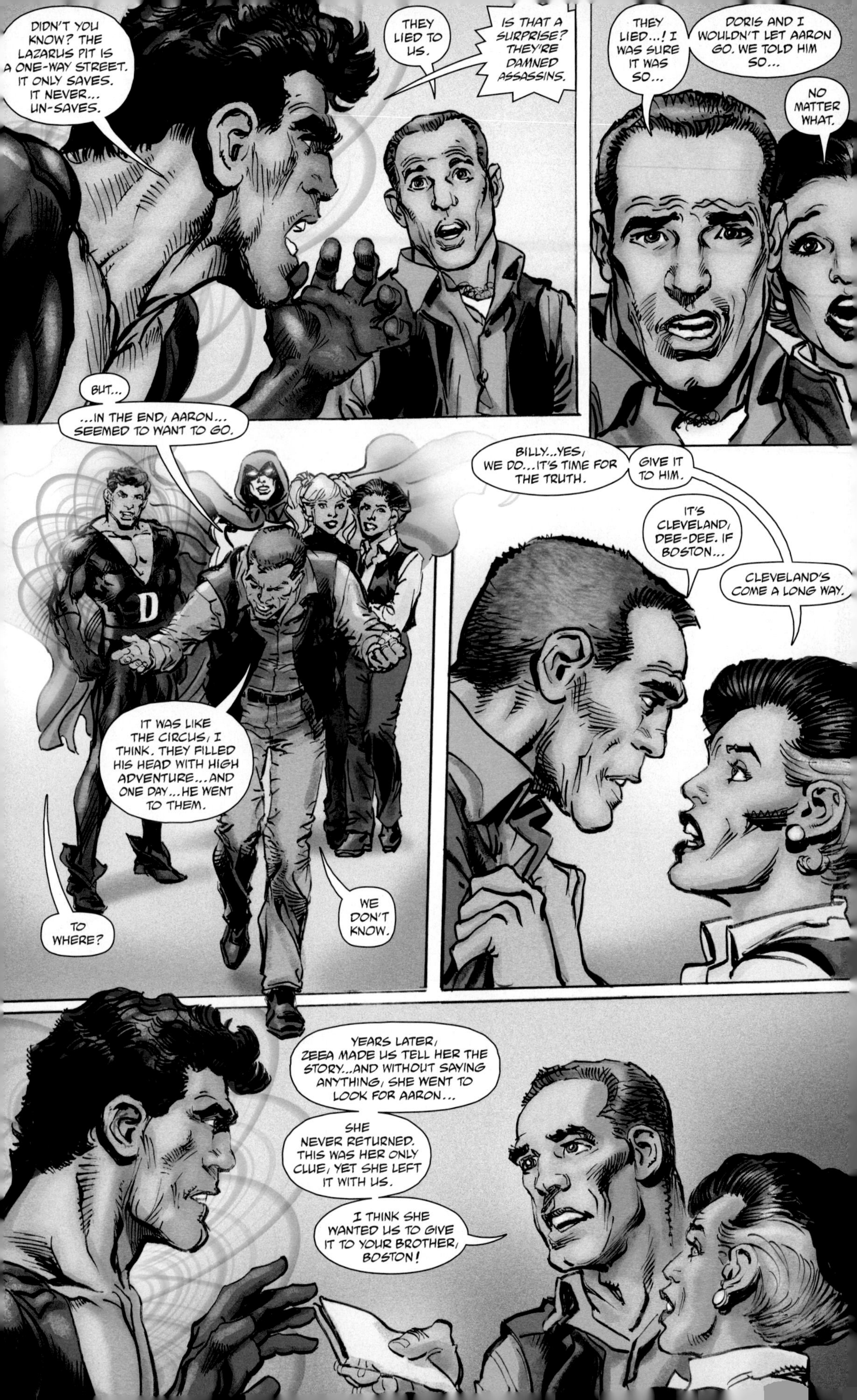

DIDN'T YOU KNOW? THE LAZARUS PIT IS A ONE-WAY STREET. IT ONLY SAVES. IT NEVER... UN-SAVES.
THEY LIED TO US.
IS THAT A SURPRISE? THEY'RE DAMNED ASSASSINS.
THEY LIED...! I WAS SURE IT WAS SO...
DORIS AND I WOULDN'T LET AARON GO. WE TOLD HIM SO...
NO MATTER WHAT.
BUT...
...IN THE END, AARON... SEEMED TO WANT TO GO.
IT WAS LIKE THE CIRCUS, I THINK. THEY FILLED HIS HEAD WITH HIGH ADVENTURE...AND ONE DAY...HE WENT TO THEM.
TO WHERE?
WE DON'T KNOW.
BILLY...YES, WE DO...IT'S TIME FOR THE TRUTH.
GIVE IT TO HIM.
IT'S CLEVELAND, DEE-DEE. IF BOSTON...
CLEVELAND'S COME A LONG WAY.
YEARS LATER, ZEEA MADE US TELL HER THE STORY...AND WITHOUT SAYING ANYTHING, SHE WENT TO LOOK FOR AARON...
SHE NEVER RETURNED. THIS WAS HER ONLY CLUE, YET SHE LEFT IT WITH US.
I THINK SHE WANTED US TO GIVE IT TO YOUR BROTHER, BOSTON!

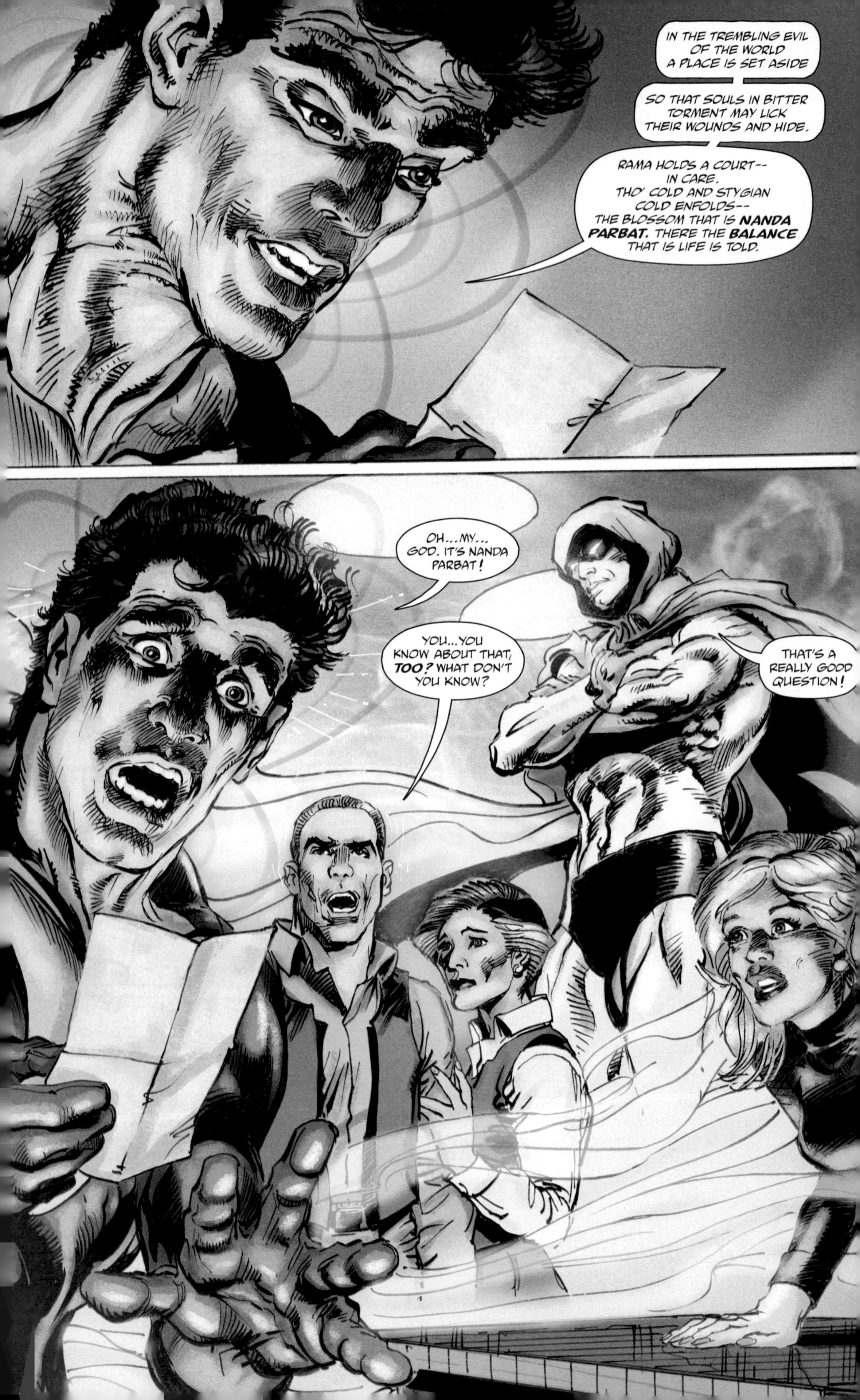
IN THE TREMBLING EVIL OF THE WORLD A PLACE IS SET ASIDE
SO THAT SOULS IN BITTER TORMENT MAY LICK THEIR WOUNDS AND HIDE.
RAMA HOLDS A COURT-- IN CARE. THO' COLD AND STYGIAN COLD ENFOLDS-- THE BLOSSOM THAT IS **NANDA PARBAT.** THERE THE **BALANCE** THAT IS LIFE IS TOLD.
OH...MY... GOD. IT'S NANDA PARBAT!
YOU...YOU KNOW ABOUT THAT, ***TOO?*** WHAT DON'T YOU KNOW?
THAT'S A REALLY GOOD QUESTION!

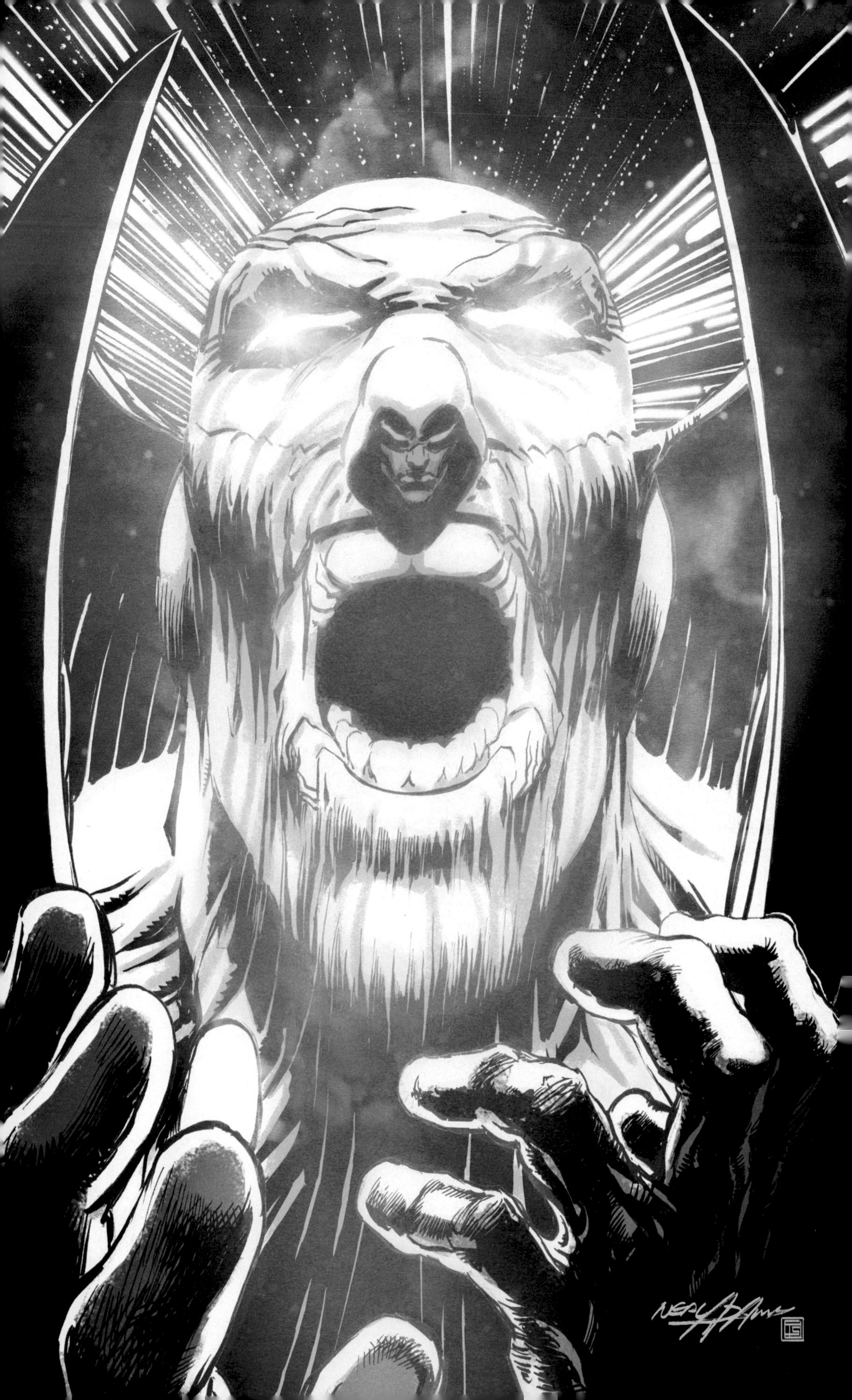

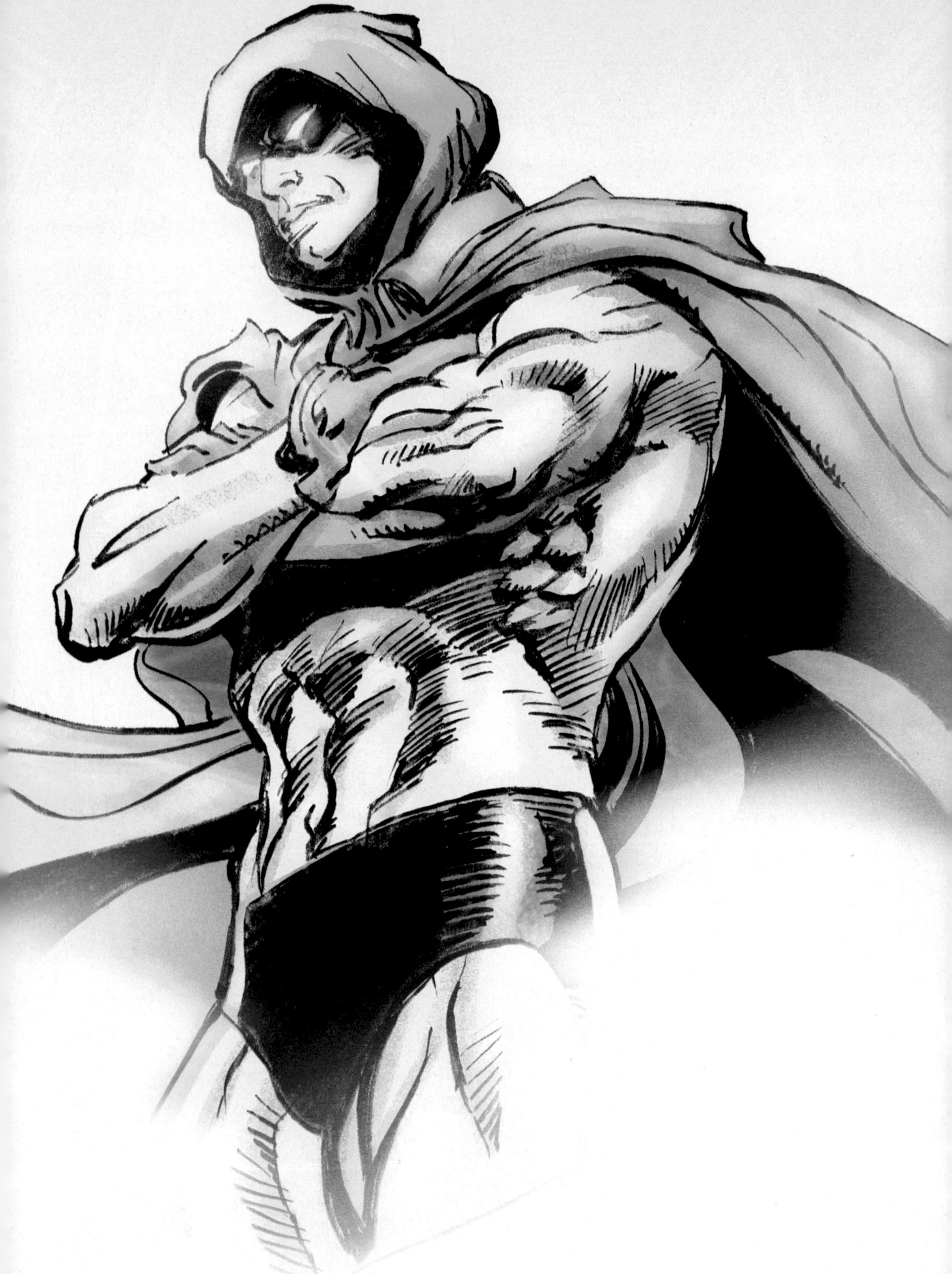

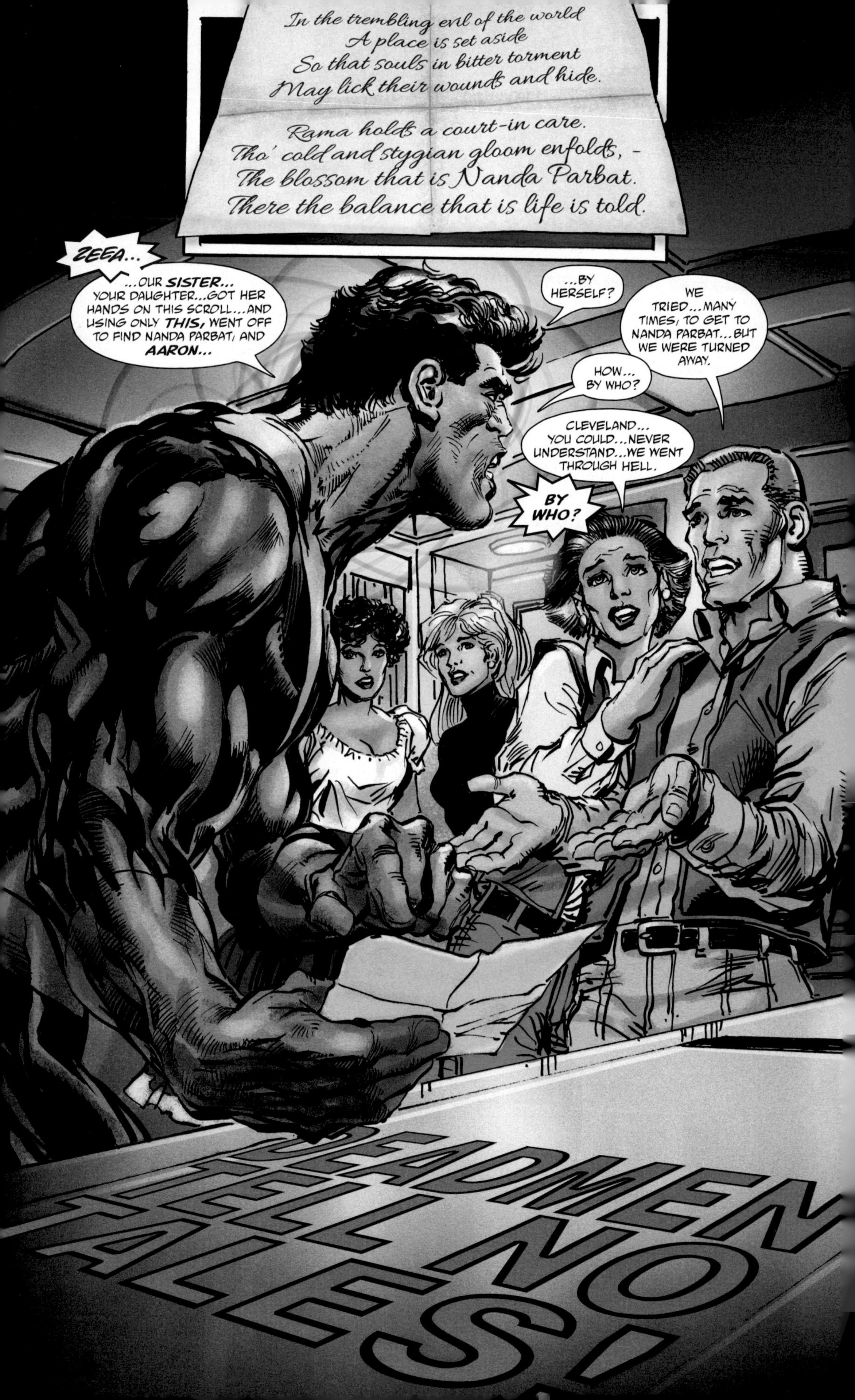
In the trembling evil of the world
A place is set aside
So that souls in bitter torment
May lick their wounds and hide.
Rama holds a court-in care.
Tho' cold and stygian gloom enfolds, -
The blossom that is Nanda Parbat.
There the balance that is life is told.
ZEEA...
...OUR SISTER... YOUR DAUGHTER...GOT HER HANDS ON THIS SCROLL...AND USING ONLY THIS, WENT OFF TO FIND NANDA PARBAT, AND AARON...
...BY HERSELF?
WE TRIED...MANY TIMES, TO GET TO NANDA PARBAT...BUT WE WERE TURNED AWAY.
HOW... BY WHO?
CLEVELAND... YOU COULD...NEVER UNDERSTAND...WE WENT THROUGH HELL.
BY WHO?
DEADMEN TELL NO TALES!

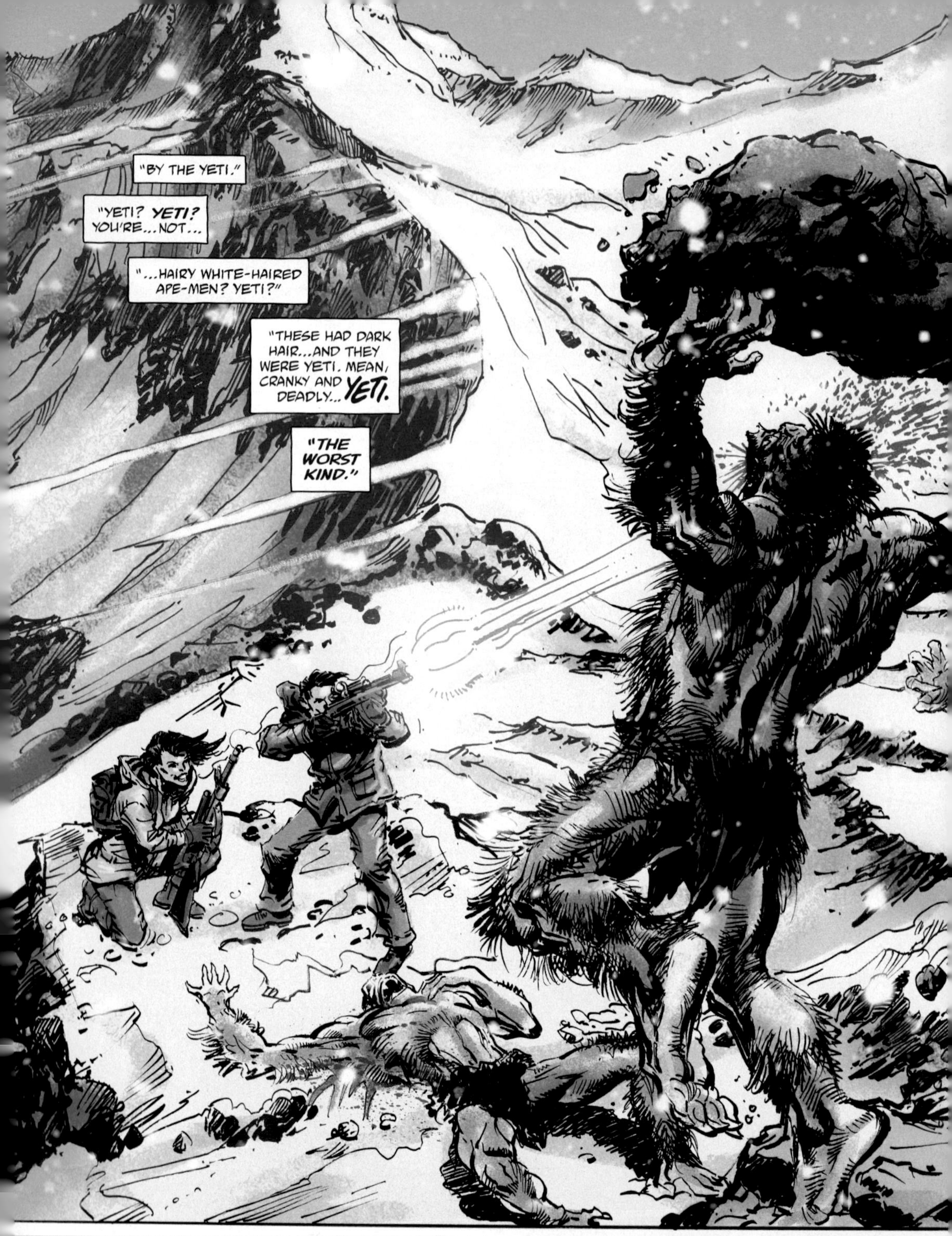
"BY THE YETI."
"YETI? YETI? YOU'RE...NOT...
"...HAIRY WHITE-HAIRED APE-MEN? YETI?"
"THESE HAD DARK HAIR...AND THEY WERE YETI. MEAN, CRANKY AND DEADLY...YETI.
"THE WORST KIND."

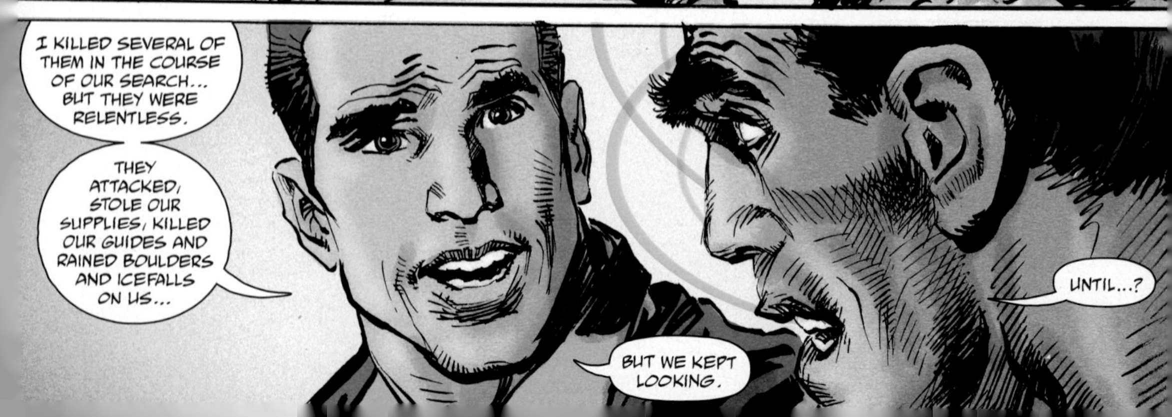
I KILLED SEVERAL OF THEM IN THE COURSE OF OUR SEARCH... BUT THEY WERE RELENTLESS.
THEY ATTACKED, STOLE OUR SUPPLIES, KILLED OUR GUIDES AND RAINED BOULDERS AND ICEFALLS ON US...
BUT WE KEPT LOOKING.
UNTIL...?

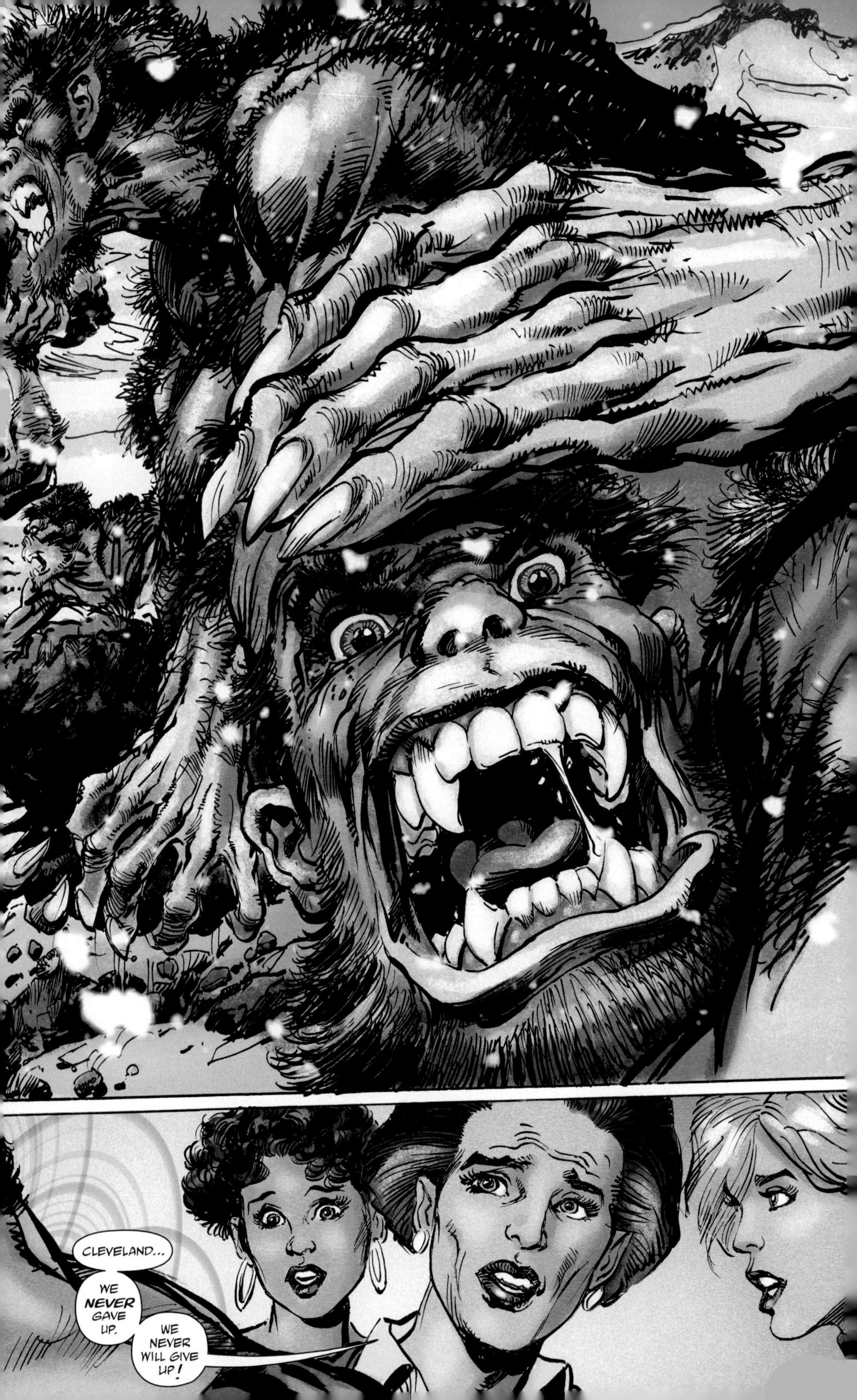
CLEVELAND...
WE NEVER GAVE UP.
WE NEVER WILL GIVE UP!

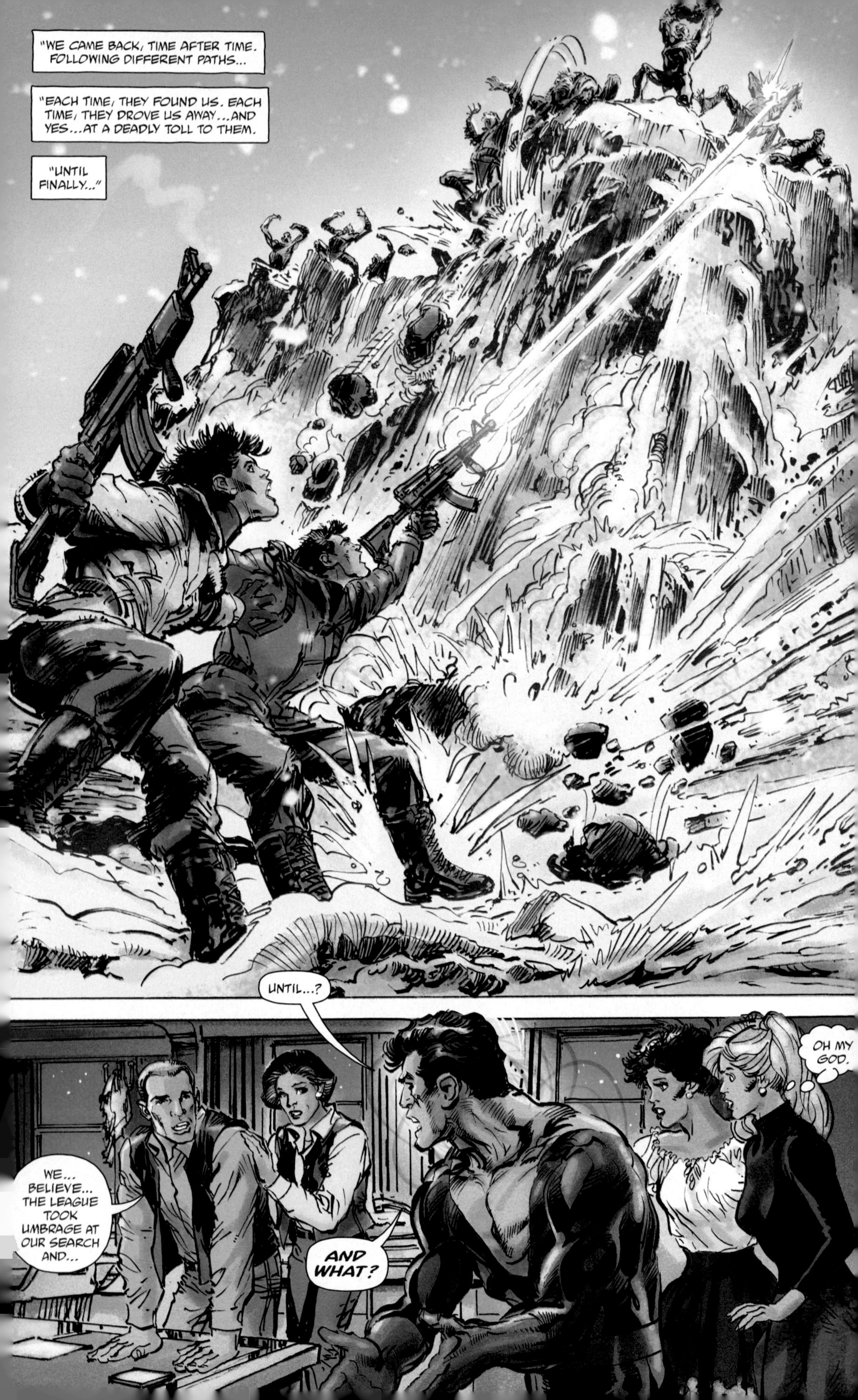
"WE CAME BACK, TIME AFTER TIME. FOLLOWING DIFFERENT PATHS...
"EACH TIME, THEY FOUND US. EACH TIME, THEY DROVE US AWAY...AND YES...AT A DEADLY TOLL TO THEM.
"UNTIL FINALLY..."
UNTIL...?
OH MY GOD.
WE... BELIEVE... THE LEAGUE TOOK UMBRAGE AT OUR SEARCH AND...
AND WHAT?

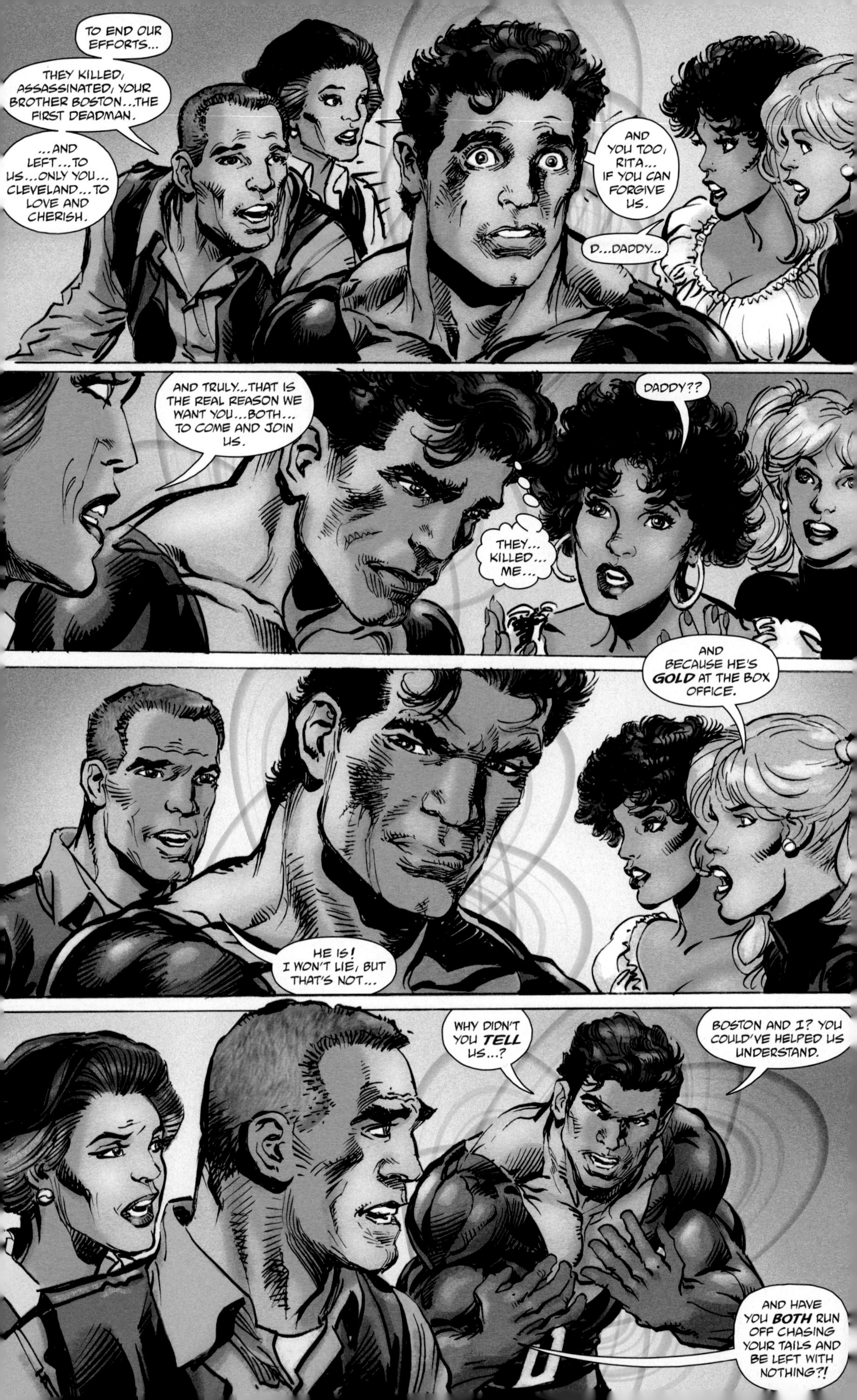
TO END OUR EFFORTS...
THEY KILLED, ASSASSINATED, YOUR BROTHER BOSTON...THE FIRST DEADMAN.
...AND LEFT...TO US...ONLY YOU... CLEVELAND...TO LOVE AND CHERISH.
AND YOU TOO, RITA... IF YOU CAN FORGIVE US.
D...DADDY...
AND TRULY...THAT IS THE REAL REASON WE WANT YOU...BOTH... TO COME AND JOIN US.
DADDY??
THEY... KILLED... ME...
AND BECAUSE HE'S **GOLD** AT THE BOX OFFICE.
HE IS! I WON'T LIE, BUT THAT'S NOT...
WHY DIDN'T YOU **TELL** US...?
BOSTON AND I? YOU COULD'VE HELPED US UNDERSTAND.
AND HAVE YOU **BOTH** RUN OFF CHASING YOUR TAILS AND BE LEFT WITH NOTHING?!

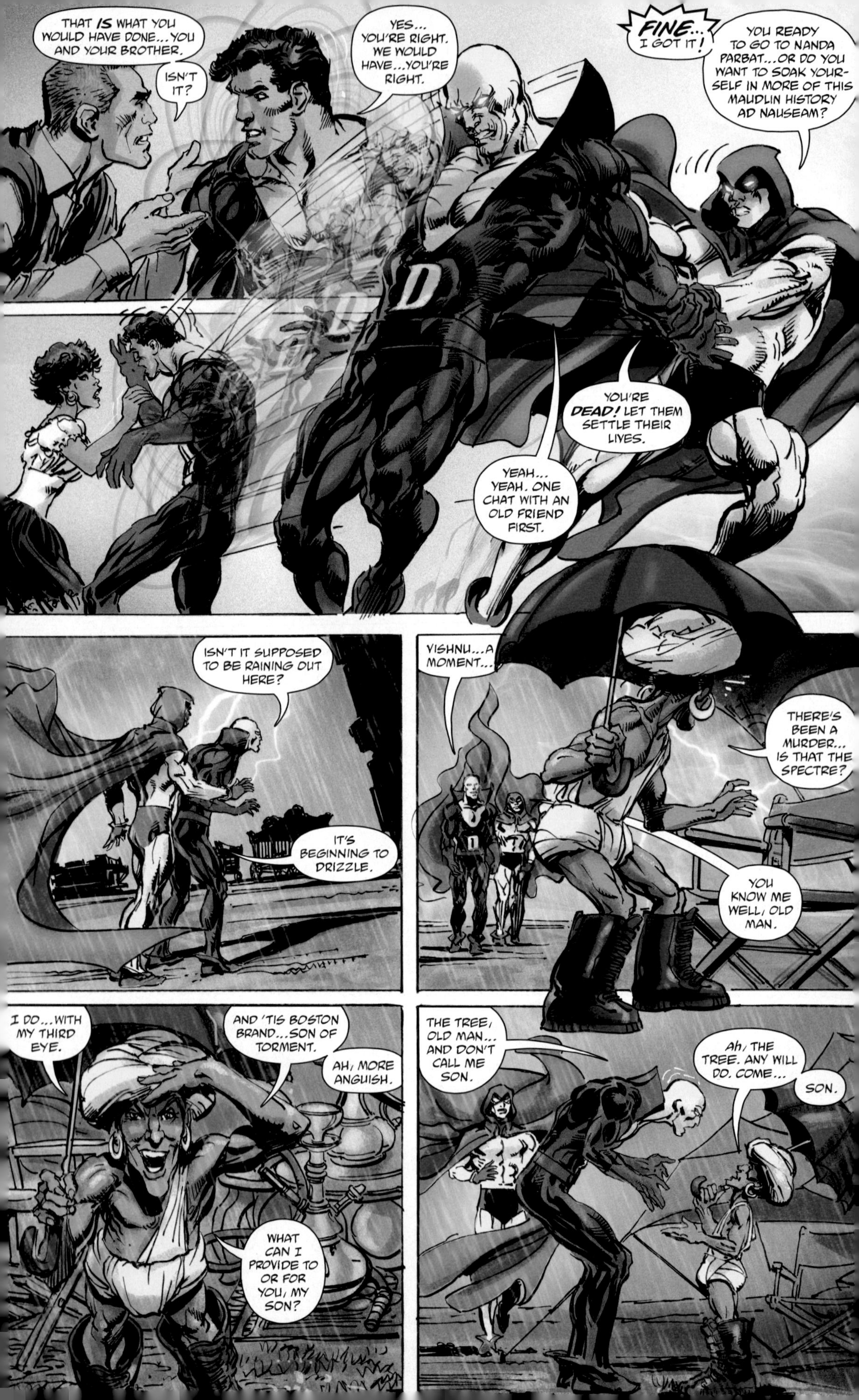
THAT IS WHAT YOU WOULD HAVE DONE...YOU AND YOUR BROTHER.
ISN'T IT?
YES... YOU'RE RIGHT. WE WOULD HAVE...YOU'RE RIGHT.
FINE... I GOT IT!
YOU READY TO GO TO NANDA PARBAT...OR DO YOU WANT TO SOAK YOURSELF IN MORE OF THIS MAUDLIN HISTORY AD NAUSEAM?
YOU'RE DEAD! LET THEM SETTLE THEIR LIVES.
YEAH... YEAH. ONE CHAT WITH AN OLD FRIEND FIRST.
ISN'T IT SUPPOSED TO BE RAINING OUT HERE?
IT'S BEGINNING TO DRIZZLE.
VISHNU...A MOMENT...
THERE'S BEEN A MURDER... IS THAT THE SPECTRE?
YOU KNOW ME WELL, OLD MAN.
I DO...WITH MY THIRD EYE.
AND 'TIS BOSTON BRAND...SON OF TORMENT.
AH, MORE ANGUISH.
WHAT CAN I PROVIDE TO OR FOR YOU, MY SON?
THE TREE, OLD MAN... AND DON'T CALL ME SON.
AH, THE TREE. ANY WILL DO. COME...
SON.

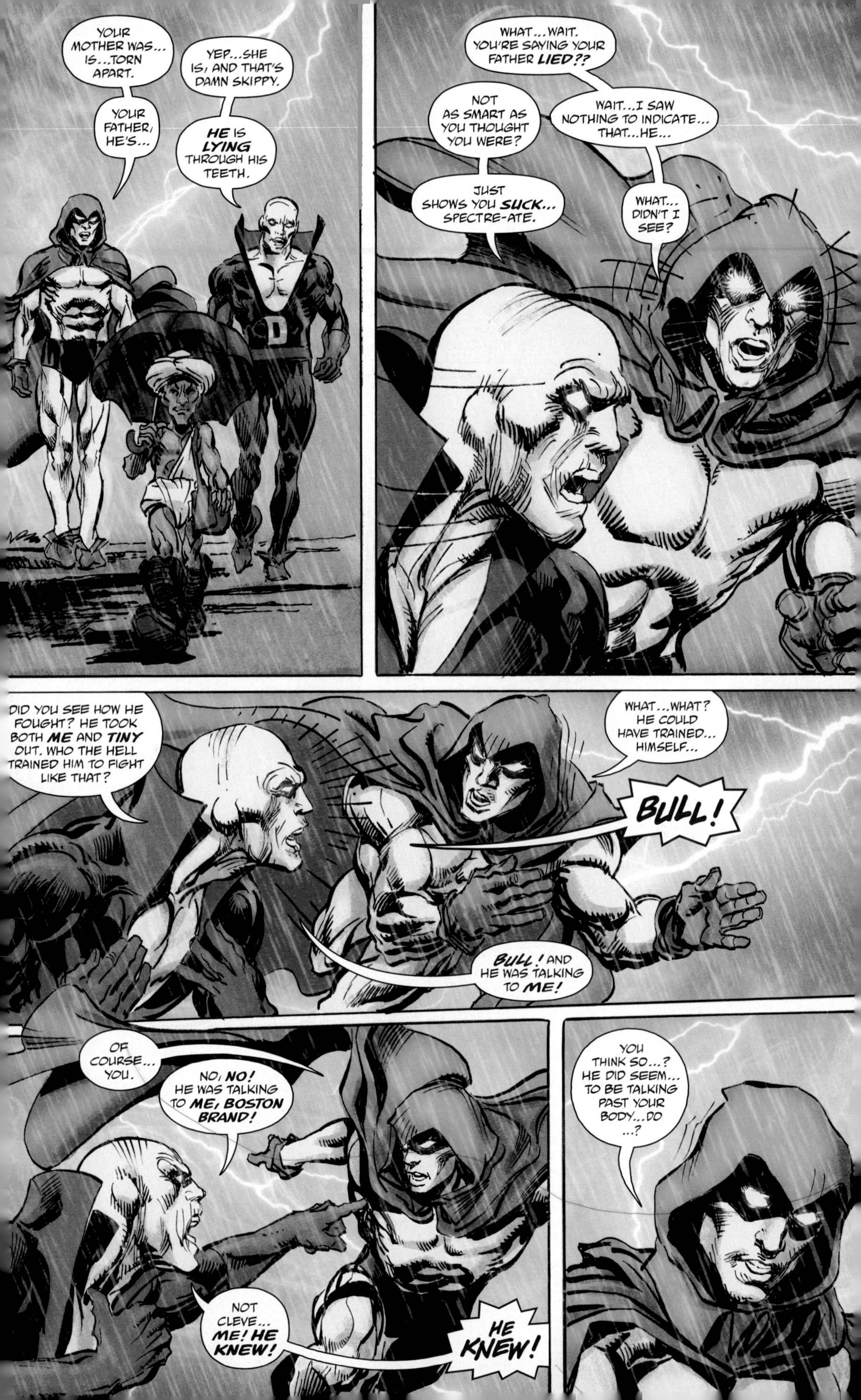
YOUR MOTHER WAS... IS...TORN APART.
YEP...SHE IS, AND THAT'S DAMN SKIPPY.
YOUR FATHER, HE'S...
HE IS LYING THROUGH HIS TEETH.
WHAT...WAIT. YOU'RE SAYING YOUR FATHER LIED??
NOT AS SMART AS YOU THOUGHT YOU WERE?
WAIT...I SAW NOTHING TO INDICATE... THAT...HE...
JUST SHOWS YOU SUCK... SPECTRE-ATE.
WHAT... DIDN'T I SEE?
DID YOU SEE HOW HE FOUGHT? HE TOOK BOTH ME AND TINY OUT. WHO THE HELL TRAINED HIM TO FIGHT LIKE THAT?
WHAT...WHAT? HE COULD HAVE TRAINED... HIMSELF...
BULL!
BULL! AND HE WAS TALKING TO ME!
OF COURSE... YOU.
NO, NO! HE WAS TALKING TO ME, BOSTON BRAND!
NOT CLEVE... ME! HE KNEW!
HE KNEW!
YOU THINK SO...? HE DID SEEM... TO BE TALKING PAST YOUR BODY...DO ...?

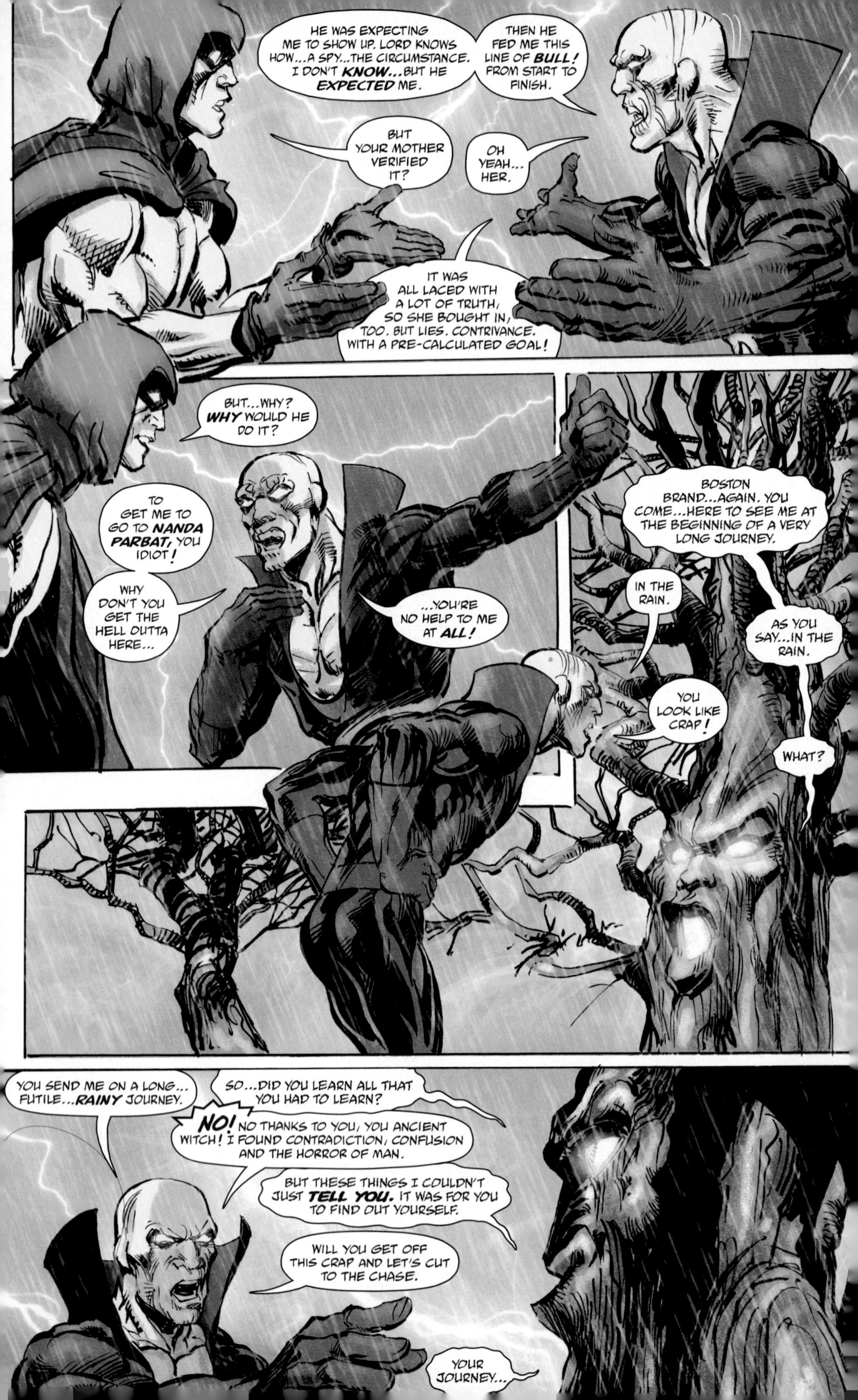
HE WAS EXPECTING ME TO SHOW UP. LORD KNOWS HOW...A SPY...THE CIRCUMSTANCE. I DON'T KNOW...BUT HE EXPECTED ME.
THEN HE FED ME THIS LINE OF BULL! FROM START TO FINISH.
BUT YOUR MOTHER VERIFIED IT?
OH YEAH... HER.
IT WAS ALL LACED WITH A LOT OF TRUTH, SO SHE BOUGHT IN, TOO. BUT LIES. CONTRIVANCE. WITH A PRE-CALCULATED GOAL!
BUT...WHY? WHY WOULD HE DO IT?
TO GET ME TO GO TO NANDA PARBAT, YOU IDIOT!
WHY DON'T YOU GET THE HELL OUTTA HERE...
...YOU'RE NO HELP TO ME AT ALL!
BOSTON BRAND...AGAIN. YOU COME...HERE TO SEE ME AT THE BEGINNING OF A VERY LONG JOURNEY.
IN THE RAIN.
AS YOU SAY...IN THE RAIN.
YOU LOOK LIKE CRAP!
WHAT?
YOU SEND ME ON A LONG... FUTILE...RAINY JOURNEY.
SO...DID YOU LEARN ALL THAT YOU HAD TO LEARN?
NO! NO THANKS TO YOU, YOU ANCIENT WITCH! I FOUND CONTRADICTION, CONFUSION AND THE HORROR OF MAN.
BUT THESE THINGS I COULDN'T JUST TELL YOU. IT WAS FOR YOU TO FIND OUT YOURSELF.
WILL YOU GET OFF THIS CRAP AND LET'S CUT TO THE CHASE.
YOUR JOURNEY...

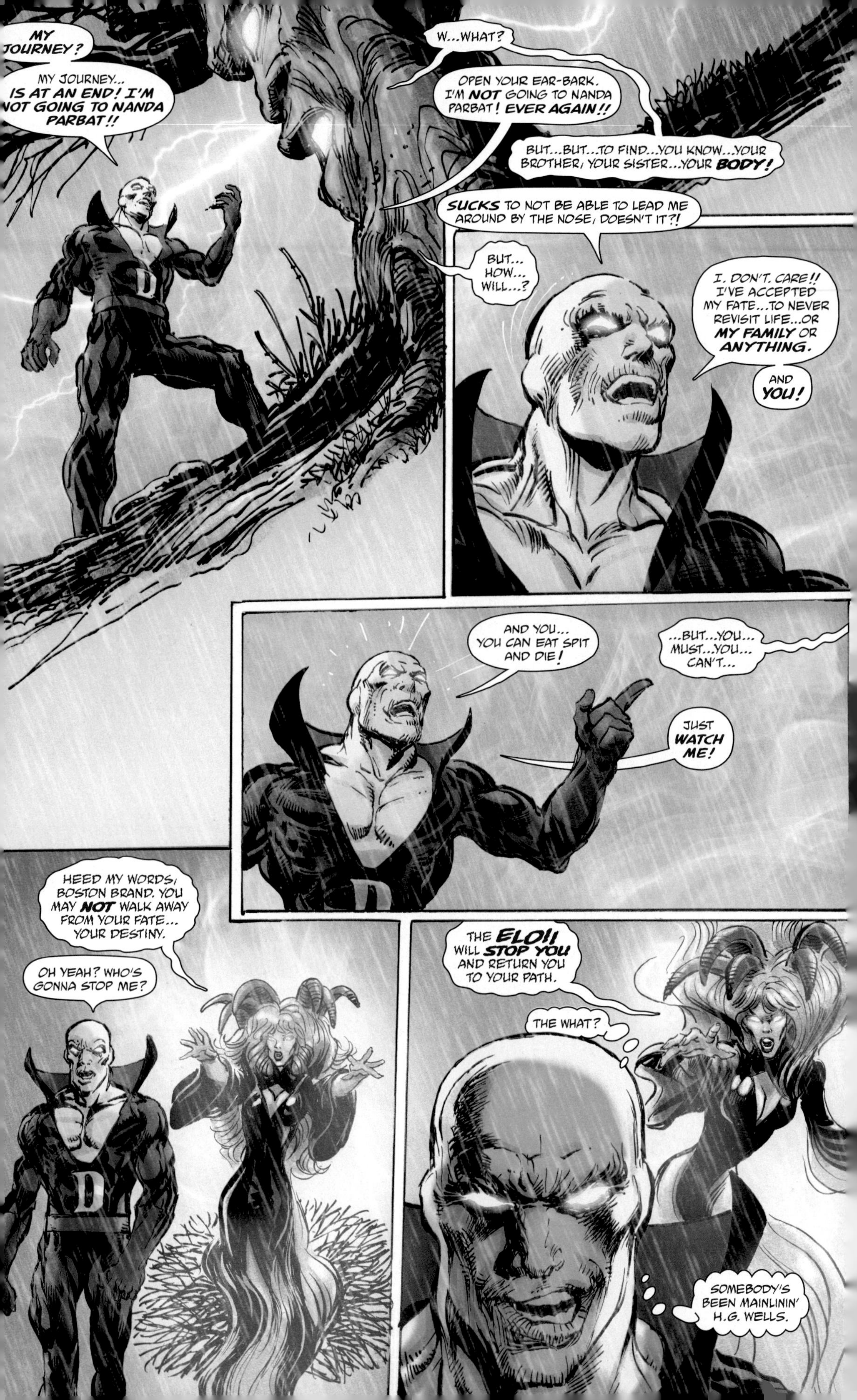

MY JOURNEY?
MY JOURNEY... IS AT AN END! I'M NOT GOING TO NANDA PARBAT!!
W...WHAT?
OPEN YOUR EAR-BARK. I'M NOT GOING TO NANDA PARBAT! EVER AGAIN!!
BUT...BUT...TO FIND...YOU KNOW...YOUR BROTHER, YOUR SISTER...YOUR BODY!
SUCKS TO NOT BE ABLE TO LEAD ME AROUND BY THE NOSE, DOESN'T IT?!
BUT... HOW... WILL...?
I. DON'T. CARE!! I'VE ACCEPTED MY FATE...TO NEVER REVISIT LIFE...OR MY FAMILY OR ANYTHING.
AND YOU!
AND YOU... YOU CAN EAT SPIT AND DIE!
...BUT...YOU... MUST...YOU... CAN'T...
JUST WATCH ME!
HEED MY WORDS, BOSTON BRAND. YOU MAY NOT WALK AWAY FROM YOUR FATE... YOUR DESTINY.
OH YEAH? WHO'S GONNA STOP ME?
THE ELOI! WILL STOP YOU AND RETURN YOU TO YOUR PATH.
THE WHAT?
SOMEBODY'S BEEN MAINLININ' H.G. WELLS.

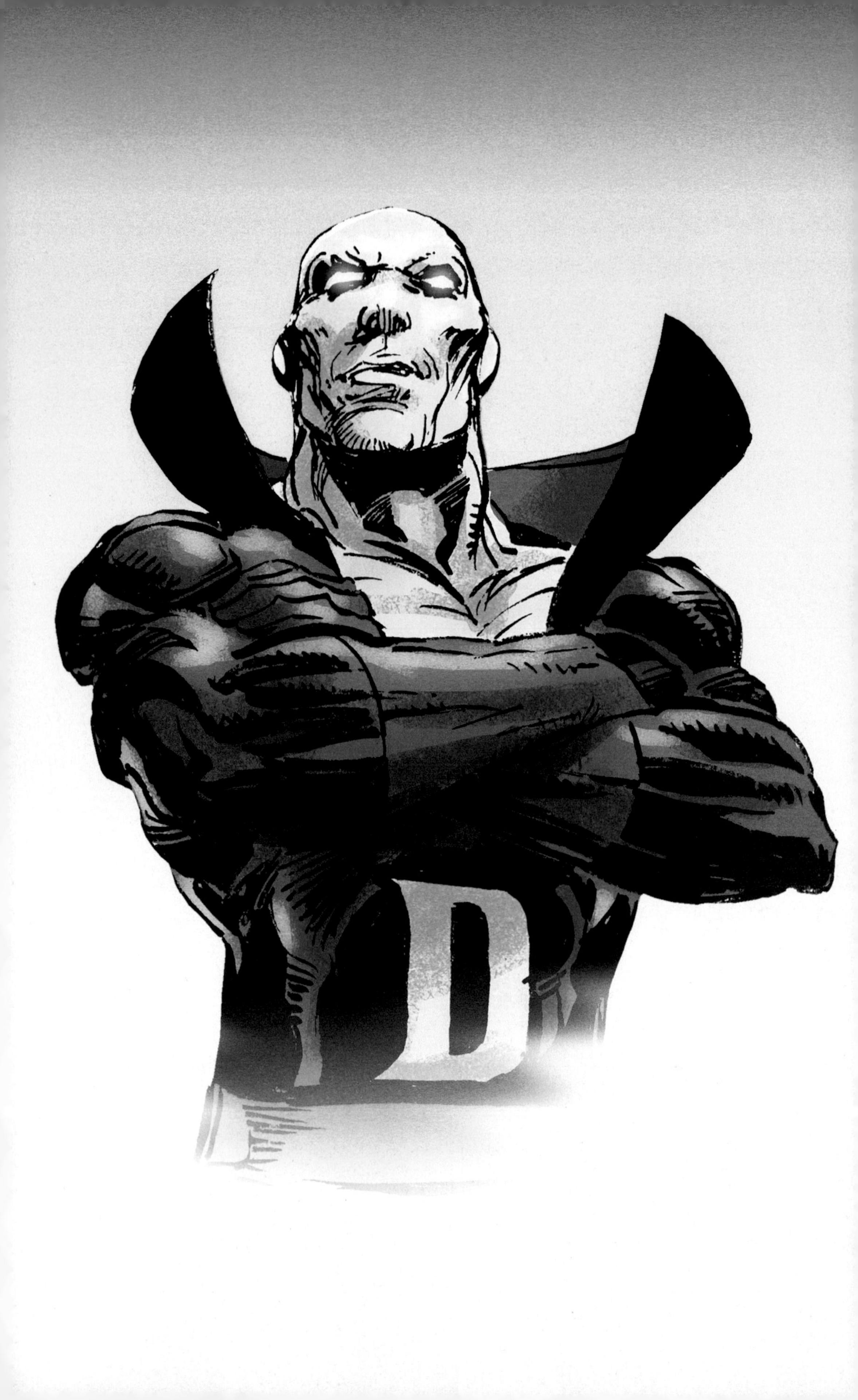

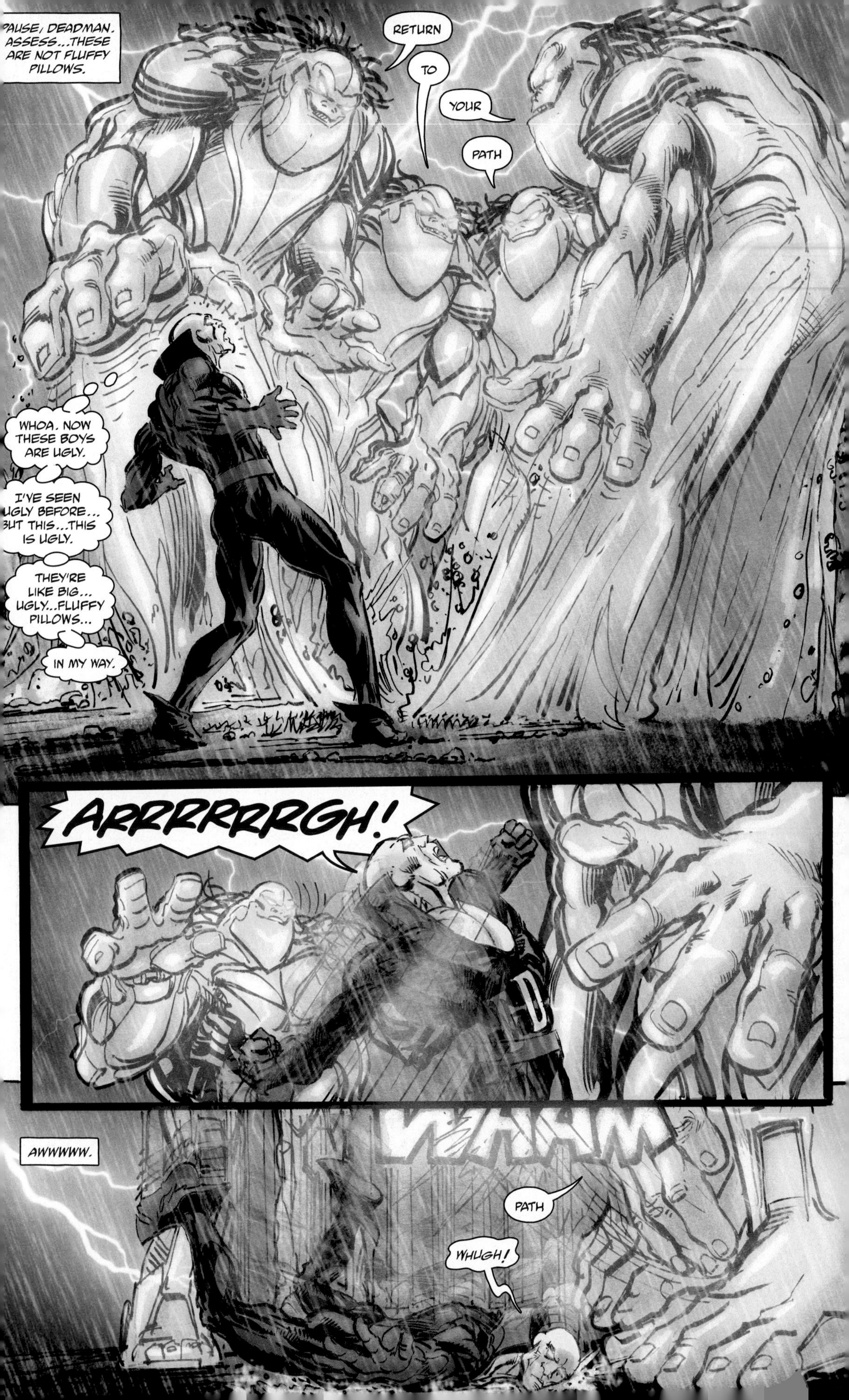
PAUSE, DEADMAN. ASSESS...THESE ARE NOT FLUFFY PILLOWS.
RETURN
TO
YOUR
PATH
WHOA. NOW THESE BOYS ARE UGLY.
I'VE SEEN UGLY BEFORE... BUT THIS...THIS IS UGLY.
THEY'RE LIKE BIG... UGLY...FLUFFY PILLOWS...
IN MY WAY.
ARRRRRRGH!
AWWWWW.
PATH
WHUGH!

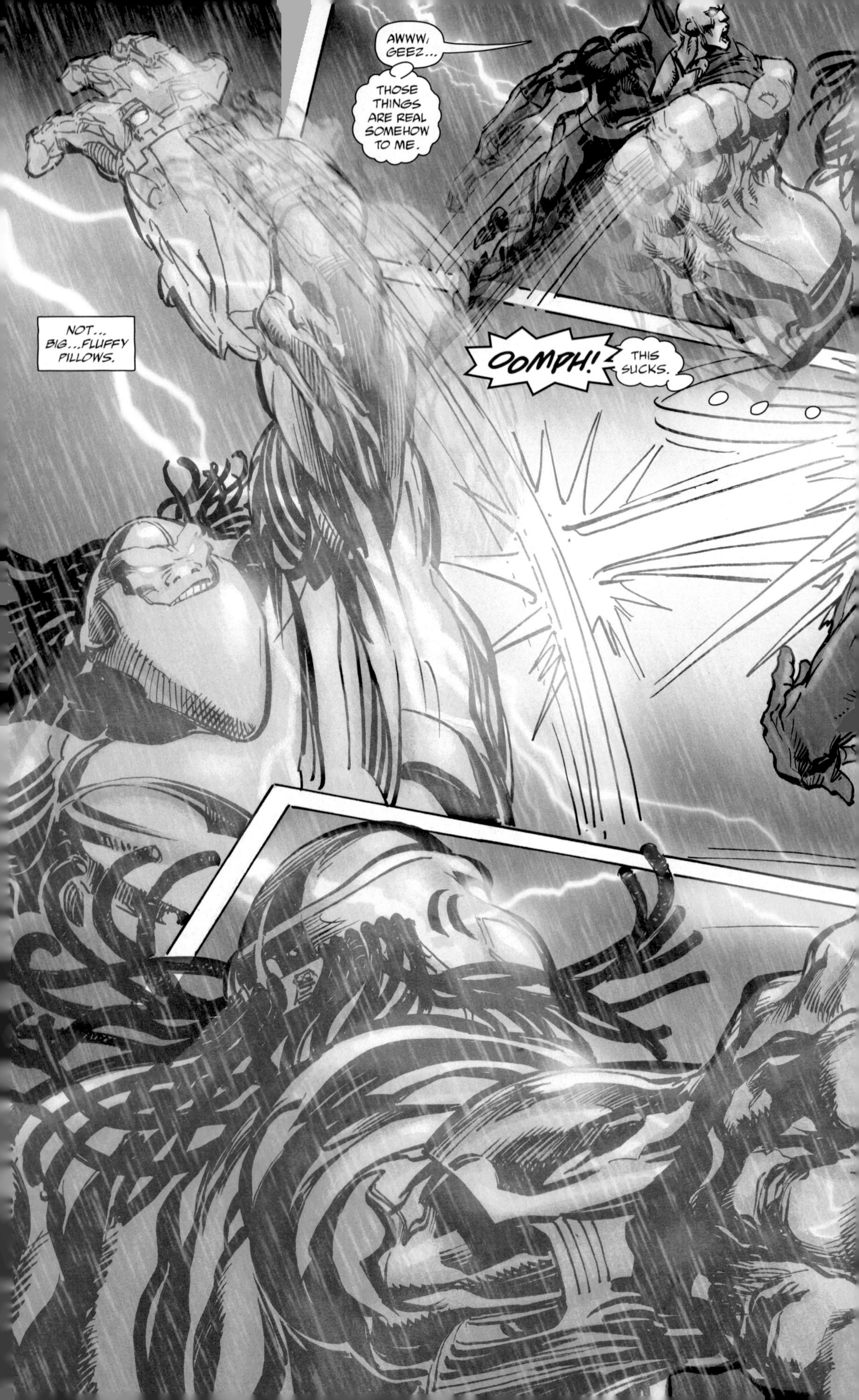
AWWW, GEEZ...
THOSE THINGS ARE REAL SOMEHOW TO ME.
NOT... BIG...FLUFFY PILLOWS.
OOMPH!
THIS SUCKS.

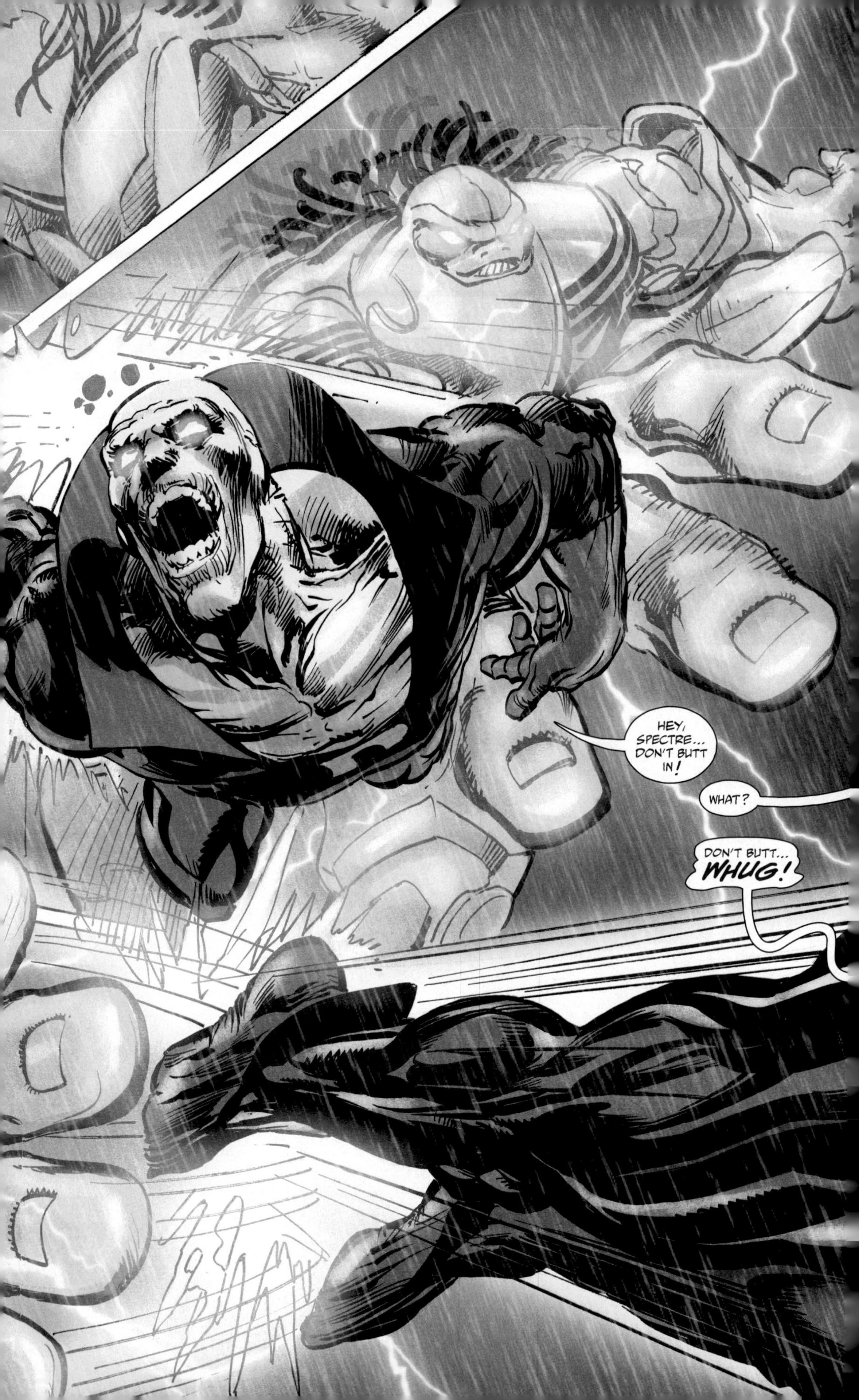
HEY, SPECTRE... DON'T BUTT IN!
WHAT?
DON'T BUTT... WHUG!

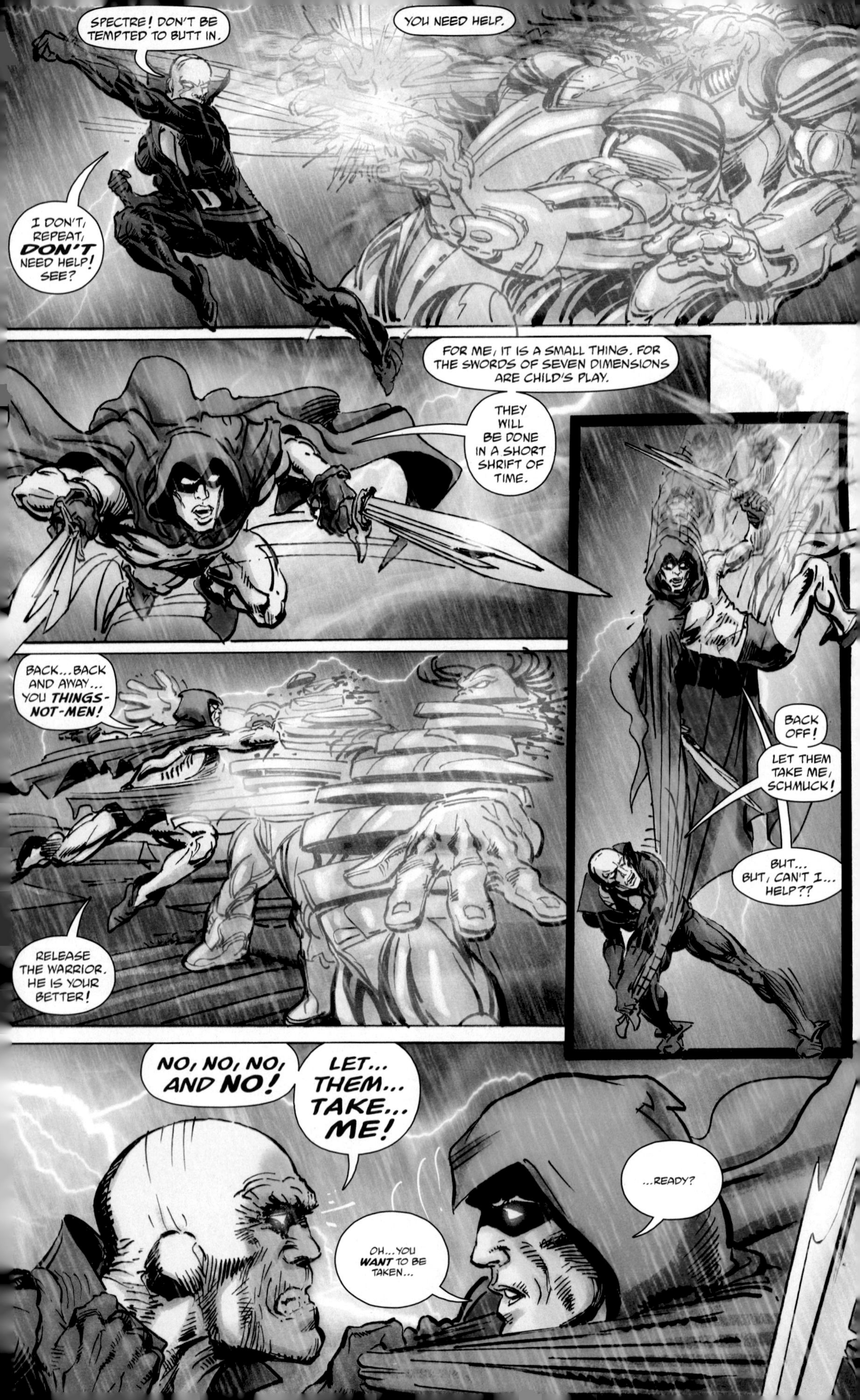
SPECTRE! DON'T BE TEMPTED TO BUTT IN.
YOU NEED HELP.
I DON'T, REPEAT, DON'T NEED HELP! SEE?
FOR ME, IT IS A SMALL THING. FOR THE SWORDS OF SEVEN DIMENSIONS ARE CHILD'S PLAY.
THEY WILL BE DONE IN A SHORT SHRIFT OF TIME.
BACK... BACK AND AWAY... YOU THINGS-NOT-MEN!
RELEASE THE WARRIOR. HE IS YOUR BETTER!
BACK OFF!
LET THEM TAKE ME, SCHMUCK!
BUT... BUT, CAN'T I... HELP??
NO, NO, NO, AND NO!
LET... THEM... TAKE... ME!
OH... YOU WANT TO BE TAKEN...
...READY?

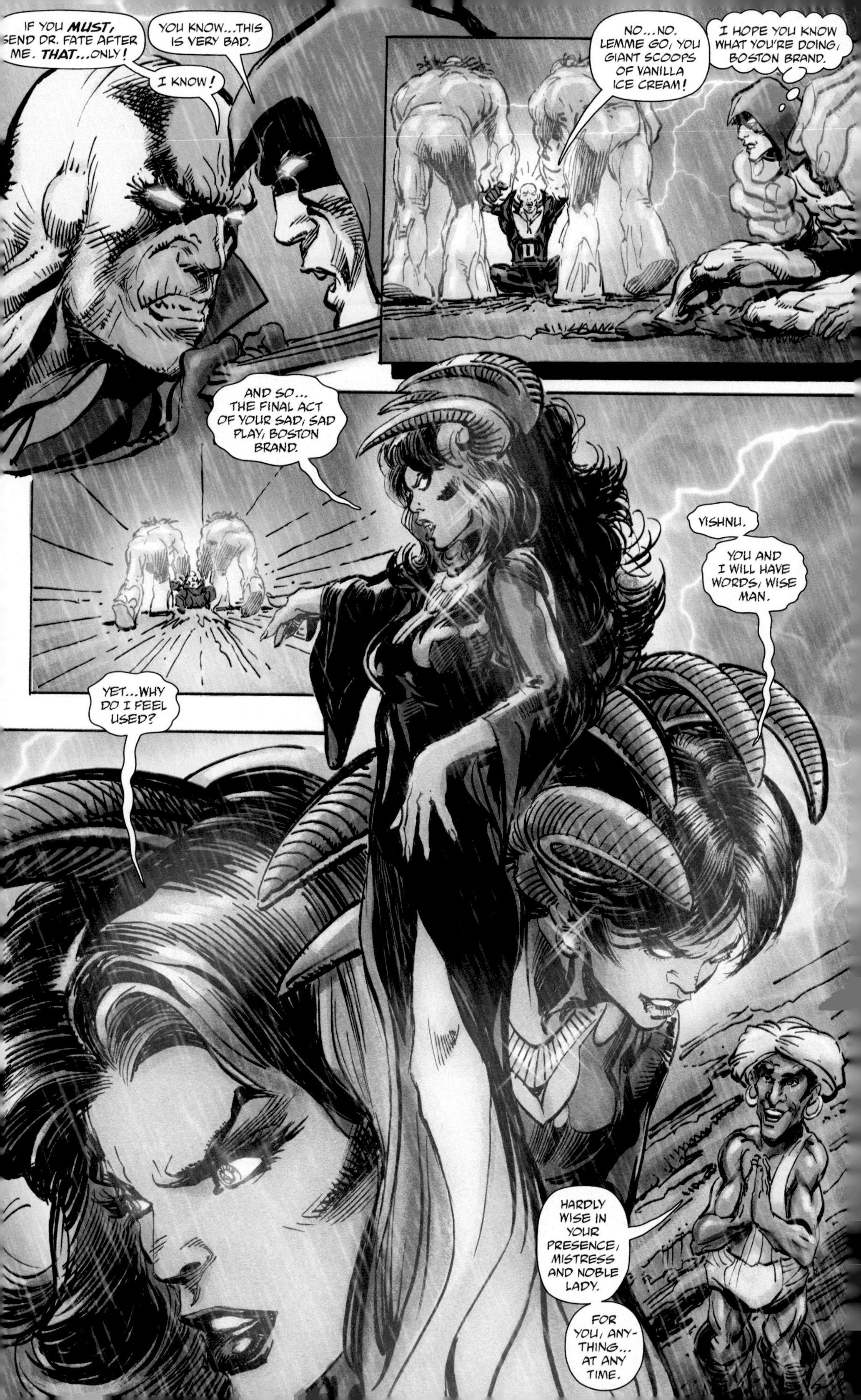
IF YOU MUST, SEND DR. FATE AFTER ME. THAT...ONLY!
YOU KNOW...THIS IS VERY BAD.
I KNOW!
NO...NO. LEMME GO, YOU GIANT SCOOPS OF VANILLA ICE CREAM!
I HOPE YOU KNOW WHAT YOU'RE DOING, BOSTON BRAND.
AND SO... THE FINAL ACT OF YOUR SAD, SAD PLAY, BOSTON BRAND.
YET...WHY DO I FEEL USED?
VISHNU.
YOU AND I WILL HAVE WORDS, WISE MAN.
HARDLY WISE IN YOUR PRESENCE, MISTRESS AND NOBLE LADY.
FOR YOU, ANY-THING... AT ANY TIME.

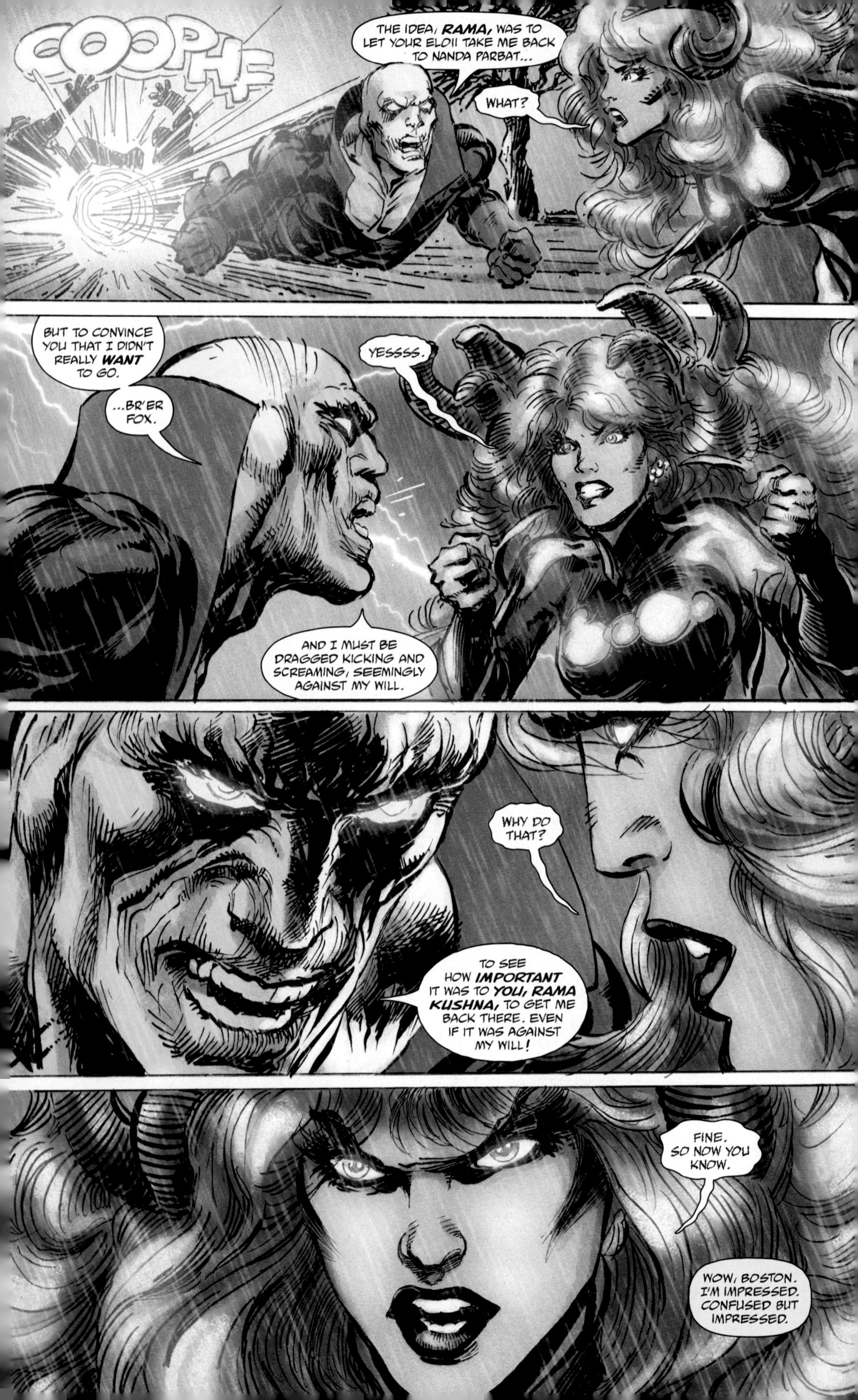
GOOPH
THE IDEA, RAMA, WAS TO LET YOUR ELOII TAKE ME BACK TO NANDA PARBAT...
WHAT?
BUT TO CONVINCE YOU THAT I DIDN'T REALLY WANT TO GO.
...BR'ER FOX.
YESSSS.
AND I MUST BE DRAGGED KICKING AND SCREAMING, SEEMINGLY AGAINST MY WILL.
WHY DO THAT?
TO SEE HOW IMPORTANT IT WAS TO YOU, RAMA KUSHNA, TO GET ME BACK THERE. EVEN IF IT WAS AGAINST MY WILL!
FINE. SO NOW YOU KNOW.
WOW, BOSTON. I'M IMPRESSED. CONFUSED BUT IMPRESSED.

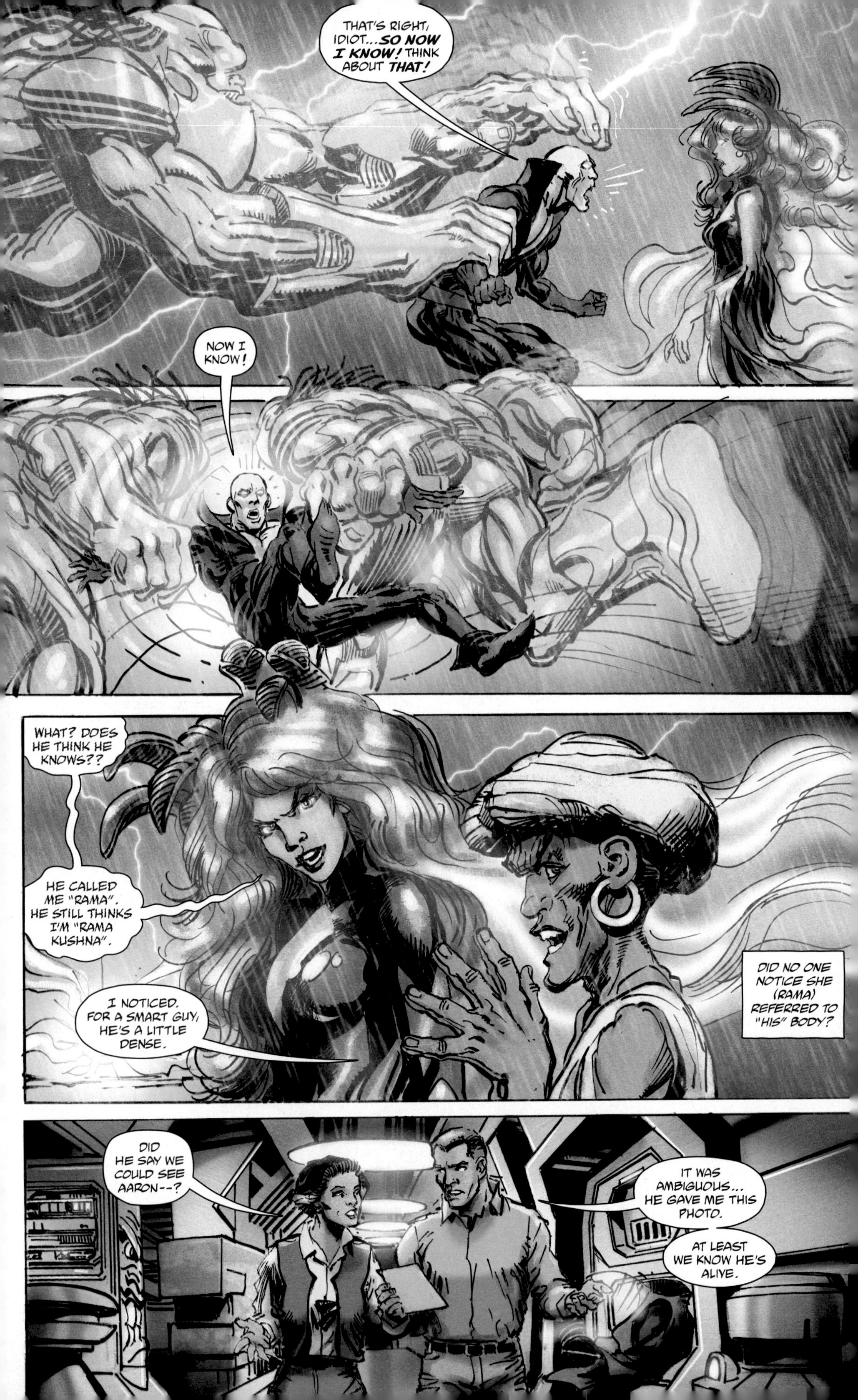
THAT'S RIGHT, IDIOT... SO NOW I KNOW! THINK ABOUT THAT!
NOW I KNOW!
WHAT? DOES HE THINK HE KNOWS??
HE CALLED ME "RAMA". HE STILL THINKS I'M "RAMA KUSHNA".
I NOTICED. FOR A SMART GUY, HE'S A LITTLE DENSE.
DID NO ONE NOTICE SHE (RAMA) REFERRED TO "HIS" BODY?
DID HE SAY WE COULD SEE AARON--?
IT WAS AMBIGUOUS... HE GAVE ME THIS PHOTO.
AT LEAST WE KNOW HE'S ALIVE.

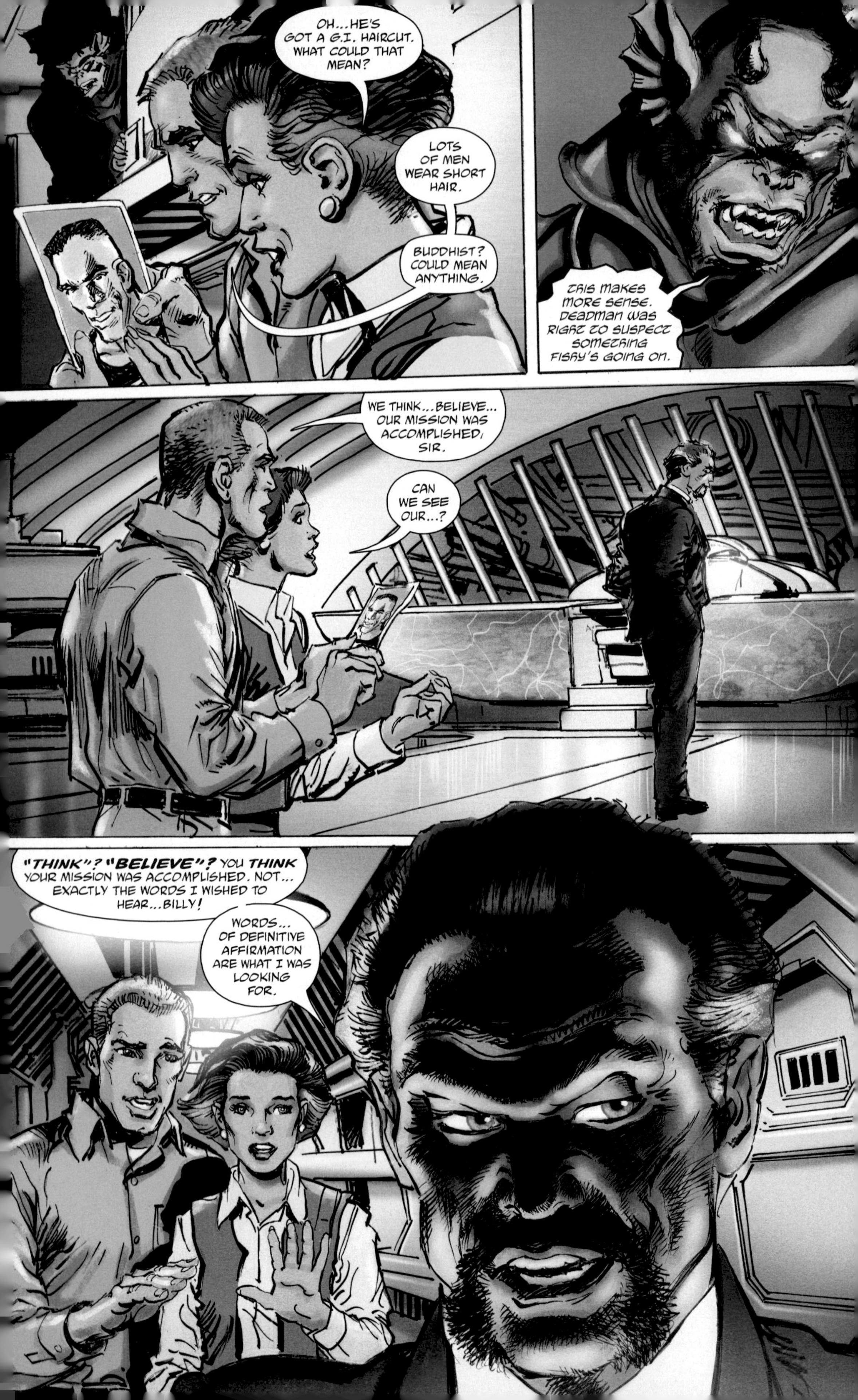
OH...HE'S GOT A G.I. HAIRCUT. WHAT COULD THAT MEAN?
LOTS OF MEN WEAR SHORT HAIR.
BUDDHIST? COULD MEAN ANYTHING.
THIS MAKES MORE SENSE. DEADMAN WAS RIGHT TO SUSPECT SOMETHING FISHY'S GOING ON.
WE THINK...BELIEVE... OUR MISSION WAS ACCOMPLISHED, SIR.
CAN WE SEE OUR...?
"THINK"? "BELIEVE"? YOU THINK YOUR MISSION WAS ACCOMPLISHED. NOT... EXACTLY THE WORDS I WISHED TO HEAR...BILLY!
WORDS... OF DEFINITIVE AFFIRMATION ARE WHAT I WAS LOOKING FOR.

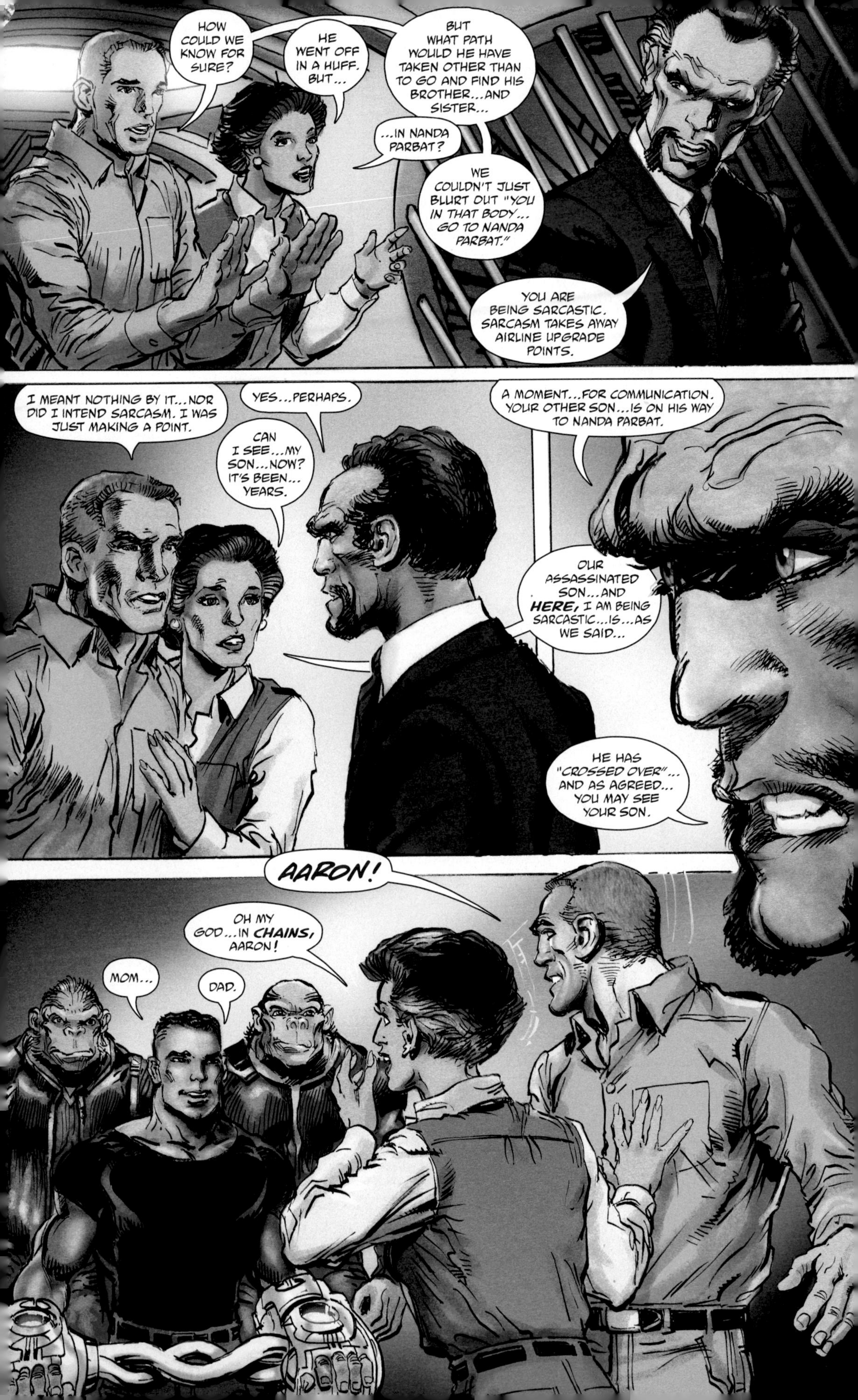
HOW COULD WE KNOW FOR SURE?
HE WENT OFF IN A HUFF. BUT...
BUT WHAT PATH WOULD HE HAVE TAKEN OTHER THAN TO GO AND FIND HIS BROTHER...AND SISTER...
...IN NANDA PARBAT?
WE COULDN'T JUST BLURT OUT "YOU IN THAT BODY... GO TO NANDA PARBAT."
YOU ARE BEING SARCASTIC. SARCASM TAKES AWAY AIRLINE UPGRADE POINTS.
I MEANT NOTHING BY IT...NOR DID I INTEND SARCASM. I WAS JUST MAKING A POINT.
YES...PERHAPS.
CAN I SEE...MY SON...NOW? IT'S BEEN... YEARS.
A MOMENT...FOR COMMUNICATION. YOUR OTHER SON...IS ON HIS WAY TO NANDA PARBAT.
OUR ASSASSINATED SON...AND HERE, I AM BEING SARCASTIC...IS...AS WE SAID...
HE HAS "CROSSED OVER"... AND AS AGREED... YOU MAY SEE YOUR SON.
AARON!
OH MY GOD...IN CHAINS, AARON!
MOM...
DAD.

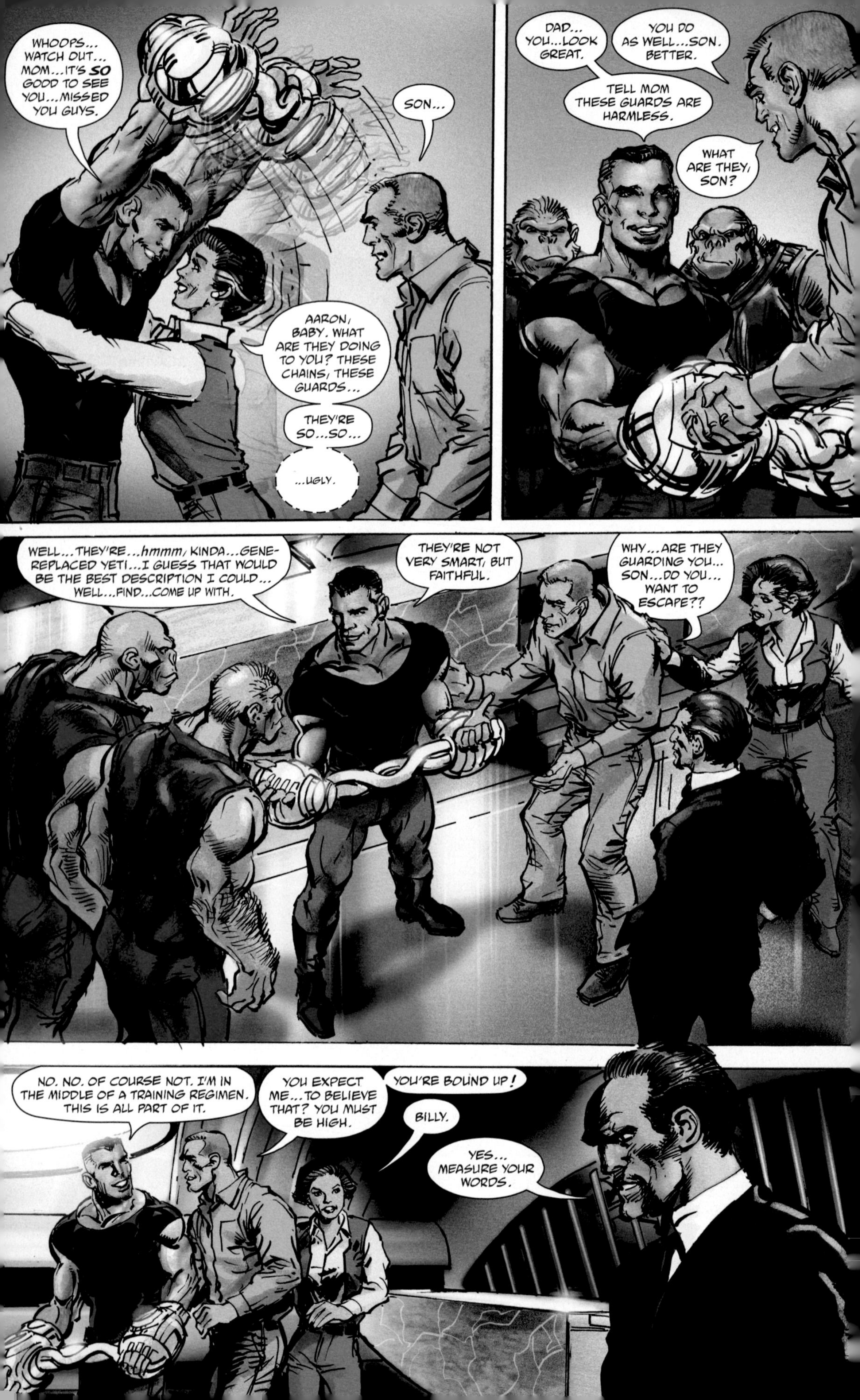
WHOOPS... WATCH OUT... MOM...IT'S SO GOOD TO SEE YOU...MISSED YOU GUYS.
SON...
AARON, BABY. WHAT ARE THEY DOING TO YOU? THESE CHAINS, THESE GUARDS...
THEY'RE SO...SO...
...UGLY.
DAD... YOU...LOOK GREAT.
YOU DO AS WELL...SON. BETTER.
TELL MOM THESE GUARDS ARE HARMLESS.
WHAT ARE THEY, SON?
WELL...THEY'RE...*hmmm*, KINDA...GENE-REPLACED YETI...I GUESS THAT WOULD BE THE BEST DESCRIPTION I COULD... WELL...FIND...COME UP WITH.
THEY'RE NOT VERY SMART, BUT FAITHFUL.
WHY...ARE THEY GUARDING YOU... SON...DO YOU... WANT TO ESCAPE??
NO. NO. OF COURSE NOT. I'M IN THE MIDDLE OF A TRAINING REGIMEN. THIS IS ALL PART OF IT.
YOU EXPECT ME...TO BELIEVE THAT? YOU MUST BE HIGH.
YOU'RE BOUND UP!
BILLY.
YES... MEASURE YOUR WORDS.

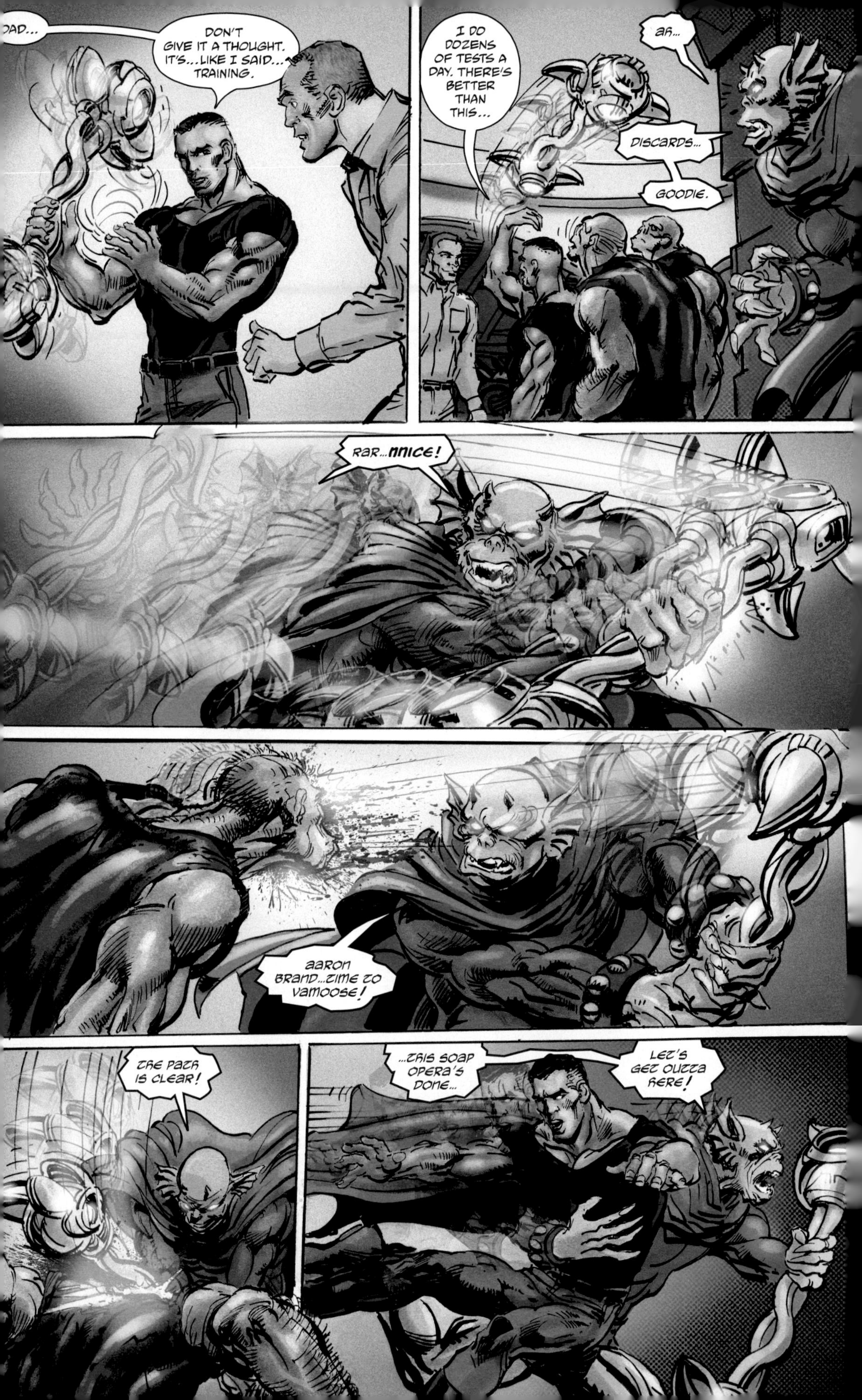
DAD...
DON'T GIVE IT A THOUGHT. IT'S...LIKE I SAID... TRAINING.
I DO DOZENS OF TESTS A DAY. THERE'S BETTER THAN THIS...
AR...
DISCARDS...
GOODIE.
RAR...NNICE!
AARON BRAND...TIME TO VAMOOSE!
THE PATH IS CLEAR!
...THIS SOAP OPERA'S DONE...
LET'S GET OUTTA HERE!

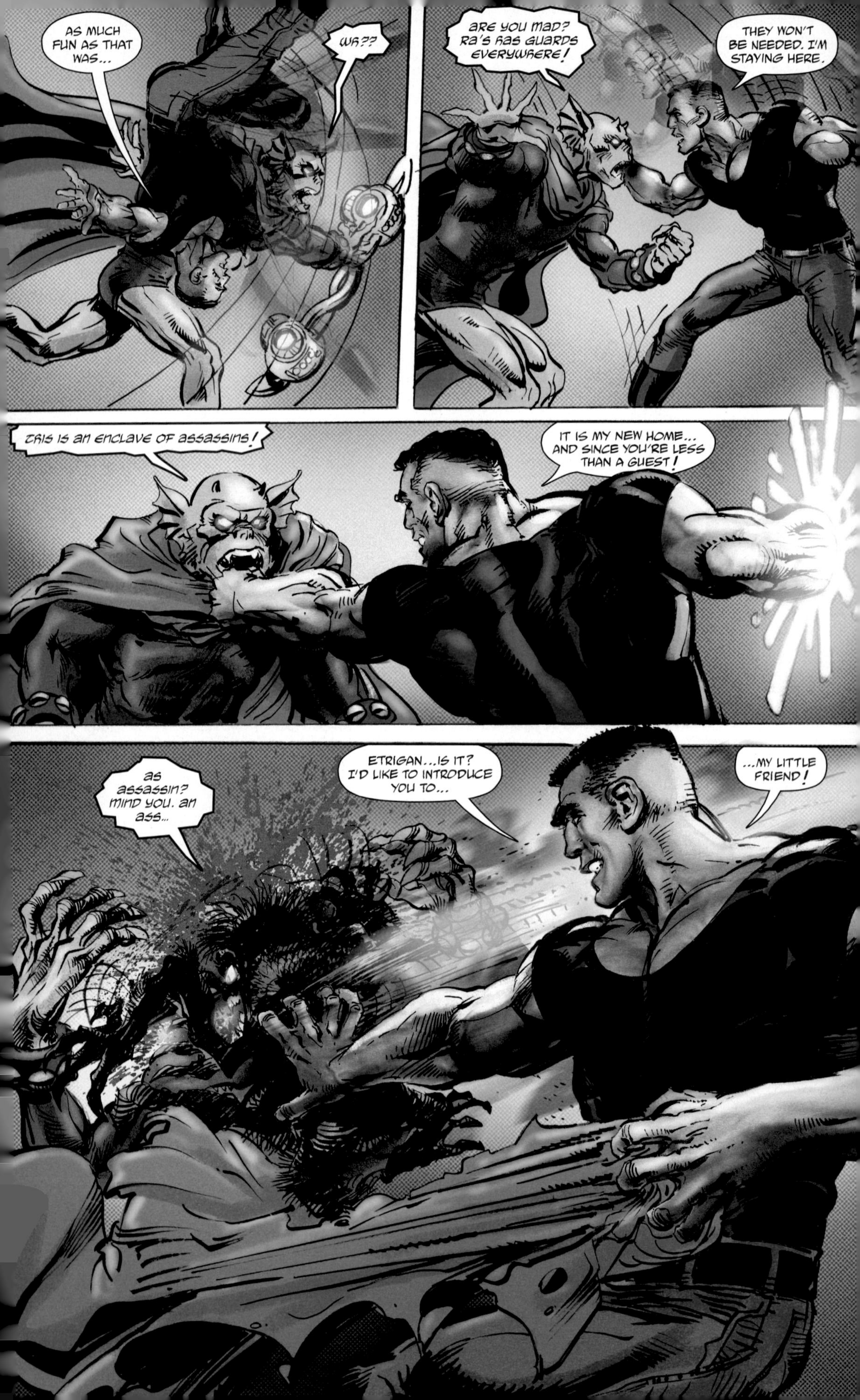
AS MUCH FUN AS THAT WAS...
WH??
ARE YOU MAD? RA'S HAS GUARDS EVERYWHERE!
THEY WON'T BE NEEDED. I'M STAYING HERE.
THIS IS AN ENCLAVE OF ASSASSINS!
IT IS MY NEW HOME... AND SINCE YOU'RE LESS THAN A GUEST!
ETRIGAN...IS IT? I'D LIKE TO INTRODUCE YOU TO...
...MY LITTLE FRIEND!
AS ASSASSIN? MIND YOU. AN ASS...

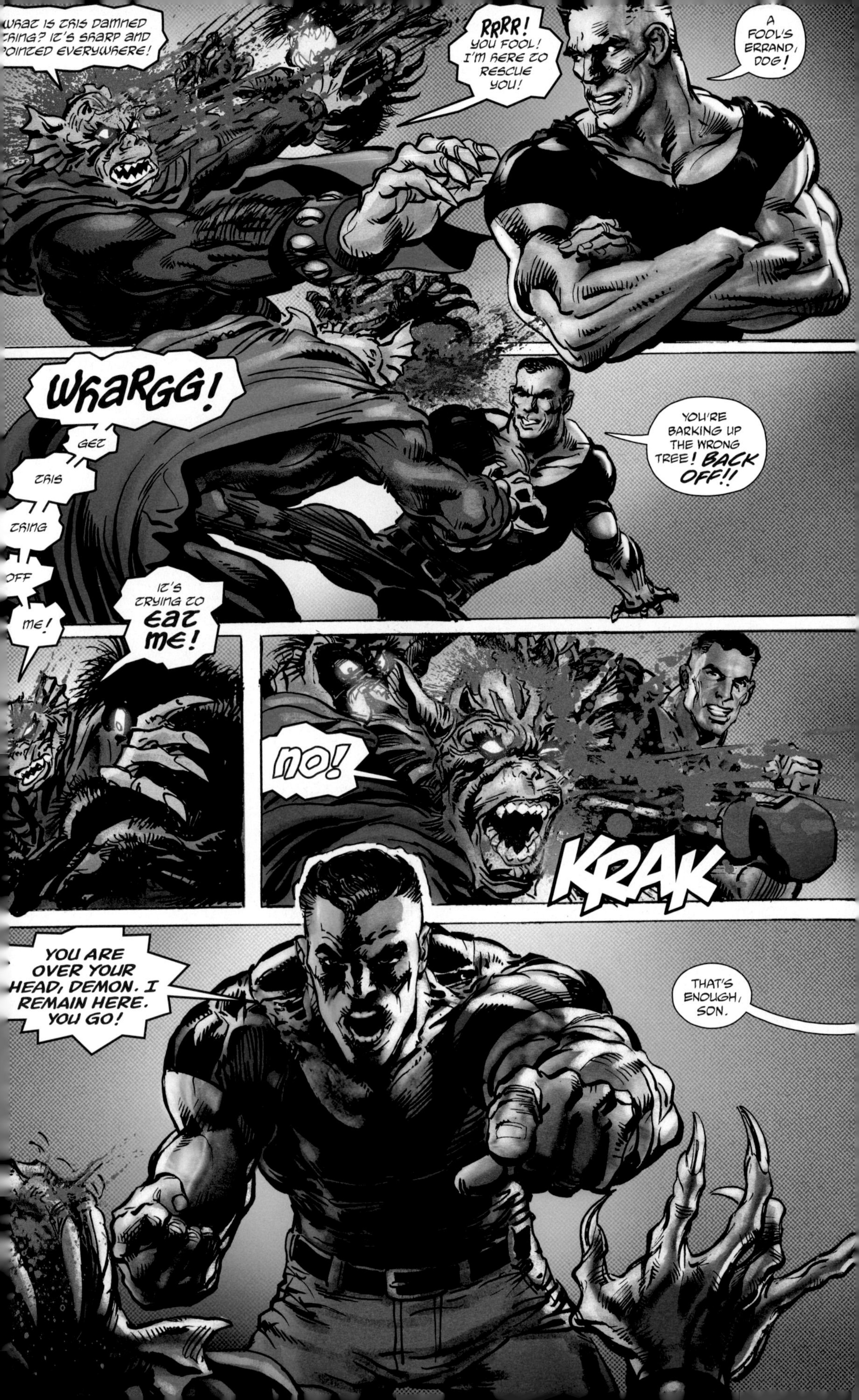
WHAT IS THIS DAMNED THING? IT'S SHARP AND POINTED EVERYWHERE!
RRRR! YOU FOOL! I'M HERE TO RESCUE YOU!
A FOOL'S ERRAND, DOG!
WHARGG!
GET
THIS
THING
OFF
ME!
YOU'RE BARKING UP THE WRONG TREE! BACK OFF!!
IT'S TRYING TO EAT ME!
NO!
KRAK
YOU ARE OVER YOUR HEAD, DEMON. I REMAIN HERE. YOU GO!
THAT'S ENOUGH, SON.

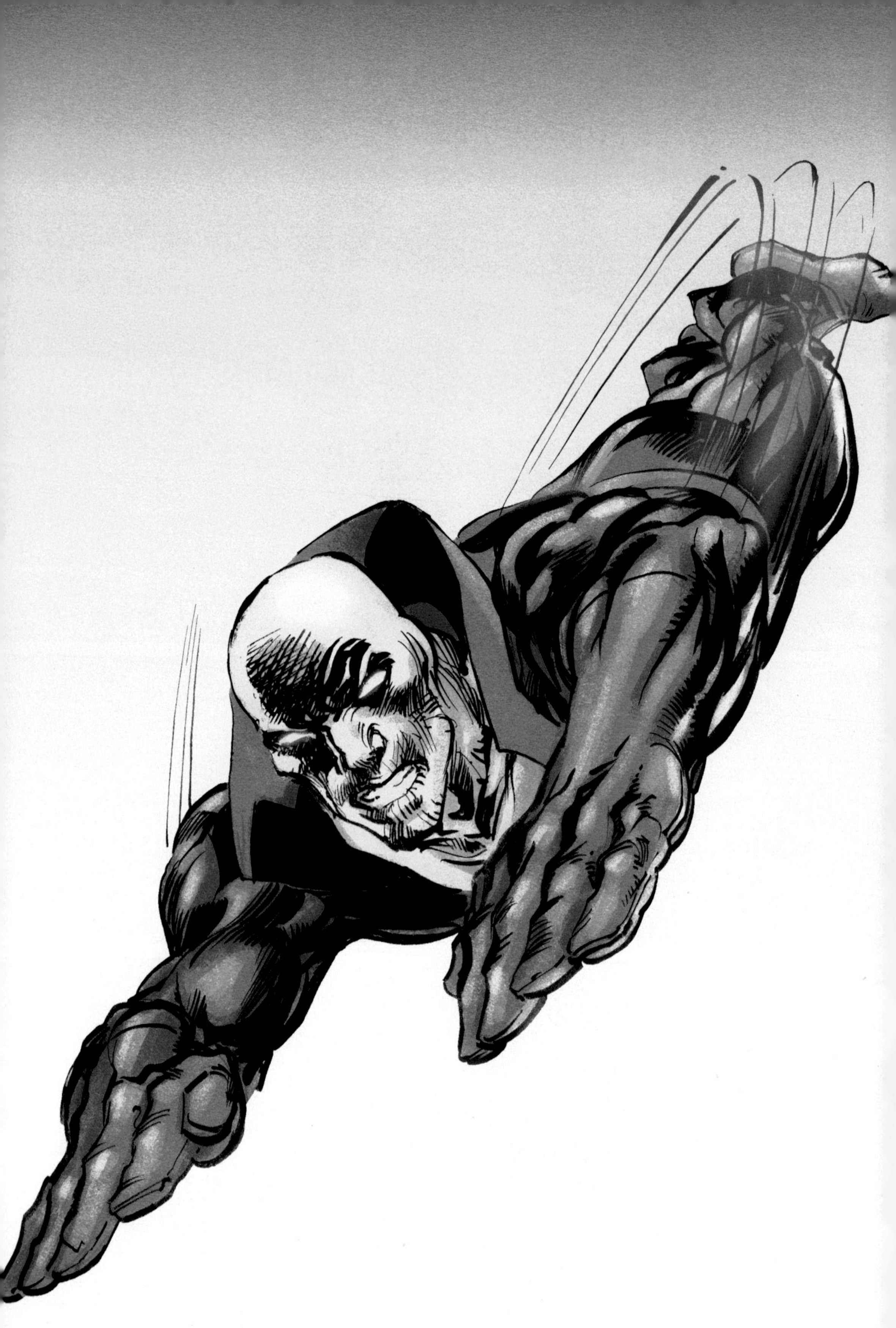

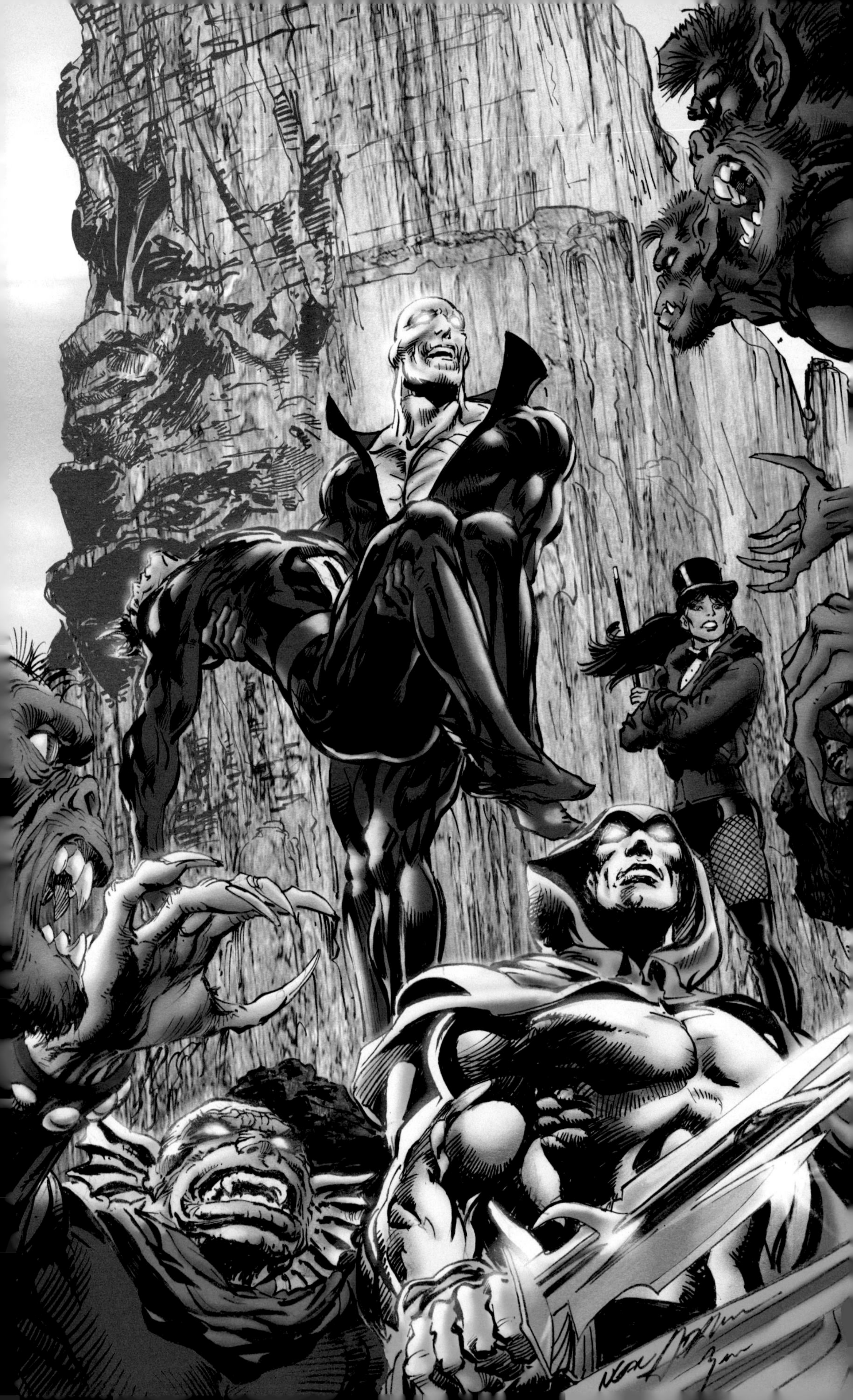

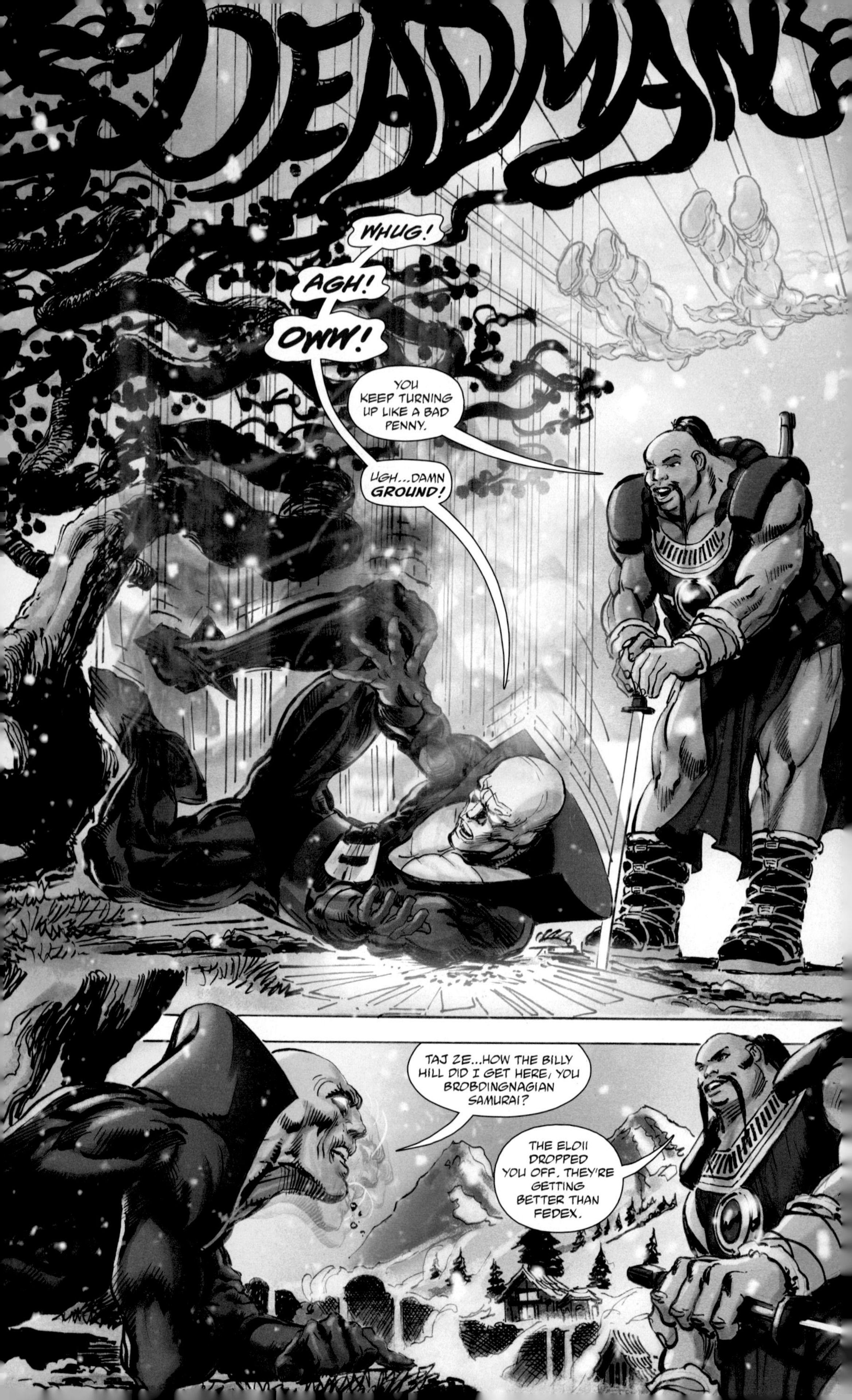
DEADMAN
WHUG!
AGH!
OWW!
YOU KEEP TURNING UP LIKE A BAD PENNY.
UGH...DAMN GROUND!
TAJ ZE...HOW THE BILLY HILL DID I GET HERE, YOU BROBDINGNAGIAN SAMURAI?
THE ELOII DROPPED YOU OFF. THEY'RE GETTING BETTER THAN FEDEX.

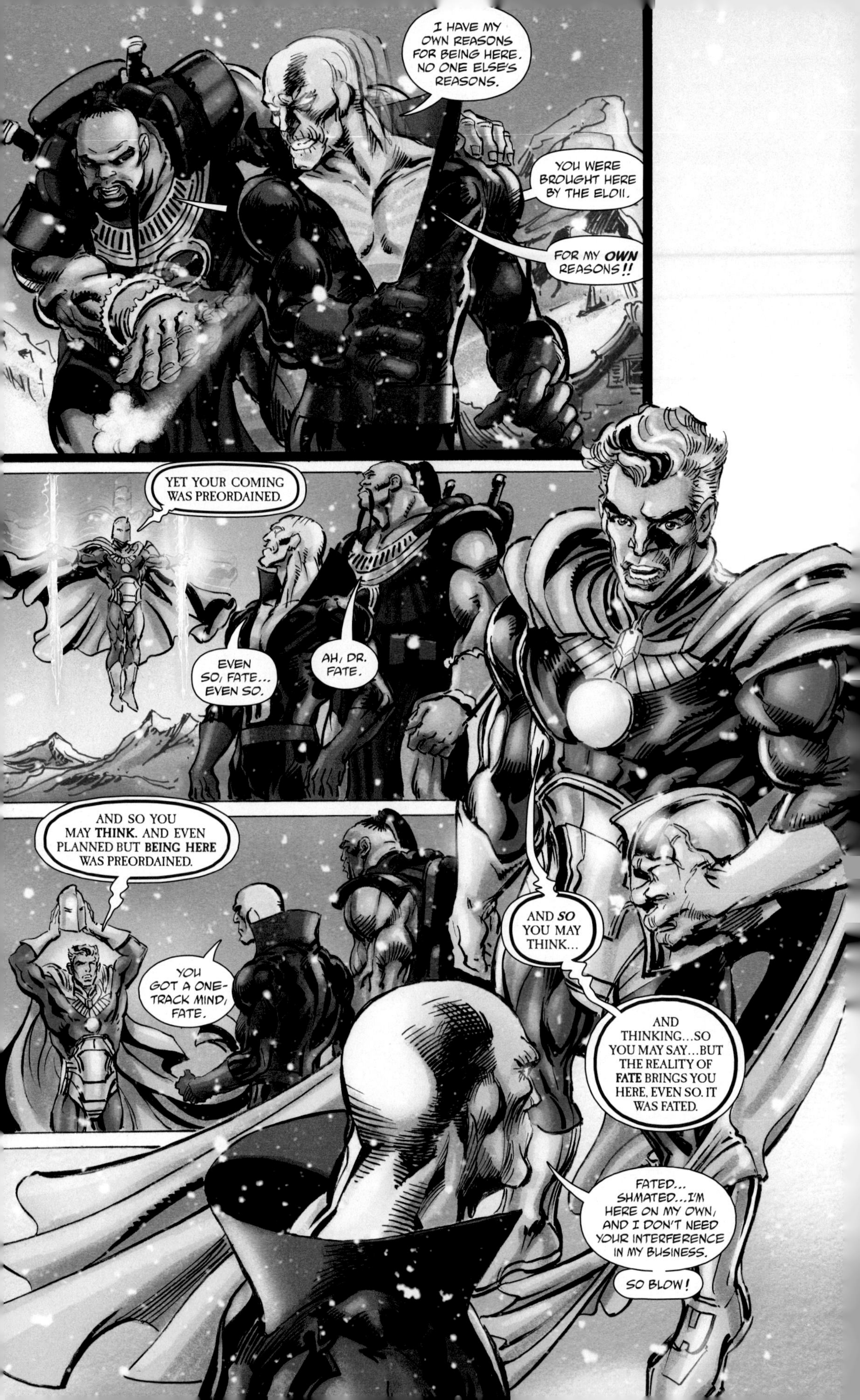
I HAVE MY OWN REASONS FOR BEING HERE. NO ONE ELSE'S REASONS.
YOU WERE BROUGHT HERE BY THE ELOII.
FOR MY OWN REASONS!!
YET YOUR COMING WAS PREORDAINED.
AH, DR. FATE.
EVEN SO, FATE... EVEN SO.
AND SO YOU MAY THINK. AND EVEN PLANNED BUT BEING HERE WAS PREORDAINED.
YOU GOT A ONE-TRACK MIND, FATE.
AND SO YOU MAY THINK...
AND THINKING...SO YOU MAY SAY...BUT THE REALITY OF FATE BRINGS YOU HERE, EVEN SO. IT WAS FATED.
FATED... SHMATED...I'M HERE ON MY OWN, AND I DON'T NEED YOUR INTERFERENCE IN MY BUSINESS.
SO BLOW!

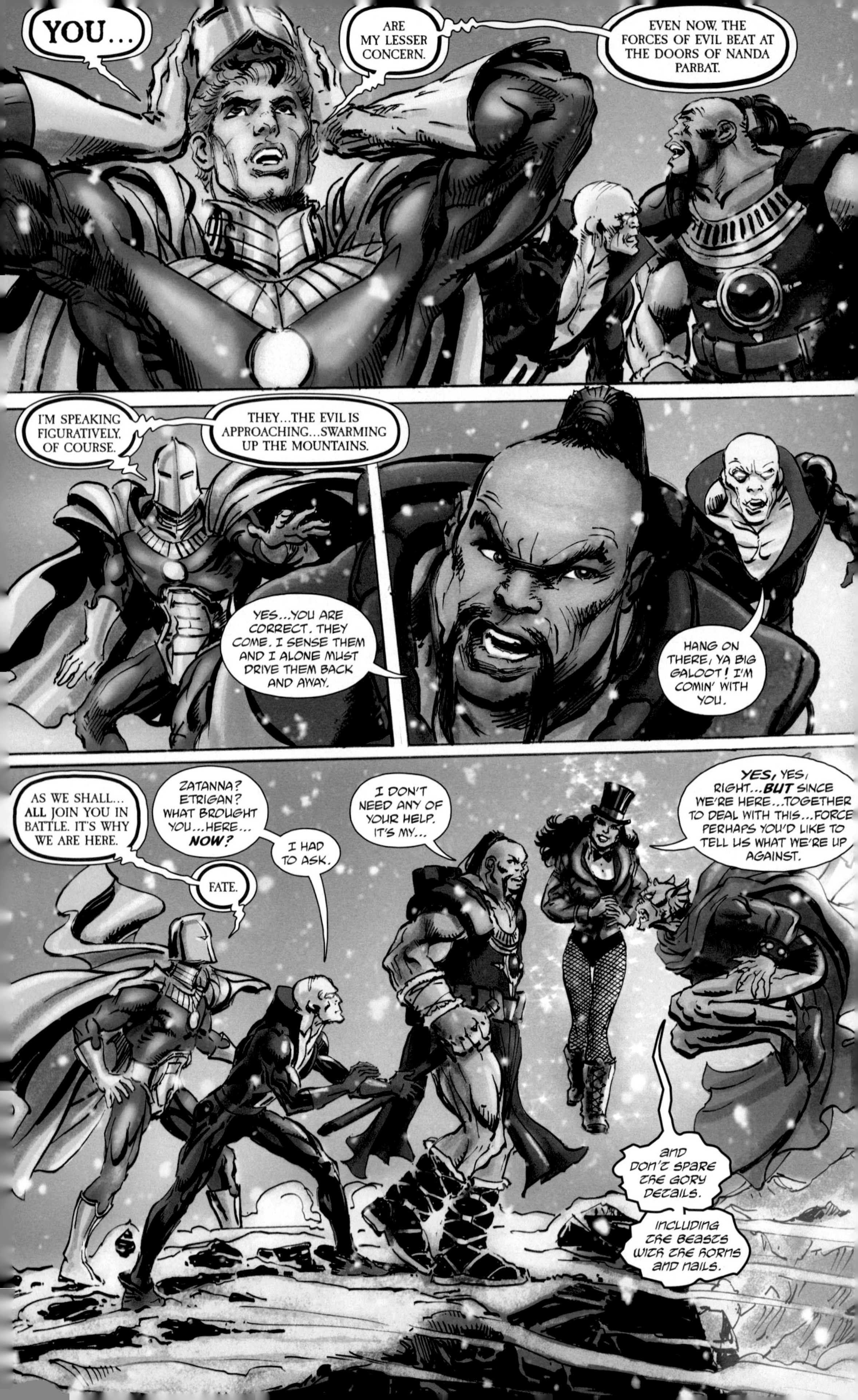
YOU...
ARE MY LESSER CONCERN.
EVEN NOW, THE FORCES OF EVIL BEAT AT THE DOORS OF NANDA PARBAT.
I'M SPEAKING FIGURATIVELY, OF COURSE.
THEY...THE EVIL IS APPROACHING...SWARMING UP THE MOUNTAINS.
YES...YOU ARE CORRECT. THEY COME. I SENSE THEM AND I ALONE MUST DRIVE THEM BACK AND AWAY.
HANG ON THERE, YA BIG GALOOT! I'M COMIN' WITH YOU.
AS WE SHALL... ALL JOIN YOU IN BATTLE. IT'S WHY WE ARE HERE.
FATE.
ZATANNA? ETRIGAN? WHAT BROUGHT YOU...HERE... NOW?
I HAD TO ASK.
I DON'T NEED ANY OF YOUR HELP. IT'S MY...
YES, YES, RIGHT...BUT SINCE WE'RE HERE...TOGETHER TO DEAL WITH THIS...FORCE PERHAPS YOU'D LIKE TO TELL US WHAT WE'RE UP AGAINST.
AND DON'T SPARE THE GORY DETAILS.
INCLUDING THE BEASTS WITH THE HORNS AND NAILS.

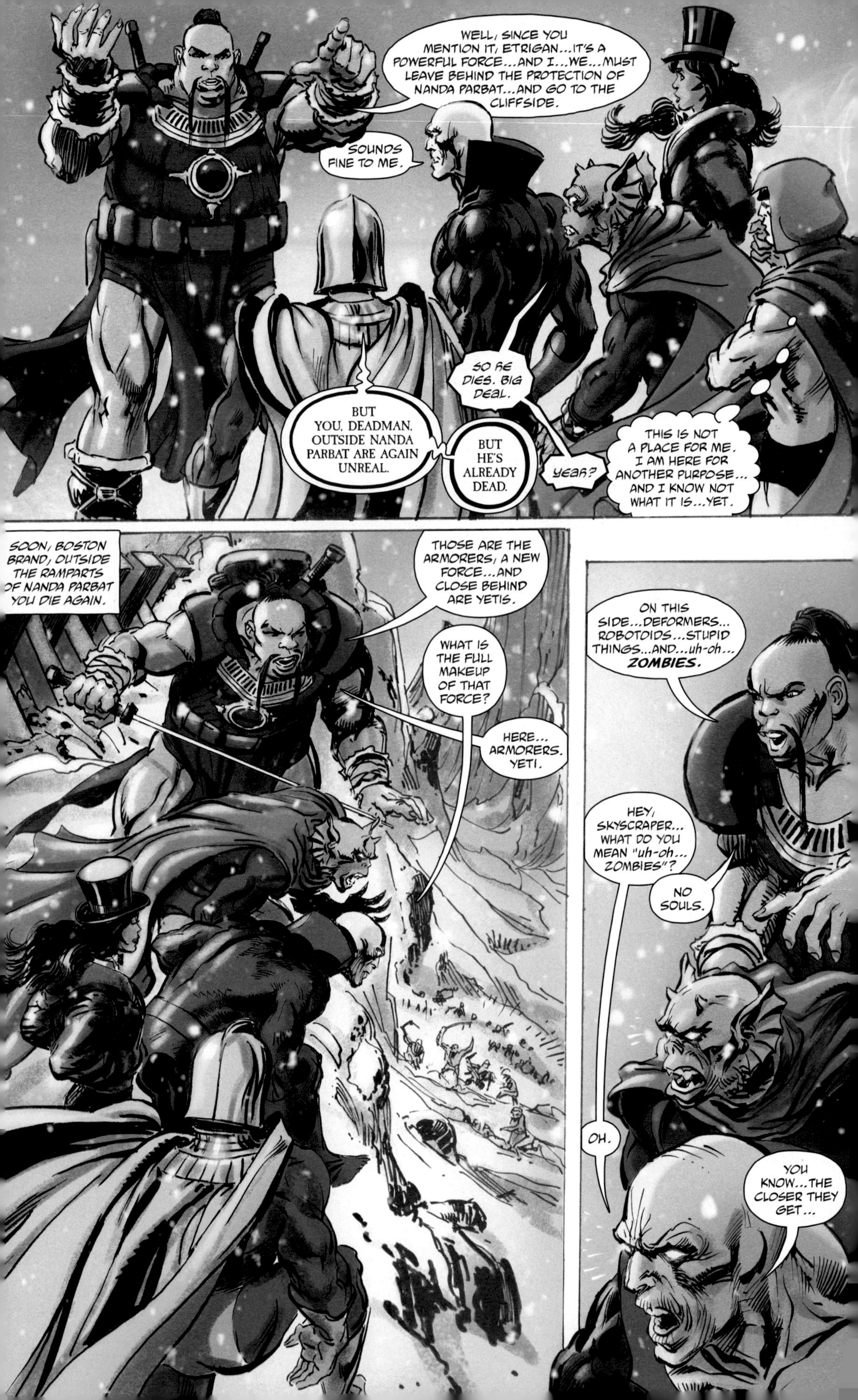

WELL, SINCE YOU MENTION IT, ETRIGAN...IT'S A POWERFUL FORCE...AND I...WE...MUST LEAVE BEHIND THE PROTECTION OF NANDA PARBAT...AND GO TO THE CLIFFSIDE.
SOUNDS FINE TO ME.
BUT YOU, DEADMAN, OUTSIDE NANDA PARBAT ARE AGAIN UNREAL.
BUT HE'S ALREADY DEAD.
SO HE DIES. BIG DEAL.
YEAH?
THIS IS NOT A PLACE FOR ME. I AM HERE FOR ANOTHER PURPOSE... AND I KNOW NOT WHAT IT IS...YET.
SOON, BOSTON BRAND, OUTSIDE THE RAMPARTS OF NANDA PARBAT YOU DIE AGAIN.
THOSE ARE THE ARMORERS, A NEW FORCE...AND CLOSE BEHIND ARE YETIS.
WHAT IS THE FULL MAKEUP OF THAT FORCE?
HERE... ARMORERS. YETI.
ON THIS SIDE...DEFORMERS... ROBOTOIDS...STUPID THINGS...AND...uh-oh... ZOMBIES.
HEY, SKYSCRAPER... WHAT DO YOU MEAN "uh-oh... ZOMBIES"?
NO SOULS.
OH.
YOU KNOW...THE CLOSER THEY GET...

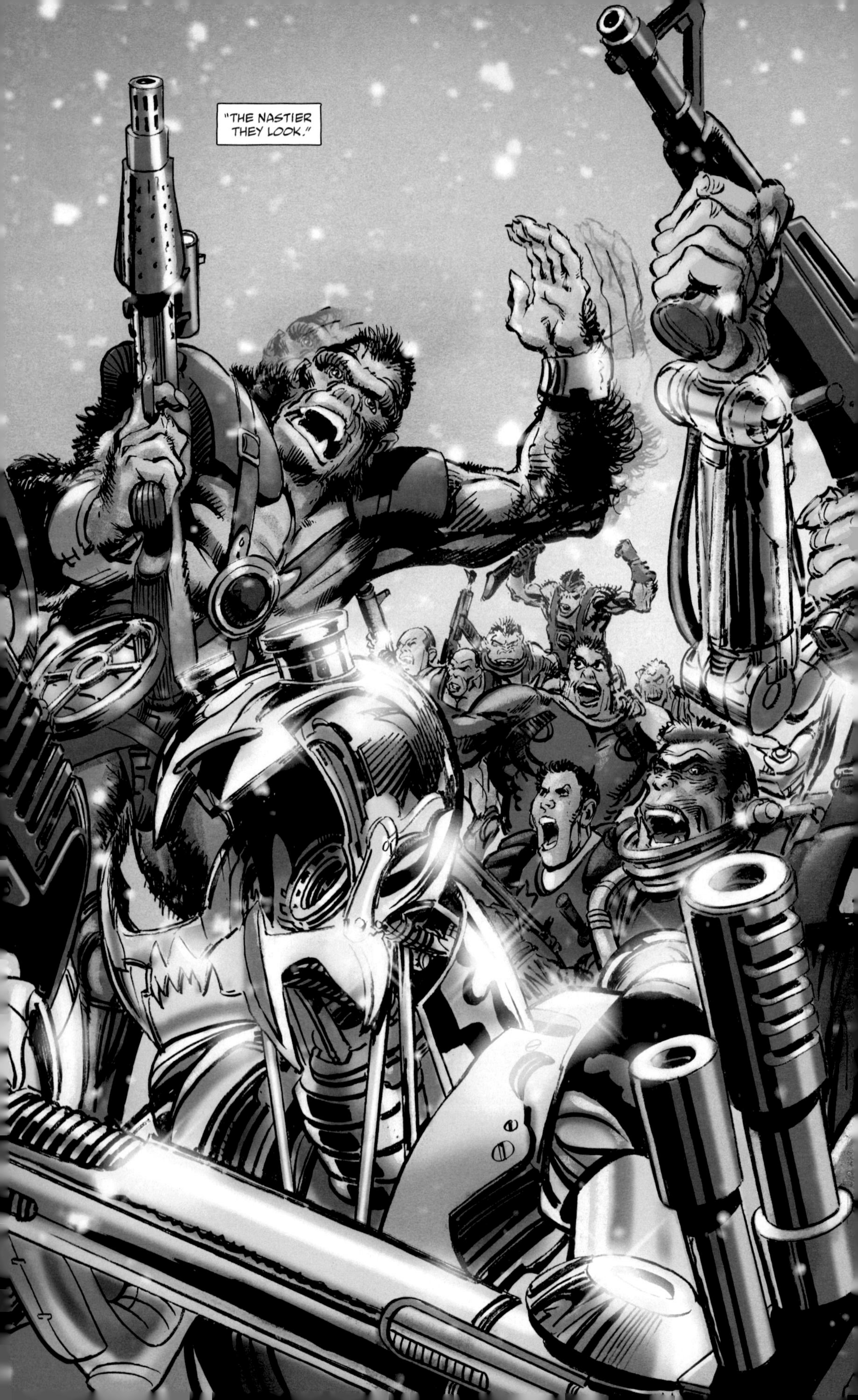
"THE NASTIER THEY LOOK."

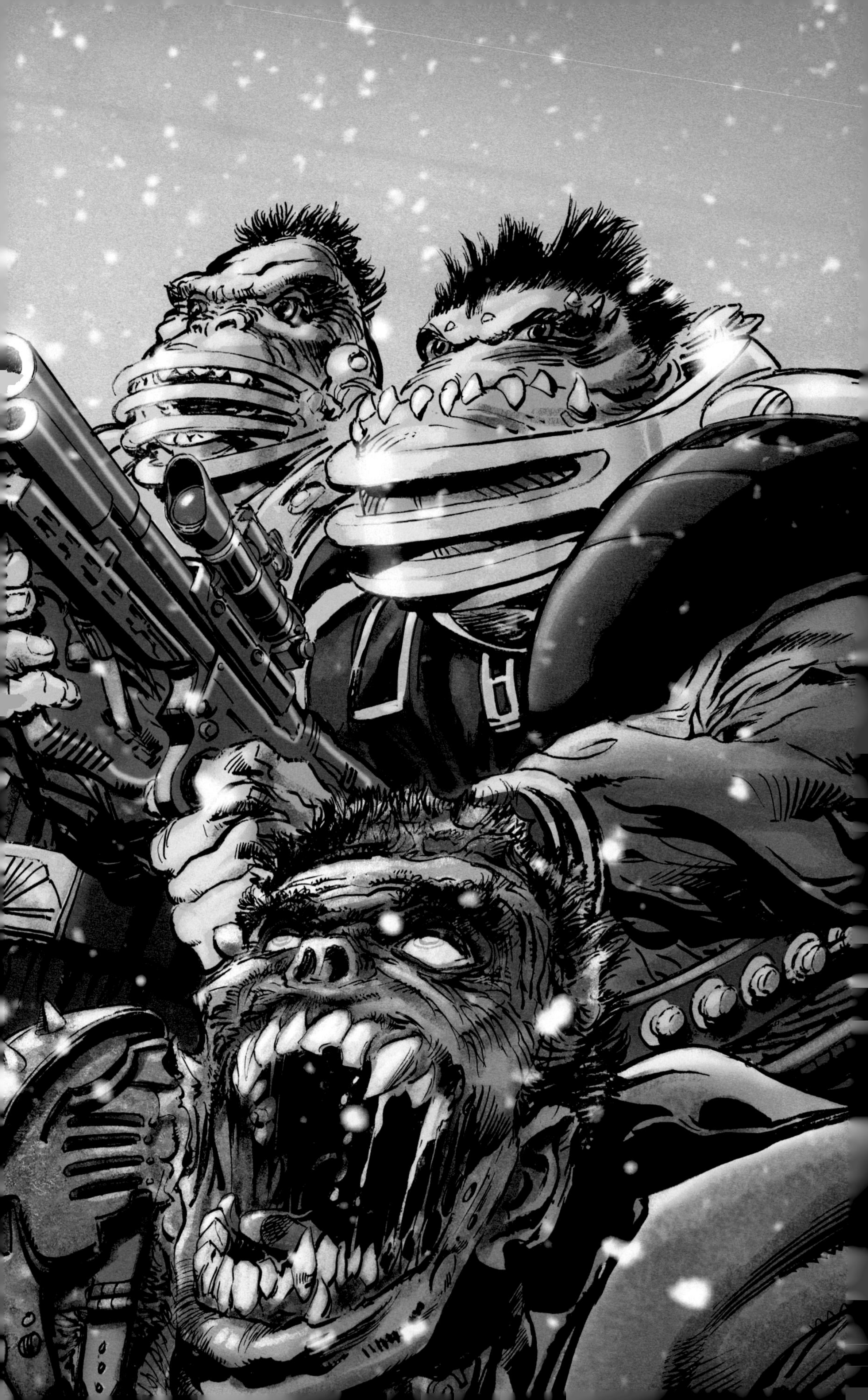

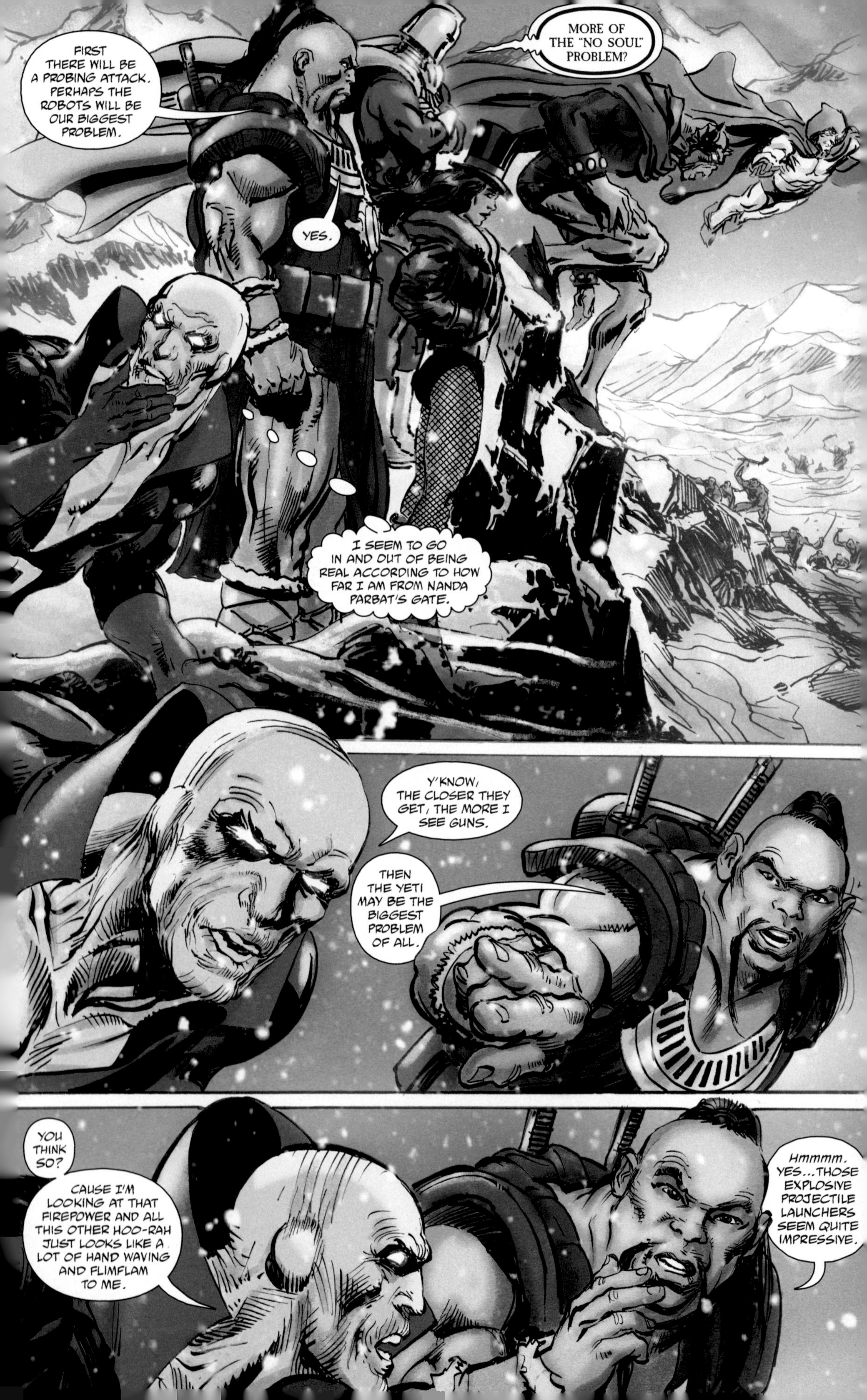

FIRST THERE WILL BE A PROBING ATTACK. PERHAPS THE ROBOTS WILL BE OUR BIGGEST PROBLEM.
MORE OF THE "NO SOUL" PROBLEM?
YES.
I SEEM TO GO IN AND OUT OF BEING REAL ACCORDING TO HOW FAR I AM FROM NANDA PARBAT'S GATE.
Y'KNOW, THE CLOSER THEY GET, THE MORE I SEE GUNS.
THEN THE YETI MAY BE THE BIGGEST PROBLEM OF ALL.
YOU THINK SO?
CAUSE I'M LOOKING AT THAT FIREPOWER AND ALL THIS OTHER HOO-RAH JUST LOOKS LIKE A LOT OF HAND WAVING AND FLIMFLAM TO ME.
Hmmmm. YES...THOSE EXPLOSIVE PROJECTILE LAUNCHERS SEEM QUITE IMPRESSIVE.

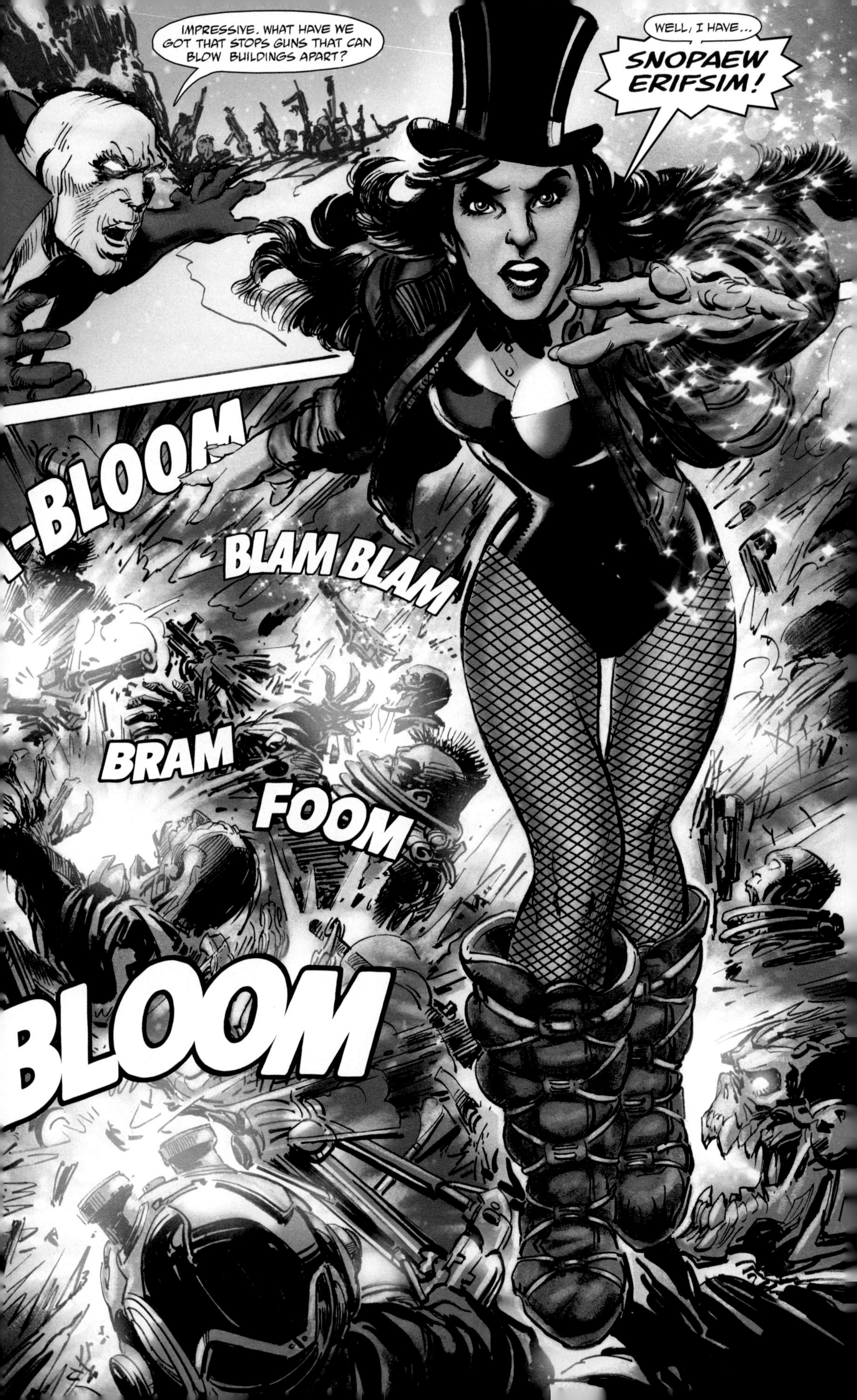
IMPRESSIVE. WHAT HAVE WE GOT THAT STOPS GUNS THAT CAN BLOW BUILDINGS APART?
WELL, I HAVE...
SNOPAEW ERIFSIM!
-BLOOM
BLAM BLAM
BRAM
FOOM
BLOOM

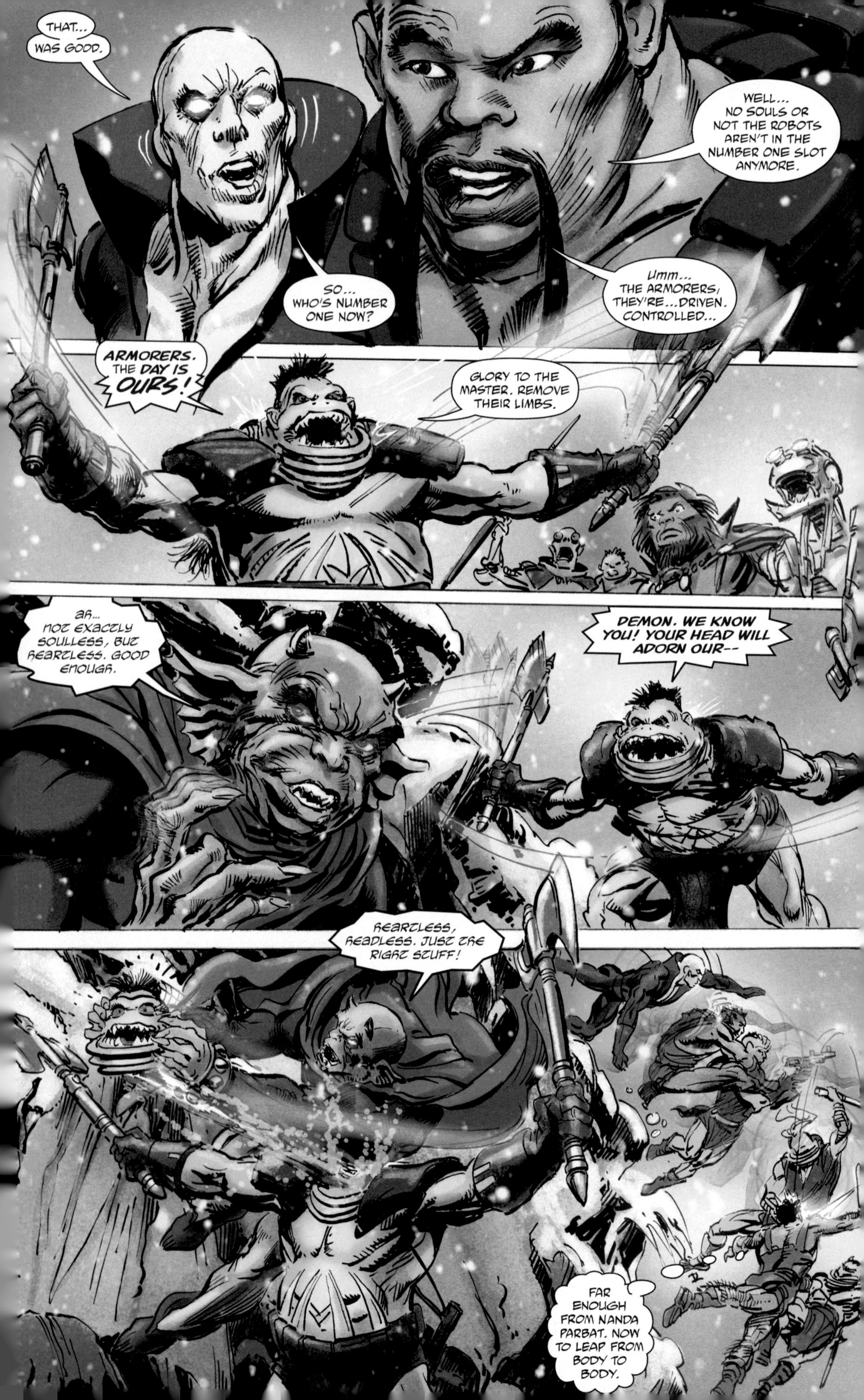
THAT... WAS GOOD.
WELL... NO SOULS OR NOT THE ROBOTS AREN'T IN THE NUMBER ONE SLOT ANYMORE.
SO... WHO'S NUMBER ONE NOW?
UMM... THE ARMORERS, THEY'RE...DRIVEN. CONTROLLED...
ARMORERS. THE DAY IS OURS!
GLORY TO THE MASTER. REMOVE THEIR LIMBS.
AH... NOT EXACTLY SOULLESS, BUT HEARTLESS. GOOD ENOUGH.
DEMON. WE KNOW YOU! YOUR HEAD WILL ADORN OUR--
HEARTLESS, HEADLESS. JUST THE RIGHT STUFF!
FAR ENOUGH FROM NANDA PARBAT. NOW TO LEAP FROM BODY TO BODY.

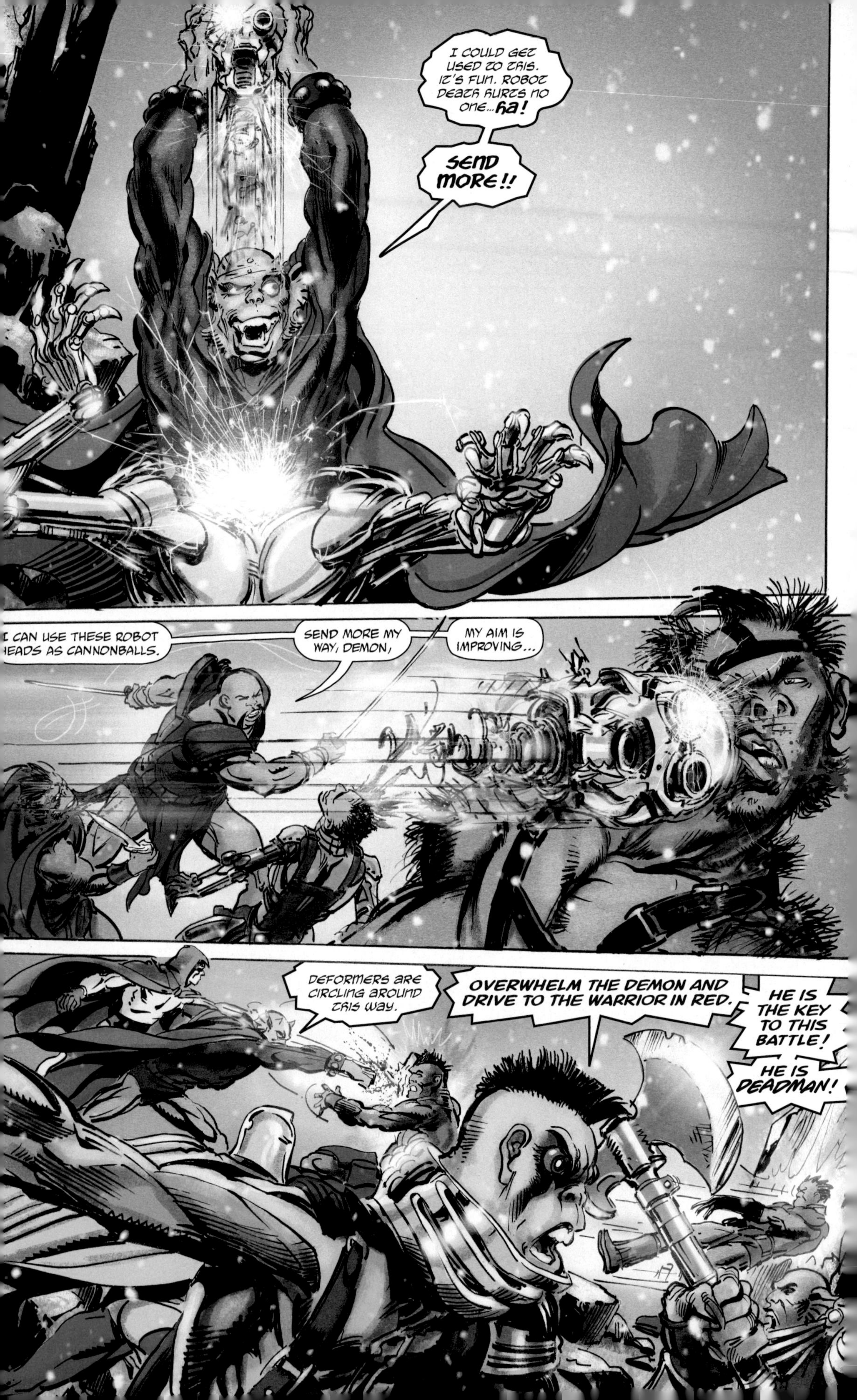
I COULD GET USED TO THIS. IT'S FUN. ROBOT DEATH HURTS NO ONE...HA!
SEND MORE!!
I CAN USE THESE ROBOT HEADS AS CANNONBALLS.
SEND MORE MY WAY, DEMON,
MY AIM IS IMPROVING...
DEFORMERS ARE CIRCLING AROUND THIS WAY.
OVERWHELM THE DEMON AND DRIVE TO THE WARRIOR IN RED.
HE IS THE KEY TO THIS BATTLE!
HE IS DEADMAN!

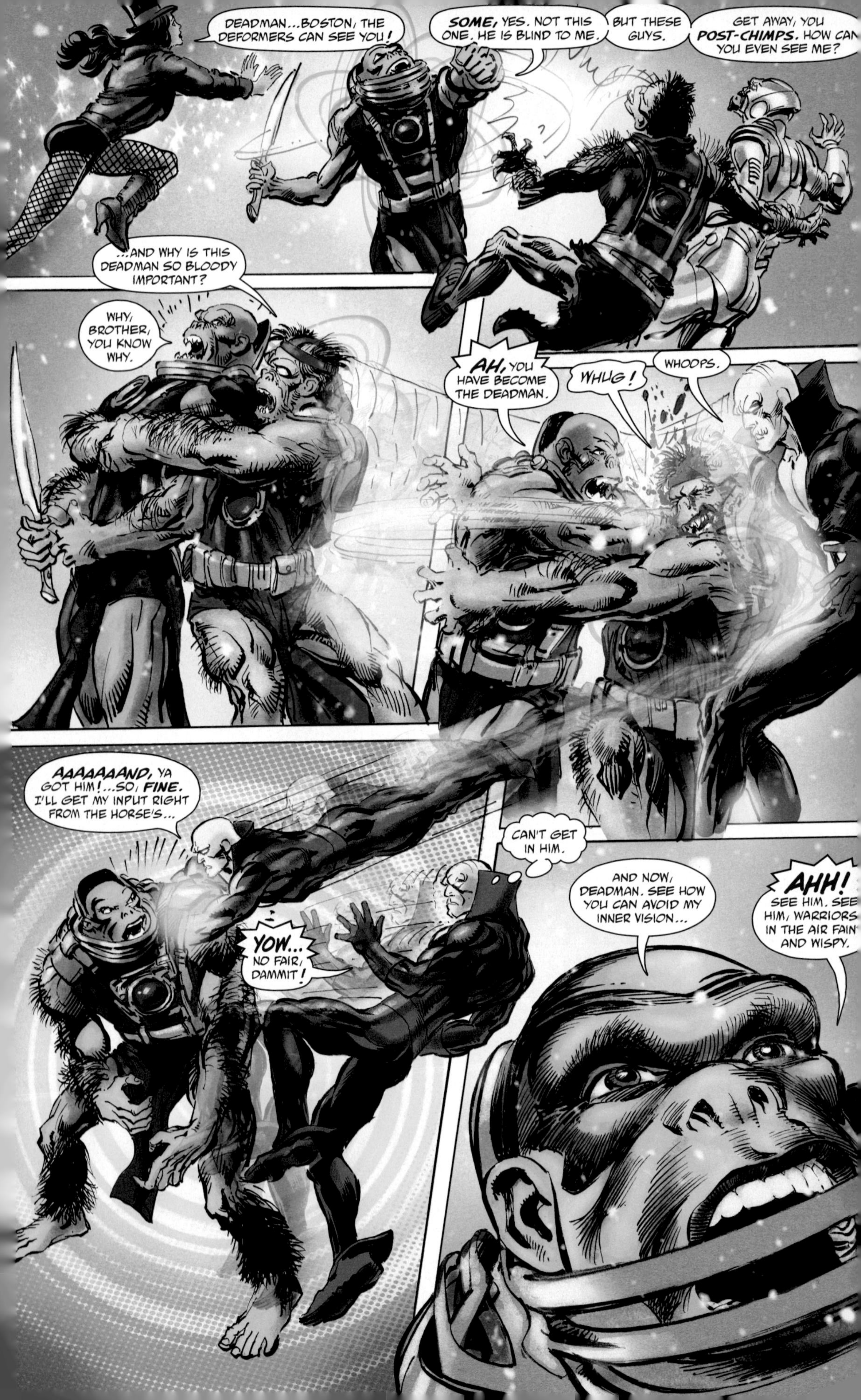
DEADMAN...BOSTON, THE DEFORMERS CAN SEE YOU!
SOME, YES. NOT THIS ONE. HE IS BLIND TO ME.
BUT THESE GUYS.
GET AWAY, YOU POST-CHIMPS. HOW CAN YOU EVEN SEE ME?
...AND WHY IS THIS DEADMAN SO BLOODY IMPORTANT?
WHY, BROTHER, YOU KNOW WHY.
AH, YOU HAVE BECOME THE DEADMAN.
WHUG!
WHOOPS.
AAAAAAAND, YA GOT HIM!...SO, FINE. I'LL GET MY INPUT RIGHT FROM THE HORSE'S...
CAN'T GET IN HIM.
YOW... NO FAIR, DAMMIT!
AND NOW, DEADMAN. SEE HOW YOU CAN AVOID MY INNER VISION...
AHH!
SEE HIM. SEE HIM, WARRIORS IN THE AIR FAIN AND WISPY.

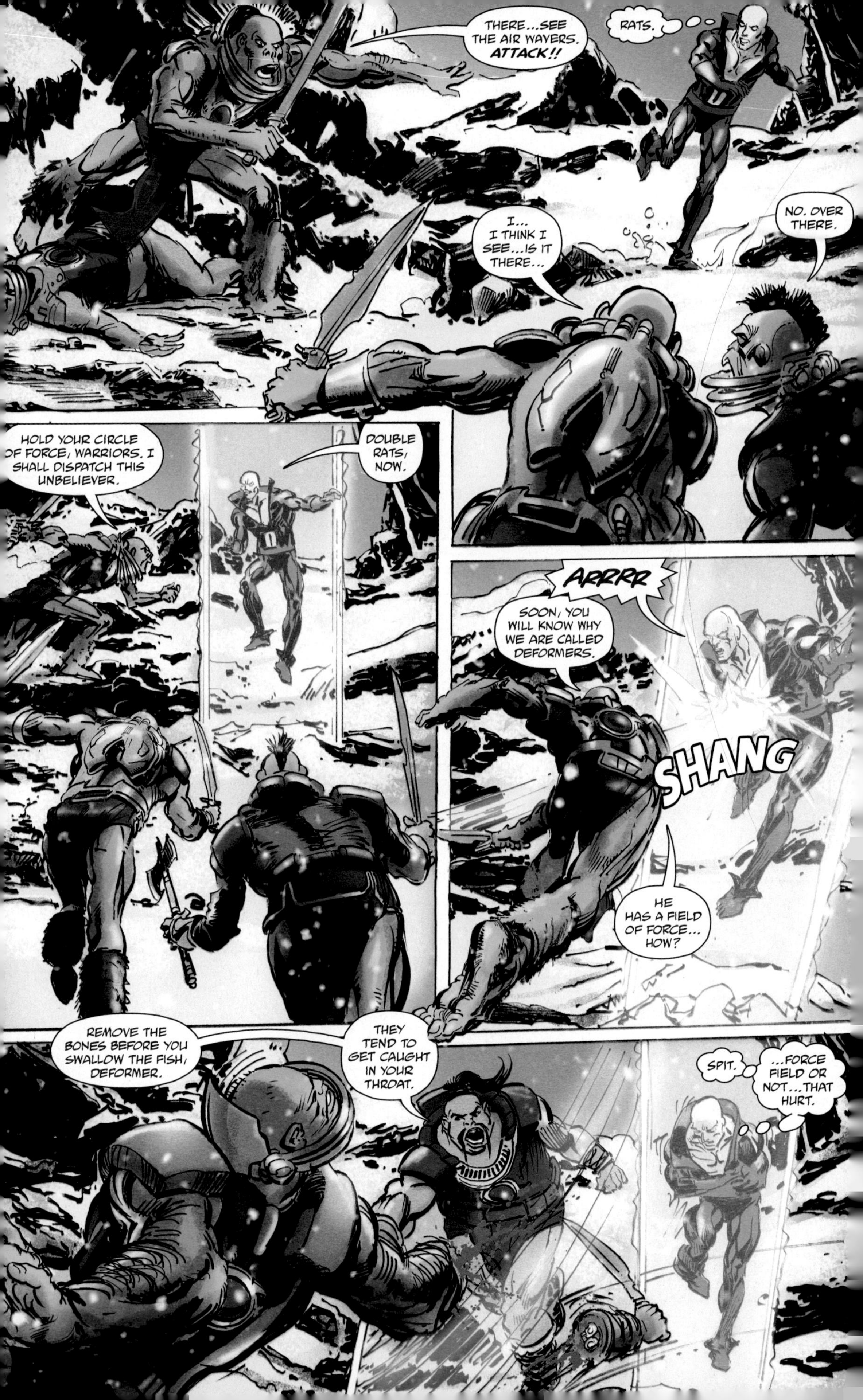
THERE...SEE THE AIR WAYERS. ATTACK!!
RATS.
I... I THINK I SEE...IS IT THERE...
NO. OVER THERE.
HOLD YOUR CIRCLE OF FORCE, WARRIORS. I SHALL DISPATCH THIS UNBELIEVER.
DOUBLE RATS, NOW.
ARRRR
SOON, YOU WILL KNOW WHY WE ARE CALLED DEFORMERS.
SHANG
HE HAS A FIELD OF FORCE... HOW?
REMOVE THE BONES BEFORE YOU SWALLOW THE FISH, DEFORMER.
THEY TEND TO GET CAUGHT IN YOUR THROAT.
SPIT.
...FORCE FIELD OR NOT...THAT HURT.

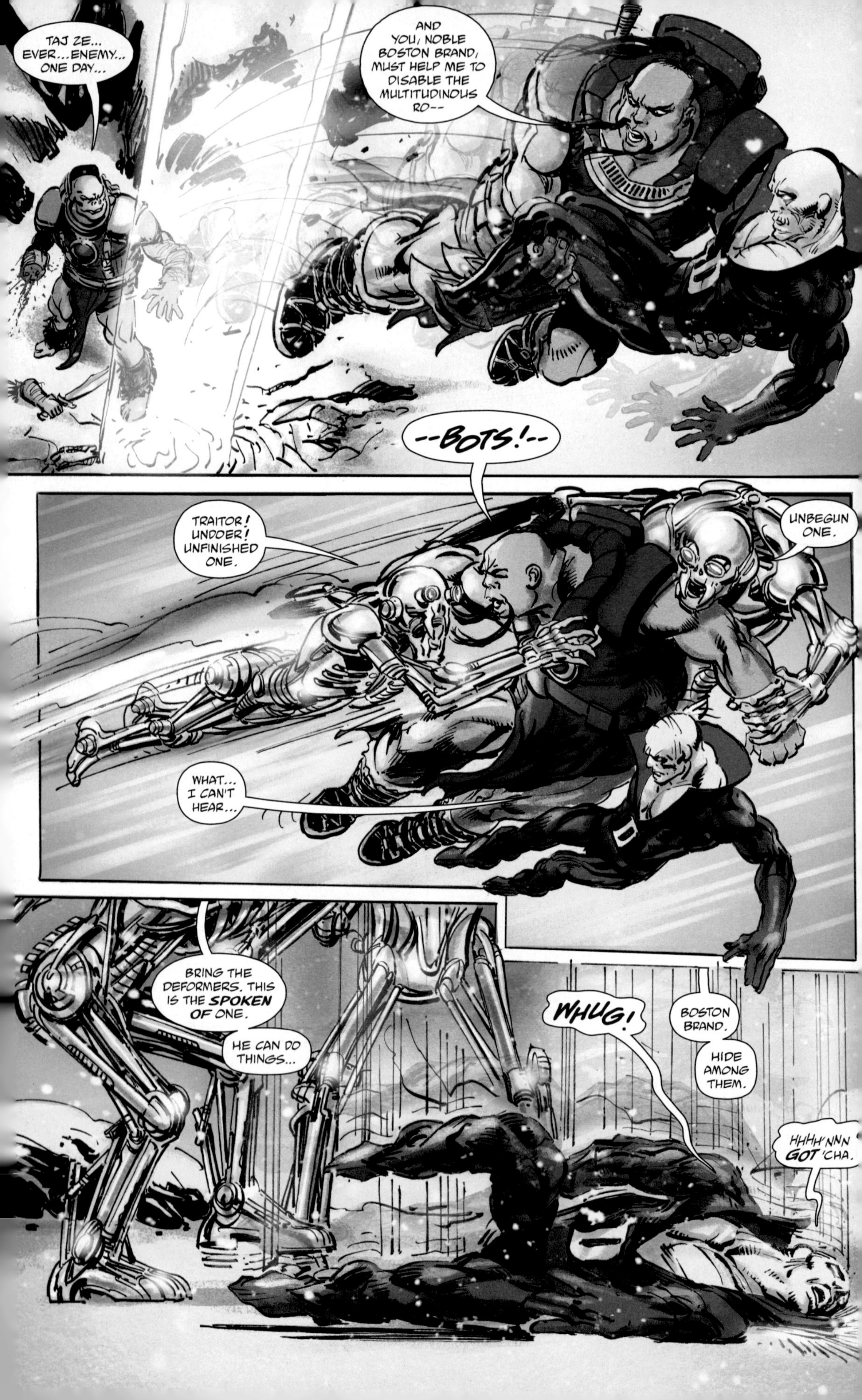
TAJ ZE... EVER...ENEMY... ONE DAY...
AND YOU, NOBLE BOSTON BRAND, MUST HELP ME TO DISABLE THE MULTITUDINOUS RO--
--BOTS!--
TRAITOR! UNDOER! UNFINISHED ONE.
UNBEGUN ONE.
WHAT... I CAN'T HEAR...
BRING THE DEFORMERS. THIS IS THE SPOKEN OF ONE.
HE CAN DO THINGS...
WHUG!
BOSTON BRAND.
HIDE AMONG THEM.
HHHH'NNN GOT 'CHA.

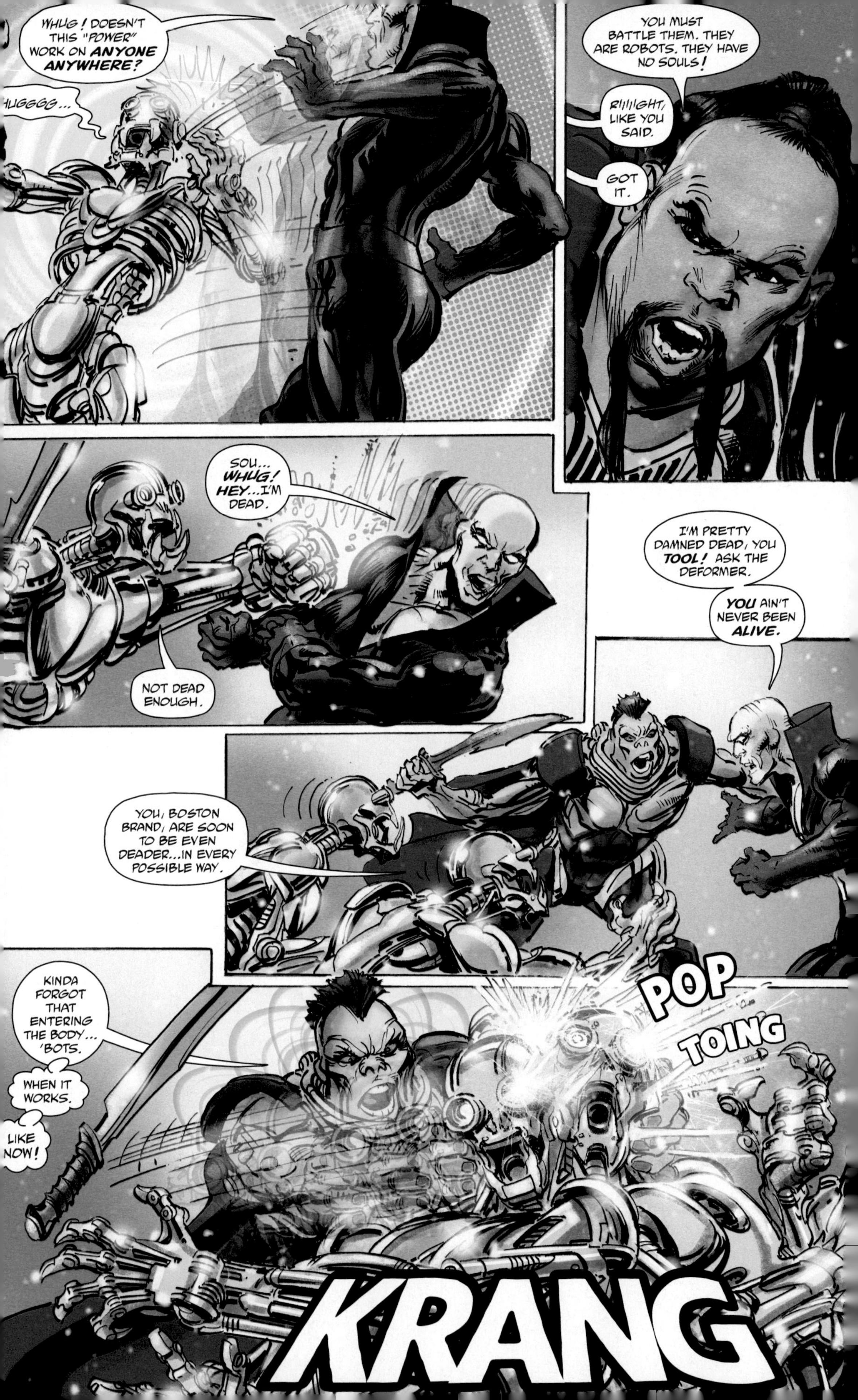
WHUG! DOESN'T THIS "POWER" WORK ON ANYONE ANYWHERE?
HUGGGG...
YOU MUST BATTLE THEM. THEY ARE ROBOTS. THEY HAVE NO SOULS!
RIIIIGHT, LIKE YOU SAID.
GOT IT.
SOU... WHUG! HEY...I'M DEAD.
NOT DEAD ENOUGH.
I'M PRETTY DAMNED DEAD, YOU TOOL! ASK THE DEFORMER.
YOU AIN'T NEVER BEEN ALIVE.
YOU, BOSTON BRAND, ARE SOON TO BE EVEN DEADER...IN EVERY POSSIBLE WAY.
KINDA FORGOT THAT ENTERING THE BODY... 'BOTS.
WHEN IT WORKS.
LIKE NOW!
POP
TOING
KRANG

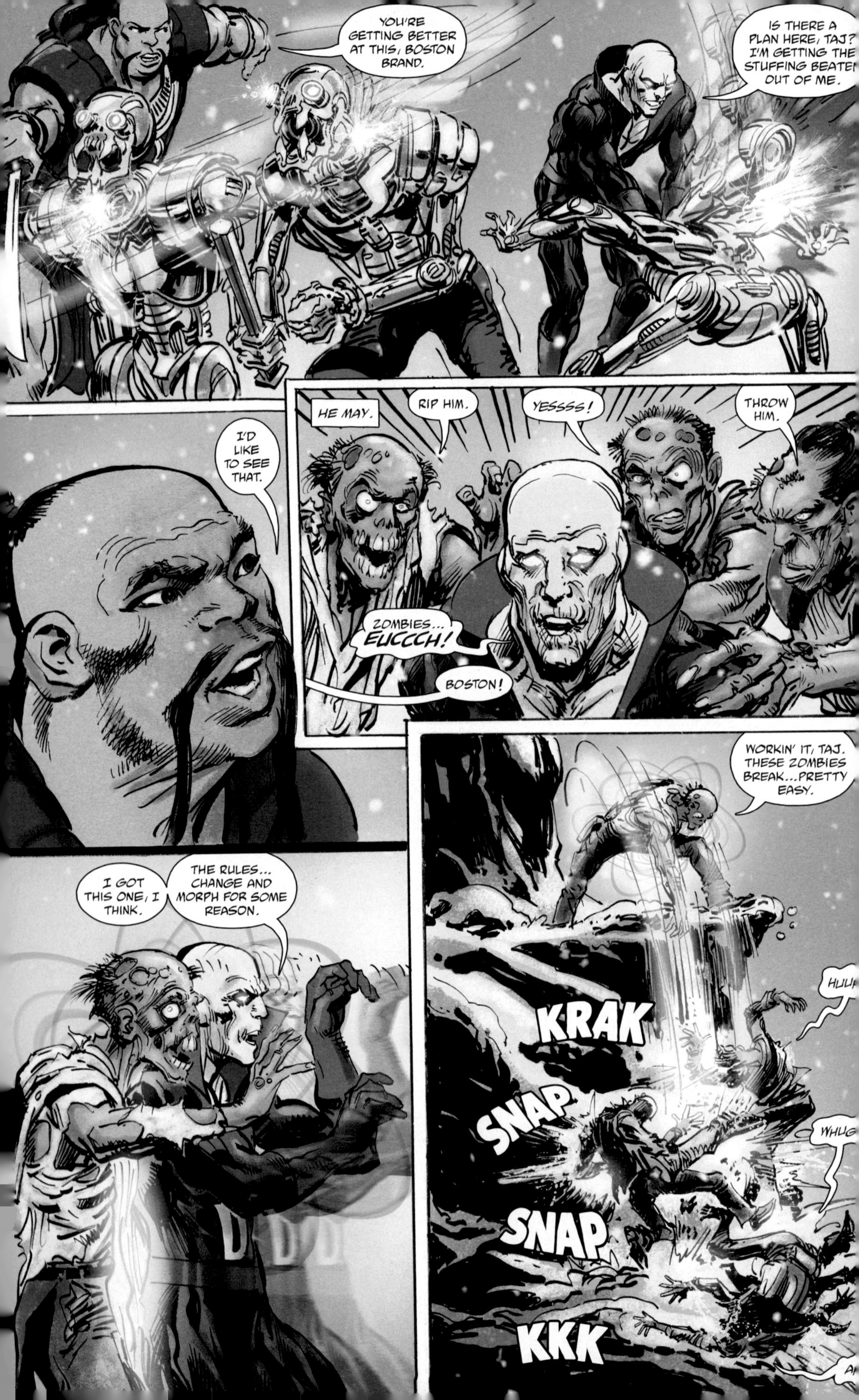
YOU'RE GETTING BETTER AT THIS, BOSTON BRAND.
IS THERE A PLAN HERE, TAJ? I'M GETTING THE STUFFING BEATEN OUT OF ME.
HE MAY.
RIP HIM.
YESSSS!
THROW HIM.
I'D LIKE TO SEE THAT.
ZOMBIES... EUCCCH!
BOSTON!
WORKIN' IT, TAJ. THESE ZOMBIES BREAK...PRETTY EASY.
I GOT THIS ONE, I THINK.
THE RULES... CHANGE AND MORPH FOR SOME REASON.
KRAK
SNAP
SNAP
KKK

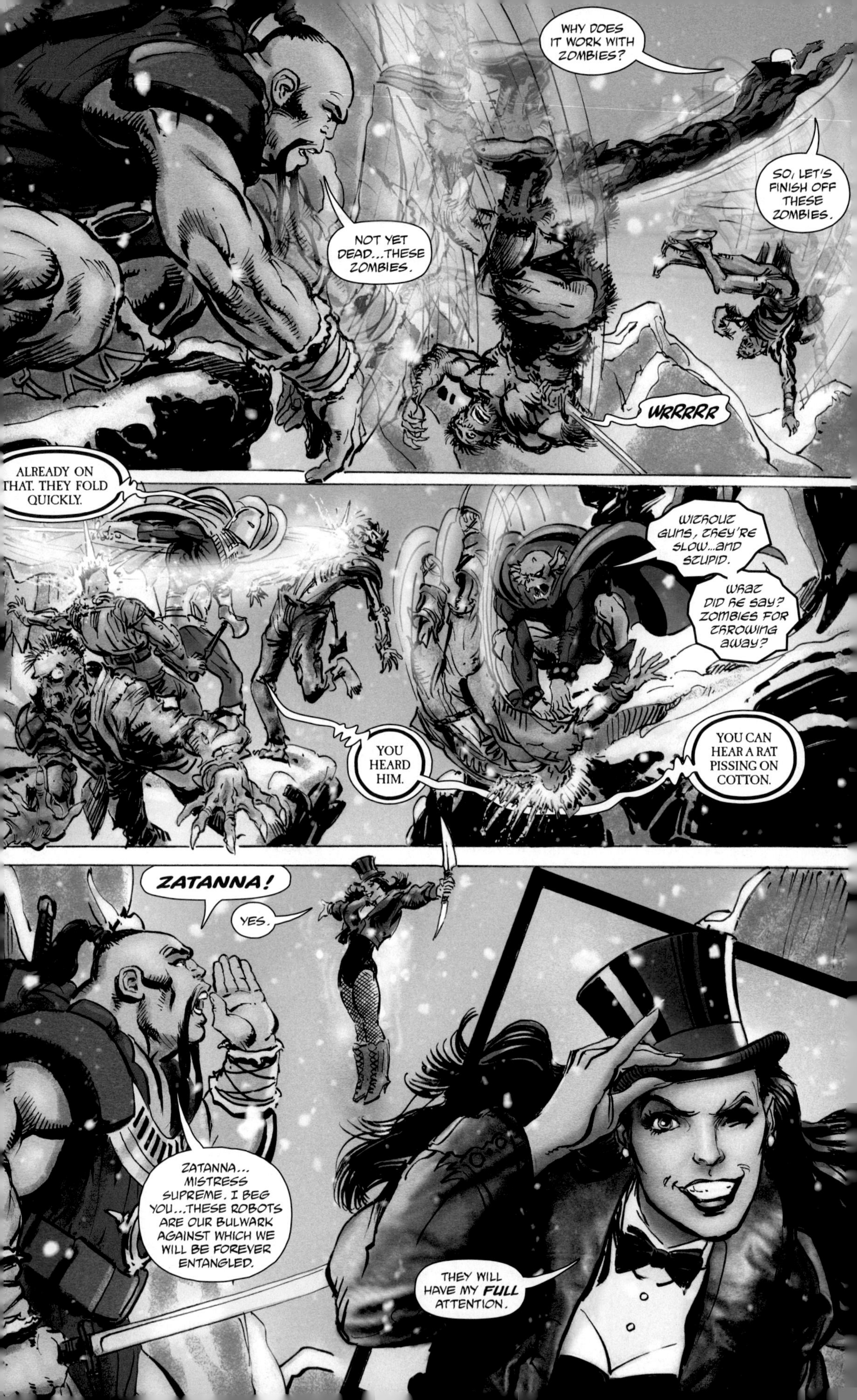
WHY DOES IT WORK WITH ZOMBIES?
NOT YET DEAD...THESE ZOMBIES.
SO, LET'S FINISH OFF THESE ZOMBIES.
WRRRRR
ALREADY ON THAT. THEY FOLD QUICKLY.
WITHOUT GUNS, THEY'RE SLOW...AND STUPID.
WHAT DID HE SAY? ZOMBIES FOR THROWING AWAY?
YOU HEARD HIM.
YOU CAN HEAR A RAT PISSING ON COTTON.
ZATANNA!
YES.
ZATANNA... MISTRESS SUPREME. I BEG YOU...THESE ROBOTS ARE OUR BULWARK AGAINST WHICH WE WILL BE FOREVER ENTANGLED.
THEY WILL HAVE MY FULL ATTENTION.

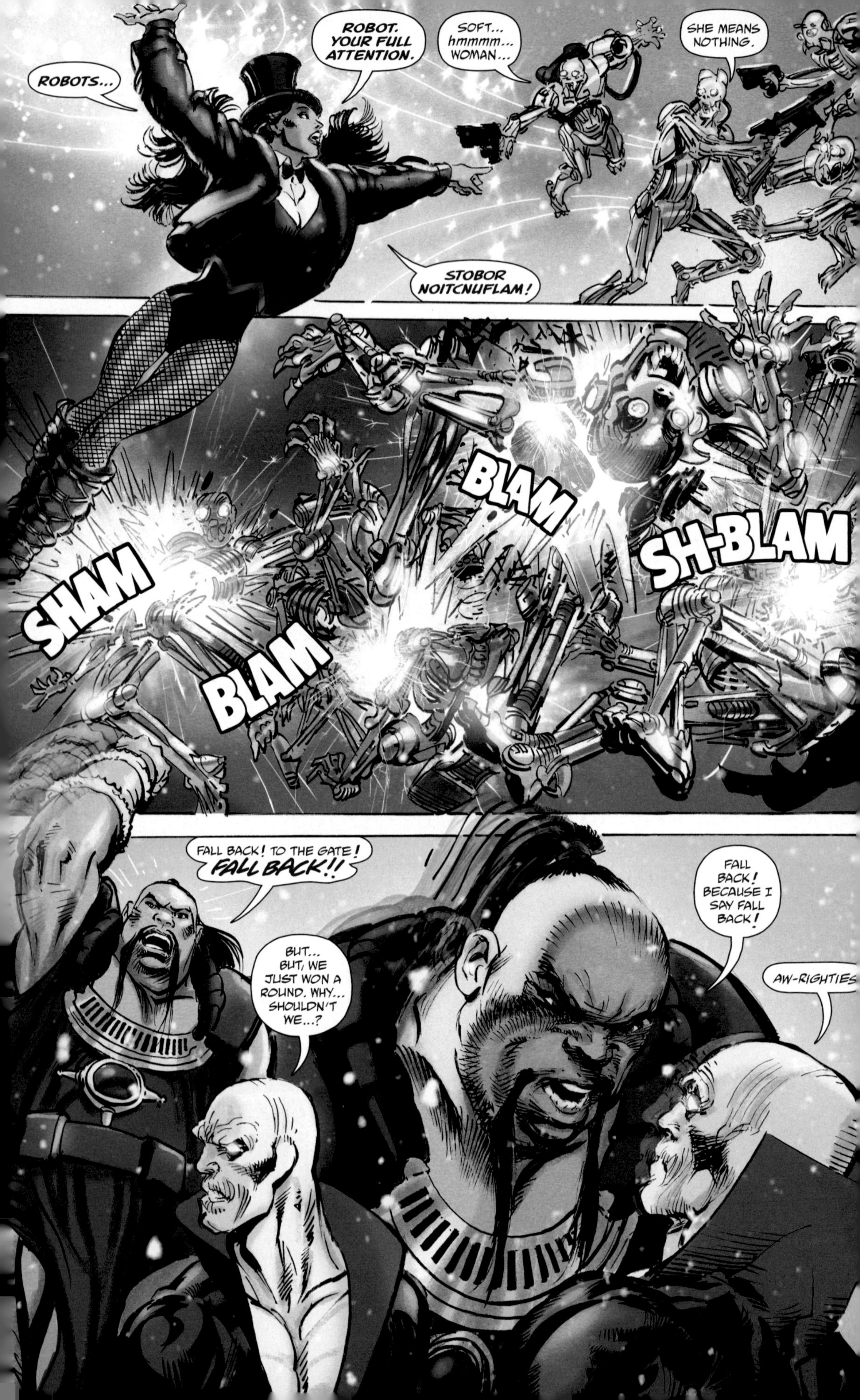
ROBOTS...
ROBOT. YOUR FULL ATTENTION.
SOFT... hmmmm... WOMAN...
SHE MEANS NOTHING.
STOBOR NOITCNUFLAM!
BLAM
SH-BLAM
SHAM
BLAM
FALL BACK! TO THE GATE! FALL BACK!!
BUT... BUT, WE JUST WON A ROUND. WHY... SHOULDN'T WE...?
FALL BACK! BECAUSE I SAY FALL BACK!
AW-RIGHTIES

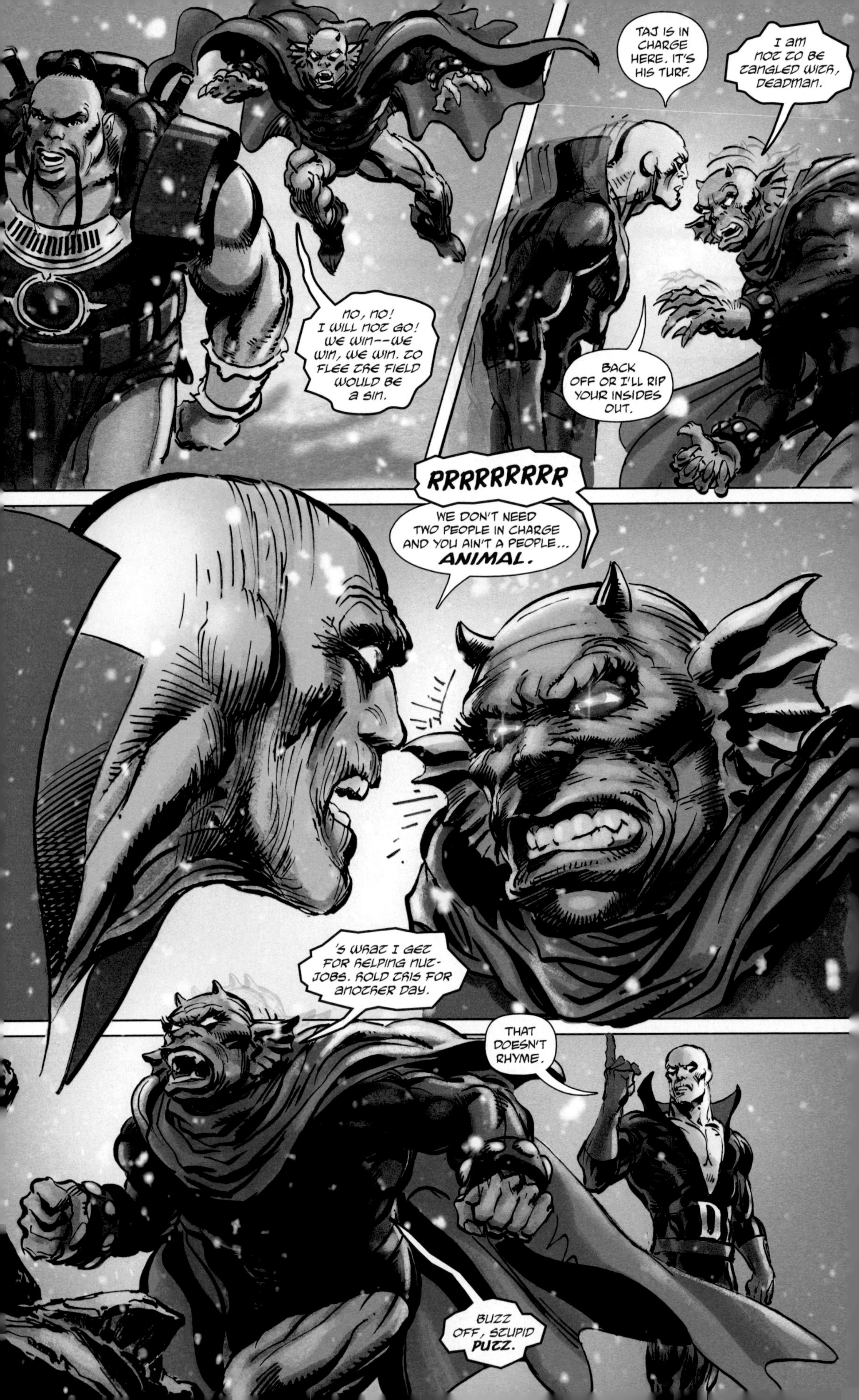
NO, NO! I WILL NOT GO! WE WIN--WE WIN, WE WIN. TO FLEE THE FIELD WOULD BE A SIN.
TAJ IS IN CHARGE HERE. IT'S HIS TURF.
I AM NOT TO BE TANGLED WITH, DEADMAN.
BACK OFF OR I'LL RIP YOUR INSIDES OUT.
RRRRRRRRR
WE DON'T NEED TWO PEOPLE IN CHARGE AND YOU AIN'T A PEOPLE... ANIMAL.
'S WHAT I GET FOR HELPING NUT-JOBS. HOLD THIS FOR ANOTHER DAY.
THAT DOESN'T RHYME.
BUZZ OFF, STUPID PUTZ.

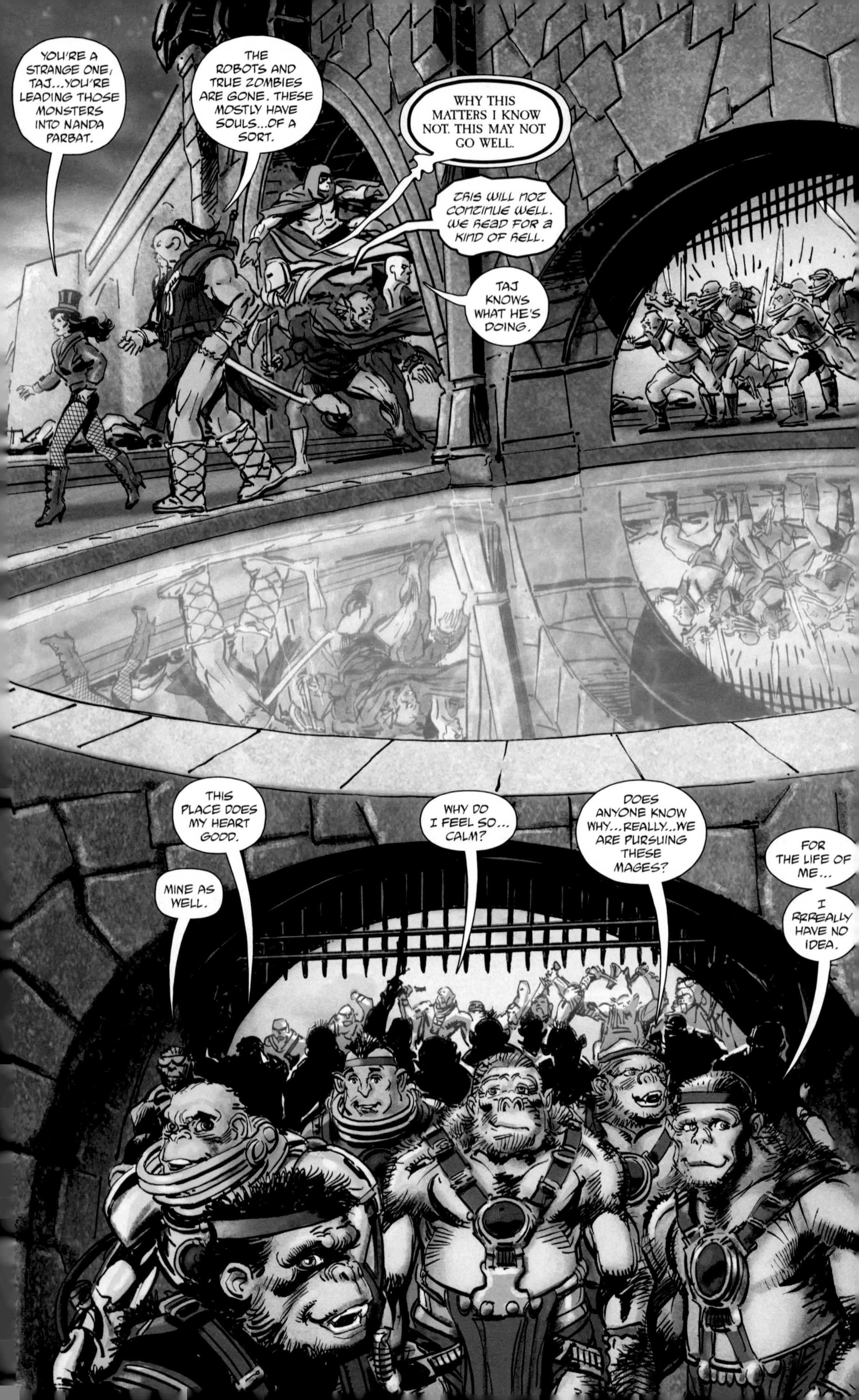
YOU'RE A STRANGE ONE, TAJ...YOU'RE LEADING THOSE MONSTERS INTO NANDA PARBAT.
THE ROBOTS AND TRUE ZOMBIES ARE GONE. THESE MOSTLY HAVE SOULS...OF A SORT.
WHY THIS MATTERS I KNOW NOT. THIS MAY NOT GO WELL.
THIS WILL NOT CONTINUE WELL. WE HEAD FOR A KIND OF HELL.
TAJ KNOWS WHAT HE'S DOING.
THIS PLACE DOES MY HEART GOOD.
MINE AS WELL.
WHY DO I FEEL SO... CALM?
DOES ANYONE KNOW WHY...REALLY...WE ARE PURSUING THESE MAGES?
FOR THE LIFE OF ME...
I RRREALLY HAVE NO IDEA.

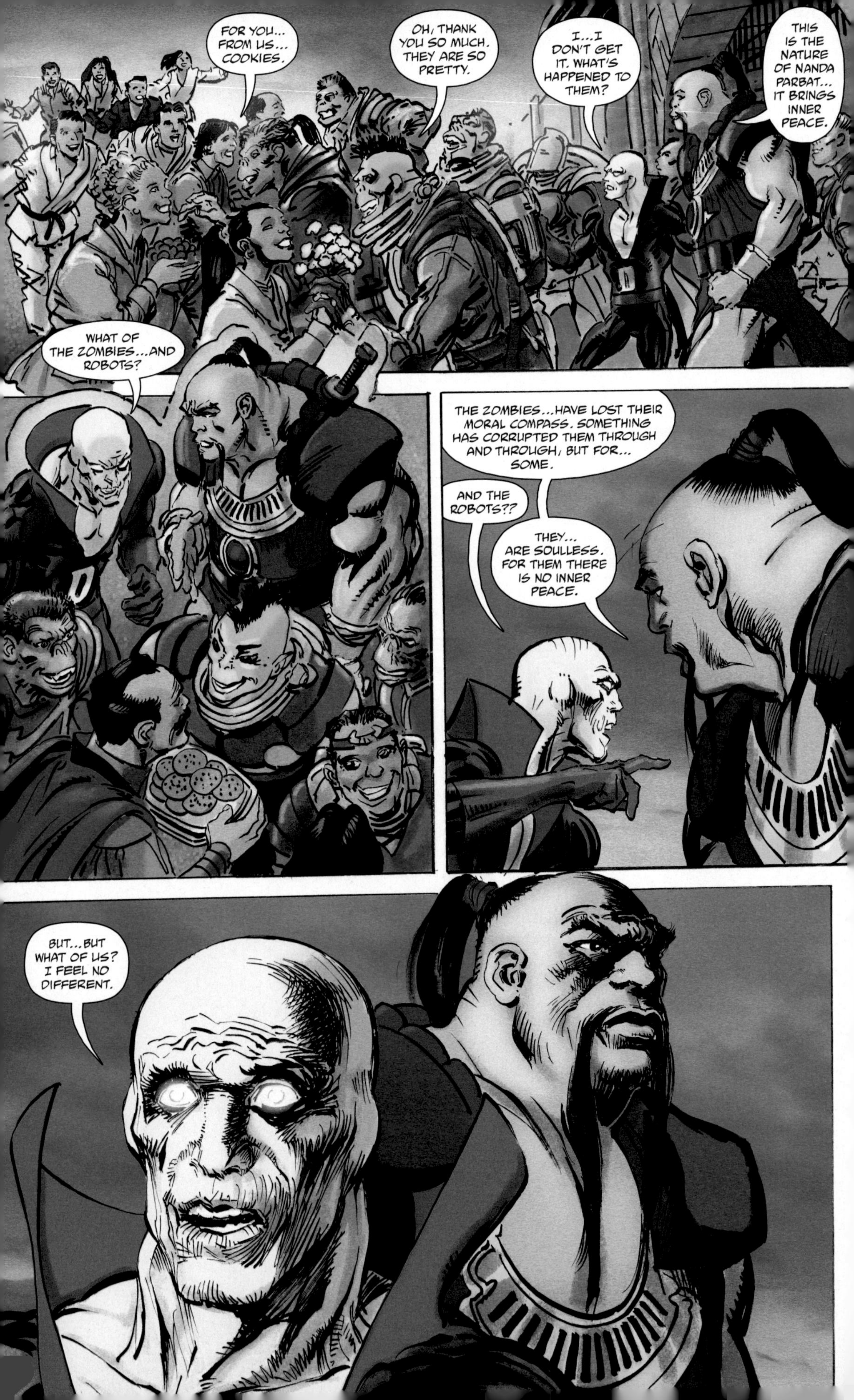
FOR YOU... FROM US... COOKIES.
OH, THANK YOU SO MUCH. THEY ARE SO PRETTY.
I...I DON'T GET IT. WHAT'S HAPPENED TO THEM?
THIS IS THE NATURE OF NANDA PARBAT... IT BRINGS INNER PEACE.
WHAT OF THE ZOMBIES...AND ROBOTS?
THE ZOMBIES...HAVE LOST THEIR MORAL COMPASS. SOMETHING HAS CORRUPTED THEM THROUGH AND THROUGH, BUT FOR... SOME.
AND THE ROBOTS??
THEY... ARE SOULLESS. FOR THEM THERE IS NO INNER PEACE.
BUT...BUT WHAT OF US? I FEEL NO DIFFERENT.

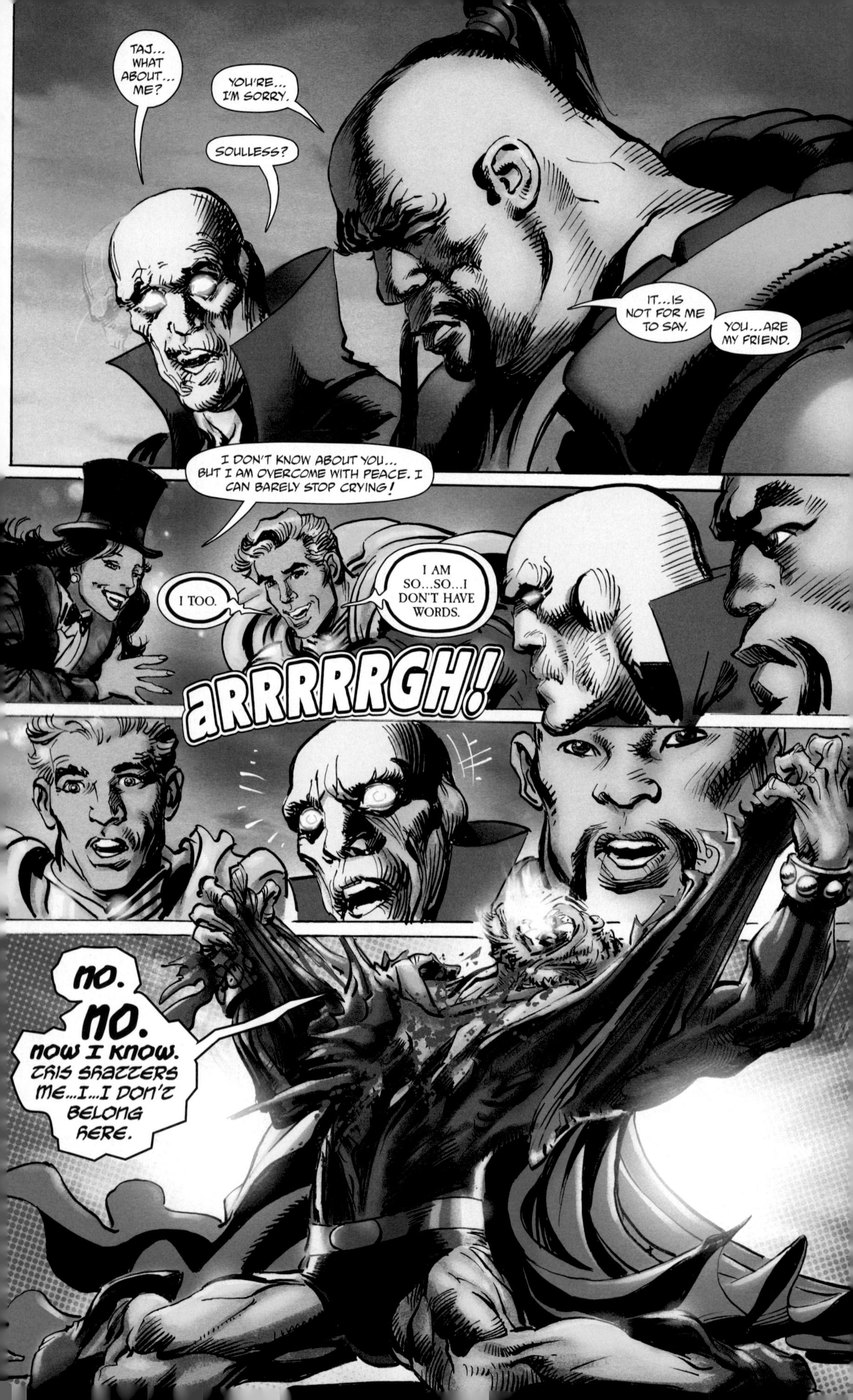
TAJ... WHAT ABOUT... ME?
YOU'RE... I'M SORRY.
SOULLESS?
IT...IS NOT FOR ME TO SAY.
YOU...ARE MY FRIEND.
I DON'T KNOW ABOUT YOU... BUT I AM OVERCOME WITH PEACE. I CAN BARELY STOP CRYING!
I TOO.
I AM SO...SO...I DON'T HAVE WORDS.
aRRRRRGH!
no. no. now I know. This shatters me...I...I don't belong here.

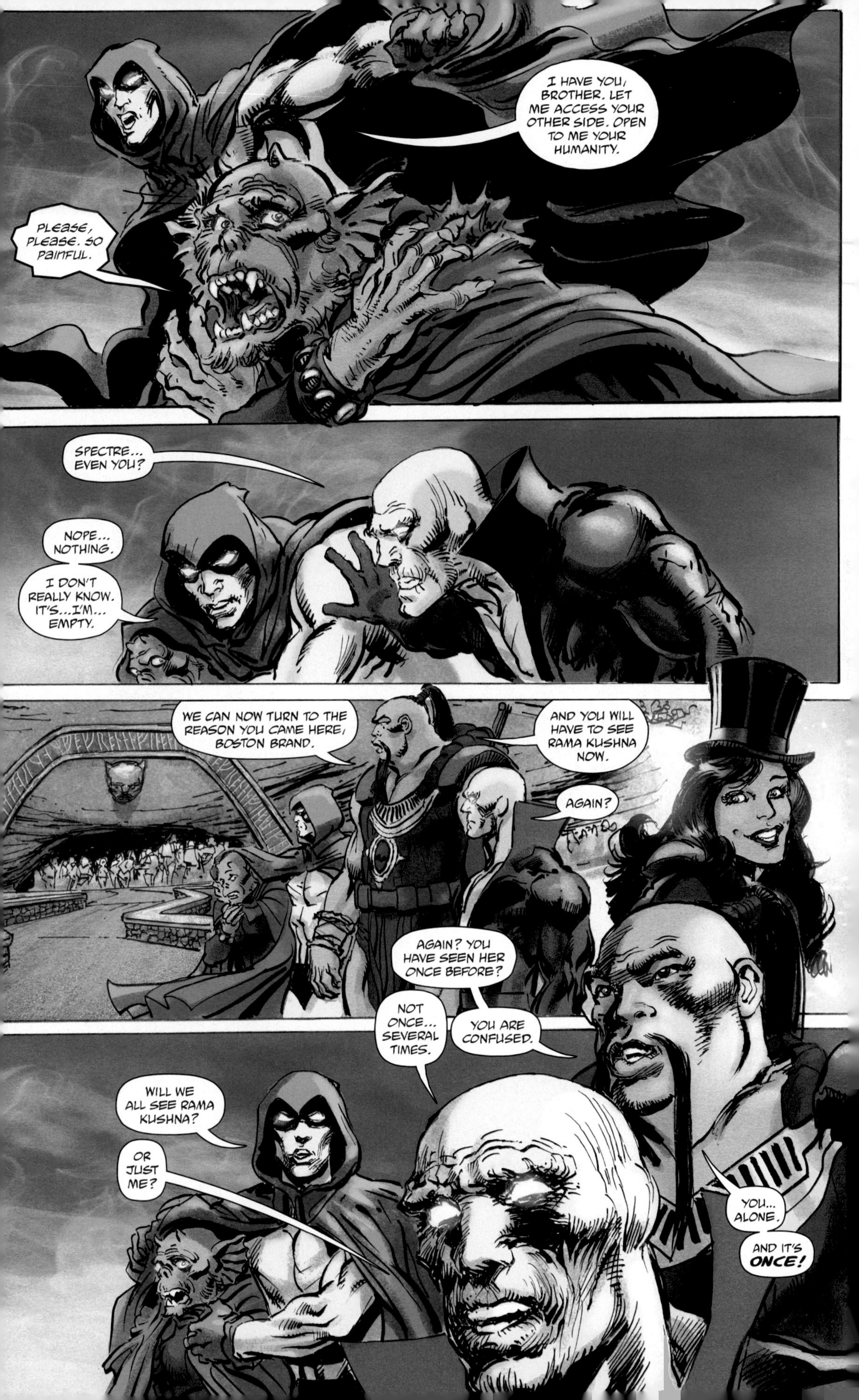
I HAVE YOU, BROTHER. LET ME ACCESS YOUR OTHER SIDE. OPEN TO ME YOUR HUMANITY.
PLEASE, PLEASE. SO PAINFUL.
SPECTRE... EVEN YOU?
NOPE... NOTHING.
I DON'T REALLY KNOW. IT'S...I'M... EMPTY.
WE CAN NOW TURN TO THE REASON YOU CAME HERE, BOSTON BRAND.
AND YOU WILL HAVE TO SEE RAMA KUSHNA NOW.
AGAIN?
AGAIN? YOU HAVE SEEN HER ONCE BEFORE?
NOT ONCE... SEVERAL TIMES.
YOU ARE CONFUSED.
WILL WE ALL SEE RAMA KUSHNA?
OR JUST ME?
YOU... ALONE.
AND IT'S ONCE!

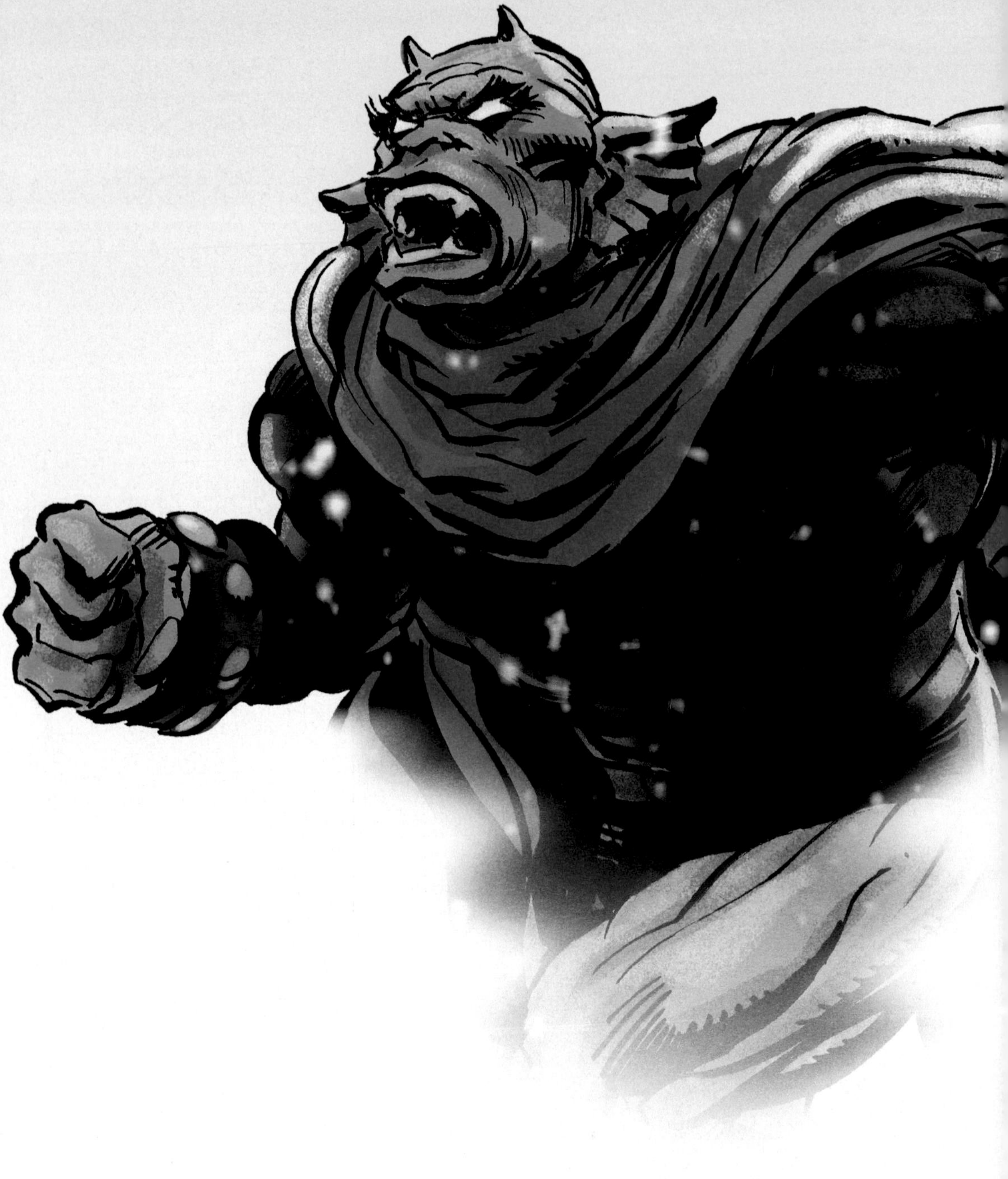

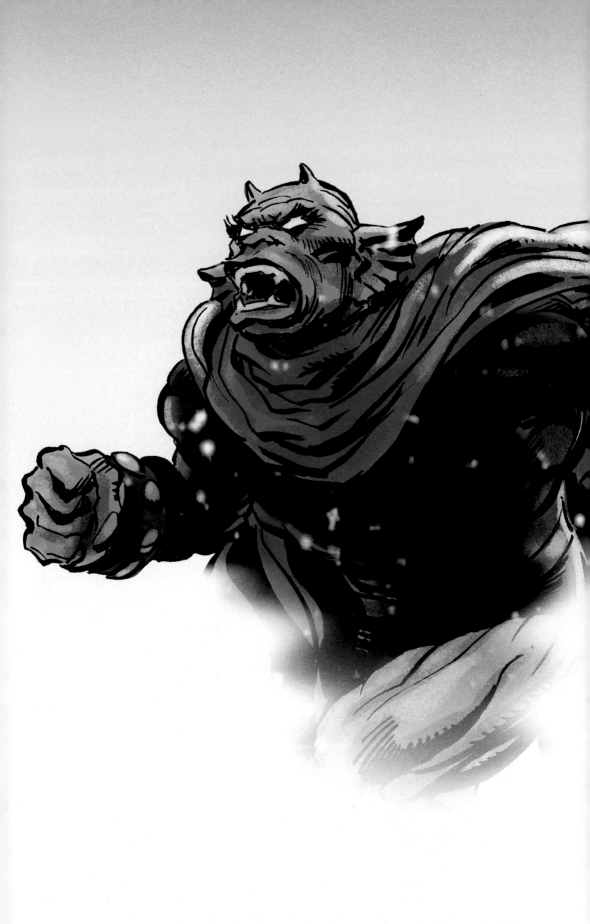

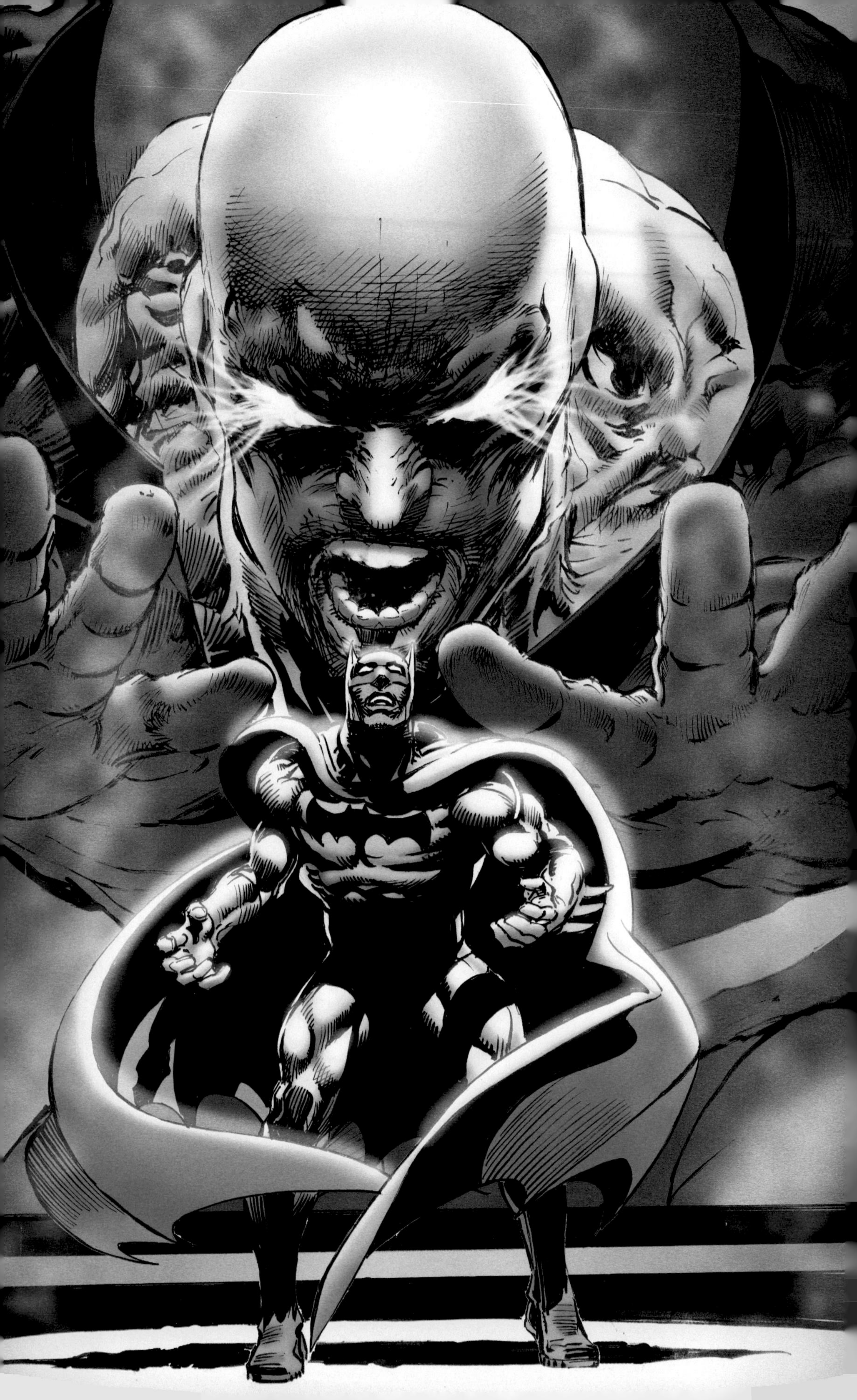

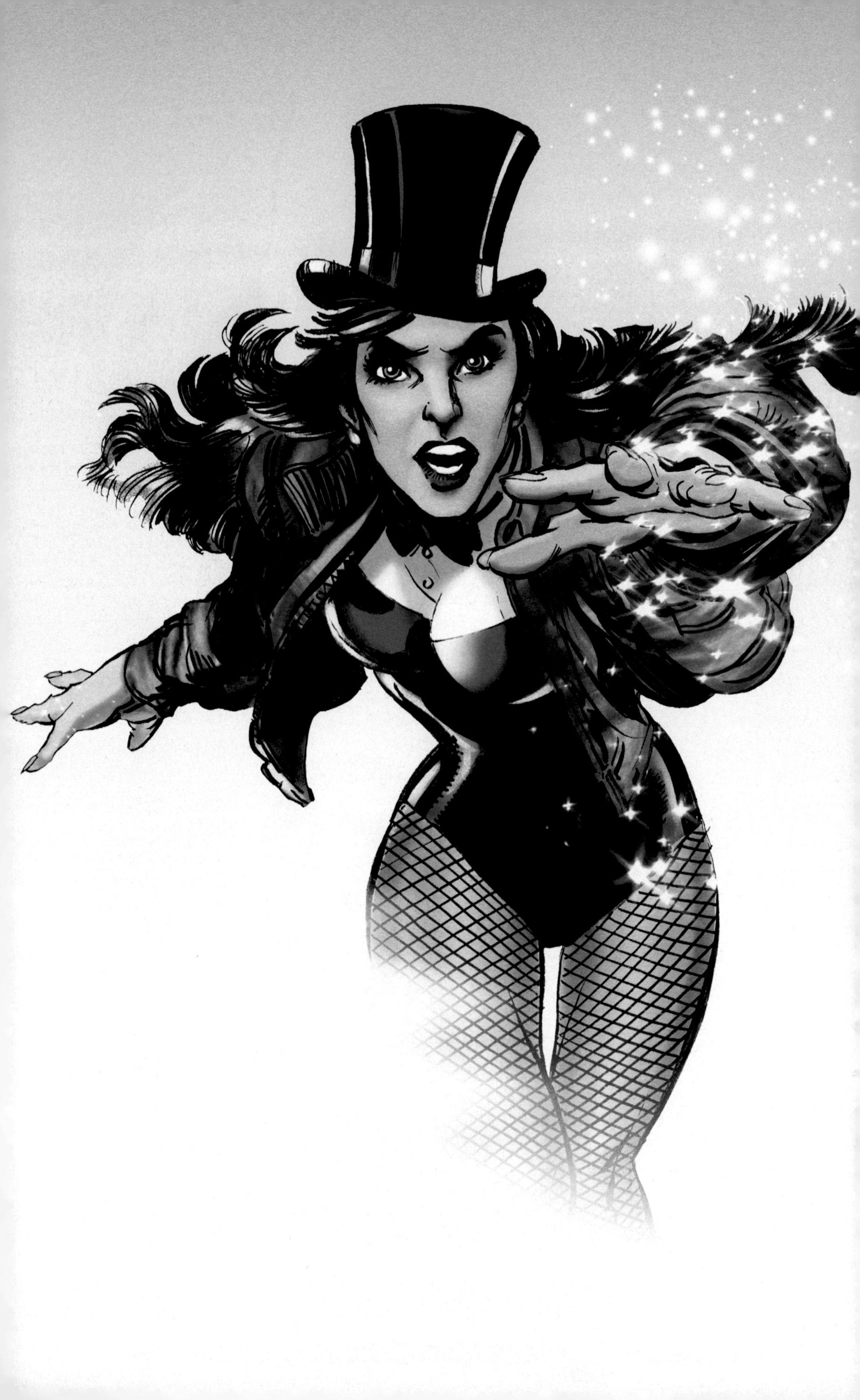

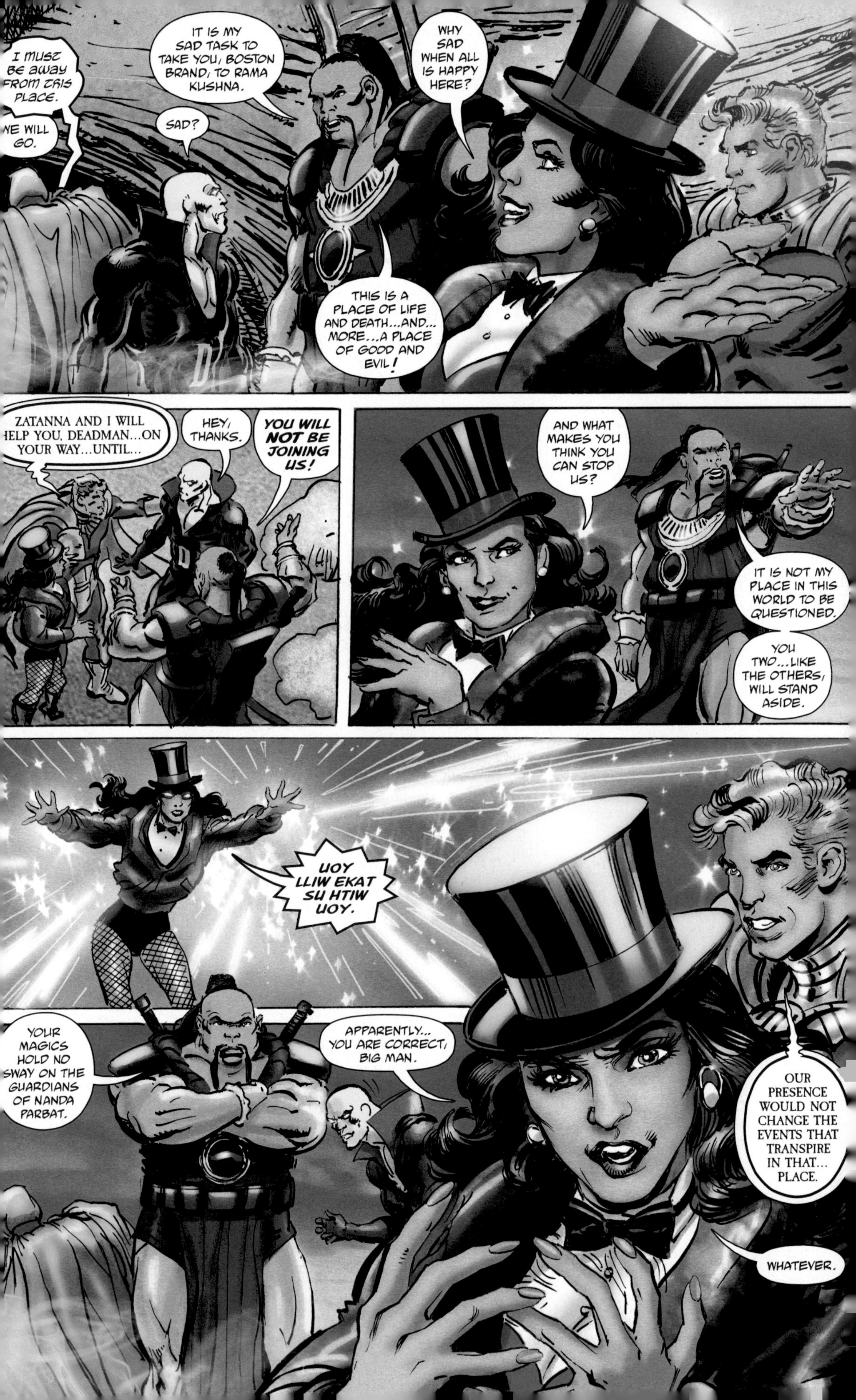

I MUST BE AWAY FROM THIS PLACE.
WE WILL GO.
IT IS MY SAD TASK TO TAKE YOU, BOSTON BRAND, TO RAMA KUSHNA.
SAD?
WHY SAD WHEN ALL IS HAPPY HERE?
THIS IS A PLACE OF LIFE AND DEATH...AND... MORE...A PLACE OF GOOD AND EVIL!
ZATANNA AND I WILL HELP YOU, DEADMAN...ON YOUR WAY...UNTIL...
HEY, THANKS.
YOU WILL NOT BE JOINING US!
AND WHAT MAKES YOU THINK YOU CAN STOP US?
IT IS NOT MY PLACE IN THIS WORLD TO BE QUESTIONED.
YOU TWO...LIKE THE OTHERS, WILL STAND ASIDE.
UOY LLIW EKAT SU HTIW UOY.
YOUR MAGICS HOLD NO SWAY ON THE GUARDIANS OF NANDA PARBAT.
APPARENTLY... YOU ARE CORRECT, BIG MAN.
OUR PRESENCE WOULD NOT CHANGE THE EVENTS TRANSPIRE IN THAT... PLACE.
WHATEVER.

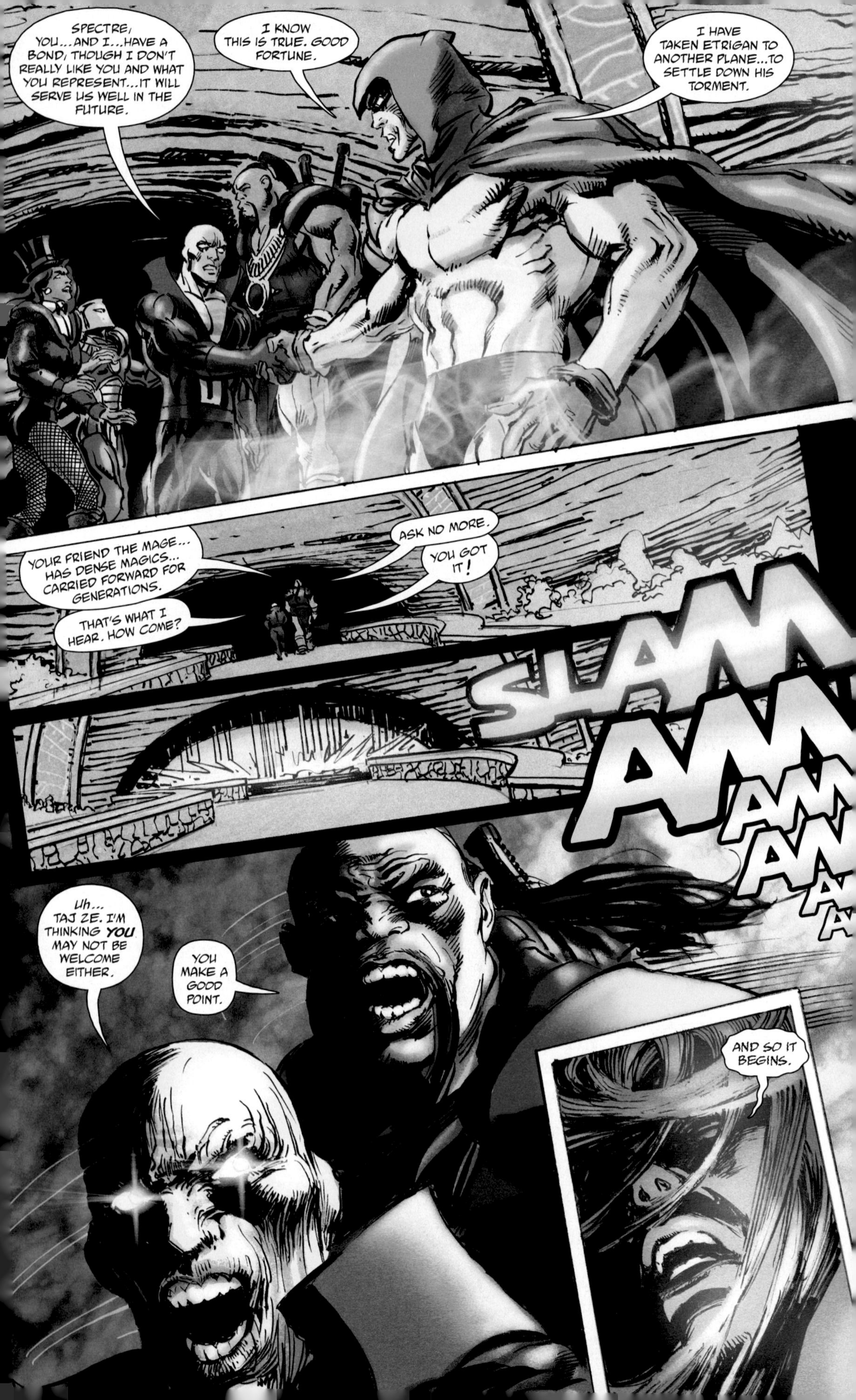
SPECTRE, YOU...AND I...HAVE A BOND, THOUGH I DON'T REALLY LIKE YOU AND WHAT YOU REPRESENT...IT WILL SERVE US WELL IN THE FUTURE.
I KNOW THIS IS TRUE. GOOD FORTUNE.
I HAVE TAKEN ETRIGAN TO ANOTHER PLANE...TO SETTLE DOWN HIS TORMENT.
YOUR FRIEND THE MAGE... HAS DENSE MAGICS... CARRIED FORWARD FOR GENERATIONS.
THAT'S WHAT I HEAR. HOW COME?
ASK NO MORE.
YOU GOT IT!
SLAAMAAAAA
Uh... TAJ ZE. I'M THINKING YOU MAY NOT BE WELCOME EITHER.
YOU MAKE A GOOD POINT.
AND SO IT BEGINS.

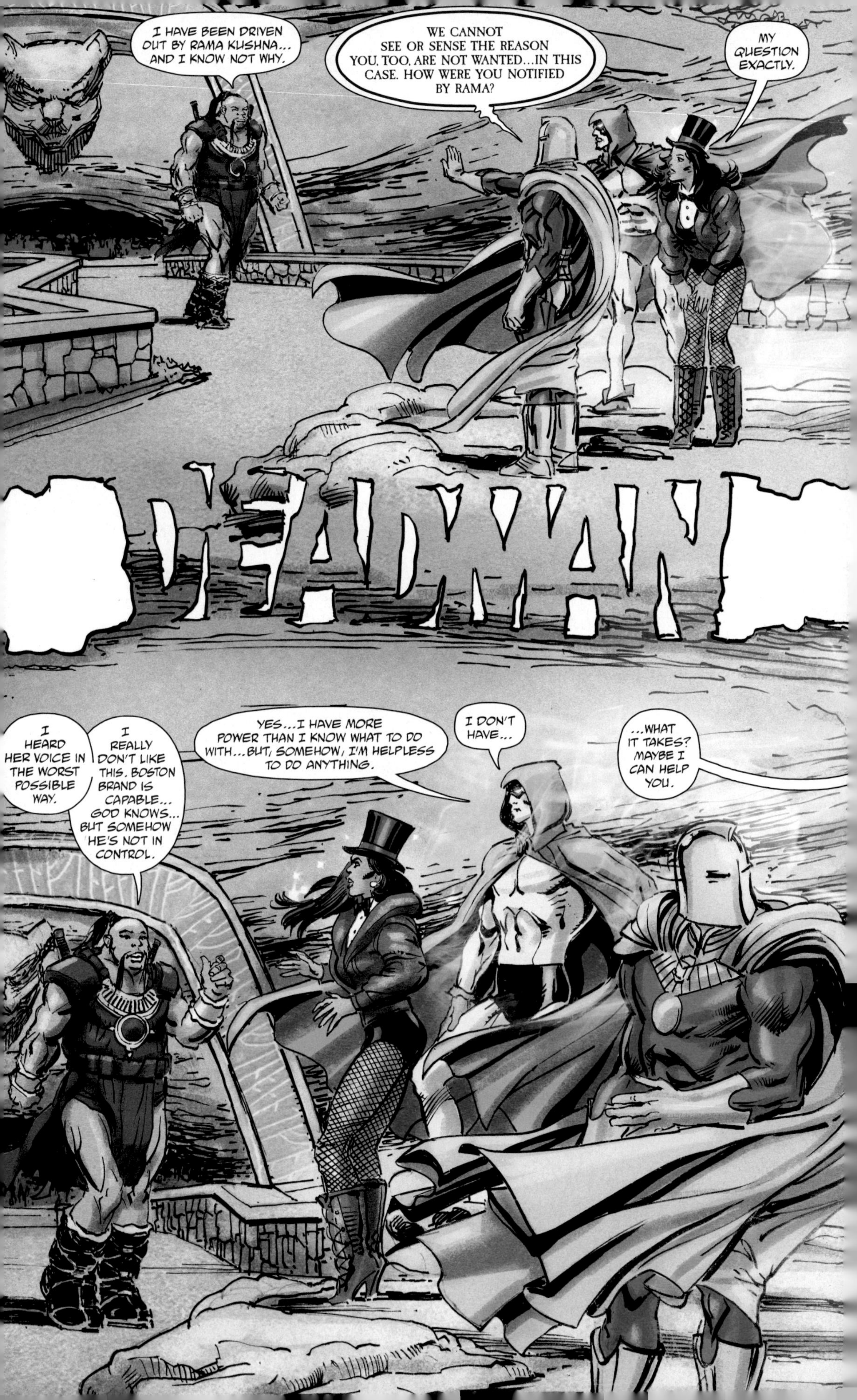
I HAVE BEEN DRIVEN OUT BY RAMA KUSHNA... AND I KNOW NOT WHY.
WE CANNOT SEE OR SENSE THE REASON YOU, TOO, ARE NOT WANTED...IN THIS CASE. HOW WERE YOU NOTIFIED BY RAMA?
MY QUESTION EXACTLY.
DEADMAN
I HEARD HER VOICE IN THE WORST POSSIBLE WAY.
I REALLY DON'T LIKE THIS. BOSTON BRAND IS CAPABLE... GOD KNOWS... BUT SOMEHOW HE'S NOT IN CONTROL.
YES...I HAVE MORE POWER THAN I KNOW WHAT TO DO WITH...BUT, SOMEHOW, I'M HELPLESS TO DO ANYTHING.
I DON'T HAVE...
...WHAT IT TAKES? MAYBE I CAN HELP YOU.

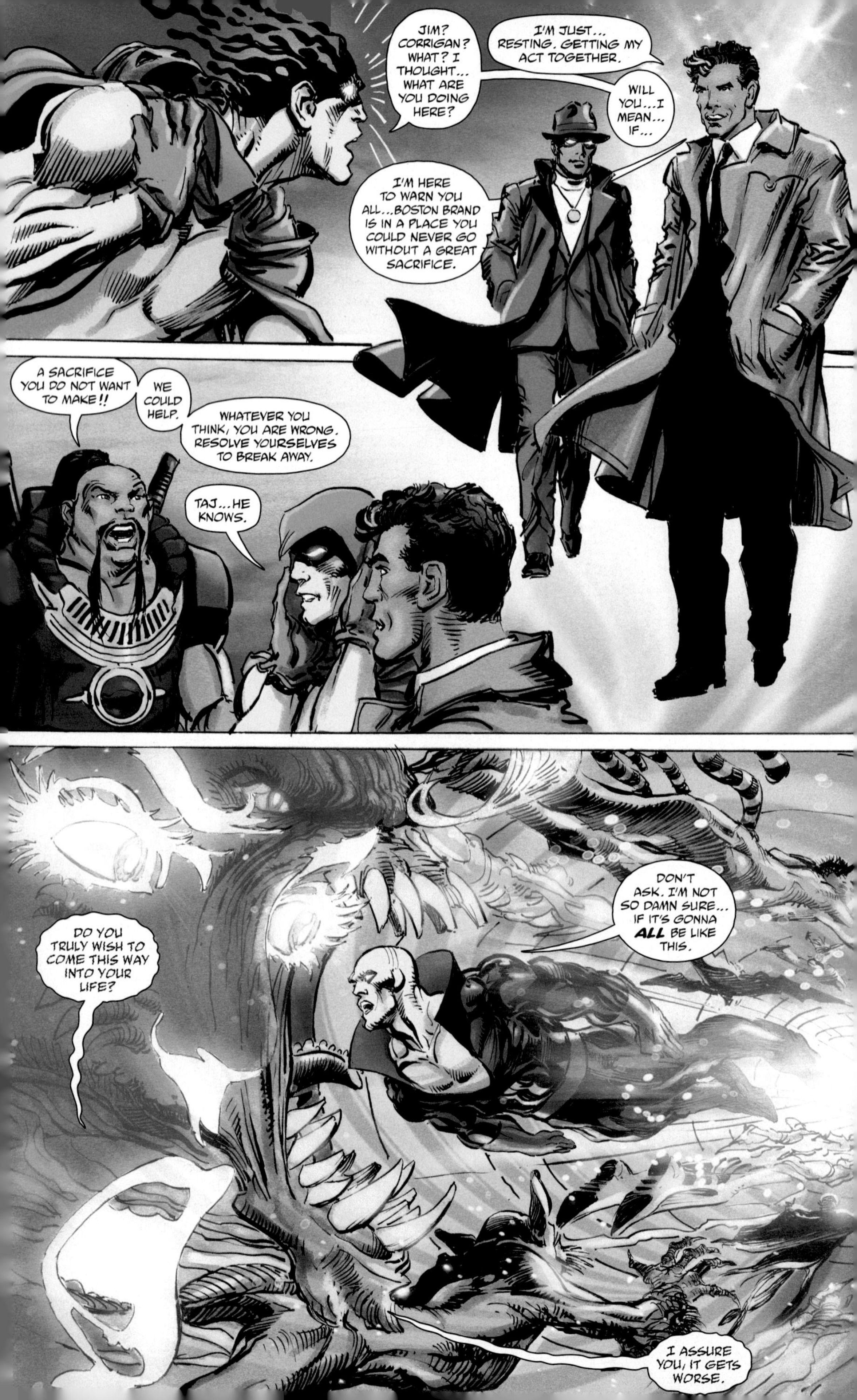
JIM? CORRIGAN? WHAT? I THOUGHT... WHAT ARE YOU DOING HERE?
I'M JUST... RESTING. GETTING MY ACT TOGETHER.
WILL YOU...I MEAN... IF...
I'M HERE TO WARN YOU ALL...BOSTON BRAND IS IN A PLACE YOU COULD NEVER GO WITHOUT A GREAT SACRIFICE.
A SACRIFICE YOU DO NOT WANT TO MAKE!!
WE COULD HELP.
WHATEVER YOU THINK, YOU ARE WRONG. RESOLVE YOURSELVES TO BREAK AWAY.
TAJ...HE KNOWS.
DO YOU TRULY WISH TO COME THIS WAY INTO YOUR LIFE?
DON'T ASK. I'M NOT SO DAMN SURE... IF IT'S GONNA **ALL** BE LIKE THIS.
I ASSURE YOU, IT GETS WORSE.

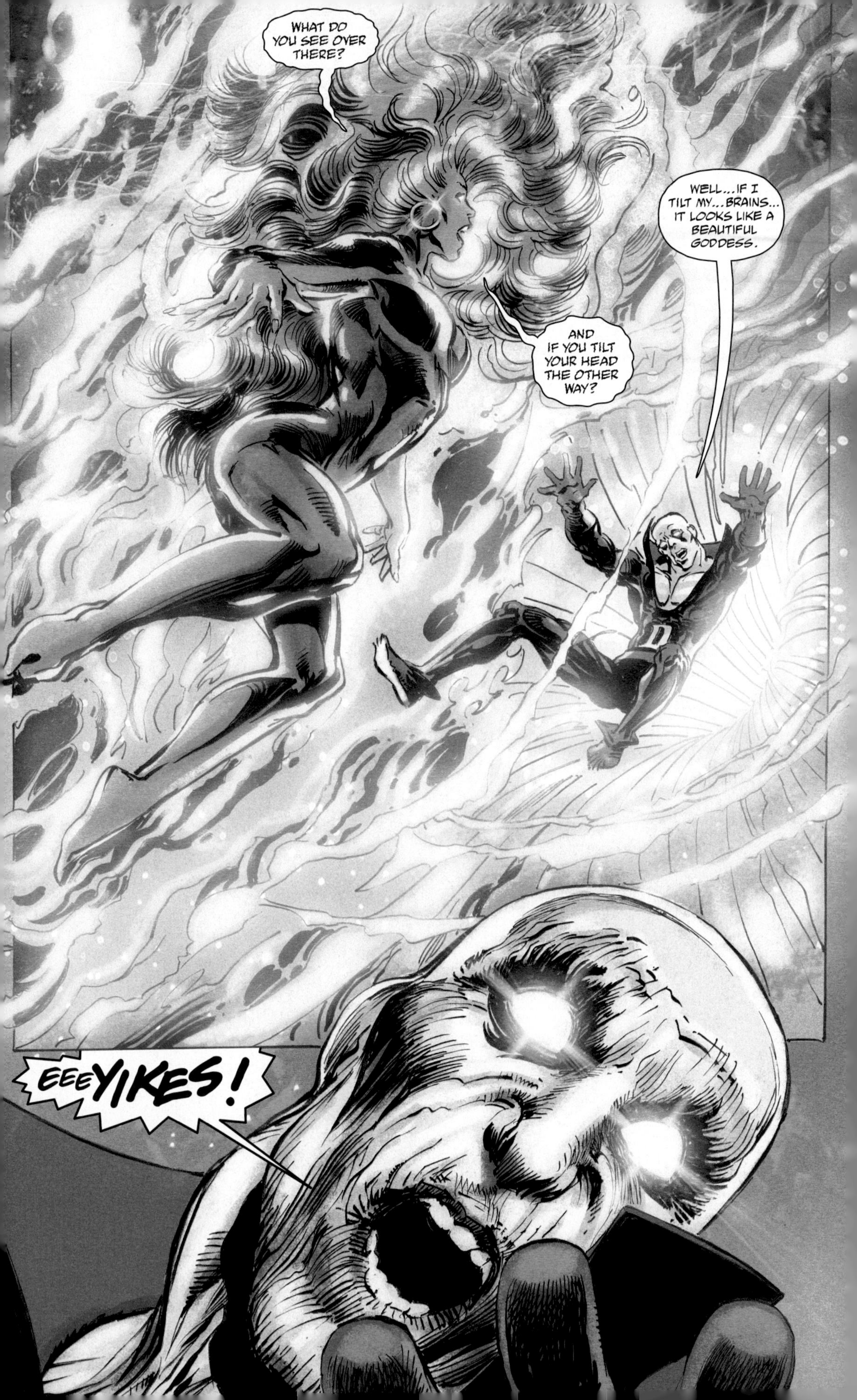
WHAT DO YOU SEE OVER THERE?
WELL...IF I TILT MY...BRAINS... IT LOOKS LIKE A BEAUTIFUL GODDESS.
AND IF YOU TILT YOUR HEAD THE OTHER WAY?
EEEYIKES!

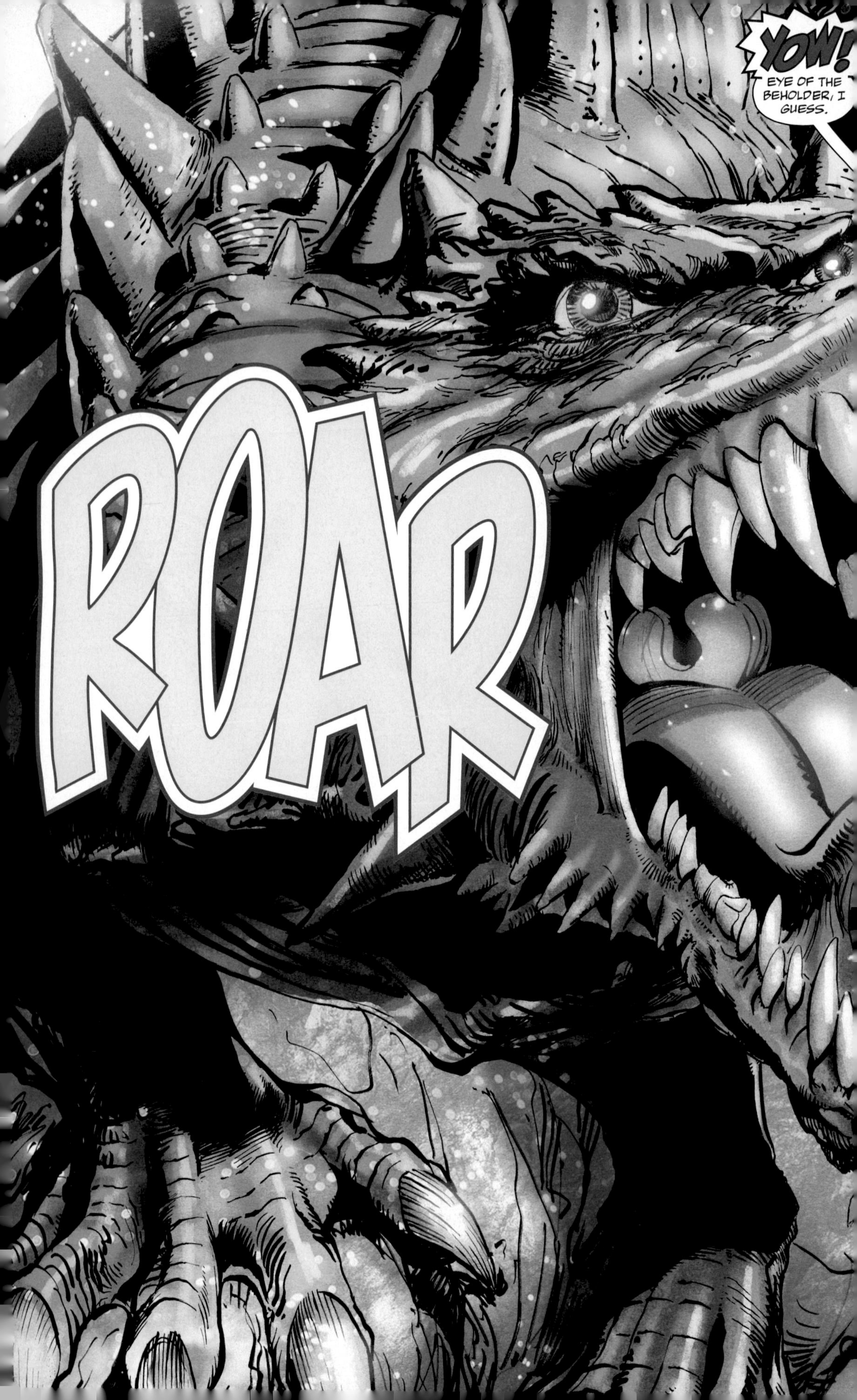
YOW!
EYE OF THE BEHOLDER, I GUESS.
ROAR

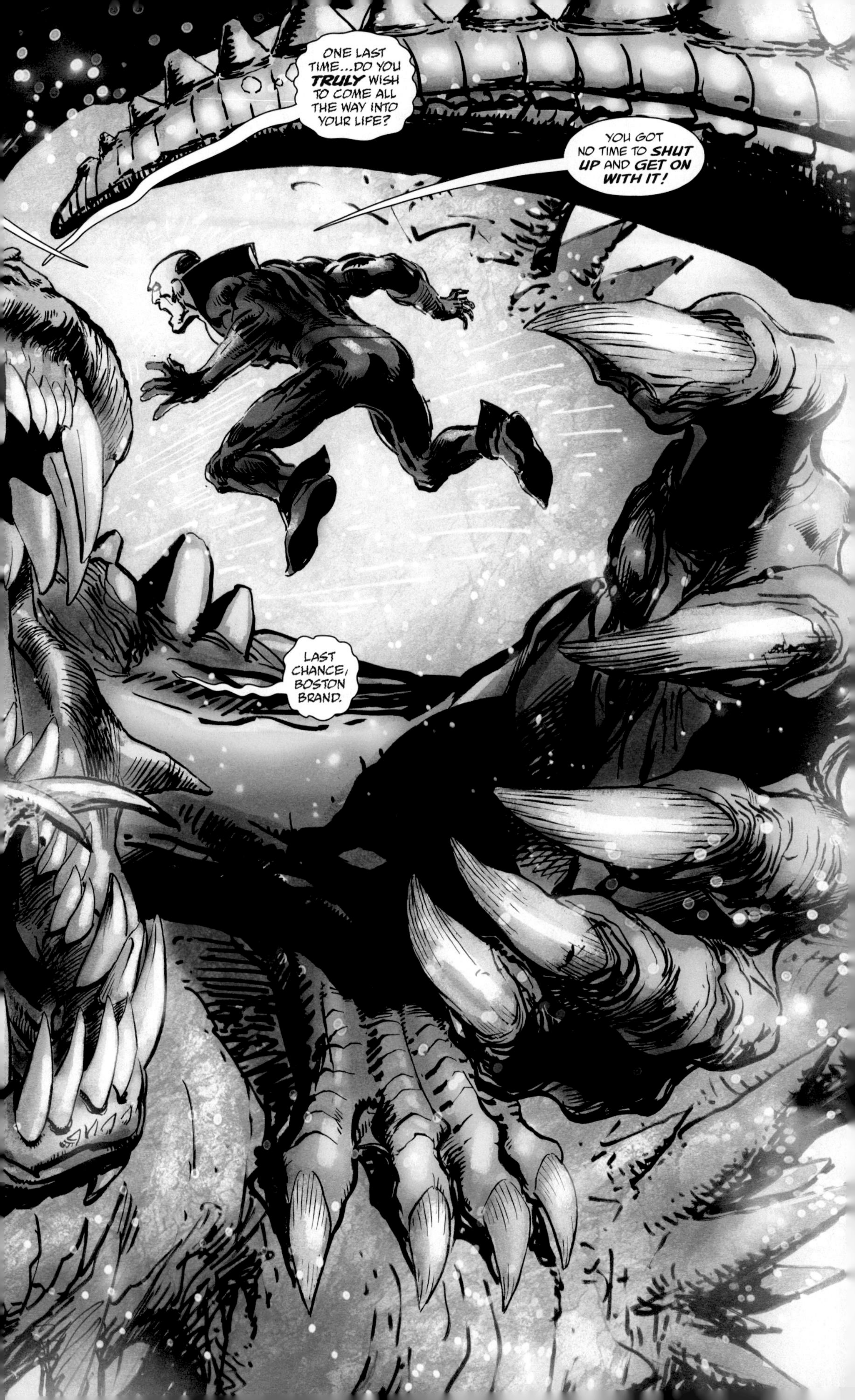
ONE LAST TIME...DO YOU TRULY WISH TO COME ALL THE WAY INTO YOUR LIFE?
YOU GOT NO TIME TO SHUT UP AND GET ON WITH IT!
LAST CHANCE, BOSTON BRAND.

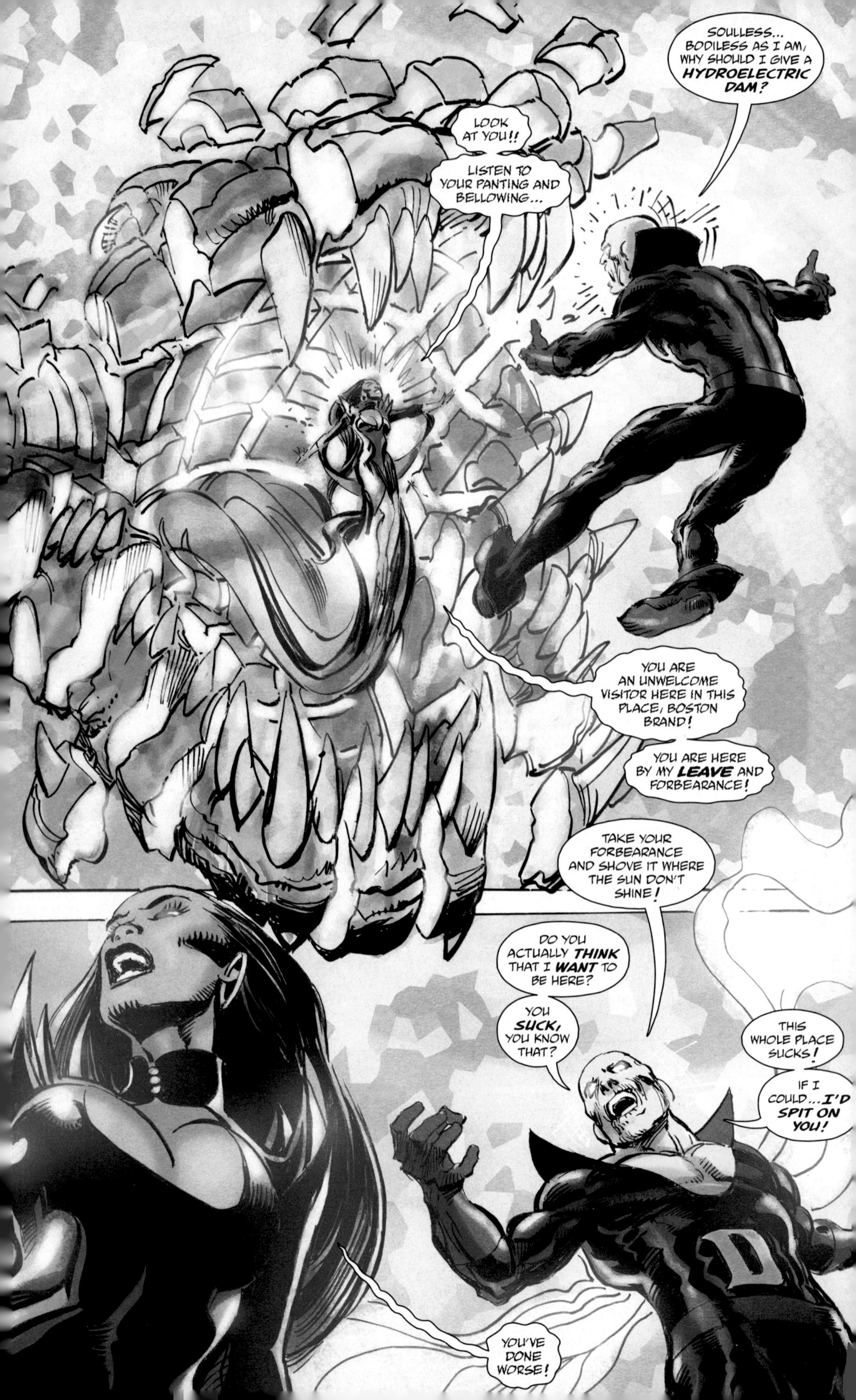

SOULLESS... BODILESS AS I AM, WHY SHOULD I GIVE A **HYDROELECTRIC DAM?**
LOOK AT YOU!!
LISTEN TO YOUR PANTING AND BELLOWING...
YOU ARE AN UNWELCOME VISITOR HERE IN THIS PLACE, BOSTON BRAND!
YOU ARE HERE BY MY **LEAVE** AND FORBEARANCE!
TAKE YOUR FORBEARANCE AND SHOVE IT WHERE THE SUN DON'T SHINE!
DO YOU ACTUALLY **THINK** THAT I **WANT** TO BE HERE?
YOU **SUCK,** YOU KNOW THAT?
THIS WHOLE PLACE SUCKS!
IF I COULD...**I'D SPIT ON YOU!**
YOU'VE DONE WORSE!

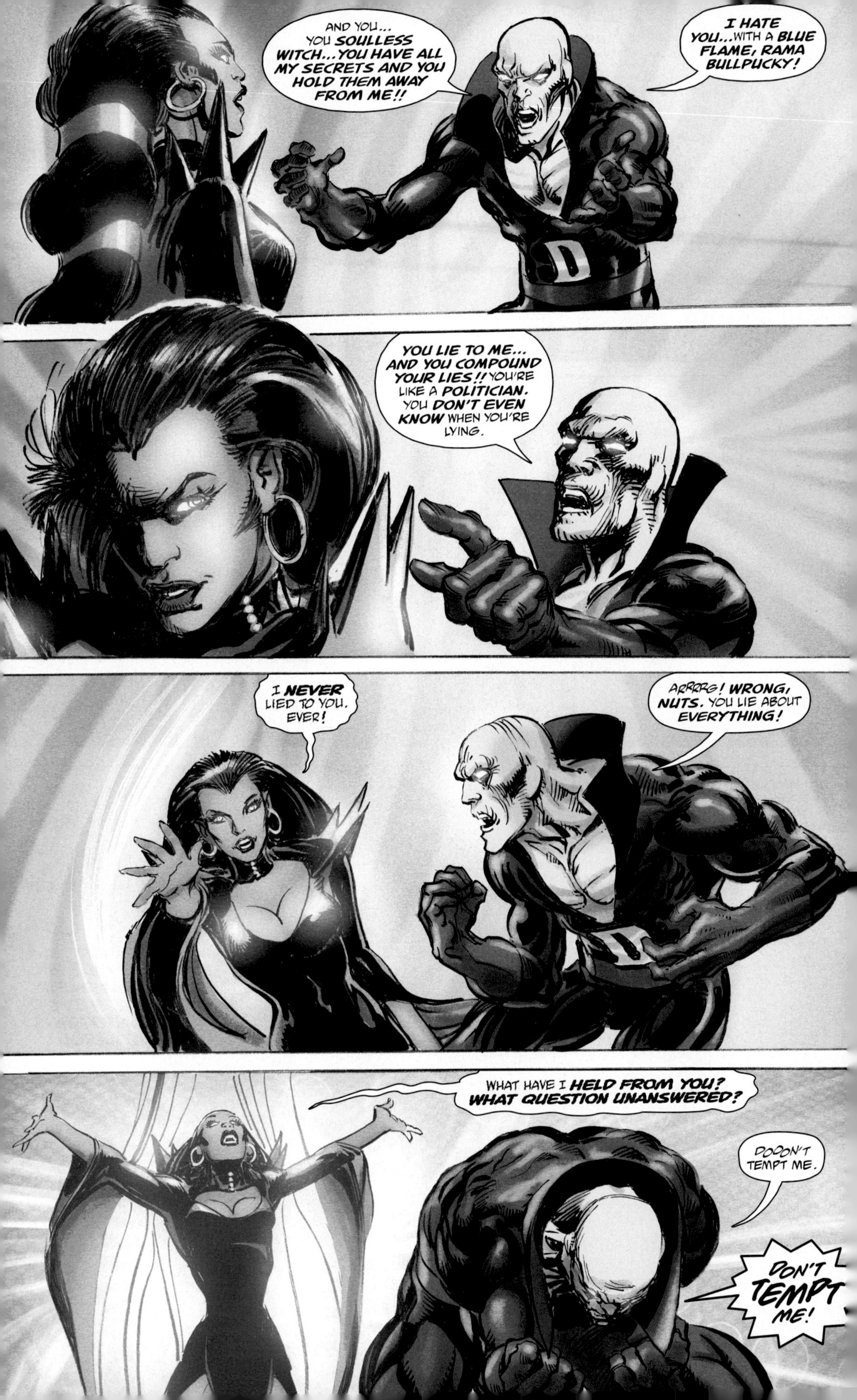
AND YOU... YOU SOULLESS WITCH...YOU HAVE ALL MY SECRETS AND YOU HOLD THEM AWAY FROM ME!!
I HATE YOU...WITH A BLUE FLAME, RAMA BULLPUCKY!
YOU LIE TO ME... AND YOU COMPOUND YOUR LIES!! YOU'RE LIKE A POLITICIAN. YOU DON'T EVEN KNOW WHEN YOU'RE LYING.
I NEVER LIED TO YOU. EVER!
ARRRRG! WRONG, NUTS. YOU LIE ABOUT EVERYTHING!
WHAT HAVE I HELD FROM YOU? WHAT QUESTION UNANSWERED?
DOOON'T TEMPT ME.
DON'T TEMPT ME!

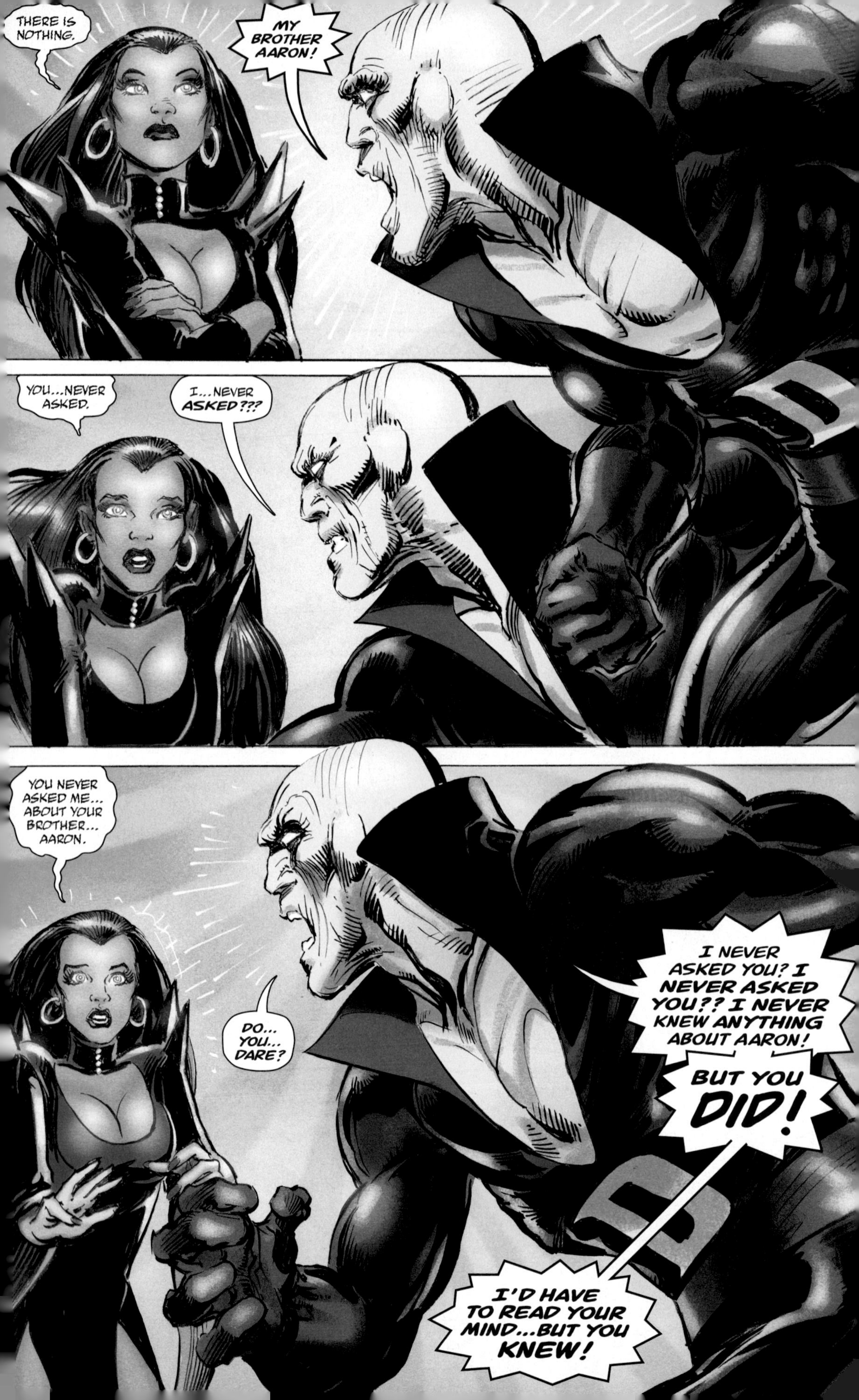
THERE IS NOTHING.
MY BROTHER AARON!
YOU...NEVER ASKED.
I...NEVER ASKED???
YOU NEVER ASKED ME... ABOUT YOUR BROTHER... AARON.
DO... YOU... DARE?
I NEVER ASKED YOU? I NEVER ASKED YOU?? I NEVER KNEW ANYTHING ABOUT AARON!
BUT YOU DID!
I'D HAVE TO READ YOUR MIND...BUT YOU KNEW!

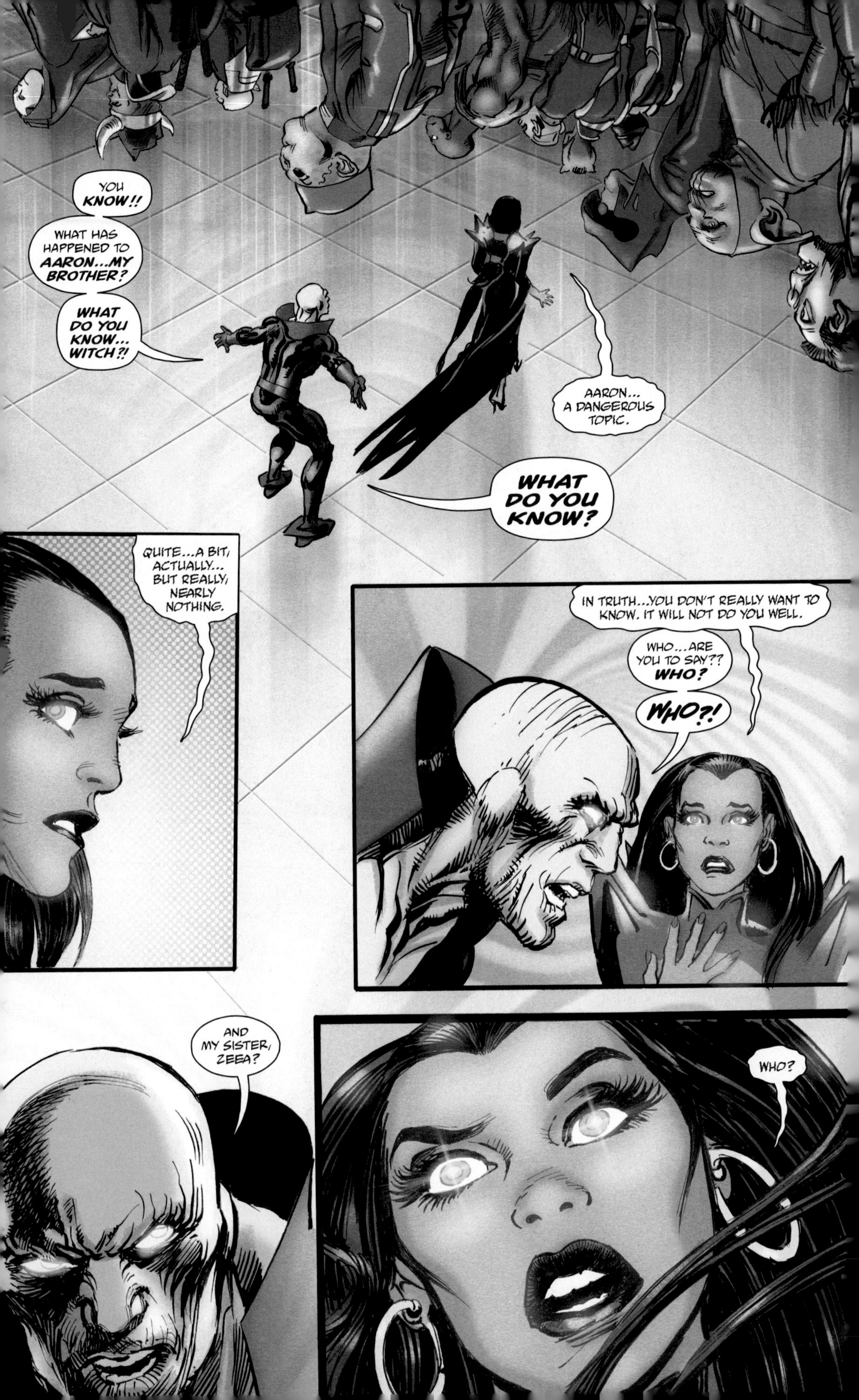
YOU KNOW!!
WHAT HAS HAPPENED TO AARON...MY BROTHER?
WHAT DO YOU KNOW... WITCH?!
AARON... A DANGEROUS TOPIC.
WHAT DO YOU KNOW?
QUITE...A BIT, ACTUALLY... BUT REALLY, NEARLY NOTHING.
IN TRUTH...YOU DON'T REALLY WANT TO KNOW. IT WILL NOT DO YOU WELL.
WHO...ARE YOU TO SAY?? WHO?
WHO?!
AND MY SISTER, ZEEA?
WHO?

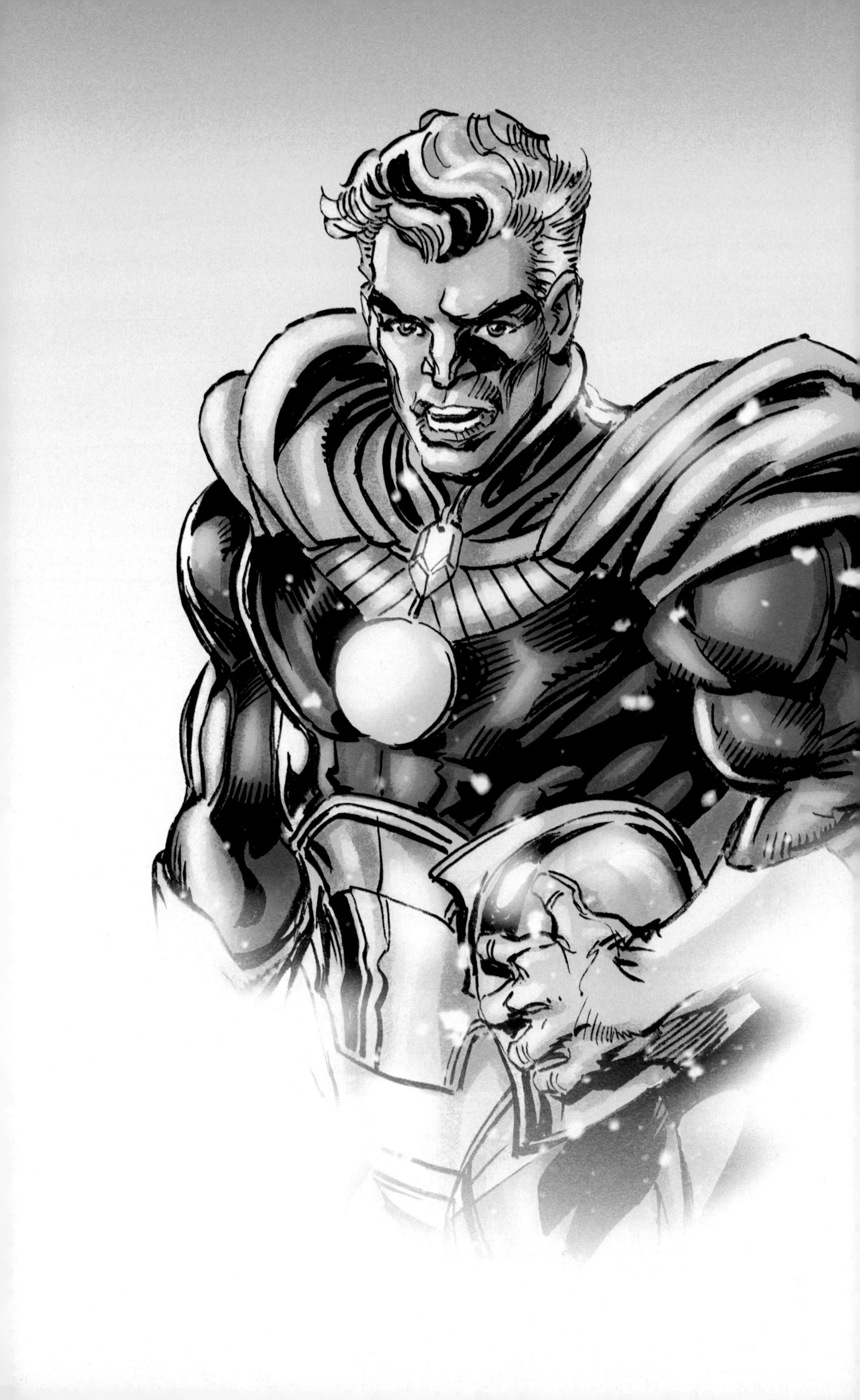

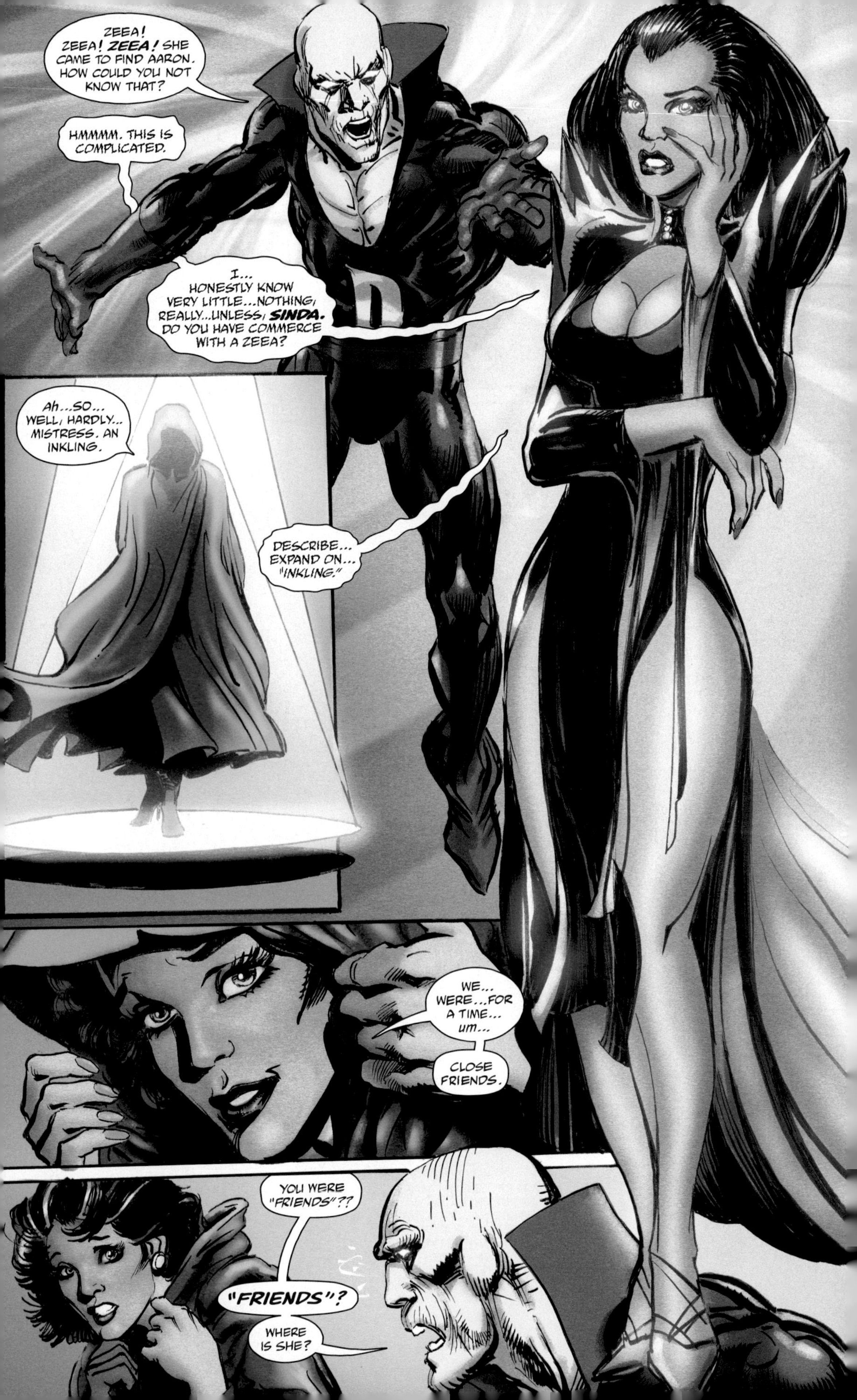
ZEEA! ZEEA! **ZEEA!** SHE CAME TO FIND AARON. HOW COULD YOU NOT KNOW THAT?
HMMMM. THIS IS COMPLICATED.
I... HONESTLY KNOW VERY LITTLE...NOTHING, REALLY...UNLESS, **SINDA.** DO YOU HAVE COMMERCE WITH A ZEEA?
Ah...SO... WELL, HARDLY... MISTRESS. AN INKLING.
DESCRIBE... EXPAND ON... "INKLING."
WE... WERE...FOR A TIME... um...
CLOSE FRIENDS.
YOU WERE "FRIENDS"??
"FRIENDS"?
WHERE IS SHE?

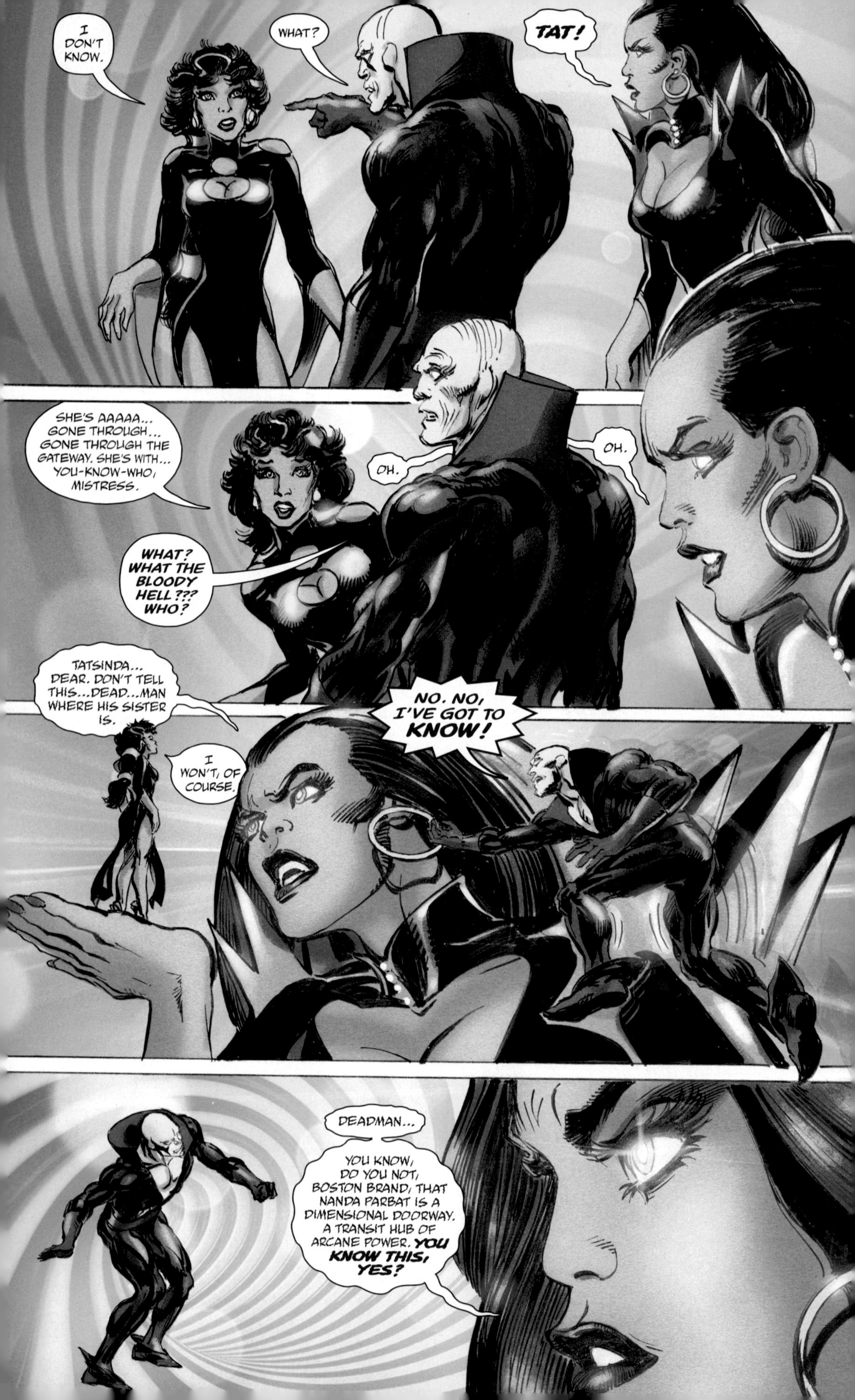
I DON'T KNOW.
WHAT?
TAT!
SHE'S AAAAA... GONE THROUGH... GONE THROUGH THE GATEWAY. SHE'S WITH... YOU-KNOW-WHO, MISTRESS.
OH.
OH.
WHAT? WHAT THE BLOODY HELL??? WHO?
TATSINDA... DEAR. DON'T TELL THIS...DEAD...MAN WHERE HIS SISTER IS.
I WON'T, OF COURSE.
NO. NO, I'VE GOT TO KNOW!
DEADMAN...
YOU KNOW, DO YOU NOT, BOSTON BRAND, THAT NANDA PARBAT IS A DIMENSIONAL DOORWAY. A TRANSIT HUB OF ARCANE POWER. YOU KNOW THIS, YES?

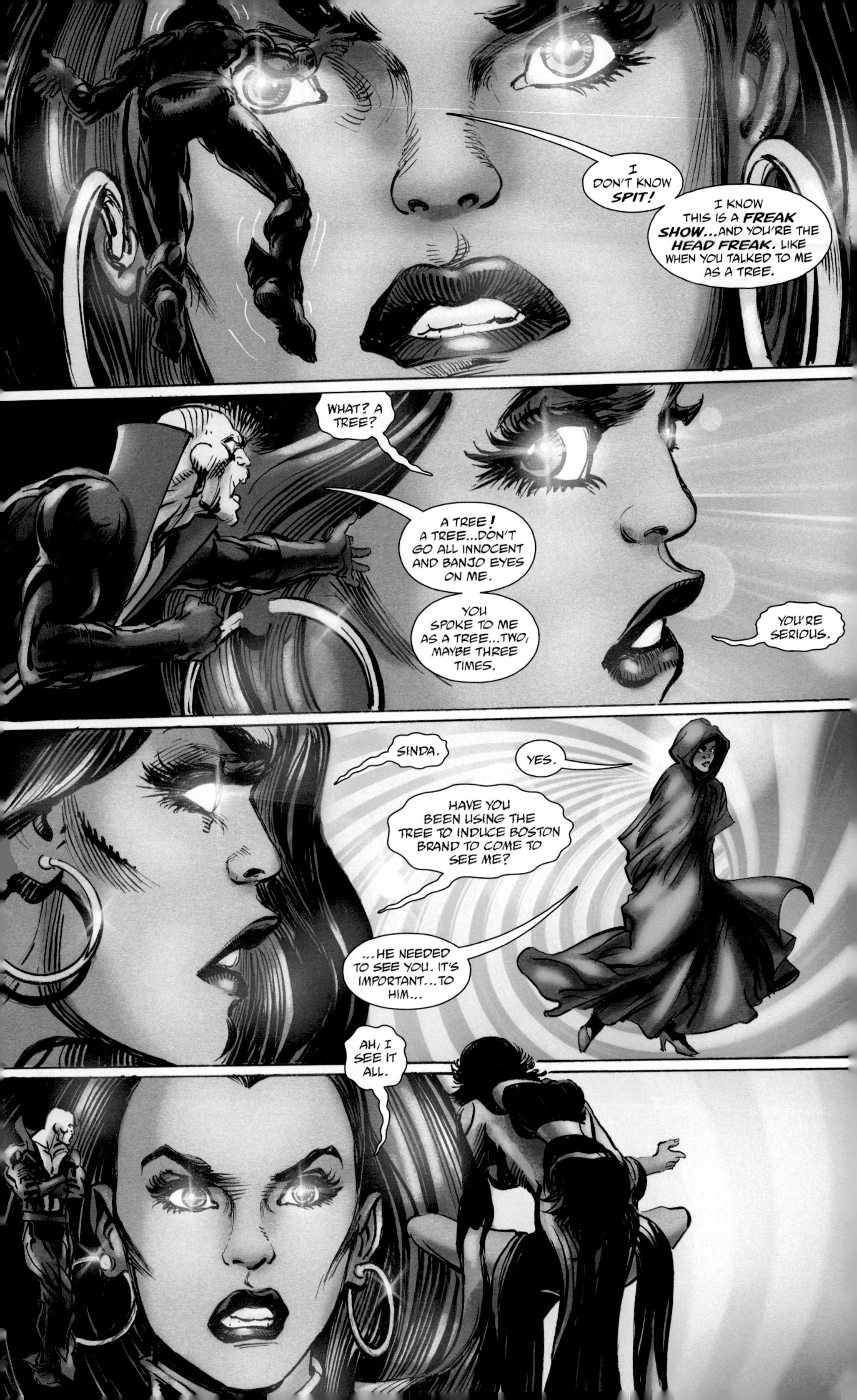
I DON'T KNOW SPIT!
I KNOW THIS IS A FREAK SHOW...AND YOU'RE THE HEAD FREAK. LIKE WHEN YOU TALKED TO ME AS A TREE.
WHAT? A TREE?
A TREE! A TREE...DON'T GO ALL INNOCENT AND BANJO EYES ON ME.
YOU SPOKE TO ME AS A TREE...TWO, MAYBE THREE TIMES.
YOU'RE SERIOUS.
SINDA.
YES.
HAVE YOU BEEN USING THE TREE TO INDUCE BOSTON BRAND TO COME TO SEE ME?
...HE NEEDED TO SEE YOU. IT'S IMPORTANT...TO HIM...
AH, I SEE IT ALL.

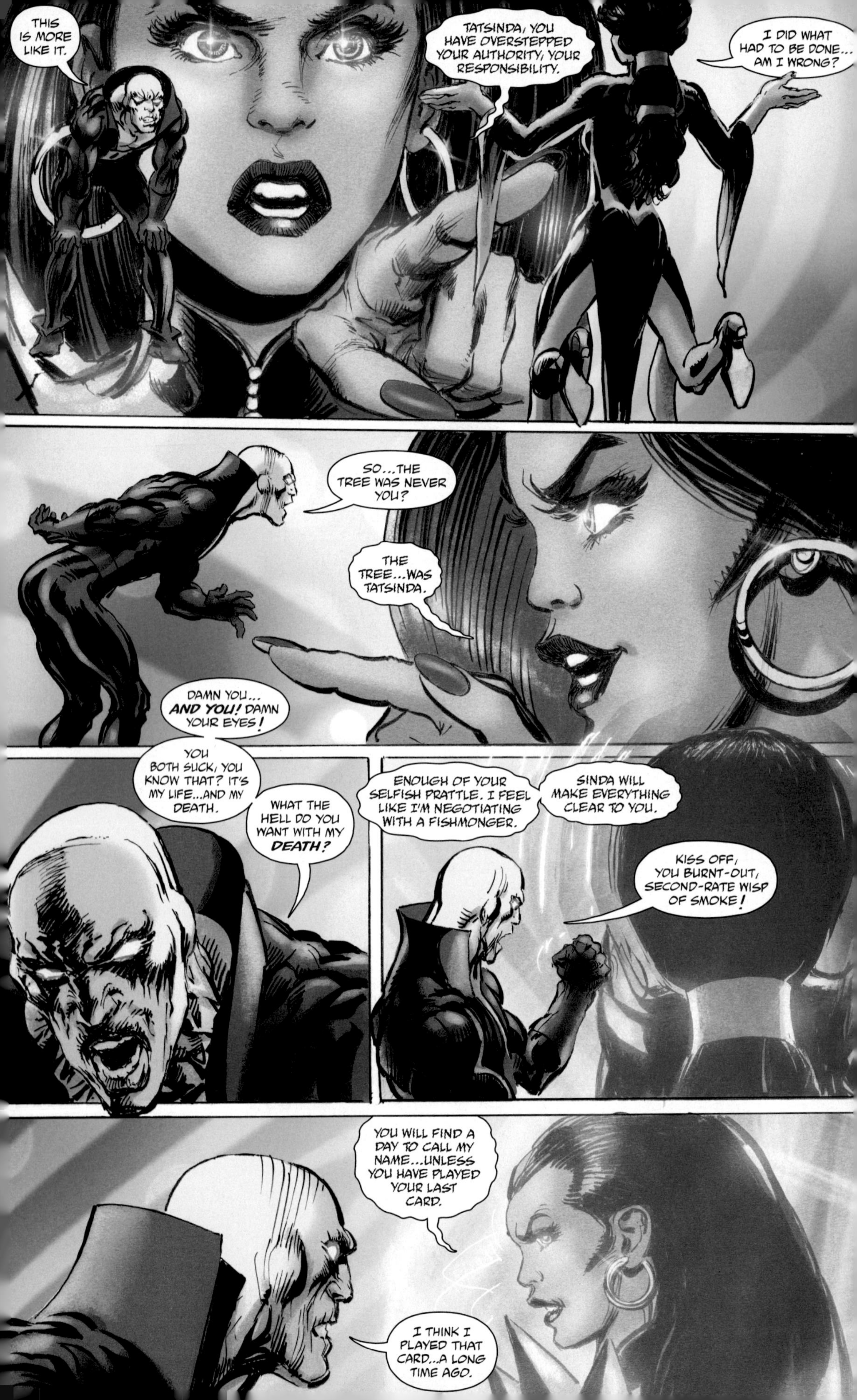
THIS IS MORE LIKE IT.
TATSINDA, YOU HAVE OVERSTEPPED YOUR AUTHORITY, YOUR RESPONSIBILITY.
I DID WHAT HAD TO BE DONE... AM I WRONG?
SO...THE TREE WAS NEVER YOU?
THE TREE...WAS TATSINDA.
DAMN YOU... AND YOU! DAMN YOUR EYES!
YOU BOTH SUCK, YOU KNOW THAT? IT'S MY LIFE...AND MY DEATH.
WHAT THE HELL DO YOU WANT WITH MY DEATH?
ENOUGH OF YOUR SELFISH PRATTLE. I FEEL LIKE I'M NEGOTIATING WITH A FISHMONGER.
SINDA WILL MAKE EVERYTHING CLEAR TO YOU.
KISS OFF, YOU BURNT-OUT, SECOND-RATE WISP OF SMOKE!
YOU WILL FIND A DAY TO CALL MY NAME...UNLESS YOU HAVE PLAYED YOUR LAST CARD.
I THINK I PLAYED THAT CARD...A LONG TIME AGO.

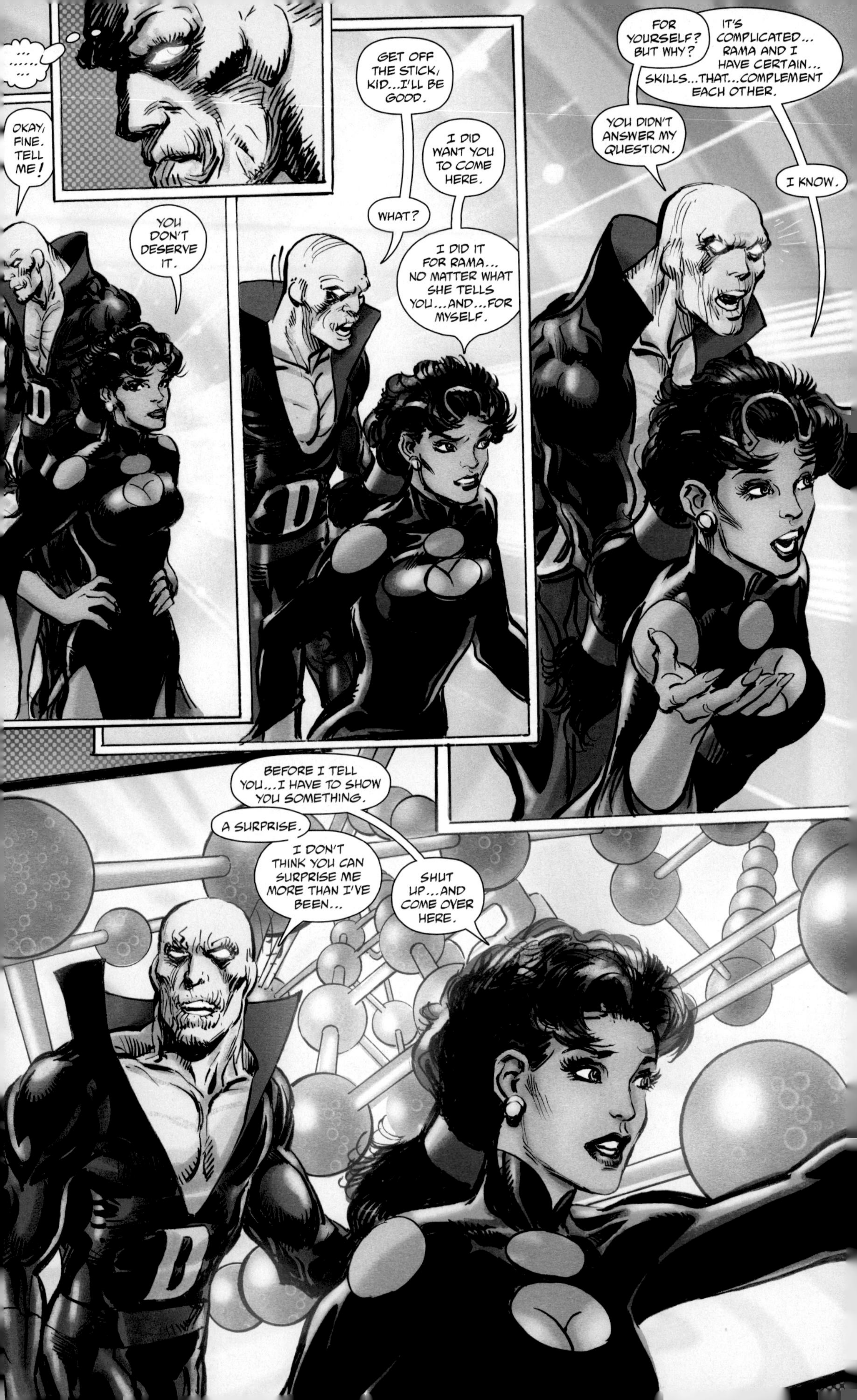
...
......
...
OKAY, FINE. TELL ME!
YOU DON'T DESERVE IT.
GET OFF THE STICK, KID...I'LL BE GOOD.
WHAT?
I DID WANT YOU TO COME HERE.
I DID IT FOR RAMA... NO MATTER WHAT SHE TELLS YOU...AND...FOR MYSELF.
FOR YOURSELF? BUT WHY?
IT'S COMPLICATED... RAMA AND I HAVE CERTAIN... SKILLS...THAT...COMPLEMENT EACH OTHER.
YOU DIDN'T ANSWER MY QUESTION.
I KNOW.
BEFORE I TELL YOU...I HAVE TO SHOW YOU SOMETHING.
A SURPRISE.
I DON'T THINK YOU CAN SURPRISE ME MORE THAN I'VE BEEN...
SHUT UP...AND COME OVER HERE.

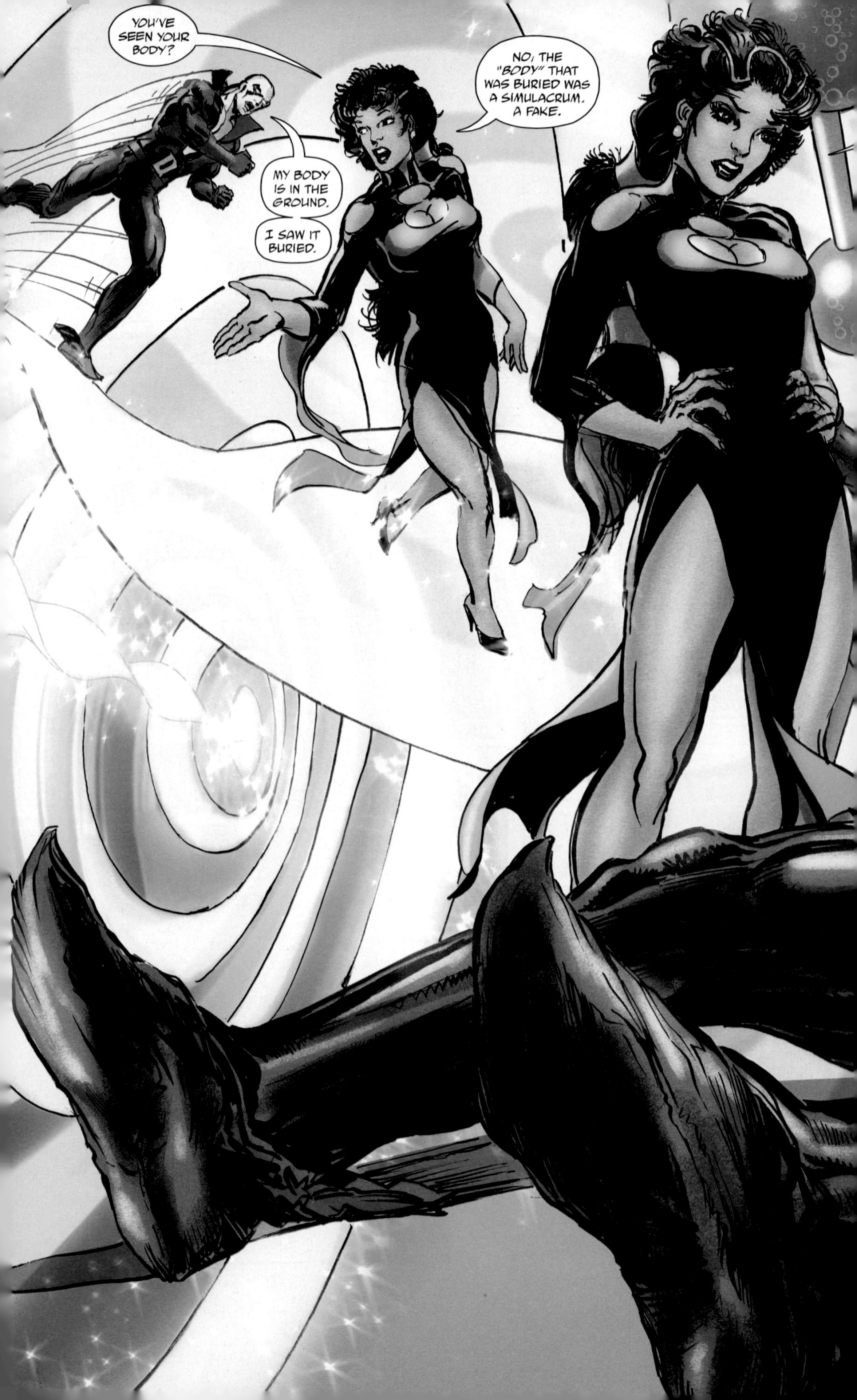
YOU'VE SEEN YOUR BODY?
MY BODY IS IN THE GROUND.
I SAW IT BURIED.
NO, THE "BODY" THAT WAS BURIED WAS A SIMULACRUM. A FAKE.

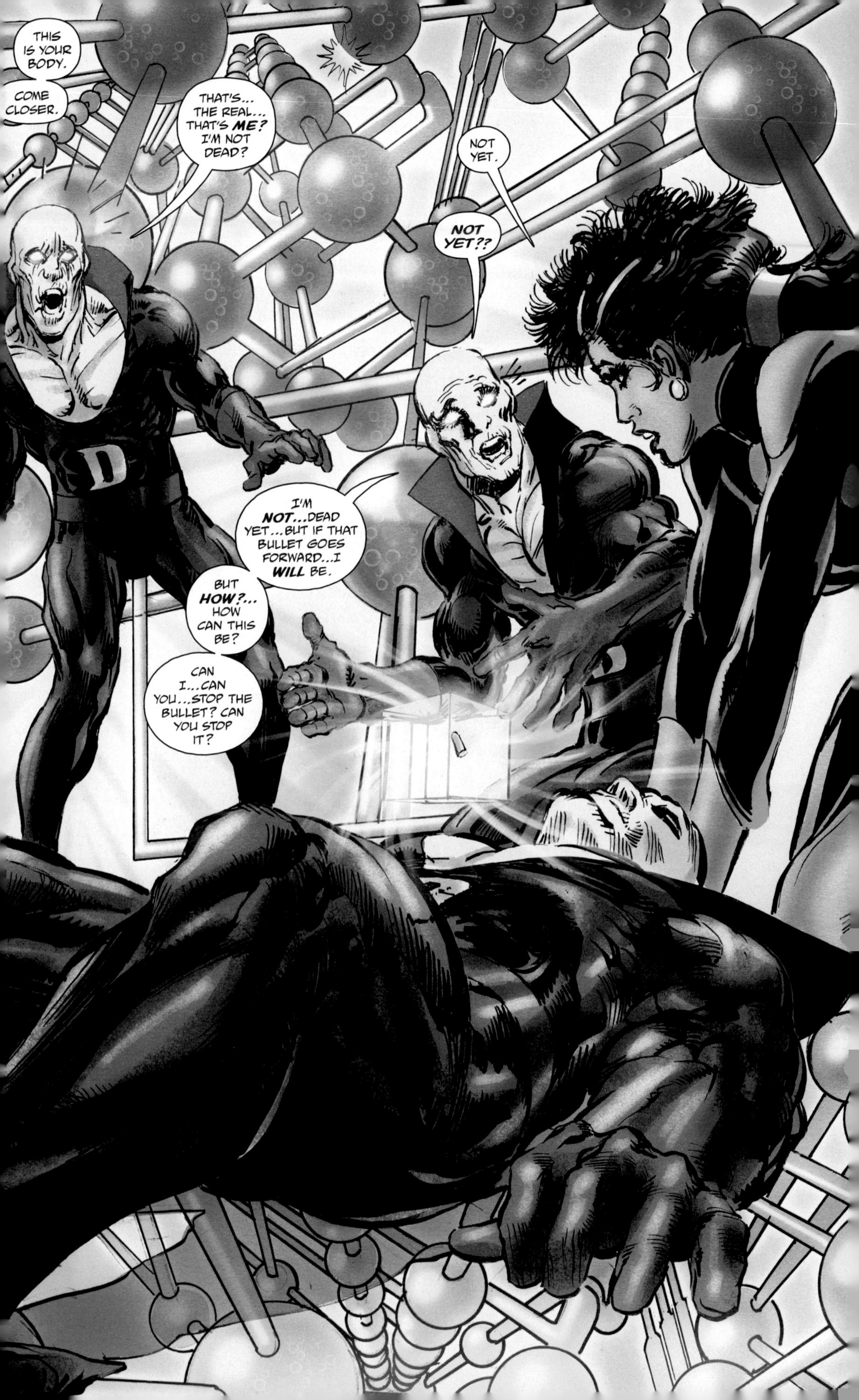
THIS IS YOUR BODY.
COME CLOSER.
THAT'S... THE REAL... THAT'S ME? I'M NOT DEAD?
NOT YET.
NOT YET??
I'M NOT...DEAD YET...BUT IF THAT BULLET GOES FORWARD...I WILL BE.
BUT HOW?... HOW CAN THIS BE?
CAN I...CAN YOU...STOP THE BULLET? CAN YOU STOP IT?

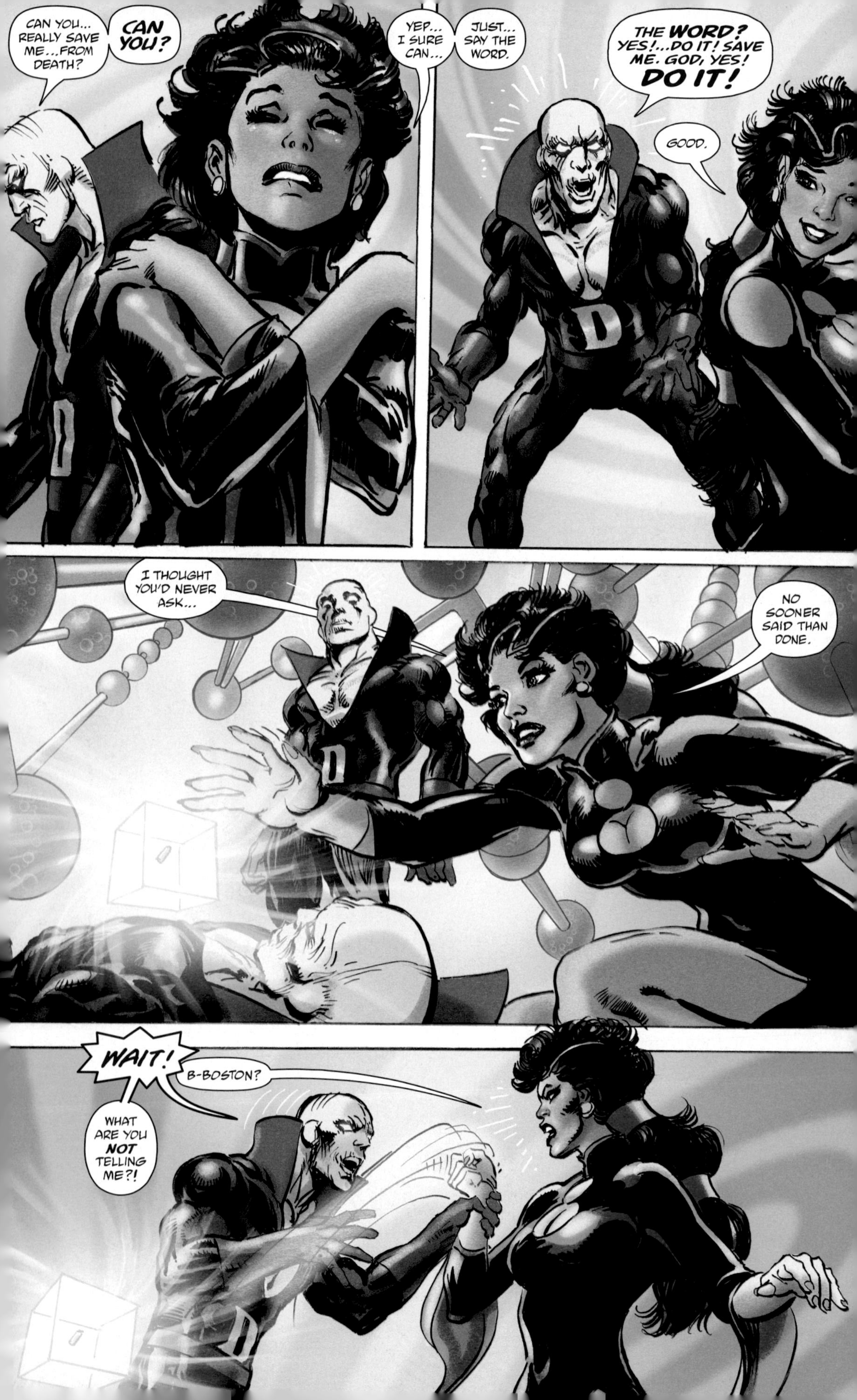
CAN YOU... REALLY SAVE ME...FROM DEATH?
CAN YOU?
YEP... I SURE CAN...
JUST... SAY THE WORD.
THE WORD? YES!...DO IT! SAVE ME. GOD, YES! DO IT!
GOOD.
I THOUGHT YOU'D NEVER ASK...
NO SOONER SAID THAN DONE.
WAIT!
B-BOSTON?
WHAT ARE YOU NOT TELLING ME?!

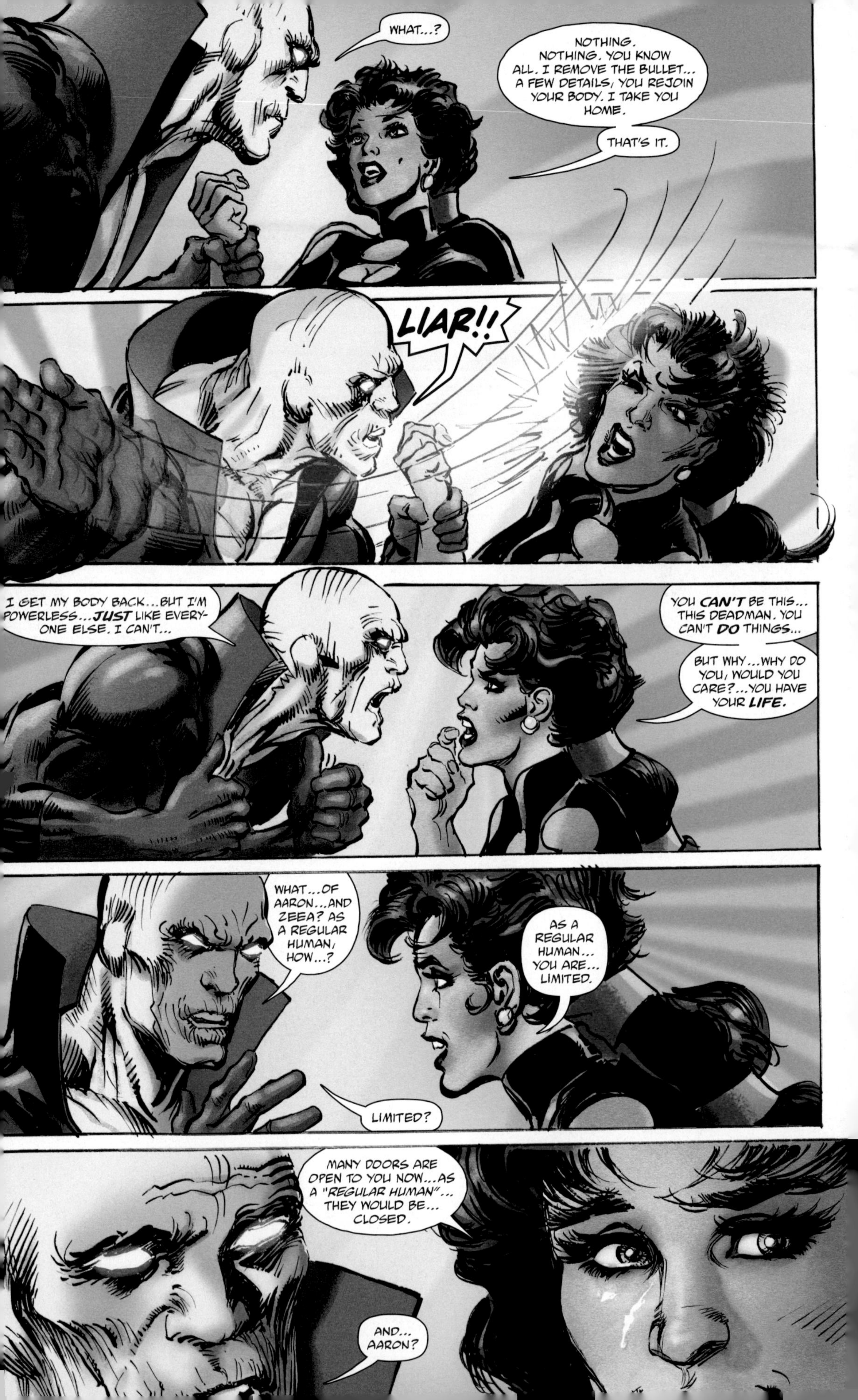
WHAT...?
NOTHING. NOTHING. YOU KNOW ALL. I REMOVE THE BULLET... A FEW DETAILS, YOU REJOIN YOUR BODY. I TAKE YOU HOME.
THAT'S IT.
LIAR!!
I GET MY BODY BACK...BUT I'M POWERLESS...JUST LIKE EVERY-ONE ELSE. I CAN'T...
YOU CAN'T BE THIS... THIS DEADMAN. YOU CAN'T DO THINGS...
BUT WHY...WHY DO YOU, WOULD YOU CARE?...YOU HAVE YOUR LIFE.
WHAT...OF AARON...AND ZEEA? AS A REGULAR HUMAN, HOW...?
AS A REGULAR HUMAN... YOU ARE... LIMITED.
LIMITED?
MANY DOORS ARE OPEN TO YOU NOW...AS A "REGULAR HUMAN"... THEY WOULD BE... CLOSED.
AND... AARON?

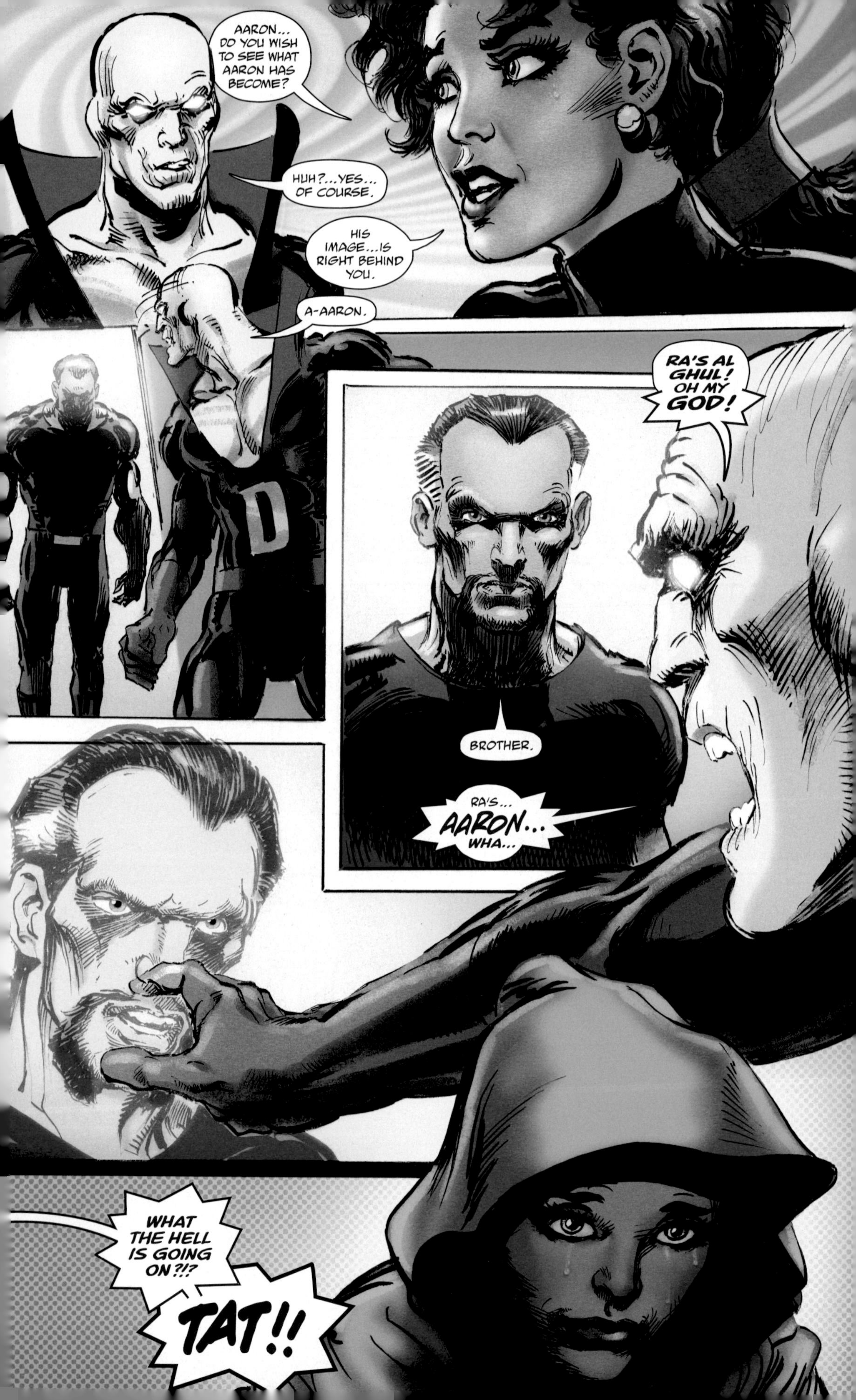
AARON... DO YOU WISH TO SEE WHAT AARON HAS BECOME?
HUH?...YES... OF COURSE.
HIS IMAGE...IS RIGHT BEHIND YOU.
A-AARON.
RA'S AL GHUL! OH MY GOD!
BROTHER.
RA'S... AARON... WHA...
WHAT THE HELL IS GOING ON?!?
TAT!!

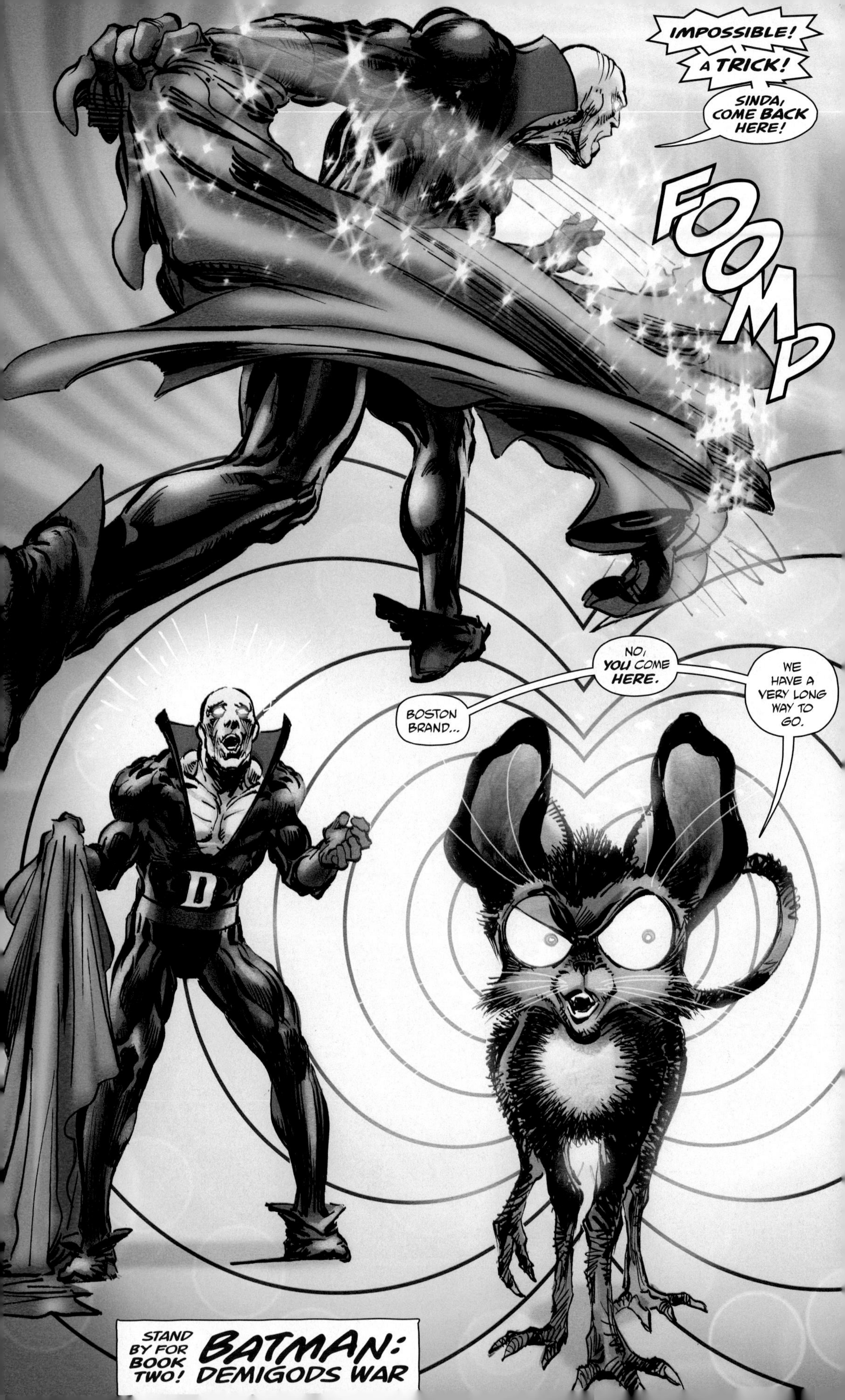
IMPOSSIBLE!
A TRICK!
SINDA, COME BACK HERE!
FOOOMP
BOSTON BRAND...
NO, YOU COME HERE.
WE HAVE A VERY LONG WAY TO GO.
STAND BY FOR BOOK TWO! BATMAN: DEMIGODS WAR

DEADMAN #1 Variant Cover by NEAL ADAMS

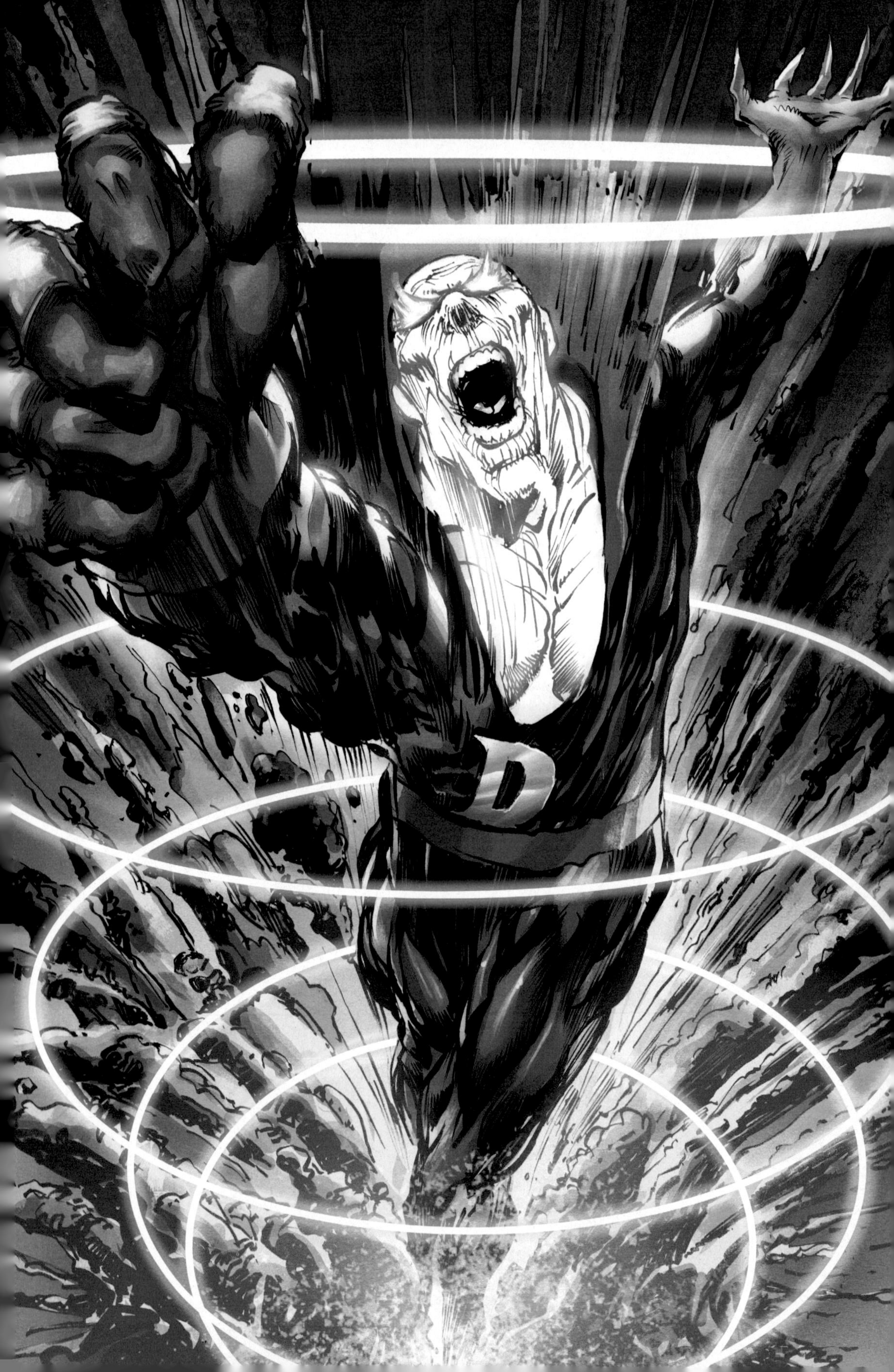

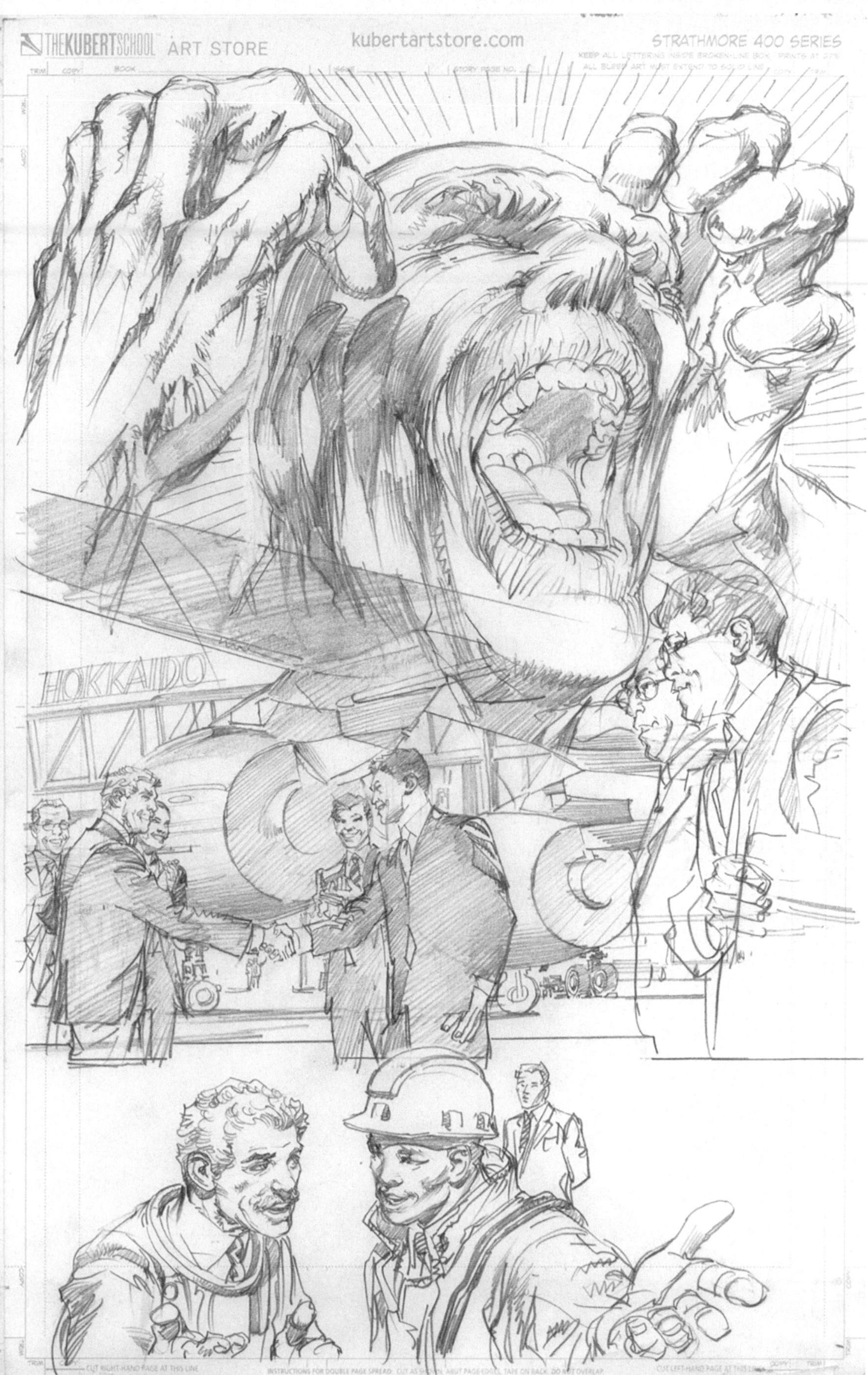
THEKUBERTSCHOOL ART STORE
kubertartstore.com
STRATHMORE 400 SERIES
HOKKAIDO

DEADMAN #1, page 1 pencils

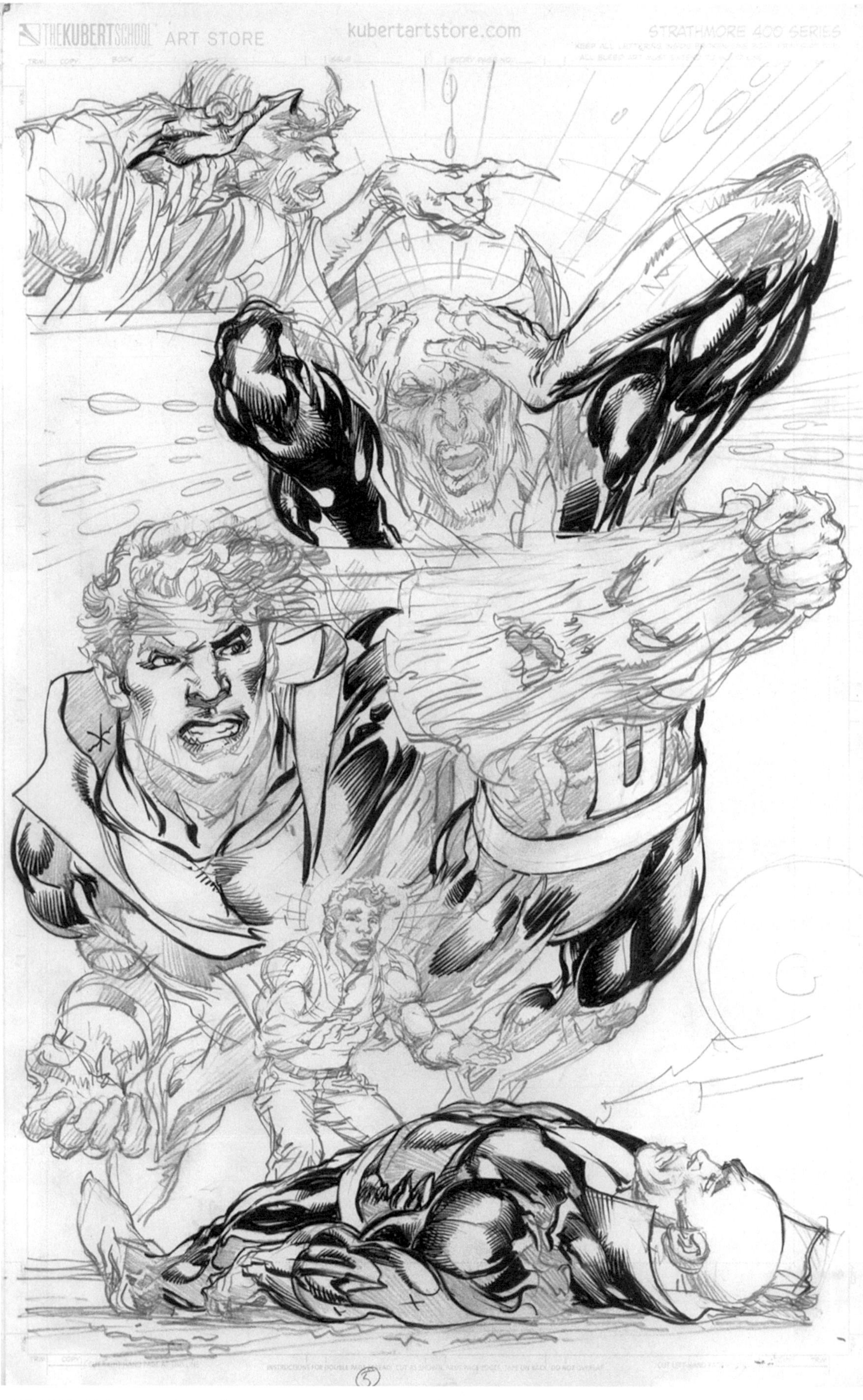
THE KUBERT SCHOOL ART STORE
kubertartstore.com
STRATHMORE 400 SERIES

DEADMAN #1, page 5 pencils

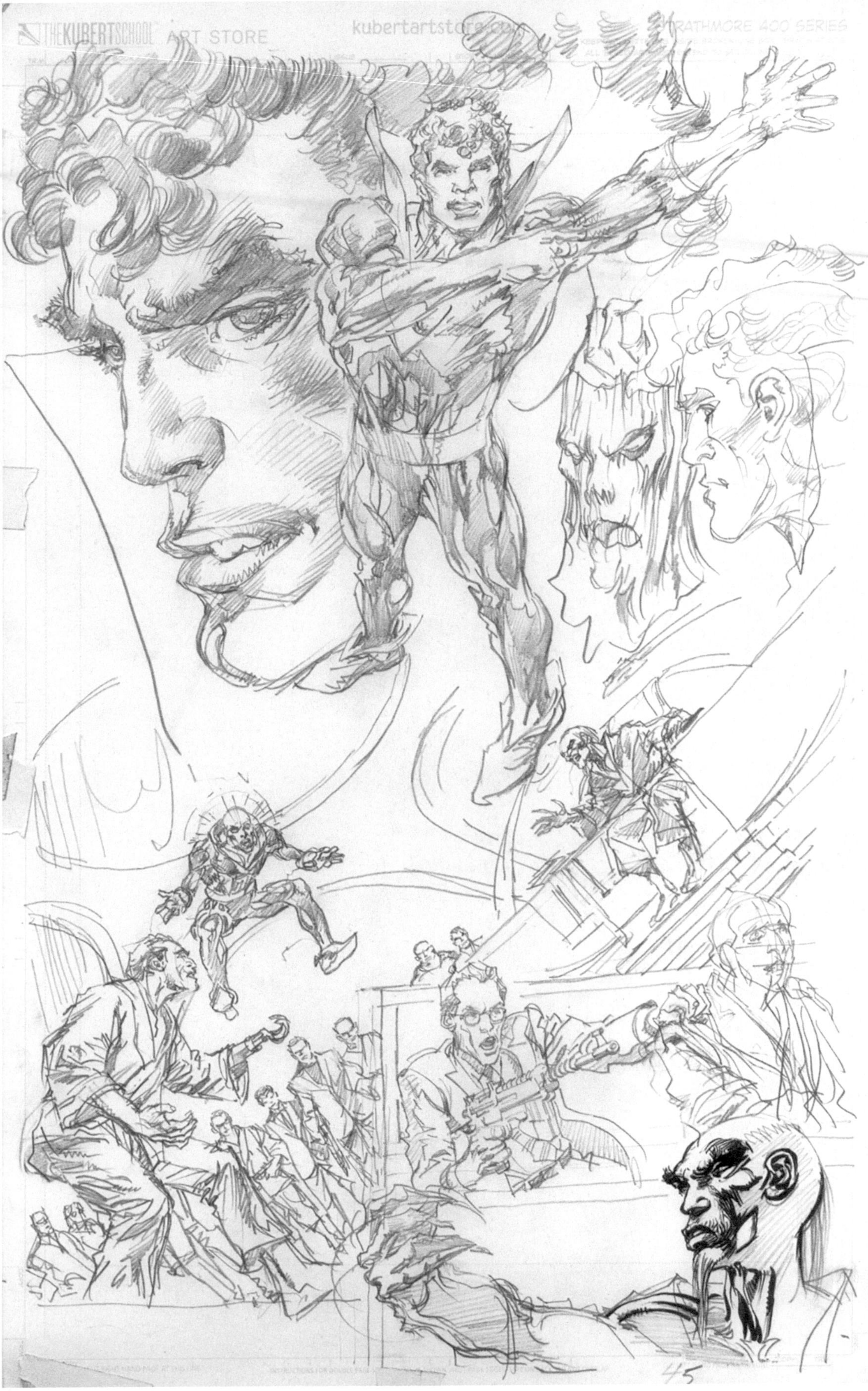

DEADMAN #1, page 6 pencils

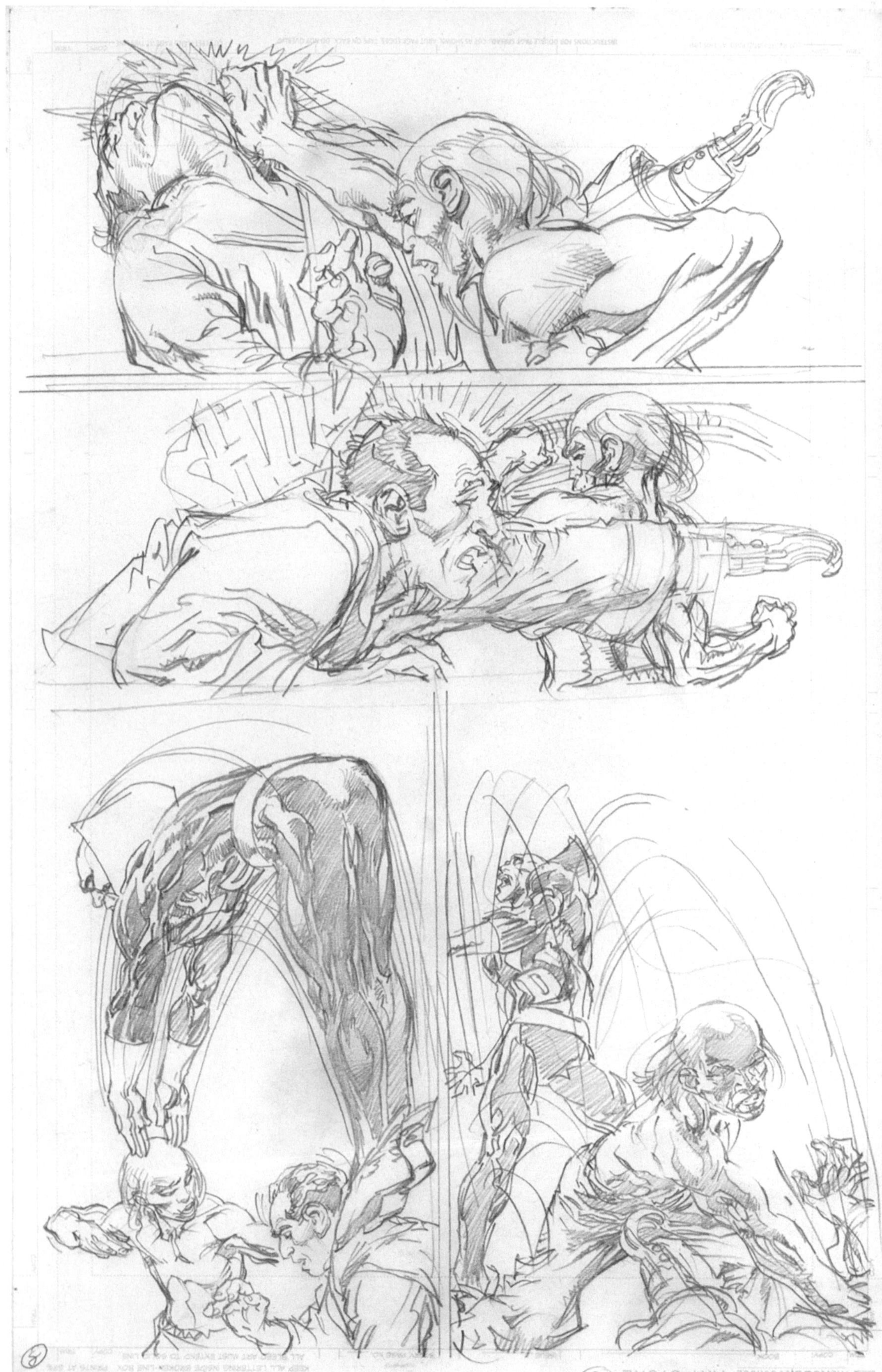

DEADMAN #1, page 8 pencils

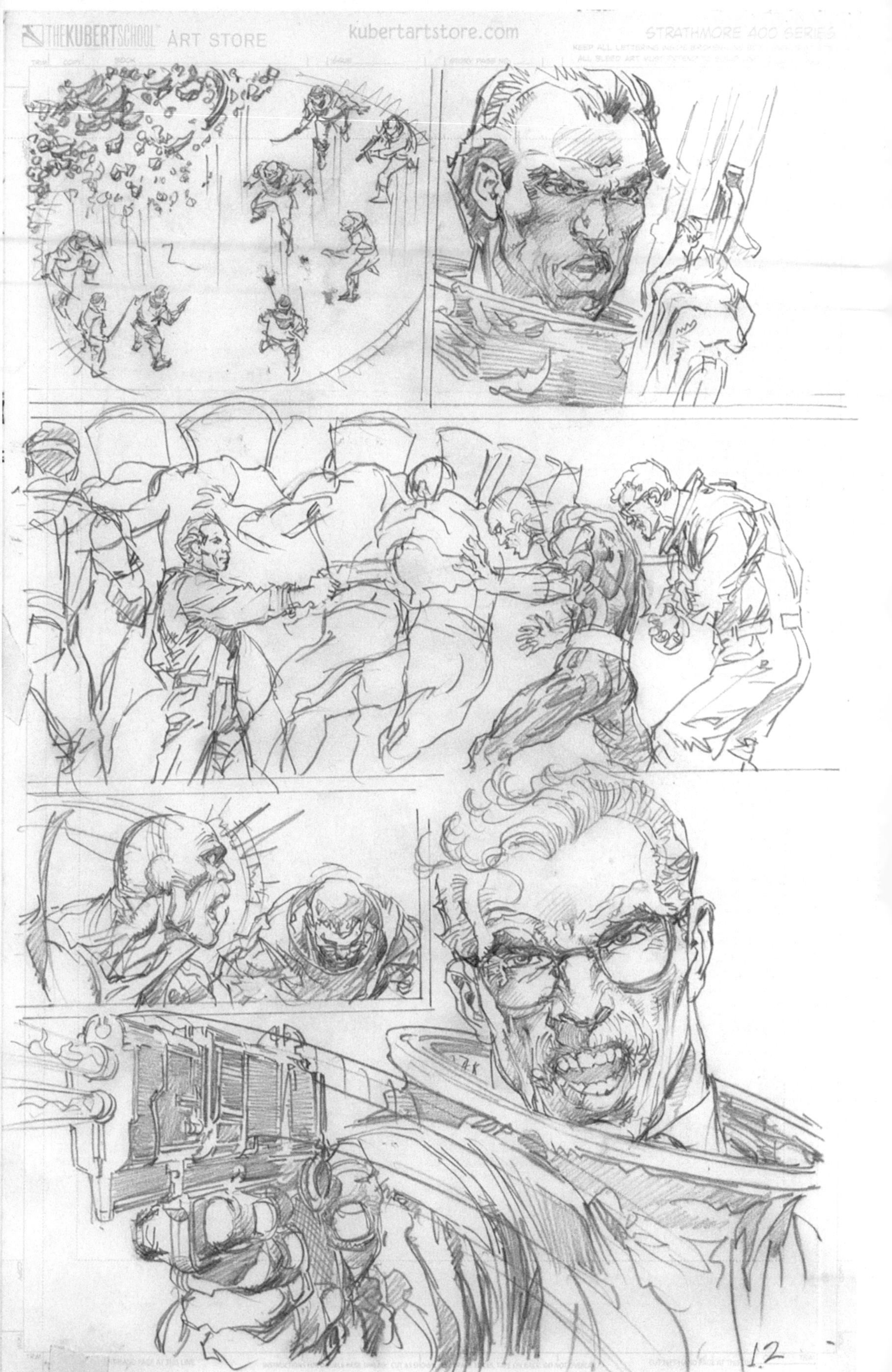
THEKUBERTSCHOOL ART STORE
kubertartstore.com
STRATHMORE 400 SERIES
12

DEADMAN #1, page 12 pencils

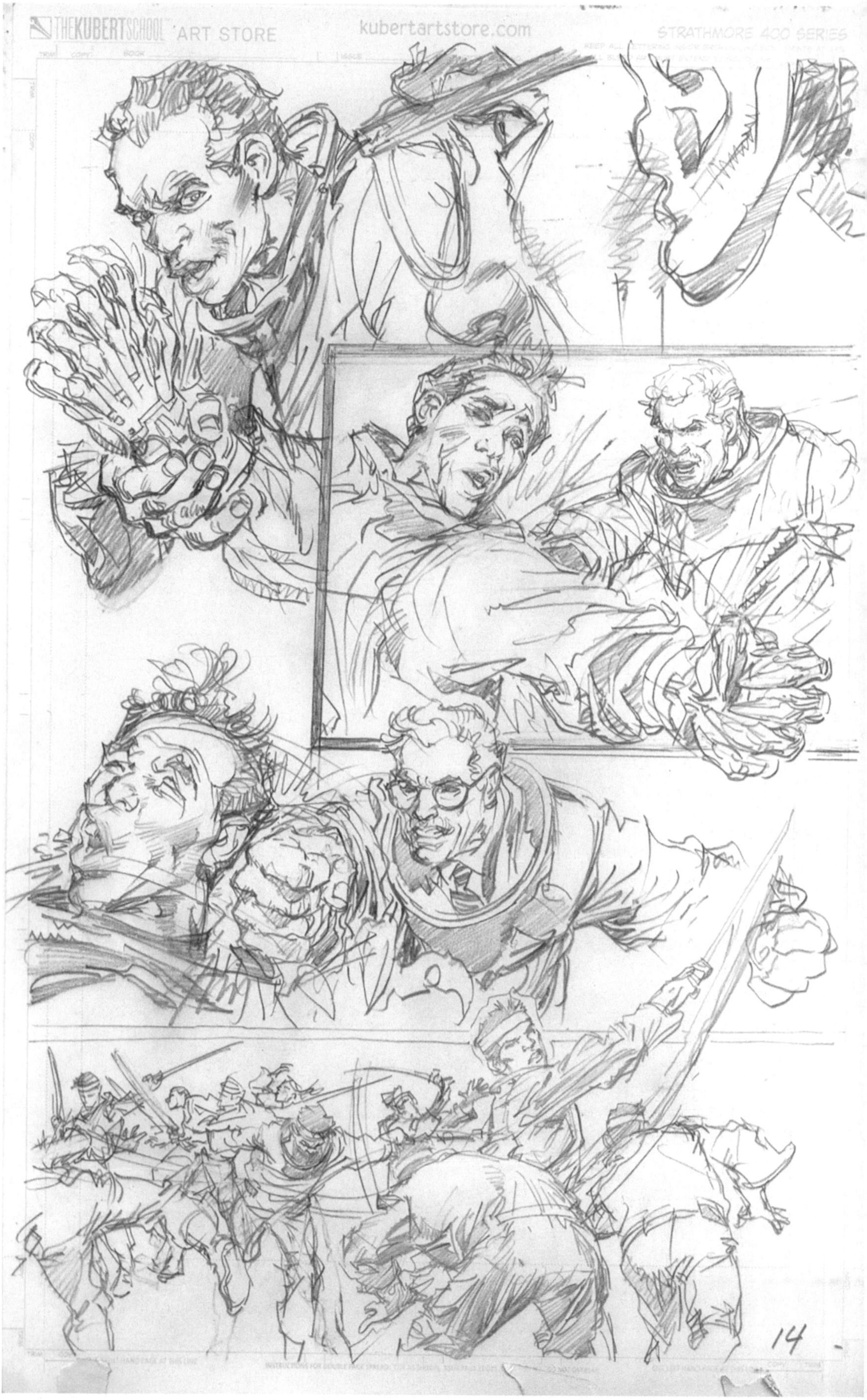
THE KUBERT SCHOOL ART STORE
kubertartstore.com
STRATHMORE 400 SERIES
14

DEADMAN #1, page 14 pencils

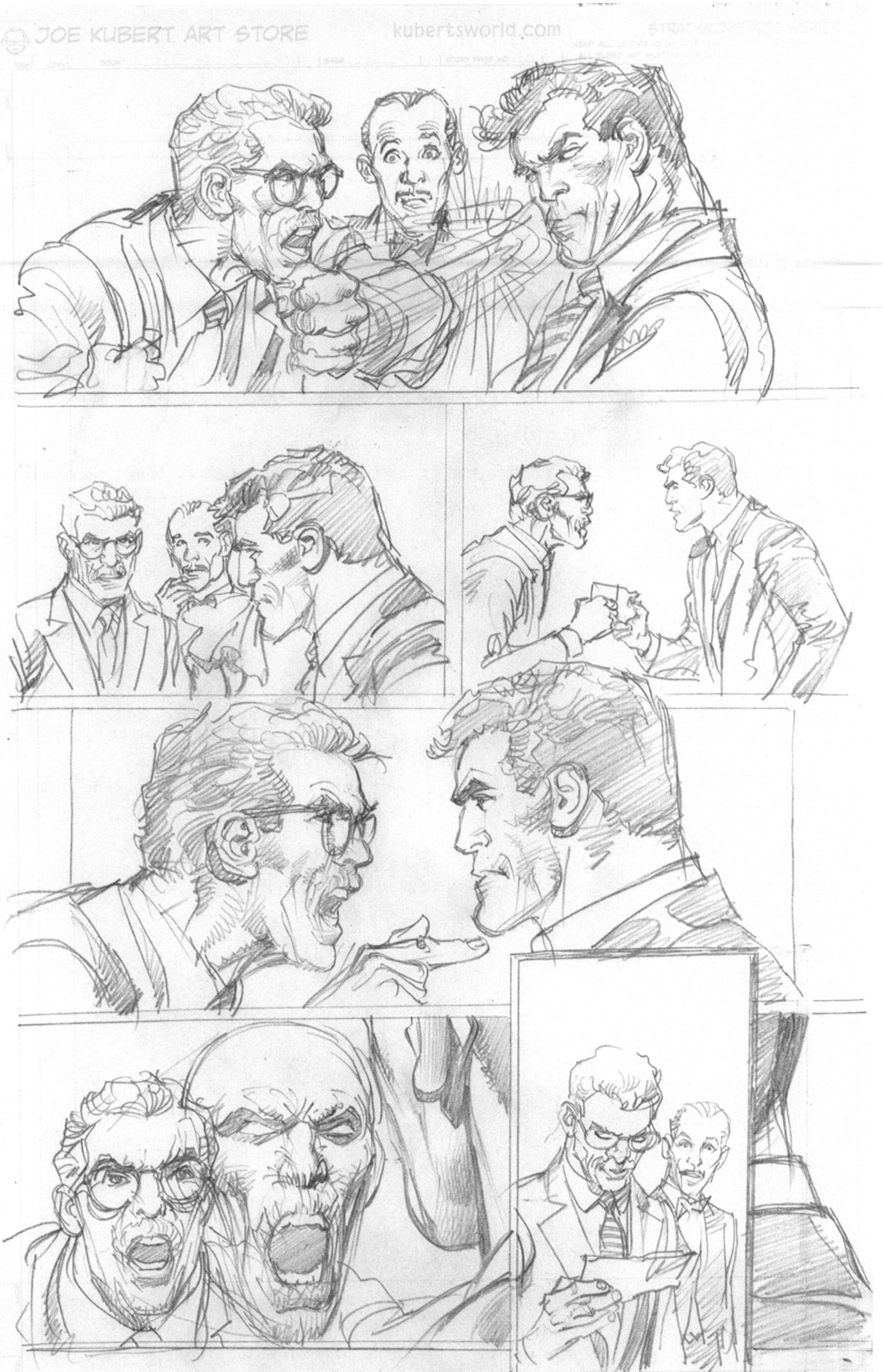
JOE KUBERT ART STORE
kubertsworld.com
20

DEADMAN #1, page 20 pencils

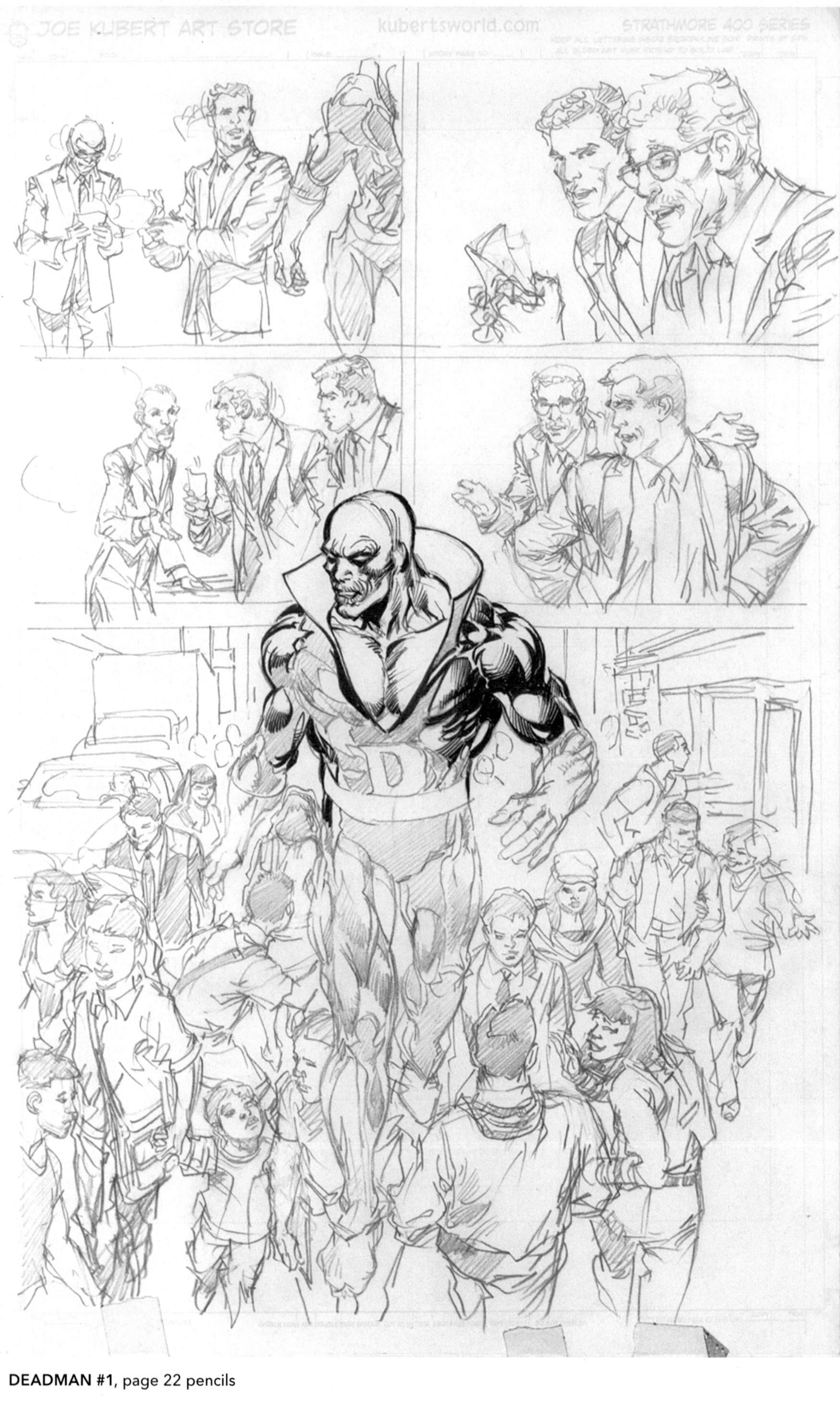
JOE KUBERT ART STORE
kubertsworld.com
STRATHMORE 400 SERIES

DEADMAN #1, page 22 pencils